NATIVE LIFE IN TRAVANCORE

PROCESSION OF GOLDEN TUB.

NATIVE LIFE IN TRAVANCORE

SAMUEL MATEER

GYAN

Published by

GYAN

Gyan Publishing House
5, Ansari Road
Daryaganj, New Delhi-110002
Phone: 011-47034999, 9811692060
E-mail: books@gyanbooks.com

Distribution Network
gyanbooks.com
India, USA, Canada, UK, Australia, France

ISBN : 978-81-212-3809-0 (PB)
First Published, London, 1883

2nd Impression 2020

Printed at: Gyan Press, Delhi.

Native Life in Travancore
Author: Samuel Mateer

NATIVE LIFE

IN

TRAVANCORE

BY

THE REV. SAMUEL MATEER, F.L.S.

Of the London Missionary Society

AUTHOR OF "THE LAND OF CHARITY," ETC.

LONDON

W. H. ALLEN & CO., 13, WATERLOO PLACE

PALL MALL, S.W.

1883

PREFACE

—o—

THIS work has been written, mainly, during a period of restriction, on account of weak health, from the more active duties of the ministry; and the hope is indulged that it may prove quite as useful, in its own way, by treasuring and presenting for general reference information regarding Travancore, as, perhaps, more direct labours in travelling and lecturing on the subject might have been. For the last twenty-five years, I have been studying that country with reference to the prosecution of missionary labour, culling facts of every kind, and accumulating notes respecting its people, history, and literature; collecting a library, English, Tamil, and Malayalam, with complete sets of Reports, some of which are now almost inaccessible to the public, and enjoying friendly intercourse with Europeans and natives of all classes. And at home, while engaged in the preparation of this book, free access has also been given, through the courtesy of the librarians, to the splendid library at the India House.

The valuable materials and knowledge thus acquired for personal use are now placed at the disposal of others; arranged, digested, and condensed so as to give, if it were possible, a whole library in a single volume—providing reliable matter for future investigation and practical application—throwing light especially on those points affecting the social and moral condition of the people on which the statesman or philanthropist would wish to be informed—furnishing materials for a true history of the country—and giving a photograph of strange manners and usages that are rapidly passing away under the influence of modern enlightenment and the spread of Christianity. The history of the past increases our intellectual wealth in each generation, and should be handed on to the next.

No pains have been spared in the careful collation of facts and records; and much care has been taken to ensure accuracy, and avoid a mere surface view of things, as well as to simplify and elucidate every topic discussed, and give a true reflection of the present state of native society. Still, in such a mass of detail, minor errors may exist, arising from varying or incomplete accounts supplied by native helpers and friends. Any mistakes have only to be pointed out for rectification in a second edition, if called for.

I have still much material on hand which it was found impossible to include in this volume—further particulars of Castes and Ceremonies, and chapters on the more abstract and statistical topics of Legislation and Judicial Administration, Land Tenures, Taxation and Revenue, &c. On such a diversified population, an exhaustive work in a single volume is impracticable; and a great and expensive book is not wanted. Only a few typical castes, therefore, have been selected for detailed description, and a few cardinal topics discussed.

In some sense it may be said that the same ground is gone over as in a former work—"The Land of Charity" (Snow & Co., London). But while either book is complete in itself, the matter in each is quite distinct, as I have endeavoured to put nothing in this volume that is in the former one; and the two works should go together, each being the complement of the other. The one discusses chiefly the religious, the other the social and moral aspect of Travancore. The former book was intended chiefly for the friends of missions in England; the present one for readers in India, interested in the welfare of the native population, and desirous to have a correct view of their actual condition, and to use any influence they may possess for the furtherance of solid progress and reform. Though speaking plainly and frankly of the evils which prevail and of the need of a speedy remedy, I am conscious of having written throughout with the desire and aim to be fair to all parties, and with affection and sympathy for all classes in Travancore, whither I hope shortly to return to continue my labours as life and health may be afforded.

Brief quotations and sentences taken from innumerable books and papers which have been freely consulted, abstracted, or utilized for the advantage of the reader, have not been specially marked, as this appeared to be mere waste of labour, and an encumbrance of the printed page.

Special acknowledgments, however, are due to the Government of Travancore for copies of the Administration Reports and the Census Report as each was issued—and to my missionary brethren and other friends, both English and native, for reports and papers keeping me *au courant* with the state of affairs during my absence on leave in England. Also to Rev. W. J. Richards for valuable notes on the Pulayars, &c., in North Travancore—to Rev. R. Collins, M.A., and Rev. R. H. Maddox, B.D., for the loan of photographs for engraving, mostly taken by the former gentleman—and to the Secretaries of the London Missionary Society for twelve illustrations; the Church Missionary Society for five illustrations; the Wesleyan Missionary Society for engraving of Oil Mill; and the Religious Tract Society for engraving of Krishna, kindly permitted by them to be used in this work. The other illustrations have been specially engraved for it.

Indian words and technical terms used in the Travancore official reports are mostly printed in italics, and the exact meaning will readily be found on reference to the Glossary at the end of the volume. The long *á* is pronounced like *a* in *father*, and the short *a* like *u* in *drum*; *é* like *a* in fate; *i* as it is pronounced in *pique*; and *u* generally like *oo* in *food*.

This work is sent forth now in humble reliance on God's gracious guidance, and in the hope that it may prove really helpful to all who desire accurate and recent information on the subject of it, and may thus ultimately tend to raise the social condition and advance the moral and spiritual welfare of the native population of Travancore.

S. MATEER.

London, 9th August, 1883.

ERRATUM.

Page 20, fifth line from bottom, for *town* read *tower*.

Principal works referred to, in addition to those named in "Land of Charity":—

Barbosa's Description of East Africa and Malabar. Hakluyt Society. London, 1866.

Standing Information of Madras Government. Maclean. Madras, 1879.

Canter Visscher's Letters from Malabar. Drury. Madras, 1862.

Missionary Enterprise in the East. Collins. London, 1873.

Lingerings of Light in a Dark Land. Whitehouse. London, 1873.

Indian Caste. Dr. John Wilson. Edinburgh, 1877.

Political History of Tinnevelly. Caldwell. Madras, 1881.

The Vedic Religion. Macdonald. Calcutta, 1882.

Wilson's Glossary of Indian Terms. Allen. London, 1855.

Asiatic Studies. Lyall. London, 1882.

Hindoo Music. Ghose. Calcutta, 1874.

Six Principal Ragas. Tagore. Calcutta.

Mal. History of Travancore. Páchu Múttathu. Trevandrum, *M.E., 1043*.

Maroomakatayum; or, Law of Inheritance among the Sudras of Malabar. P. Moothookristna Naidoo. Cottayam, 1871.

Kéralávagása Kramam. G. K. Va-mman Tirumulpád. Trevandrum *M.E. 1051*.

Asiatic Researches.

Indian Antiquary.

Western Star, Cochin; and Travancore Times, Nagercoil.

Indian Evangelical Review.

Madras C. M. Record; and Travancore Diocesan Gazette.

CONTENTS.

—o—

LIST OF ILLUSTRATIONS.

—o—

NATIVE LIFE IN TRAVANCORE.

CHAPTER I.

THE COUNTRY—DESCRIPTIVE.

THE small but picturesque country of Travancore in South India, though little known in England and even in some distant parts of India, from which it is distinguished by its humid climate, perpetual verdure, and rich vegetable productions, its ancient Hindu Government, and a population of surprising variety, is full of deepest interest to those who have had occasion to reside there, or who have directed their regards closely to the subject. The exhaustive study of the physical features of the country—its multifarious population, with their languages and literature, their strange customs and religions—its flourishing Christian missions and rising civilization—would be the work of a lifetime, and could not fail, so far as it is prosecuted, to draw out the profoundest moral sympathy with the people of all classes and with those on whom devolves the duty of governing them.

Travancore abounds with attractions to the student of nature, of religion, and of mankind. The sportsman and the naturalist will find an endless variety in the fauna—elephants and tigers, for instance, so numerous in some parts that the hillmen are obliged to build their huts in the tops of trees—wild oxen and deer, monkeys, crocodiles, snakes, birds, fishes, and insects. The botanist will find much to interest and delight in the flora: the frequent tropical rains make most of the country a sea of verdure and luxuriant vegetation; and gardening is a pastime uninterrupted by any dreary fall of the leaf or inclemency of winter. The land is crowded with graceful palms, and is one of the head-quarters of the ginger and pepper tribes. It was to procure these spices and other valuable products that the servants of King Solomon visited Malabar in the golden age of the Jewish nation ; and it was these that, in the Providence of God, attracted Europeans first to the Western Coast of India, induced persevering efforts to open more direct communication with the Indies, led to the discovery of the Cape route as well as America and the West Indies, and ultimately to the establishment of the great Indian Empire of the British Crown. Dense forests of teak, blackwood, and other useful timbers clothe the hill regions—fruit-trees, some of them bearing fruits of enormous size, or in extraordinary abundance, are grown in every garden—the medicinal plants deserve fuller investigation and trial—and economic products such as coffee, tea, chocolate, and chinchona are now being largely introduced and developed by enterprising English planters.

The historian and the antiquarian have yet, it may be said, to begin their labours in Travancore, examining ancient but hitherto inaccessible temples, with their undeciphered inscriptions, and investigating records and usages which may throw light upon the origin of its strange laws. The ethnologist will have a wide sphere for study in the varied and mutually contrasting manners and customs of the four hundred and twenty Hindu castes of the population, besides the mixed descendants of the Portuguese, Dutch, and other nations—quite a museum of races—and in the comparison of these with customs prevailing in other parts of the world. Some of these castes are, from their exclusive habits and insulation, inaccessible to the European, and nearly so to their own countrymen of other classes.

The merchant and the manufacturer may find here a market for their commodities as civilization and comfort spread, and an opening for new and varied forms of industry ; and the statesman will be interested in the social and political condition of a country where the great problem is to decide how far, and by what successive steps, the people shall be freed from barbarous and unequal laws, endowed with civil liberty, and ultimately entrusted with some share in the government of their country.

Above all, the Christian philanthropist cannot but mourn over the gross idolatry and demon worship, and the miserable superstitions which corrupt and darken all that is otherwise fair and pleasant—the dense popular ignorance, oppressions, and abject wretchedness of the lower castes, and the debasement of females amongst most classes of society ; and he will rejoice over the incipient enlightenment, the spread of education, and the establishment of living and active Christian churches throughout the land.

The religions of Travancore are strangely diverse, comprising both popular Hinduism, and demon, ancestral, serpent, and sun worship—Muhammadanism of a low and imperfect type—Jews, the history of whose settlement in India dates back to, perhaps, the time of the destruction of Jerusalem, or even earlier—Roman Catholics of three centuries' standing—the Malabar Syrian Church, very much resembling in rites and ecclesiastical government the Greek Church, and whose founders and ancestors came to Malabar fully fifteen hundred years ago—and last, but not least in importance for the future welfare of the country, Protestant Christians connected with the London Missionary Society in the South, and with the Church Mission in the North, brought under the influence of the Gospel within the last sixty or seventy years. It is a remarkable fact that over one-fifth of the population are nominally Christian, while the Malayálam Sudras, who constitute the mass of the respectable population, the landowners and employers of labour, the agricultural and military classes, are quite outnumbered by the native Christians; and the Brahmans, who enjoy immense power and prestige in social and political matters, and almost divine honours as the representatives of the deity and the sole competent priestly celebrants of religious rites, number only forty thousand in a total population of nearly two millions and a half. Travancore is thus an Oriental microcosm, a representative land, a country of striking contrasts. In its scenery, sea-coast and mountain range, wood and water, hill and dale, river and lake are all combined in comparatively small compass. The primeval forests, where the elephant, tiger, and wild ox roam unchecked, lie not many miles distant from the capital, with its public offices, English college, and museum; and the almost savage denizen of the woods and hills, clad in green leaves or fringes of long grass, is found not far from the Brahman official or Sudra noble, who lectures on modern science, and writes the English language as well as any of us.

To introduce and to illustrate particulars of the manners and customs, the social and civil condition of the people, some descriptive account of the country seems required. Let us enter it from the north, and travel right through by the main and most frequented route, parallel with the coast, to the southernmost extremity at Cape Comorin, observing the physical features which it presents to our notice as we pass along.

The nearest railway station on the way from Madras is at Shoranoor in the extreme north of Cochin, where we cross the Beypore river over a long bridge, which, it is hoped, will some day be utilized for the extension of the railroad to Cochin:

thence we proceed by bullock cart southwards some twenty miles to Trichoor. The road passes in places through dense forest, and is in parts adorned and sheltered by avenues of magnificent over-arching trees, especially banyans, forming natural Gothic arches draped and festooned with epiphytal ferns and orchids, and gorgeous flowering creepers depending from the branches. At Trichoor, "the key of Cochin," we enter upon the "backwater" communication by lagoons, canals, and rivers to Trevandrum, separated generally by but a narrow strip of land from the sea—a very cheap and convenient mode of travelling, though rather slow. In stormy weather, when winds and waves rock the shallow canoe and threaten to overturn it, or beat hard upon the cabin-boat, this mode of travel is unpleasant or even unsafe; but nothing could be more delightful in favourable weather, in the rich glow of the golden sunset, in the bright moonlight, or the cool dawn of day.

In the daytime we meet or pass numerous freight and passenger-boats, large and small, going in various directions; and stop for a short time at convenient places of call to procure provisions, or to allow the boatmen to cook their food. Pretty little mullet fish, silvery and glistening, may be seen leaping out of the water, sometimes in shoals; and occasional specimens leap into the boat. At night all is calm and still, except the conversation of passengers in boats gliding past, or the salutations of boatmen one to another, the sound of drumming and play in distant villages, the croaking of great frogs close by, not unlike the cawing of crows, and the shrill ceaseless stridulation of the Cicada in the trees.

Passing the ruins of the fort of Cranganore, once the scene of European warfare and diplomacy, and a settlement of the Jews and Syrian Christians, but now desolate, except for a noted temple, which is the annual resort of multitudes to offer sacrifices of cocks to the goddess Bhagavathi, we enjoy a pretty view of the backwater, studded with low islands covered with grass and sedges, the banks carefully cultivated, or overgrown with fine jungle containing handsome convolvulus or other creepers, rattans, and flowering shrubs, and the mountains in the distance. On the other side of the backwater we see the Travancore military "lines" or defensive hedge running inland, which was some obstacle to the Mysore forces on the invasion of Tippu Saib about a century ago, but now presents the appearance simply of a raised roadway with a few small bambus growing upon it. The Travancore territory extends to about this parallel of latitude, some dozen miles north of the town of Cochin; but a narrow strip along the coast belonging to the Cochin Rajah runs into the Travancore State.

Boats and boatmen can readily be changed or procured at the busy and flourishing port and commercial emporium of British Cochin, the history of whose vicissitudes and conflicts under native rule, and under the Portuguese and the Dutch, is full of interest. Here European vessels lie in the roads, or in the harbour formed by the estuary where the inland waters meet the sea. Coasting steamers call weekly, and crowds of native craft lie at anchor in the backwater, which is here about two miles in width, the banks very low and covered with palms and other vegetation. Were the shores higher, this sheet of water would be a magnificent sight. The Cochin Rajah's public offices and schoolhouse, and several Roman Catholic churches show well at Ernaculam on the eastern bank of the backwater. Native huts and villages nestle under the shade of the trees; mangroves send their curious arched roots into the mud: overhead, flocks of green parrokeets scream as they fly across; and gorgeous kingfishers sit perched on the branches, attentively watching for fish in the water beneath. Great flocks of cranes settle in the rice-fields around. The native town of Cochin extends southwards for a mile or two to the remarkable settlements of white and black Jews, to which most travellers endeavour to pay a visit in passing.

South of Cochin, the water communication varies in width, but, on the whole, gradually expands into a considerable lake, called the Vembanád backwater, on the eastern side of which lies the important mission station of Cottayam, with its English college and vernacular Seminary, its numerous congregations and Protestant bishop—the head-quarters also of the Syrian Christian church; and on the western side the busy town of Alleppy with its fine lighthouse, coir factories, shipping, and population of 30,000, largely Muhammadan. This sheet of water is about thirteen miles long and nine in breadth, almost an inland sea. Here, and in other waters of sufficient expanse, sails may be set when the wind is favourable, and a speed of some six or eight miles an hour may be attained. Along the banks of the lake, and on the sea-beach, the dense forest of cocoanut trees is surprising, in some places not a spot of earth to be seen unoccupied, nor scarcely a house visible through the crowded plantations. There seems no end of cocoanut palms, until ultimately one gets rather tired of the monotony, valuable as are the trees to the inhabitants. In the monsoon floods, some of these places look like large sheets of water studded with small islands full of cocoanut trees and human habitations.

Rice-fields are formed by reclaiming the swamps by the side of the backwater, so that a season of unusual drought, which injuriously affects the crops in the south, is helpful in drying up the low-lying lands in the north of Travancore, which are covered with several feet deep of water in the rainy season. In some places these are a couple of feet lower than the level of the canal, the water being kept out by mud banks, and irrigation wheels, turned by the feet of men sitting on the frames, are at work in many places. Where necessary, the water is carried up through a sloping trough, half the distance by one wheel, and the other half by a second. The field serfs are often seen working up to the neck in water deepening the canals, or lifting up mud from the bottom to repair the banks at the sides.

Here and there vicious looking crocodiles lie on the low banks in the sun, with the mouth wide open, "to catch flies," say the natives. They are rarely over ten feet in length, not being permitted now-a-days to live so long as in former times when these formidable reptiles were used in ordeals, and human life was less valued.

The distance from Cochin to Quilon, ninety miles, is done at a stretch in twenty-four hours, or less, by cabin boat, and in a couple of days by canoe. On the way we pass near to various populous towns—which might be visited if time permits—many hamlets, farm-houses, and shops where betel-leaf, tobacco, arrack, fruits, and cooked rice are purchased by the boatmen and passengers who are not of high caste; and after some miles of narrow canal, uniting the Káyenkulam Lake with that at Quilon, we enter this beautiful piece of water, with arms reaching in various directions, high red cliffs of laterite; and near Quilon, several handsome houses belonging to the native gentry and English officers.

From the landing-place at Quilon an avenue of pretty feathery-foliaged casuarina trees leads to the British Cantonment, a wide sandy plain intersected by roads and surrounded by the bungalows of the sepoy officers, the barracks, English church, hospital, mosque, &c. The market is held in an open square in the town, adorned and sheltered by several noble banyan trees in the centre. Crowds of large bats hang on these trees, fighting for the best places, and incessantly squeaking towards evening. At night they take flight in search of fruits and other food. Thence three or four streets branch off, one leading down through long rows of shops to the native town. Here and there are little pyramids of clay for demon-worship, and temples of Ganesha and other Hindoo deities, to which the British sepoys stationed here, or the inhabitants, make their offerings. Tall, military-looking men strut about, and a sepoy guard is stationed in the principal street. The native town proper contains a palace, public offices, and temple, with a population of some fifteen thousand.

Leaving Quilon by a narrow canal with high sandy banks near the town, on the inland side of which are situated several large bungalows, we proceed parallel with the sea-coast, and after two or three miles come again into an open lake, separated from the sea by a narrow strip of beach covered with cocoanut plantations. At Paravúr there is another outlet for the back-water into the turbulent sea, and the lake is very deep, so that the poles used to push along the canoes do not reach to the bottom. At such places boats are sometimes overturned by the irresistible current when the waters are swollen by the rush of torrents from the hills during the long-continued rains of the monsoon. Here again we have a fine display of tropical vegetation of diverse foliage and hue, the beautiful green flowing foliage of the cocoanut intermingling with the glossy laurel nut (*Calophyllum*) and mango, the cerbera and pandanus, with lilies, great acrostichum ferns and masses of sedge (*Cyperus*) at the edge of the water and within it—a lovely country, to which Nature has been bountiful; would that it were filled with a truly Christian people!

Up to 1881, a hilly barrier of four miles existed at Wurkally to the water navigation, that seemed to be insurmountable; and it has in fact been overcome only by a heavy expenditure of over sixteen lacs of rupees by the State. Passengers and goods had to be carried across the portage and transhipped. After many years of surveying, consultation, criticism, and labour, the canal has been taken for two or three miles by a circuitous route through the valleys at either end, and two portions of hill intervening have been pierced with tunnels, one over a thousand feet, and the other over two thousand feet in length, furnishing a clear water way five feet deep and sixteen broad. The open cuttings through the laterite are in some parts no less than sixty or seventy feet in depth. A curious deposit of lignite or primeval forest was found here under thirty feet of earth and below the present sea-level, some of it only of the consistence of clay, but a few stumps of huge trees in fair preservation and capable of being worked into furniture. This tunnel is the first of the kind that has been attempted in India, and its cost has been thought to be disproportionate, but certainly the relief to commerce and travel, and the admission of better boats from the north into the Trevandrum Canal has been a benefit impossible to estimate in money value. By this tunnel the line of water communication is completed from

Trevandrum northwards to the ports of Alleppey and Cochin, and the whole of the northern districts of Travancore and the railway station at Tiroor, a distance of 228 miles. Small steamboats of light draught are also running on the backwater between Cochin and Alleppy.

A few miles beyond the tunnel we pass close to the old British fort and town of Anjengo, now quite decayed, but still owned by the British Government. The first political and commercial relation of Travancore with the East India Company was in 1673, when the Company established a factory at Anjengo. The old tombs of former English officials and their families are interesting, and were repaired and enclosed through the efforts of Mr. G. A. Ballard when Resident. Further on, quantities of cocoanut husks may be seen steeping in the water, enclosed in nets—or rather they may be smelt, giving forth a horrible stench. Poor people sit under the shade of the trees beating out the coir fibre, or twist it into yarn.

The last ten miles of the journey to Trevandrum are through a canal, the sandy banks of which are prettily covered with the pandanus or screw-pine, with masses of odorous flowers and large scarlet fruit, exactly resembling the pineapple, but utterly useless; the Cerbera odallam with its long leaves, large white fragrant flowers and green fruit, just like the mango, but poisonous; the Barringtonia, with pendulous strings of pink tassel-like flowers; the cashew, with its fragrant blossoms and nuts growing on the outside of the apple, and other trees, often covered with convolvulus and other creepers, and with climbing ferns as the *Drymoglossum* and *Stenochlænum*, and the long grass-like *Vittaria* fern. The white-flowered crinum and the water-lily abound along with various aquatic and floating plants, and a pretty fine-leaved fern, *Ceratopteris thalictroides*, perhaps the only fern which grows *in* the water.

To give some idea of the external aspect of Trevandrum and its people, we cannot do better than quote freely from a vivid description, evidently written by a lady, in "India's Women," July, 1881:—"The first thing that strikes a new-comer is that the streets are shut in on each side by walls. Now these walls are very varied, the better kind being made of red brick with a white stone coping at the top; the next in grade, of laterite from our quarries, plastered, whitewashed, and generally thatched with plaited palm leaves to protect them from the rain; while the third are simply made of lumps of the reddish-brown soil for which Travancore, like Devonshire, is famous, and are also thatched at the top. These latter, though not very durable in monsoon time, are to my mind much more picturesque than either of the others, especially when contrasted with the strip of bright green grass bordering the roads during the rains, or adorned, as they often are, by tiny ferns and moss. Not only have we no pavements, but there is no visible line between the carriage road and that for foot passengers ; this appears, however, to cause them no anxiety ; they move leisurely along, apparently quite indifferent whether they are run over or not.

The houses behind these walls are built in very irregular fashion. Some are pretentious-looking two-storied buildings with balconies and verandahs, tiled roofs and brilliant whitewashed fronts, while near them may be seen an old-fashioned hut, with its deep roof of palm-leaf, one small window and door, and surrounded by the inevitable plantain tree. Next we may come to a large compound with no house visible, though there probably is one buried among the trees, but screened from view by a thick plantation of coffee bushes, their branches laden with snow-white blossom in the early part of the year. A little further on are some shops ; in one, sacks of grain of different kinds, rice, grain for horses, and cotton seed for bullocks. The sacks are arranged in a row at the edge of the narrow verandah, upright and open-mouthed to show their contents, while their owner generally reclines among them waiting for customers, with no great anxiety to secure them. The vegetable shops with their large bunches of red, green, or golden plantains, their mounds of bright scarlet or green chillies, their huge pumpkins, yams, gourds, and brinjals, are worth more than a passing glance, and they are commonly surrounded by a crowd of eager buyers, bargaining in loud voices to effect as cheap a sale as possible. Some vendors of English tinned meats, wines, &c., make no show, but are content to hang a black board with the word *Shop* printed on it, outside what looks like a private house with the front door open.

Now a break in the street will occur, and we come to a large compound shut in by handsome iron-railings, containing a fine block of buildings designed by an English engineer, and used as Government offices. Opposite, at some little distance from the road, is the telegraph-office, and a little higher up a small whitewashed building with 'Post-Office' in large letters on the front. In between the houses are groups of palms, the feathery cocoanut, the slender areca with its small graceful head, and the broad-leaved fan palm tamarind trees, which are both ornamental and useful, the scarlet flowering Poinsettia, the Bougainvillea, and other gay shrubs adorn our streets ; while some of them are hedged in, instead of being walled, by the orange lantana, and bordered by rows of casuarina and other trees, affording grateful shade to all, but especially prized by the poor cooly toiling at noon under his heavy load. For his convenience, too, rests are erected, consisting of a horizontal slab of granite, supported by two upright blocks; on the top his burden is often to be seen, while he sits placidly down in the shade close at hand.

Sacred trees, remnants of the most ancient worship known in this land, are to be met with in the roads here and there. They are generally large banyans (*Ficus Bengalensis* or *F. religiosa*) and have a platform, often raised from the ground by several steps built of stone and carefully whitewashed, at their roots. On festival nights, at the four corners lights are placed, and a crowd of poor deluded worshippers gather there. Great daubs of red ochre are put on the tree, and the spirit further propitiated with fireworks. Besides these trees, there are roadside temples, mere sheds with pictures of gods drawn in red and blue by the most primitive of artists on their outer walls, and two or three pointed stones with red ochre on the top inside.

The most interesting of all our streets are those within the walls of the fort, where reside Brahman and other high-caste families. You enter by a gate, wide open, though guarded by a sepoy with fixed bayonet, and pass into a road swept every morning as carefully as a drawing-room. To your right and left are the quaint dwellings of the Brahmans, with a row of small windows above, just large enough for one head to peep out, but so high as to ensure that no passer-by can look in. Tiny verandahs raised to some height above the road are painted in stripes of red and white, while before each door on the passengers' foot-way is a square of black, which has been rubbed with a mixture of cow-dung and charcoal, and when dry adorned with a neat geometrical pattern in white; the appearance is that of a drawing on a slate, and very even and straight the lines usually are. On festival days these ornaments are most elaborate, and a little red is often added to improve the effect. There seems to be a pleasant rivalry amongst the women of the neighbourhood as to who shall produce the best and most studied designs. They are rubbed away by night, but are carefully renewed every morning.

The verandah is always occupied by men in various attitudes, one muttering prayers from a book, but ready to look off every minute at what is going forward, another cleaning his teeth most vigorously, or perhaps a bright-faced schoolboy learning his lesson aloud. In and out among the grown people, looking as happy as any bird, are boys and girls unencumbered by any clothing, except a string or perhaps a chain round their fat little bodies.

We go a little further and see the street well, with a group of graceful women, dressed in clothes of shaded brown and yellow,

SCENE IN THE FORT, TREVANDRUM

red, or plain dark blue, and amongst them we can always distinguish the widow by her having one end of her cloth drawn round her shaven head, as a kind of veil. They have but one meal a day, and are despised for having brought disgrace into their families by some sin committed in a former state of being. Now we meet a group of women of all ages, followed by an attendant with towels, dry cloths, &c., evidently on their way to the large tank, where they will enjoy their morning bath in a corner by themselves, but quite in sight of men performing their ablutions. They are slightly clothed when in the water, and appear quite unconscious of any impropriety in choosing so public a place. It is sacred, near the great pagoda, and close to the holy stones, before which lights are burned every night. What place then could be better for holy women, they would argue. At the tank during the bathing hour incessant noise is heard, talking, laughing, muttering of *mantrams* or prayers, and the monotonous sound of beating their clothes against stones for the purpose of washing them, for the Brahman could not wear a garment washed by a man of lower caste than himself; he, therefore, goes through the performance every morning while bathing.

Passing on from the tank we come to a large walled-in garden, with grand bunches of plantains hanging over the road, and a bread-fruit tree with its large handsome leaves and solid looking green fruit; and are made aware by a heap of white stars on the road of the presence of jessamine, so largely cultivated for garlands.

The guard-house for sepoys, opposite to the Dewán's residence, is open, and about a dozen men of the Náyar Brigade, in red coats and black trousers, but no boots, are lounging about. They do not look very warlike, but doubtless, if occasion offered, would fight bravely to defend their fields and homes.

Now a mendicant Brahman passes by, and we note the copper vessel slung round his neck to contain the rice he is sure to get from house to house. He carries two little brass cups in his hands, which he strikes together to give notice of his approach, that the people may get their offerings ready. Street vendors there are, too, hawking their wares—a woman with a large pot of buttermilk, which she ladles out to all who call her to their doors; a boy with lucifer matches; and a man with a round basket on his shoulder containing bread, which he announces by lusty cries.

The streets of the fort are delightful in the early morning; the sky is blue, but not cloudless; the merry grey palm-squirrels (*Sciurus palmarum*), favoured by Ráman, and bearing the impress of his fingers in the black stripes on their backs, chase one another over the tiled roofs of the houses, and play at hide-and-seek in their curiously-carved gables; the black and white robin stops in his search for food to trill forth a note of gladness and praise; and contented-looking cows and calves walk about where they please, with an air of proprietorship which only a cow in an Oriental city knows how to assume."

Proceeding from Trevandrum southwards by bullock cart, we cross the strong and handsome bridge over the Karamana river, built by a native architect, the view from which up the river and downwards is very agreeable. The banks are well-wooded, people wash clothes in the stream far beneath us, and many Brahmans are bathing at the flight of stone steps connected with the Temple, the buildings of which peep out above the luxuriant vegetation by which they are surrounded.

Avenues of umbrageous trees planted on either side shade the road, among which the most common and conspicuous are banyans, with their rootlets hanging from the branches and stems, often covered with Vanda, Cymbidium, and other epiphytal orchids and clumps of the Drynaria fern, the Thespesia or *púvarasu* tree, covered with beautiful yellow tulip-like flowers, tamarinds, mangoes, terminalia, &c. Some single specimens are remarkable for size. Here is a noble mango-tree for instance, some fifty feet in height, straight and symmetrical, with long lance-shaped leaves, quite covered with greenish flowers, sweetly fragrant in the blossoming season. Tamarinds also occur, with trunks from twelve to fifteen feet in circumference. One curious tree, Holigarna longifolia, is greatly dreaded by the people, as it causes the skin and flesh to swell when incautiously handled. In August and September the beautiful Gloriosa superba creeper abounds amongst the smaller jungle by the roadside, displaying its orange lilies in the bright sunshine. Another beautiful creeper, Ipomœa vitifolia, with bright sulphur-coloured flowers, twines through the hedgerows.

The highway or "king's path," southward from Trevandrum, being of a fair width and kept in good condition, with the exception of some annoying bits in long-continued rainy weather, our bullock cart goes along pleasantly and makes steady, if slow, progress. In wet weather, however, when the mat covering of the cart is leaking, or in the height of the hot season, when the red dust of the roads comes pouring in, bandy travelling is far from pleasant. Telegraph posts by the roadside mark the advance of civilization, and most of the land on either hand is reclaimed from waste and cultivated with tapioca roots, yams, and other vegetables, plantains, fruit-trees, and other products of domestic utility. The country, generally, is undulating, and in the valleys the road runs on a raised bank through rice fields, which look like lakes of lovely verdure.

On our left, a conical hill called Némam Hill, perhaps a thousand feet in height, is noted as a landmark for passing vessels. From it, a low range of knolls, partly cleared and cultivated, runs along for a few miles parallel with the main road. We pass through various straggling villages with their little shops and dwellings; and notice here and there idol shrines and temples, as well as open *ambalams*, or resthouses and shelters for travellers, and wells with an attendant to dispense the cooling and refreshing liquid to all applicants.

About nine miles from Trevandrum, the view is exceedingly beautiful, a wide prospect of the whole south country being visible from a high part of the road, beyond which the land seems to sink, and is spread out before us covered with rich groves of palms, verdant rice-fields, and productive gardens. The extreme south of Travancore is nearly level, drier in climate, and in several respects bearing a closer likeness to the eastern coast.

Here it may be instructive, and amusing as well, to notice the stream of passengers of various castes and classes whom we meet going to the capital. Bullock carts travel in company, if possible, in long strings, laden with provisions, cloth, and other commodities, some of them with broad green plantain leaves to be used as plates for the high castes when eating: the drivers are singing, abusing their bullocks, or perhaps half asleep. Coolies carry loads of pottery, cocoa nuts, rice, oil-jars, fowls, firewood, and other necessaries for the city. Women are returning from market with piles of baskets on their heads, balanced with wonderful nicety. Girls bring water from the nearest well. Farmers are driving their cattle homewards. Brahman families in bright dresses, except some one unfortunate enough to be a widow, and who is, therefore, deprived of every ornament, clothed in white, and her hair shaven off, go to enjoy the feasting at Trevandrum; and travellers, young and aged, men, women, and children, with their umbrellas and fans of palm-leaf, brass drinking vessels, and bundles of clothing, arrayed in various styles of dress or undress, trudge along. Notice how useful one's toes are, if people did but make use of them. There is a woman who has dropped her cloth and picks it up with her toes without the labour of stooping to lift it. Practice, indeed, makes perfect! And here and there, to remind us of the suffering masses, a wretched Pulayan man or woman, skulks along the road, afraid of approaching too near the high caste man, or of being so unmannerly as to come "betwixt the wind and his nobility."

Just beyond the Náyar town of Neyáttankara, with its palace, magistrate's cutcherry, school-house and temple, the "Butter River" is crossed by a bridge of three arches and embankment, like that at Karamana, and by the same architect, erected about twenty-five years ago. We may be said to cross at the same time, the boundary of the Malayálam language, Tamil being the vernacular of South Travancore; and here we usually change from the one tongue to the other. Farther on, a neat Mission Church stands by the roadside, with a little rest-house at the gate for travellers. Throughout Travancore, these Christian churches, emblems of true religion and instruments of vast moral and social improvement, frequently occur. Formerly we were not allowed to erect them close to the road, lest the Brahmans should be polluted by the near approach of Christians of humble birth.

A curious little temple of Ganesha, a deity more worshipped in the Tamil than in the Malayálam country, stands near the road, quite circular in form, with conical roof, an unusual model in Travancore.

Kaliakavilei may be taken as an average specimen of a village in the south. A row of small houses, including a number of shops for retail of provisions, runs along the road on either side; and in the centre of the village is an open square, where the market is held. The public buildings, such as they are, comprise a police-station, a stone ambalam or travellers' rest-house, a small temple of the demon Káli, just like a cage with wooden bars, a Roman Catholic Church for the fisher people, and the Protestant Mission Church at the far end of the village. In front of the shops tobacco, cocoa-nut kernel, and rice, are spread out on mats to dry. The inhabitants are chiefly Muhammadan and Christian, and low caste Hindus, the Brahmans always residing in separate and secluded hamlets called Agrahárams.

The market, or fair as we might call it, is held twice a week, as in many other parts of the country, when crowds of people, especially women, troop in from the surrounding neighbourhood to sell their produce and lay in a small store of provisions. The hubbub and gabble of tongues is heard afar off. The people fill the open area, while a few low sheds are occupied by the cloth dealers. The supplies are various, and sufficient for the ordinary demand, comprising rice and other grain, peas, vegetables, fruits, spices, oil, salt, palm-sugar, sweetmeats, fish, cheap ornaments, and cloth. Formerly, and still in some parts of the south, and in the whole of North Travancore, Pulayars and Pariahs were obliged to stand at a distance apart from the crowd, but in some places they mix with other common people

Brahmans never attend these markets. When this liberty was given to the low castes, Sudra women and others refrained for a while from attending market, but they are now getting accustomed to the new state of things, though they hotly declare their dislike to it. "Since the Bible came here," said one, "the slaves, and low-castes are allowed to walk near us on roads, and to approach us in the markets, and so pollute us. Better had a pestilence prevailed and swept those abominable people away."

Children perfectly naked are playing about in the blazing sun, and from hence southward one sees great numbers of women going about in nature's garb from the waist upwards. Indeed, one of the first signs of having entered Travancore territory is the sight of half-nude Chogan females watering trees, or otherwise engaged on the banks of the backwaters. Muhammadan women, on the contrary, seem rather cumbered with clothing, wearing both jacket and upper-cloth, often black with filth, or the greater portion dirty, then partly covered with one clean white cloth, making the others appear but the worse by contrast. The Brahman women are always nicely dressed. The inelegant but decent dress of the Roman Catholic fisherwomen appears to be the result of a curious compromise between barbarous laws and female modesty—they cover the bosom straight across with a cloth which runs under each arm. But we are struck with the fact that the Christian jacket seems to occur but too rarely in proportion to the number of converts, and are obliged to hope that this mark of propriety and refinement is not getting forgotten in these days of peace and prosperity. The Christians seem to prefer the respectable "upper cloth," but it is insufficient as a garment for females.

Here and there barren rocky eminences occur, and the road at times passes over high ground strewn with huge blocks of granite. Towards Nagercoil these form considerable hills of somewhat conical form, as if a great heap of black granite, rounded rocks, and stones had been poured upon the plain. At Vannúr, near Pareychaley, a Brahman temple is picturesquely perched on a solid rock, such as Hindus like to build upon.

This is also the region of diminished rainfall, and some corresponding change in the vegetation appears. The hedges are formed of aloe and prickly pear; and euphorbias and palmyra palms increase in numbers on to Cape Comorin. A curious sight is a grove of palmyras, with their black stems and their round tops many feet high in the air. As there are no branches, it looks strange to see the distant background in some places clearly through the forest of mast-like stems.

At Kulitory, twenty-one miles from Trevandrum, we come to another Sudra town, with its palace, temple, and other buildings, and a magnificent iron-girder bridge—by far the finest in Travancore—which cost some thirteen lacs of rupees. It stands thirty feet high over the bed of the river, and is protected by iron railings, and lighted by lamps on either side. The total length is nearly 700 feet in eleven spans of sixty feet each; the abutments and piers of admirable granite work, and the approaches level and well metalled. In the dry season a scanty stream wanders over a broad expanse of sand in the bed of the river; but in the monsoon the flood from the hills formerly rose over the neighbouring country to a great width, and the irresistible current was impassable by the flat-bottomed canoes of the country.

As we go southwards, and the distance between the coast and the hills diminishes, the mighty wall of the Ghauts, nearly parallel with the coast, becomes more distinctly visible, and one spur, Vély Malei, comes close to the high road. From here the prospect includes the termination of the Ghauts, and several isolated hills near Cape Comorin. Up in the hills a new Sanitarium, for Europeans and others, has recently been opened by the Maharajah, from the pleasant climate and delightful scenery of which, almost vying with Coonoor, much benefit may be anticipated by visitors from South Travancore and Tinnevelly in search of health. A fine elevated plateau, several miles in extent, situated at some distance north of Asambu, within thirty miles of Nagercoil and fifty of Trevandrum, was discovered here a few years ago, and is occasionally visited by sportsmen. It is called Muttu-kuli-váyal, "pearl pit field," from a tradition of some bright shining pebbles having been formerly dug there. Several excavations like diamond pits are observable. A stream of firstrate water runs through the plateau, surrounded by undulating knolls covered with grass and scrub. The stream has been traced descending into Travancore, to which State the land is now adjudged to belong, as the water-shed of the hills is the fixed boundary between Travancore and Tinnevelly territory. The height is about 4,000 feet above the sea level, and the view magnificent: some of the planters' bungalows and estates appear to be far beneath, and the whole country is visible as far as the Cape. "The scenery is a combination of grandeur and beauty, with its lofty adjacent peaks and magnificent valleys, open and undulating grassy slopes, from which may be seen, on the one hand, vast stretches of forest-clad hills, and, on the other, at various points, a long unbroken line of sea-shore."

Nowhere south of the Peermade Hills does there seem to be anything equal to this place. In the hottest season the air is deliciously cool, the temperature ranging from 64 to 71 degrees

BUILDINGS AT MAVELIKARA.

Fahr.; in October the average is 57° to 60°. Being open all round and high, there seems no reason to dread the malarious fevers so common on the lower hills. The ascent is made by an easy zigzag road, and roads are being made all about, so that every facility will be afforded for pedestrian exercise. Bison and other game abound in the neighbourhood, and the magnificent evergreen forests and splendid waterfalls of Pápanásam at the head of the Tambraparni river are within easy reach. Already several houses have been built and occupied.

About thirty miles south of Trevandrum a group of three places close together and near to the road, and interesting in the history of Travancore, seem worthy of a visit. The first is Palpanábhapuram fort and town, an ancient residence of the Rajahs, now containing about 4,000 inhabitants. It lies about a mile from the main road. The walls are high, not unlike those of Trevandrum fort. The old palace is a good specimen of the Malabar style, a very extensive gallery-like building, two stories high, and with tiled roof; the Durbar Hall somewhat resembling the old one at the capital, with fine polished chunám pillars, and ground floor open to the courtyard on the inside. Some of the corridors are very narrow and low-roofed, built without any regard to ventilation, the windows long and low, nearly closed with beautiful panels of carved lattice work; some bow windows are supported without on sloping brackets finely carved with grotesque figures, and are furnished inside with seats, so as to afford a convenient view to the female inmates of all public processions and visitors. The uppermost rooms are more cool and airy for sleeping in, having no walls, but open lattice work all round. There is much good solid stone-work of carved or polished granite—baths, pillars square and round, magnificent slabs of black granite, &c. In this fort there are various temples, a large tank, and houses of entertainment for Brahmans. The accompanying engraving of buildings at Mávelikara, between Alleppy and Quilon, will give a good idea of the usual style of native architecture.

Oodayagerry is a large irregular fort nearly three miles in circumference, with a hill in the centre. The bare walls only remain, and ruins of the barracks, gun-foundry, magazine, and church. The enclosure is now grown over with jungle and palmyra trees. The monuments in the old church are deeply interesting, and should be carefully preserved. Here lie the remains of D'Lanoy, with his wife and son, who was the architect of the fort, and greatly enlarged the kingdom of Travancore for Rajah Vanji Martánda Vurmah by his courage and arms, and skilful conduct of the native troops. This fort must have cost an immense sum, and much forced labour from the poor, yet proved of no value when the British forces entered Travancore in 1809, and both Oodayagerry and Palpanábhapuram forts were at once abandoned by the Travancoreans.

Outside the fort we see the rock in which a Christian martyr of the last century is now pretended to have opened a spring of water by striking the rock with his elbow. A memorial church has been erected by the Roman Catholics over the small spring (if it is a spring), and it is now being made the source of a new superstition, discrediting the cause of Christian truth just where it should be presented in its clearest and purest form. It is visited by pilgrims from various parts, who make contributions to the shrine and drink the sacred water as a cure for disease; the water is carried to various parts of South India.

Kottár is a very ancient town forty-two miles south of Trevandrum, situated in the centre of the level tract of country called the Nánjinád or "district of Nánji." The population of Kottár is about 7,000, to which should be added another 7,000 for Nagercoil, which may be regarded as virtually one with it. The bazaar is extensive, and trade with Tinnevelly and Travancore considerable: silk cloths and cotton checks are manufactured here and at the neighbouring Cháliyar village of Vadaséri. Temples of Pilleiyár or Ganesha abound as in the Tamil country, usually small buildings, but of solid stone work: these are the commonest places of worship, except demon altars. There is a handsome cathedral-like church of St. Xavier, with good stone porch, which is visited annually in December in commemoration of the saint by many thousands, and where Hindus also sometimes offer vows and supplications. The London Mission has here a reading-room, visited by thousands of readers yearly, and a neat chapel erected at the sole cost of a remarkable convert, a manufacturer of silk cloth, which the family supplied to the palace till their conversion to Christianity, when the trade was taken from them.

Nagercoil was not long since the merest hamlet, connected with the "Snake Temple," which gives its name to the place; but having been adopted as the head-quarters of the London Mission in these parts, it is now a clean, well-built, and increasing Christian town. By their intelligence and industry in various ways, and especially of late years in the coffee-planting enterprise, the native Christians are becoming wealthy, and a wonderful change has taken place. When Mr. Mault went out he "could not find four Shánárs able to read;" now the Christians themselves own and edit a newspaper in Tamil and English; and publish vernacular books. Some twenty years ago, when Mr. P. D. Déwasagáim built his neat two-story house, it was a wonder in these parts; but now there are many such, some even larger, with good rooms, upper story, and reception hall. Christian women, once forbidden by caste law to cover the person, now dress handsomely and well, and manufacture valuable pillow-lace. There are two English missionaries, one in charge of the English Seminary, a busy Press, several schools, including some for female education, which receives devoted attention and is the foundation of all the good visible, and one of the largest churches in South India, "the Exeter Hall of Travancore," in which many a noble speech and sermon have been delivered. The native congregation worshipping here is entirely self-supporting, chooses and provides for its own pastor, has not for twenty years received any pecuniary aid from the Society, and now aids a native preacher at the capital. This church was lately presided over by a remarkable and devoted Brahman pastor, and now by an eloquent Tamil preacher and writer—Rev. J. Joshua. It has long been a custom in native partnerships to insert in the deed as one of the conditions the devotal of one-tenth of the profits to religious and charitable purposes. In this and similar ways funds are freely provided for self-support and the extension of Christian truth.

Here we are in the centre of the Nánjinád—a tract of flat country, comprising about 218 square miles, shut in by hills on nearly all sides excepting the sea-coast on the south, occupying the southernmost corner of Travancore, and presenting distinctive characteristics of its own. Very little rain falls at Cape Comorin, but a small river from the hills, and several large irrigation tanks and channels supply water for numerous rice-fields. The most densely peopled and richest part of the State, and purely Tamil in language and population, it is dotted over with villages quite of the style of those on the Eastern Coast, often badly thatched or repaired, as the drier climate allows of greater carelessness in this respect. Strong winds and tracts of dry barren sand eastwards form obstacles to profitable cultivation, yet the people seem larger and better fed than those further north.

The flora naturally differs from that of the more humid Western Coast. The Ixora, Mussænda, and other shrubs are absent, except on the banks of canals, abundance of Barleria and other plants filling their place. The Colocynth spreads over the sandy wastes, and the Aloe and Sanseviera abound on the shore. Amongst trees, the acacia, margosa, laurel-nut, terminalia and umbrella tree abound.

Extraordinary legends are told of some ancient ruler of Nánjinád—of the Kuravan caste, they say, called Pándi Kuravan—how he got this territory as a present for piercing the ears of the Pandian Rajah's daughter; or according to the more common story, how this caste obtained power by the discovery of an oil-well which possessed virtue to transmute iron into gold; how they only asked as tax the shares of the old ploughs, which they at once converted into gold; how a king of this tribe desired a daughter of one of the neighbouring Vellála Muthaliárs as his wife, but was got rid of by being crushed under a stone pandal for the marriage ceremony, so contrived as to be capable of being thrown down in an instant, and so forth. It does appear that the Kuravars held power at times, and there may be some basis of fact on which these traditions are founded. W. Taylor considers that they were superseded by the Vellálars, and these by the English or Travancore authorities.

From Kottár the road to the Cape passes along a high embankment of earth, which protects the rice-fields from the small backwater at Managoody, and through Suchindram, an ancient and sacred town. Near Suchindram are several magnificent trees of terminalia, some six or seven feet in diameter. The town is surrounded by rice-fields and groves of cocoanut trees and palmyras. The "Paraya Aur," or "old river," is crossed by a curious ancient stone bridge, formed of large granite slabs, which appears to have stood long, and to be very solid work. When was it built? There are about twenty piers of long heavy stones laid on one another in the direction of the current: these are crossed by similar stones in a line with the road. A somewhat similar stone bridge, but with the centre piers higher than those at the side, crosses the river at one place between Káyenkulam and Mávelikara, and is in good condition. Several others are found in various parts of the country. The Post Bridge at Dartmoor is very similar in style.

The temple of Suchindram is of prime importance, the Maharajah being expected to fast on the day of the idol car-drawing in December till the operation is completed. A good tank, and the usual Brahman feeding-house and subsidiary buildings are attached to the temple, and it is adorned with sculptures of the ten avatars. The town has recently been rebuilt by the Sirkar at the cost of nearly a lac of rupees. The god is almost hidden under the mass of golden ornaments presented by his votaries, but these offer too great a temptation to the cupidity of the priests and attendants. A large amount of the

TEMPLE AT SUCHINDRAM

jewels disappeared recently, when a Hindu quaintly remarked: "The Christian preachers have taken away from the hearts of the people the fear of their native gods. People now rob the gods of their gold and silver jewellery, and the gods are afraid of being stolen themselves!"

Nearer the Cape lies another remarkable village, Agasteeswaram, one of the head-quarters of demon worship in these parts, and where the Shánár caste had once a nominal chieftain or headman. The soil is sandy and barren, the hedges are of Euphorbia; the principal produce the Acacia latronum or umbrella tree, curiously like an umbrella in its growth, with terrible thorns two inches in length; goats, it is said, eat the young shoots. The water here is very bad.

Before reaching the Cape we pass through the Travancore "lines" or fortified wall similar to that on the northern frontier. All is now in ruins—a mere bank of earth thinly grown over with acacia, margosa, banyan, and other trees—with, here and there, portions of walls and ruins of gates and bastions. These southern lines were described when in their best condition, in the following terms by Colonel Welsh, who took them in 1809:—"The lines by which the entrance into Travancore through the pass was defended, were about two miles in length, stretching across the gap from one range of mountains to another. They included a rugged hill to the southward, strongly fortified, and a strong rock about halfway, called the northern redoubt. The works consisted of small well-built bastions for two or three guns, joined at intervals by strong curtains, the whole cannon-proof, and protected by a thick hedge of thorn-bushes, the approach to which was difficult from the wildness of the country."

The last isolated mountain in Travancore is called by the people "Medicine Hill," being supposed to be the very hill which the monkey god Hanuman brought, as related in the Rámáyana, from a distance of fifteen hundred miles further north, and threw down here. He had been sent to it for medicinal herbs to restore the dead and wounded of Ráma's army, and not being able, in his haste, to recognize and gather the particular plants, he pulled up the mountain itself, and brought it on his shoulders. It seems, however, that in hurriedly depositing his burden he turned it upside down!

Cape Comorin being low and not discernible a great way off, this isolated hill is better visible to navigators, and is therefore sometimes called Comorin by them. The southern termination of the range of the Western Ghauts, a bold conspicuous summit and magnificent mass of solid rock, with a clear fall of many hundred feet towards the Tinnevelly side, has also been erroneously taken for the Cape, though several miles distant from it.

The road to the Cape is broad, and pleasantly shaded for some miles with banyan trees, which in many parts stretch quite across the road. Cape Comorin is supposed, along with several other noted places in India, to be very sacred, and is visited by pilgrims from all parts, though those residing near it do not share in the enchantment. In the immediate neighbourhood the whole country is a mass of palmyras, as the coast is of cocoanut palms. The land is not high, and slopes gently down into the sea. At the north end of the village stands a large Roman Catholic Church, and a village of fisher people, just such as Xavier laboured amongst so successfully three centuries ago. Several low enclosures with pyramidal stones, or demon altars, may be noticed in the vicinity.

A street of Brahman houses leads down to the travellers' rest-house, where Gosámis and other religious mendicants and pilgrims from Northern India abide, and may be heard chanting their orisons, and to the Pagoda and the bathing-places on the shore. The total population is about 2,300. Various buildings are scattered about, and minor shrines of Pilleiyár and other deities. The great temple is dedicated to Bhagavathi, or Durga, the patron goddess of the place, which is named after her Kumari, "the virgin;" and who appears to have been worshipped here as early as the time of Pliny, for he mentions the place by this name. The monthly bathing in honour of the goddess is still continued, but is not practised to the same extent as in former times. The annual expenditure of the temple is about Rs. 11,000. From without, little of it is visible except the high walls adorned with perpendicular streaks of red, and the flat terraced roofs; of course, it cannot be entered by strangers or low caste people for close inspection. In front are four remarkable stone monoliths rising into the air to the height of twenty feet, as if intended to support a portico, but left unfinished, as in Madura and Tanjore, which, it is said, is always done to neutralise the "evil eye." The festival is held for five days in the year, when the place is "wholly given to idolatry."

The passage between the Brahman Street and the Temple and Choultry has once been paved with large stones, and the pillars at the sides well carved, but these have now mostly fallen in the dust. The great stone Choultry is more accessible, and a really artistic production. It consists of a corniced roof, say eighteen feet in height, resting upon twelve carved pillars. The sides are closed in with walls, and the front partly closed with cross bars or beams of stone, leaving but a small opening for entrance. Within are two rows of dark granite pillars on each side, with good sculptures, some of them large and spirited representations of Vishnu, Brahma, Hanuman, Krishna, and other Hindu gods; figures holding a lamp in outstretched hands—a good design for an ornamental lamp—and the pillars covered on all sides with scrolls and figures. Two striking grotesque sculptures represent the fabulous Yáli, with face and body of a lion, and trunk of an elephant; underneath a smaller elephant raises his trunk, which intertwines with the proboscis of the upper one; and this elephant itself rests upon a human figure. In the mouths of the yális are stone balls which will turn round, but not come out, the whole being cleverly carved out of the solid block.

On the shore are several small bathing-places for the use of the Maharajah and Brahmans bathing in the sacred waters in honour of the goddess—small, square buildings like the ordinary roadside rest-houses, supported on stone pillars. Here may be gathered specimens of remarkable sands, one bright reddish in colour formed of rolled fragments of garnet and ruby, such as are found in larger pieces in Ceylon—another black sand formed from titaniferous iron-ore, not magnetic—and the celebrated "rice sand" with strangely worn grains of chalcedonic quartz, partly tinted with a little oxide of iron and bearing a close resemblance to rice, respecting which the priests relate some foolish legends. One version has already been recorded. (Land of Charity, p. 178.) Another is to the effect that when the god Siva was going on a certain night privately to marry the goddess, the morning unexpectedly broke, its dawn being heralded by the crowing of a cock, which compelled him to retrace his steps; and all the rice which had been prepared for the wedding was petrified and thrown on the shore. A couple of low, black rocky islets a little way out in the sea, in the centre of one of which a fresh water well is said to exist, with one or two smaller rocks, on which the sea breaks, form the last points of solid land in India.

CHAPTER II.

THE PEOPLE AND THEIR CLASSIFICATION.

THE report on the Census of Travancore, taken on May 18, 1875, supplies valuable details respecting the population of the State, and their social and religious condition. The enumeration itself caused considerable commotion amongst the people, especially the lower castes. For some months previously the rural population were in a state of complete ferment, dreading that advantage would be taken of the occasion to impose some new tax or to exercise some bitter oppression, as was often done on various occasions in the old times of cruelty and injustice. This opportunity was seized by some Muhammadans and others, to despoil the poor slave-castes of their fowls and other domestic animals, by telling them that the Sirkar was about to seize everything of the kind, and to exact a similar amount annually, so that they had better sell them off at once at any price than lose them altogether. The Súdras also sought to frighten them by the report that the Christians were to be carried off in ships to foreign parts, in which the missionaries and their native helpers would assist. When numbers were stamped upon all the houses, people thought that soon they themselves would be branded and seized by the Sirkar. Absurd reports were raised. Some said the Maharajah had promised to supply inhabitants for a country which had been desolated by famine. Others said that a certain number were to be shipped off on the 18th May. Till that date the people were whispering "To-day or to-morrow we shall be caught." For example, an old woman having shut up her grandson in her house for safety, went to call her son, weeping all the way and beating her breast. One who met her comforted her and went back with her to the house, where the child was found half-dead with fright. Many of the people left their gardens uncultivated during the panic, ate up the seed corn, sold their cattle and sheep. One man had ten fowls, and, taking them to a river, he cut off their heads, and threw them away. So dreadful is the ignorance of the people through want of education. It was even reported that the missionaries had prepared a building on the sea-coast, where a great meeting was to be held, immediately after which the people would be caught and shipped off. Many of the uneducated Sudras also in distant localities were much afraid.

The Native Government did all that was possible at the moment by issuing re-assuring proclamations to satisfy the minds of the people, but this was so far rendered nugatory by the wiles of the former slave-owners, who still hold most Government appointments, and by the amazing ignorance of the Pariahs and Pulayars, who can neither read proclamations themselves, nor ordinarily approach the places of public resort where Government notices are proclaimed. Handbills were also prepared and published by the mission in Tamil and Malayálam; and the catechists went round with the enumerators to assist them. After the final day, the excitement speedily quieted down, and the people learned a lesson as to the folly of regarding false reports of sinister designs on the part of the Government or the Christian missionaries. The foolish alarm illustrates the evils arising from caste divisions, popular ignorance, and the absence of the simplest elements of education amongst the lowest classes.

The total population was then found to be 2,311,379; of whom 1,702,805 are Hindus, 139,905 Muhammadans, 261 Europeans, 1,383 Eurasians, 151 Jews, and 466,874 Native Christians of various denominations—more than a fifth of the entire population—constituting Travancore *the most Christian country in India.*

Another enumeration was made, to fit in with the general census of British India, on 17th February, 1881, according to which the population consisted of 1,197,134 males and 1,204,024 females—total 2,401,158; but as no special report of this Census has yet been published, the previous census of 1875 must be quoted in the ensuing chapters, for statistics of particular castes, education, and other matters.

The average density of population for the whole country (comprising 6,731 square miles) is 343 to a square mile; but the different districts vary in this respect, from 1,280 near the coast, to as low as 37 to the square mile in the interior. There are 110 women to every 100 men; amongst children 85 girls to 100 boys.

Of the entire population 5·74 per cent. can read and write, but the proportion greatly varies in different classes and districts. Amongst Muhammadans it is 4·72, Hindus 5·57, and Native Christians 6·56 per cent. respectively. In the capital—the centre of government, learning and civilisation—the percentage of educated persons is 15, while in the wild and neglected districts of Múváttupura, Todupura and Shencótta, and in Pattanápuram, Chenganúr, and Sherttala, where large numbers of the low castes reside, the proportion of the entire population educated even slightly, is between three and four per cent; in Cunnattúr, where the population numbers 60,000, it falls so low as 2·79 per cent., revealing a fearful state of backwardness in this respect.

Roman Catholic Christians were put down as 109,820, and Syrian Christians 295,770; but probably some Syro-Romanists were reckoned as Syrians because of their birth, when they should have been classed as Roman Catholics in religion.

Native Christian educated females were given as 1,593 in number. But the London Mission alone could at that time have supplied lists of the names of 1,559, and the Church Mission of 627 adult females able to read and write, not to speak of Roman Catholics and Syrian Christian women. The proportion of educated women (aged 15 and upwards) amongst the Protestant Christians was, therefore, 1,243 in every ten thousand, not 78 as in the Census Report! The percentage of educated females over fifteen years of age in the London Mission is now 16·86, and in the Church Mission it is probably not much different. And this is but what might have been expected from the interest which missionaries have always taken in education.

The Native Christians (of all sects), it was said, "have 12·42 per cent. of their male population educated;" but the true ratio of educated males in the two Protestant Missions was then about 29 or 30 per cent.; in the London Mission it is now 38 per cent., besides boys under fifteen.

Of the population of Travancore, 1,902,533 speak Malayálam, and 387,909 Tamil. The total number of Hindu castes is 420, many of which are peculiar to this Coast.

The number of castes which comprise more than a thousand souls in each is 49, according to the following list; these, therefore, are numerically the principal castes. One more is added which is close upon this figure:—

In the spelling of these names of castes note that the ordinary masculine singular affix is *an*—feminine, *atti*, *ichi*, etc. The plural is generally marked by *r* for *n*, as *Ilavan—Ilavar;* sometimes *mar* or *kal.* It seems impracticable to reduce all to uniformity in an English work, as an exact transliteration from the Indian tongues would disguise several terms already familiar with a certain established orthography, as Shánárs, Pariahs, Sudras, and others. Writers in English commonly add our plural *s* to the Dravidian plural in *r*, as *Ilavar;* but *Ilavans* is also used—especially for those that form the plural in *mar.*

Castes	Numbers.	Males Educated.	Females Educated.
Malayála Brahman	10,762	10,188	241
Foreign Brahman	27,672		
Kshetrya, *Kshatriyan*	2,453	645	116
Eliathoo, *Ilayathu*	3,455	634	16
Kongani, Concan Brahmans, Sudras and others	14,260	1,178	4
Pushpaken	1,414		
Várier	2,730	1,315	65
Coorookul, *Guru*	1,534		
Márán	14,611	1,311	46
Malayála Soodra	440,932	46,373	2,656
Vellálen	24,125	4,294	30
Pándi Soodra...	18,867	2,887	6
Chetti	16,948	1,744	17
Vadooken (northerner), Naidoo, Naiken, etc.—Telugus	1,764	112	1
Patnoolkáren, Silk Weaver...	1,636	215	0
Khrishnenvaga, in the south, resembling Nánjinád Vellálars	8,298	772	6
Chálien, Weaver	6,691	305	1
Sunkum Pundárem	10,612	438	4
Pánan, Tailor...	2,225	119	0
Elavánien, *Ilavániyan*, Greengrocer ...	2,665	114	0
Vánien, Oilmonger	24,516	1,153	6
Cummálen, *Kammalan*, Artisan	20,936		
Thuttán, *Tattán*, Goldsmith	14,009		
Cunnán, *Kannán*, Brassfounder	3,193		
Cullen, *Kallan*, Stoneworker	5,223	4,266	37
Collen, *Kollan*, Blacksmith...	19,2[illegible]1		
Thatchen, *Tachan*, Sawyer	3,800		
Aushároo, *Asári*, Carpenter	29,385		
Maraven, Tinnevelly Marava	4,988	137	0
Idayan, Tinnevelly Shepherd	6,319	275	1
Koshaven, *Kusavan*, Potter	7,364	96	0
Veluthaden, Washerman	13,190	275	1
Chemmán or Chuckler, Shoemaker ...	981	14	1
Kshowraken, Barber	14,521	417	7
Cunián, *Kaniyán*, Soothsayer	9,107	1,966	34
Munnan, Hill tribe	16,256	280	9
Puraven, *Paravan*, Lime-burner	8,598	27	0
Thundán, *Tandán*	17,852	65	0
Noolian, Coir-spinner	1,495	15	0
Elooven, *Ilavan*	383,017	5,928	93
Chánnán, *Shánán*	97,730	1,924	8
Mookkooven, *Mukkuvan* and Chavalakaran, Fisherman	12,725	92	2
Cackalen	1,047	13	8
Mala Arayen, Hill tribe	11,918	28	0
Vaden, *Védan*	7,293	7	0
Pullen, *Pallan*	5,797	13	0
Oolláden, *Ulládan*, Hill tribe	2,829	6	0
Coraven, *Kuravan* or Kuruban	56,274	58	0
Purian, *Parayan*, Pariah	63,688	192	0
Poolian, *Pulayan*	18[illegible],916	183	0

Travancore thus contains a collection of living specimens of various types of humanity—a piecemeal and patchwork distribution of mankind of the most singularly complicated pattern—so that this small population of two millions and a half affords an inexhaustible field for ethnological research, and no complete account of even the whole of the principal castes is here possible. A few typical specimens only can be given in this volume, in which we seek especially to illustrate the condition of the lower castes, and of those that are peculiar to the Malayálam country.

To attempt to arrange the castes in the order of social precedence and respectability would, in the face of caste quarrels and jealousies, be as difficult as to draw up an exact lineal natural classification of all the species of plants; and its accuracy would be disputed by all but those at the head of the list.

Mr. G. Kerala Varmman Tirumulpád, however, in his vernacular work on "Malabar Laws of Inheritance," gives a curious and interesting classification of the castes, which furnishes us with such a list, showing the comparative estimate in which the respective castes are held by learned natives of high caste and of the old school. His arrangement is highly conventional, embodying some absurd prejudices and traditions, and making the number of castes to accord with theory rather than historical facts and existing circumstances.

This author discusses 72 castes, which he arranges as follows, Brahmanical castes, 8; Defective castes, 2; Intermediate castes, 12; Sudra castes, 18; Artisan castes, 6; Degraded (*pathitha*) castes, 10; Mean (*nícha*) castes, 8; in all, 64; besides other Ancient castes in Malabar, 8; total, 72.

The names of the eight **Brahman castes**, he says, are these—

1. Tamburán, Brahman rulers and high priests, as the Alvánchéri high priest.

2. A'dhyans of the Eight Houses, leaders of the aristocracy of Malabar. These are called Nambúripáds or head Nambúris, and are sacrificers and expounders of the Vedas.

3. Visishta, "distinguished," noted for rank, learning, or sanctity. These have other titles according to function and dignity, as Adutiri, Chomátiri, Akkitira, and Bhattatiri—offerers of burnt sacrifice, ascetics, and so forth.

4. Sámánya, "ordinary" Brahmans, who conduct ceremonies, serve in temples, profess magical arts, exorcism, &c.

5. Játhi Mátran, "barely in the caste," also called Nambúri, Mússu, Nambi, &c. A lower division comprising physicians, warriors, government servants, theatrical performers. Though considered inferior to the rest of the community, they are still

admitted to bathe at the same place and to meals in company with others.

6. Sángéthigan or Embrán, traditionally said to have left Malabar for a while, and returned retaining some foreign usages. This division includes the Tiruvallá Désis, the Canarese and Tulu Brahmans. They are Sánthis, or officiating priests in temples, repeat the Vedas, &c.

7. Sápagrastan, "accursed," because they doubted Parasu Rama. Commonly called Nambúris, but not allowed to study the Vedas, officiate as temple priests, nor associate with other Brahmans in meals or ceremonial observances.

8. Pápishtan, "delighters in sin," various faults being traditionally alleged against them, as insulting idols, murder, and performing sacred rites for Sudras (which seems to be thought as bad as murder)! They are in low estimation as to Brahmanhood; and not allowed to perform divine service.

The first to the third of these divisions are usually spoken of under the general name of Nambúris. Some of the fourth and fifth are called Póttis: some of the last, and the fifth classes, Pandárattillam. All these eight kinds are not found in Travancore. Pattars are foreign Brahmans, generally from Coimbatore.

Kshatriyas of the Lunar race alone exist in this age. There are three royal families—Tiruppáppúr, Travancore; Perumpadappu, Cochin; and Kóla, Colattiri. Kshatriyas are Rajahs, Koil Pandárams and Tirumulpads, not high enough to associate with the Brahmans, nor so low as to be put on a level with Sudras.

The two **Defective Castes** are Ilayathu, "junior," or Nambiyátiri, chiefly priests to Sudras; and Mutthathu, "senior," or Agriman; who carry idols in procession, clean the courts of temples, &c. Among these property descends from father to son. The Ilayathus are said to have once been Nambúris and degraded in caste for the crime of having informed a Sudra what rites should be performed in favour of his deceased ancestors.

The twelve **Antarála, "intermediate" castes** between Brahmans and Sudras, generally called Ambalavási, "temple dwellers," officiate as Levites or temple servants. They mostly follow the nepotistic law. They are—

1. Adi, "slaves," appointed to offer Siva worship in the groves of Bhadrakáli, and exorcise devils, who have therefore lost Brahmanhood and become Ambalavásis. Very few in number.

2. Pushpagan "florist," or Unni, brings flowers and garlands for temple worship. The next two classes are sometimes included with these, viz.:—

3. Nambisán, teachers, &c.

4. Púpalli.

5. Pishárodi, tie garlands in temples of Vishnu. They do not wear the sacred thread or the kudumi, and their bodies are, after death, buried with salt.

6. Váriyan, perform the same service as Pushpagan.

7. Chákkiyár recite poems and dramas before gods and Brahmans, sometimes also representing the personages themselves.

8. Nambiyár, play the drum and assist the preceding.

9. Tíyáttunni, "fire-dancer;" degraded from Brahmans because they jump through fire in honour of Bhadrakáli.

10. Pidáran or Mússen, resembling Adis above mentioned, make offerings of flesh, spirits, &c., to Bhadrakáli.

11. Kuru or Guru, provide milk and ghee for temples, and sweep and cleanse them. Most numerous in the South.

12. Náttu Pattan or Unni, tie garlands and sweep temples.

All Ambalavásis abstain from animal food of every kind.

The eighteen **Sudra castes** are—

1. Kiriyattil Náyar, called also Kuruppu, Keimmal, and Menon — the offspring of temple women by Brahmans. Though now generally poor they are said to be descendants of statesmen, accountants, generals, &c. They occupy the foremost place and need not serve the Brahmans.

2. Illakár, servants in Brahman houses; and,

3. Swarúpakár, in Kshatriya houses; and,

4. Pádamangalam, in temples.

5. Tamil Pádakar.

6. Idachéri Náyar, shepherds and dairymen.

7. Márán, drummers and musicians in temples, attendants at ceremonies of Brahmans and Kshatriyas. They abstain from flesh-meat, and are, therefore, considered superior to other Sudras, yet are not allowed to eat with the higher classes of Sudras.

8. Chembukotti, copper utensil makers; and,

9. Odatta Náyar, tile makers for temples.

10. Madavan or Puliyatta Náyar, servants of Brahmans and others down to Ambalavási.

11. Kalamkotti, potters, and 12. Chakkála, oil-mongers for temples.

13. Pallichán, palankeen bearers for Rajahs and Brahmans.

14. Asthikurichi, subordinate to Márán, perform funeral rites for Sudras.

The next four, our author says, are Sudras, but inferior to the preceding, and cause pollution to those Sudras who approach them, viz.:—

15. Chetti, merchants, selling curry stuffs and other goods.

16. Cháliyan, weaver.

17. Veluttedan, washerman ; happily the cloths washed and handled by them are not prohibited as unclean, and may be received into pagodas and worn by all!

18. Kshourakár, barbers for all down to Sudras.

Outside the sixty-four regular castes are the following "**extra**" **castes**:—

1. Ammóman, villagers of Payanúr.
2. Nambadi or Nambidi wearing the thread ; and
3. Nambidi, without the sacred cord, a little below Ambalavásis and above Súdras—assist in sacrifices. These are not found in Travancore.
4. Pothuvál, storekeepers in temples. Sometimes numbered with the Mútthathus.
5. Pilápalli, reduced from Brahmanhood by their ancestors accidentally receiving a fish as a present! Only a few families residing at Ambalapula and without the privileges of the Ambalavásis.
6. Sámantran, as the Zamorin and other rulers ; those without rule are called Unittiri, Unyátiri, Erádi, Vellodi, Nedungadi, &c. Sometimes numbered with the Ambalavásis.
7. Karuvélam Náyar, resembling Illakár—treasury and palace guards. Said to have been brought from Kólatnád.
8. Naujinád Vellálan, agricultural settlers in Travancore.

The **Kammalar, or "artisan" castes** are—1. Asári, carpenter, 2. Kallan or Kallásári, stonecutter. 3. Kannán or Músári, brazier. 4. Tattán, goldsmith and jeweller. 5. Kollan, blacksmith. 6. Tachan, sawyer. Of these, only goldsmiths and braziers can approach the Sudras without polluting them.

The **Pathita or "degraded" castes**, fabled to have arisen from the unlawful intercourse of persons of differing and higher castes are ten, viz.—

1. Kaniyán, astrologer.
2. Vil Kuruppu, bowmaker and painter.
3. Vélan or Mannán, sorcerer, removes rubbish from Brahman houses.
4. Kuruppu.
5. Tol Kuruppu, make shields and other articles of leather.
6. Pánan, tailor.
7. Paravan, limeburner.
8. Ilavan, cocoa-nut tree cultivator and distiller ; and
9. Shánnán, the same for the palmyra tree.
10. Válan, boatmen ; some are called Arayan and Kanakkan.

The **Nicha. or "polluted" castes** are—Of the plains, four :

1. Parayan, or Pariah, labourers and basket-makers. 2. Pulayan, slave labourers. 3, Náyadi, beggars. 4. Ulládan, woodcutters.

And of the hills four: 1. Védan. 2. Kaniyán, hunters. 3. Kuruban, or Kuravan or Kurumban. 4. Mala Arayan, hill cultivators. The Kurubans sometimes work for the Arayans.

What a marvellous schedule this Hindu writer furnishes of gradations of hierarchy, nobility, gentry, artisans, cultivators, labourers, slaves, and outcasts!

CHAPTER III.

THE PULAYARS.

THE Pulayar, or Pooliar, caste of Travancore, Cochin, and Malabar appear to be identical with those who are called Holiers in Coorg and Canara. The term is derived from *pula*, "ceremonial pollution," taint or defilement, especially by a case of birth, or by touching a dead body.

In Cochin these form the largest part of the Cherumar, or former slave population, which, according to the census of 1875, numbers over 52,000 in a total population of 601,000.

In Travancore this caste numbers 188,916, which is one-twelfth of the entire population. They are next in number to the Ilavars. "They are distributed over the whole land, north of Nánjinád. Their number is greatest in the Tiruvella district, where they muster 15,399; in Moováttupuley they number 15,124; in Cunnattúr 14,592; the lowest number is four in Shencotta. They are a Malayálam speaking race, and are, therefore, sparse in the Tamil Talooks of Nánjinád and Shencotta."

Besides the above, there are some ten or twelve thousands of the same race under the instruction of the Church and London Missionary Societies, who are classed in the census under the head of "Protestant Christians."

The Pulayars are peculiar to the Western Coast, and unknown in the British provinces on the East. They belong to the very lowest grades in caste, having been formerly slaves and still deeply degraded, as education and civilization have not yet largely affected them, and their former masters do not wish them to rise to independence or full liberty. Their customs and usages are full of the deepest interest to the ethnologist, while their social condition calls for the profoundest sympathy of the philanthropist.

Origin.—Bishop Caldwell rightly regards the Pulayars as representatives of the same class as the Pariahs and Pallars of Tinnevelly. He remarks, "Perhaps the best representatives at present of the earliest race of inhabitants are those long-oppressed tribes, now considered the lowest in the social scale. It is a noticeable circumstance that there is no tradition whatever of the arrival in the country at any time of the Pallas and Paraiyas." And again, "I consider the black, low caste races of Southern India not Turanians or immigrants of any sort, but aborigines like the negroid aborigines of the Eastern Islands and Australia."

About Trevandrum, their own tradition, evidently impressed upon them by their masters, is expressed in words uttered by one of this class. "We are content to remain in our present circumstances for Bhagaván (God), after having created the higher castes, considered what to do with the surplus earth, when Párvathi advised him to create therewith a low class to serve the higher ones."

Another account is given in one of the Mackenzie MSS, as held by the Pulayars residing near Kánjerapalli. When Parasu Ráman had made slaughter in his wars, the widows lamented their being without husbands, and besought him to supply others, which he effected by calling in strangers, from which origin the Pulayars are derived.

The Pulayars of Malabar are in a far lower condition than the Pariahs of the Tamil country. The reason seems to be the same as produced the extreme conservatism and bigoted retention of Hindu caste and primitive customs of the inhabitants of the Western Coast—the physical conformation of the country shutting them off from intercourse with their neighbours. While in the Carnatic serfs could run away from one king to another (as some Pariahs are known to have come seven generations ago to Nánjinád for greater freedom and safety); here in Malabar they were hemmed in by impassable mountains and forests and by the sea—deep rivers to cross, Nairs everywhere on the watch, and no possibility of escape. So they sank from generation to generation. And of this tribe the lowest and most debased are now found on the strip of land between Alleppy and Cochin, where they are entirely isolated between the sea and the backwater.

G. K. Vurma classes the Pulayars as one of eight *Nícha* or polluted castes. They were brought, he says, into Malabar by Parasu Raman for the service of Brahmans and others. The law of inheritance of Pariahs and Ulládars is by sons—that of Pulayars, Náyádis, and the four jungle tribes, part by sons, part by sisters' sons.

In the neighbourhood of Trevandrum, Pulayars are accustomed to boast of having once had a chieftain or rajah of their own, who resided in a fort not far off. There certainly are some remains on the summit of a hill near Vély of a mud wall and ditch, some 60 or 70 feet square, enclosing a small level plot of ground now overgrown with scrub and having a deep well inside. This is commonly called Pulayanár Kótta, and a Sudra family in the neighbourhood are called by their fellows "the Pulayan's Accountants," and freely admit that their ancestors did hold that office.

Perhaps this was the nick-name of some ancient chieftain, as has been suggested in explanation of such names as Chakkilian (shoemaker's) Fort in North Arcot, and others in the Tamil country. Or, as Head Pulayars were appointed by the Travancore Government to be responsible for the others in all matters of business, there may have been one chief head of all near the capital, to whom, as a politic means of ruling the others, some special privileges, and a small mud walled fort might have been allowed, as it was to the head of the Shánárs at Agatíswaram. But it seems impossible to believe that any of this unfortunate race could have been within the last few centuries in possession of independent authority.

Sub-divisions.—The caste is divided into several sections and local clans, varying in different parts of the country.

For instance, a few miles south and east of Trevandrum, a class numbering a few hundreds, are called Ina (real or first-class) Pulayars. They consider themselves superior to the others, whom they call Vada or Northern Pulayars; but the latter assert that the Ina people are the inferiors, and that their name should properly be Hína—base. The Ina Pulayars will not eat or intermarry with the others. Such is pride amongst some of the lowest of the human family!

Near Alleppy a remarkable section of the caste is found, of whom an interesting description is given by Rev. W. J. Richards in the "Indian Antiquary." He says:—

"The men of the Tandu Pulayans (who wear the *tandu* grass) wear the ordinary lower cloth of the kind worn in this country, but the distinctive name of the tribe comes from the women's dress, which is a very primitive article indeed. The leaves of a certain water plant (*Isolepis articulata*, Nees) are cut into lengths of a foot long, and tied round the waist in such a fashion that the strings unwoven hang in a bushy tail behind, and present the same appearance in front, reaching nearly to the knees. This dress is accounted for by a tradition that in former days a certain high caste man of that region had been sowing grains and planting vegetables in his fields, but found that his daily work was in some unknown way frustrated; for whatever he planted or sowed in the day was carefully picked up and taken 'when men slept.' So he set a watch, and one night he saw coming out of a hole hitherto unknown to him certain beings like men, but quite naked, who set to work destroying his hopes of a crop. Pursuing them, he succeeded in catching a man and a woman; and he was so impressed with shame at their condition that he gave the man his own upper-cloth, which was hanging on his shoulder, and made him put it on, but not having one to spare for the woman, she made herself an apron of grass as above described. These were the progenitors of the numerous slaves who are found there at this day. They are also called Kuri or 'Pit' Pulayans, from having originated as above said.

"Their language is Malayálam. They worship the sun and heavenly bodies, and I have seen among them a little temple, about the size of a large rabbit-hutch, in which was a plank for the spirits of their deceased ancestors to come and rest upon. The spirits are also supposed to fish in the backwater, and the phosphorescent appearance seen sometimes on the surface of the water, is taken as an indication of their presence.

"The food of these Pulayans is fish, often cooked with arrack and with the liliaceous roots of certain water plants. When visited about eleven to one o'clock in the day, they are found intoxicated, especially the men.

"They live south of Cochin, between the backwater and the sea. Another division of them is found more south than Alleppy, who are called Kanna Pulayans. These wear rather better and more artistically-made 'aprons.' When a girl of the Tandu Pulayans puts on this garment—a sign of maturity—for the first time, there is a ceremony called the Tandu marriage. The state of these poor people is still virtually that of slavery, though some of them possess property."

These people remind us of the Juangs or Patnas (leaf-wearers) of Orissa, whose women also wear no clothes—only a few strings of beads round the waist with a bunch of leaves tied before and behind. But the British Government took the trouble to provide a cotton cloth for each of the women to put on; then they gathered the bunches of leaves into a heap and set fire to it. Oddly enough, the Tandu Pulayan women are much opposed to the change of "grass" for cloth: they appear to think they might as well be out of the world as out of the fashion!

Further information respecting these Pulayars, also called Kanna or Cunna Pulayars (*kannan*, barbarian), is given by the Rev. W. Johnson to the following effect:—

The Cunnar Pulayars live only four miles north of Alleppy, yet they are about the most uncivilized people that one could meet with in any part of India. The very appearance of a European in their midst causes a fearful alarm. The men are dressed as the lowest class of natives usually are; but the women dress in long grass split to the texture of horsehair, which hangs gracefully over their bodies, and these, with a few red glass beads, form their whole attire. Their houses are of the simplest nature; and at night they rest on the bosom of mother earth, and have but few comforts. They speak in a dialect peculiar to themselves, and which cannot be well understood even by natives of Alleppy. Yet they are proud and consider their grass dress the acme of perfection for the fashionable world.

They are perfectly ignorant as to how they came to their present settlement, so also as to another world after death. They number about 150 souls in the neighbourhood above referred to, and about the same number twelve miles off. They have a headman or ruler who is also looked upon as high-priest. It is remarkable that they have no graven or molten image, whatever. Unhewn blocks of white granite form the object of their worship. These unsightly blocks are placed under little sheds close to where their relations are buried, near to their own huts. The barber of the tribe acts as sexton and grave-digger.

They acknowledge an author of good, whom they reverence, and an author of evil, whose fury they constantly strive to appease by votive offerings of poultry, afterwards eating the bodies of the birds which they have offered in sacrifice. They have a traditional reverence for the seventh day, which corresponds with our Sunday. On this day they stay in their own settlements as much as possible, and will not set out on journeys.

On the twenty-eighth day after the birth of a child, it is brought to the house and named. Up to this day both mother and child are kept in a small shed, in which one would hardly like to trust a good-bred dog during the rainy season. One good feature about this race is, that they give their women ample opportunities of gaining their livelihood, for they make their whole grass attire, which takes them ten whole days with close application; and then they have their time taken up in making mats, which they sell, or barter for rice and tobacco, and thus aid their husbands, to whom they are not indebted for a single cash towards their wardrobe or their food.

When a youth of the tribe wishes to enter wedlock, he delegates his powers to a friend of about the same age, or younger than himself. The delegate has then to make all necessary arrangements, and to pay from his own hands the sum of fifty-one chuckrams, or about one rupee and three-quarters, to the father of the bride, which, being paid, the bride is by her friends conducted to the bridegroom's house; the bridegroom promising his successful delegate that should he ever be in want of a person to act for him in the same way, he will do so, and also pay the required sum.

They are a happy and cheerful-looking set of persons on the whole, naturally very intelligent, and both boys and girls, when brought to the mission school, most anxious to learn to read and write. They are very proud of their origin, which they consider as perfectly unique among Hindus, regard themselves as far superior to all others who bear the designation of Pulayars; and practice ablutions whenever they come in contact with any persons whom they consider lower than themselves. The members of their caste intermarry very much among themselves. Their masters are Sudras.

The two great divisions of this caste, however, are the Eastern and Western Pulayars. The former are found principally about Changanácheri and at Mallapalli, and other hilly parts. Their customs seem to point them out as virtually Pariahs, as the Pallar colonies in Travancore are often called Pulayars; and in Cochin the highest class of Pulayars is said to be called Vallava, which is well-known to be a title belonging to the Pariah caste. The term "eastern" also perhaps implies that they came more recently from the eastern side of South India, unless it means simply eastward towards the hills of Travancore. There seem to be some traces also of Tamil forms in their language, as *vandu* for *vannu.* Yet a marked difference exists between them and the recognized Pariahs of the country.

These Eastern Pulayars are still more degraded than the "Western" Pulayars and the Pariahs, who would consider themselves polluted by coming in contact with them. Most went about in former days, and some do still, without any other clothing than a string of large thick leaves round the loins; or if they got a cotton cloth, they wore it over this, or as a headcloth. They hang a large quantity of strings of beads or cowries round the neck. The *kudumi* is not worn.

The Eastern Pulayars eat beef and such refuse as the Pariahs eat. In fact many Pulayars from about Quilon northwards generally eat beef, and appear to be rather a kind of Pariahs. Eastern and Western Pulayars will not eat together, but the Easterns will eat what is cooked by the others.

The Eastern Pulayars celebrate marriage with the pandal or Hindu festive bower, and with tying of the *minnu* or *táli* marriage-badge, not the Malayálam *mundu* or "cloth" given to a concubine. They always give so many *rasis* (=ten chuckrams each) for the girl. Their devil-dancers, or priests, have idols, bells, swords, belts, crowns made of peacock's feathers, &c., These are considered better servants than other Pulayars, and consequently are valued at a higher rate.

Their own tradition is that they were the slaves of Suyodhana and his brothers, while the Western Pulayars belonged to the Pandus—the two rival parties in the great war of the Mahabharata—and the defeat of Suyodhana is alleged to be the cause of the greater degradation of the former.

The Western Pulayars prevail near Cottyam. They do not eat beef, nor wear so many beads as the Eastern. They "give

PULAYARS.

cloth" for concubinage, and were formerly nepotists as to the law of inheritance, but are now adopting "*makkatáyam*" usages.

The whole caste is divided into Illams, "houses," or lineage, as we say, "the house of Devonshire," &c. These illams are very numerous. Their denominations are such as Brahmakotta —Velli (silver)—Pallikkutachan (carpenter of the temple), and so forth. Men and women belonging to the same illam cannot intermarry; they are considered to be the descendants of one family, therefore brethren, and such marriages are regarded as incestuous. "Others would laugh at them." So it is with the Ilavars also.

General Description.—The Pulayars are inferior to Pariahs in appearance, strength and courage, perhaps from not eating flesh meat; or from having been more oppressed. The men are small, and short in stature, their complexion dark from exposure in field-work. "The forehead is low, the cheek-bones high, the mouth large, the nose rather broad, the lips thick, and the hair in some cases, slightly woolly. There is much difference between them, however, in these respects." A few may be seen fairer and with well-formed features from some slight intermixture of Muhammadan, possibly even Sudra parentage, or high-caste females in former times condemned to slavery. Aged persons appear to be comparatively few amongst this people, as their hardships are great. The women are smaller still, mostly quite diminutive and very plain-looking, but a few of them are passable looking when young. Bunches

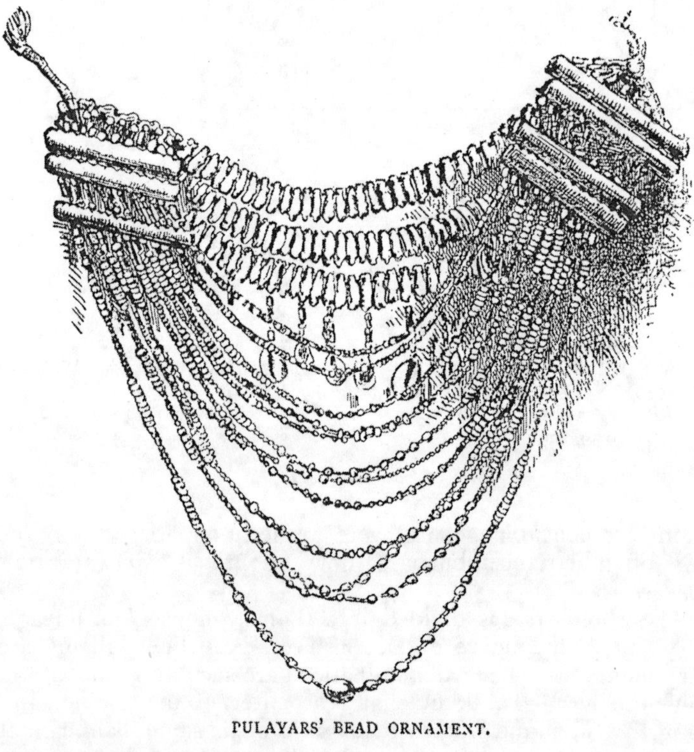

PULAYARS' BEAD ORNAMENT.

and strings of beads being worn around the women's neck and hanging on the breast, there is a demand for beads as amongst the negroes of Africa. Gold and silver ornaments are not allowed them, only brass or lead: thin flat plates of brass about an inch in diameter, with a small dot pattern, are strung round the neck. They purchase bangles, beads, shells, rings, &c., of trifling value, which are crowded on their fingers, arms, necks, and ears, in such quantity as to be almost a burden. The front teeth are filed sharp like canine teeth.

Their dress and habits are extremely filthy, as no one is willing to wash for them, and they have no washermen of their own, like other castes. Difficulty has been experienced even in getting the ordinary washing of cloths done for Christian boys in the Mission Boarding School, "on account of the disgrace of the thing" said the washermen. And even some of the degraded Pulayars had their foolish pride touched, and thought it a still deeper degradation to learn this useful employment: some who were perforce trained to it went off to other labour, being unable to bear the jeers and contempt of their fellows. As to the admirable habit of daily bathing, they are the very opposite of the Brahmans. Each washed his own cloth slightly at times, or wore it as it was till it fell off in filthy rags. This, again, was a mark of their belonging to the "great unwashed" castes, and served to point them out as polluted, besides preventing the approach of decent people on the ground of common cleanliness.

Their dwellings are miserable huts formed of sticks cut out of the woods, with walls of reed or mud, and thatched with grass or cocoa-leaf, situated by the sides of the rice swamps, or on mounds in their centre, to be out of the way of polluting respectable people. They were discouraged from having comfortable huts, in order that they might be willing to move about as required for the work of cultivation. Denied admission to the markets, they must stand apart at some distance, and make purchases or sales as well as they could.

The work of the Pulayars lies almost exclusively in the rice fields—pumping them dry, making up the embankments, hedging, digging, manuring, ploughing, weeding, transplanting, and reaping. Yet the grain is not considered as polluted, but used by the Brahmans and nobles, offered in temples, and carried into the most exclusive kitchens. Men, women, and children work together at harvest and other times; but hard work does not continue throughout the year, only about six or eight months. Sometimes after a hard day's work they have to cook their own food at night. Their master's fields also must be guarded at night from the encroachments of cattle or the depredations of wild animals, when the slaves must remain in the fields and keep awake all night, shouting to frighten away the trespassing cattle, deer, wild boars, or elephants.

Their food is chiefly rice, as they are employed in its cultivation, to which they add vegetables and fruits grown in the small plots usually allotted them by their masters. The rice is boiled and eaten with coarse curry, or only pepper and salt. It is also parched, or beaten flat, but they have no skill in baking or cookery. Even when milk and eggs are produced, they are sold rather than consumed in the household. The children consequently suffer much from diarrhœa, debility, and intestinal worms, arising from innutritious food. A considerable proportion of children die from want of proper care and attention. Adults also suffer much from disease. They pride themselves on not eating beef, and despise the Pariahs, who have the advantage in greater strength and courage. Other kinds of flesh or fish are sought—small fish, snails and shell-fish in the tanks and channels which irrigate the rice fields, crabs, rats, and so forth. In the hot season the children are often faint with hunger, and are obliged to wander into the jungles in search of wild roots and fruits.

From lack of sufficient and palatable food, it is no wonder that they have a longing for strong drink, and indulge in it too freely. Some, on being cautioned on this point, urged that their owners gave them so little food that they were obliged to dispose of a part to purchase liquor, in order to satisfy the cravings of the stomach. But of course this injures the health, and is no real remedy for their miseries. They also chew tobacco, especially the women, who then suffer from dyspepsia, headache, and convulsions. Chewing this narcotic is a more dangerous habit than smoking, and is specially injurious to a badly-fed constitution.

They possess no weapons, and have no manufactures, save that of palm-leaf umbrellas and reed baskets. The slaves about Cottayam make large mats of the beesha reed, also mats and baskets of pandanus leaf. At Mallapalli they make very good native canvas from the fibre of some tree: bags of this cloth are used by high castes.

Few have ever travelled beyond a few miles from their homes, as they had no occasion or permission to do so. They have never been able to migrate, like the Shánárs, to Ceylon or elsewhere. Their barbarous mispronunciation of Malayálam is not readily understood by others: the ludicrous errors which are made are a source of amusement to other castes. Of the total number of 188,916 Pulayars in Travancore, the census gives only 183 males and no females as able to read and write.

Yet these poor people are fairly intelligent, and readily

capable of instruction. They are sharp enough in comprehension, and heartily enjoy any good thing that is said. Some of them are entrusted with the management of cattle and agricultural details by their masters, and are set over their fellows. Others are priests, singers after a rude fashion, or natural leaders of their fellow-men.

Their improvidence, like that of most slaves and uncivilized peoples, has often been remarked, especially in their religious offerings of first fruits, powdered rice, &c., to the Five Virgins, which are merely feasts for themselves; and in eating up at once a stock of grain, which might be made to last, with economy, for months. There is a proverb that in harvest time the slave goes about, asking, "Can you sell me an elephant?" but when hard times begin he drives even his dog out of the hut. The people illustrate this by a story which they relate, or rather a parable, of a Pulayan, who went to buy an elephant. The owner told him to go and pound and eat some rice first. He did so, and stayed till all his rice was finished: then he had nothing in hand wherewith to make the purchase! It is no great wonder, however, that such half-starved people take a good feed when they can get it.

Their enslaved condition also drove them to thievery. Serious crimes they have rarely committed, but are still addicted to petty robberies. Some kind masters were liberal, and permitted their slaves to take almost what they chose from their estates; but in general they were, no doubt, sorely tempted to theft by hunger and want.

Even the degraded Pulayars have some excellent qualities. From lengthened and intimate acquaintance, we have found them just like other men—under the power of many evils engrained in them through long-continued ignorance, superstition, and oppression, but simple hearted, grateful for kindness, deeply attached to those who show themselves their friends, and improving with marked rapidity under instruction. It is sometimes difficult to make the young truthful and honest in small things; but this is a defect observable in many Hindus, and it may be expected to take two or three generations to improve and establish their moral stamina. Already some Pulayars, under the operation of Christian teaching and guidance, have become admirable characters—gentle, honourable, devout, and loving; and probably they will display a very beautiful type of character when fully christianized.

A remarkable testimony is borne to them in the Census Report, p. 206:—"They are an extremely useful and hard-working race, and are sometimes distinguished by a rare character for truth and honour, which their superiors in the caste scale might well emulate."

Some of the masters appear to appreciate individuals of this tribe as valuable servants; and the mission teachers like them very much. One expressed the opinion that "the Pariahs have more worldly cunning and intelligence, but the Pulayars are more frequently truly pious." A native missionary wrote, "The Pulayar Christians are earnest in learning to read, and in giving contributions for benevolent objects. Their desire to learn and repeat their lessons is remarkable, and they complain if instruction is not duly supplied to them. Some children glean and sell scattered stalks of rice to purchase the Scriptures. The elders sell plantains and fowls in order to be able to contribute for religious purposes." And one European missionary remarked, "There is a good deal of heart amongst Pariahs and Pulayars, such as we do not often see in the Shánárs."

Birth and Childhood.—The woman is taken to a shed at some distance, put up for the particular occasion, where she is assisted by her mother-in-law or some female friend. Any delay or unusual suffering is attributed to the malice of demons. This shed is erected because the mother is regarded as polluted during confinement. Should she not be thus set apart "others will laugh at them, and will not touch them, nor join in marriage feasts with them." It is often erected of wretched materials, exposing the unfortunate woman on all sides to the weather, so that this unfeeling custom is dropped by Christians. Men are not allowed to enter the shed. The mother remains six or seven days in it, then it is burnt. When recovered, the mother rubs the body with oil and turmeric, afterwards washes in water and re-enters her house. The husband also goes to the sea or river for a bath to cleanse from pollution. The woman returns to her work in such time as may be necessary.

As soon as an infant is born, a little cocoanut water is given to supply the deficiency of the mother's milk, which she usually gives on the third day. The child is also bathed with hot water, and for three months it is generally washed twice a day. After ten days, cocoanut oil and turmeric are used to rub the infant with twice a day, the limbs are also shaken, and the nose gently pulled out. This is continued for several months. A low head is admired.

The mother eats the usual food—rice and fish, or fowl if procurable, or pork; beef and mutton are never eaten by this caste. For about a couple of months she takes a ball morning and evening of the acid pulp of the fruit of Garcinia Roxburghii (*pinaru*), and black pepper ground.

The child is nursed for two years, sometimes much longer, which often greatly exhausts the strength of both mother and child. In the sixth month solid food is first given, for which occasion the relatives are invited. The father and grandfather and other relatives each take a small quantity of rice, and put it in the mouth of the infant. The name is at the same time given by the father, usually the name of the grandfather, or the father or other relative. The friends afterwards drink some toddy and leave.

The names in common use are not many; in any list many persons will be of the same name, and we have known two sisters both named Káli; the father had to call one "black" and the other "white" Káli. For males the most usual name is Eiyan (father or lord), then Cháttan (=Shástávu or Iyenár), Veluttán (white one), Chadayan (hairy), Kiliyan (parrot), Pálei and Arangan. For women the commonest name is Káli, Chátta (fem. of Cháttan), Eiyi (fem. of Eiyan), Velutta (fem. of Veluttan), Chakki, Natchatram (star), Kannamma, Oomala, and Mála (Garland).

The hair is first cut when the infant walks, whether male or female. The ears of girls are perforated with some ceremony. For the puberty of girls a small hut is built of jungle sticks, where the girl is sent, and no other person allowed to enter, not even the mother. Women must stand at a little distance from the shed, and food is brought and laid down a little way off. Here the girl remains for seven days, and is then brought back to the house, dressed in a new or clean cloth, and friends invited and treated with betel-nut, toddy, and arrack. When people have means, or in time of harvest when rice is always plentiful, rice flour is put on the forehead, arms, and cheeks of the girl.

Marriage is celebrated before or after maturity, according as a suitable husband may offer. Boys usually marry at the age of 14 to 18 or 20. A father likes to see his sons married during his own lifetime, so that he may arrange matters to his own satisfaction.

The father of the youth and his maternal uncle first make enquiries as to where suitable girls may be found. Coming to such a house without previous notice, the owner will ask, "What have you come for?" "To ask your daughter for our son." "Come again after a few days, and we shall arrange a day for the matter." They then hand over two or three fanams to the bride's mother or maternal uncle, and partake of some food or drink. After a few days the bridegroom goes there, taking a few fanams in hand to give to them; and they entertain him for a few days. Again the relatives accompany the youth on some auspicious day, and appoint a day for the marriage. An old man gives three fanams and beads worth, say, two fanams into the hands of the girl's father, and proclaims, "from such a date this girl is betrothed to be the wife of this youth." Then the girl's father sends a pot of toddy and three measures of parched rice to the relations of the youth; and their acceptance of these present confirms the betrothal.

On the day of the wedding, after the bride is dressed (which is done at the cost of the bridegroom), 16 fanams, or 22, are paid to a middle-man, who divides the money amongst the maternal relatives of the bride. The mother also gets her share of this, perhaps one fanam. But if the mother or the younger sisters of the bride were to approach the bridegroom, this would cause ceremonial pollution. On the day of the wedding any woman may attend, except the mother and maternal aunts of the bride. Therefore, one fanam and some betel-leaf, &c., are laid on some spot by the bridegroom for the mother. He walks off to some distance, and she takes up the presents. Sometimes a cow, or other present, is given to the bride's family—is it not a kind of purchase money, or payment for the rearing of the bride?

A wedding *pandal* or shed is put up at the bride's house, and by invitation the relatives of both families and the neighbours assemble. The affair begins in the evening and continues till morning. They begin by drinking some toddy or arrack; then sit and talk awhile. For the feast 22 edungalies of rice are given by the father of the bridegroom and other relatives, along with baskets, mats, pots, and curry stuffs. This is cooked by two of the bridegroom's party. While the rice is being cooked, four or five of the men will dance in a circle with drumming and singing.

The sister of the bridegroom ties the *táli*, or marriage badge corresponding to our wedding ring (usually a bead of glass purchased from a Muhammadan dealer), on the neck of the bride.

The male and female guests sit apart, and in order for the feast, with plantain leaves laid before them for use as plates. The newly-married husband and wife eat a little, in the presence of all, out of one vessel. But Pulayar husbands and wives commonly do eat together at the same time. Afterwards all wash hands and partake of betel-nut. This feast takes place about midnight. Then there is more play but no more drinking till dawn. The play consists of dancing and leaping, several persons together.

At dawn, a conch shell is put in a sieve, and spun round to

see whether the marriage will turn out a lucky one. The interpretation is given by wise men of their own caste. If the shell falls to the north, it is an omen of good fortune ; if to the east, still more so. The west is not considered specially favourable, but the south is the most unpropitious. In the morning the sun is worshipped with a salam by the bride and others. This is a daily practice. She also bows to her father (not to her husband's father) and to her maternal uncle, then to the four quarters ; to the east first, next north, thirdly west, and lastly, south ; thus not going round with the sun.

A new house is not built specially for the newly-married couple. Several families may reside in one house, that is, in several huts built close together. The bridegroom's party, and two or three of the bride's, accompany the young people home and put them into their house. Her nearest relatives will drink a little and go home. Nothing is given to others. If they continue to live affectionately together, the wife remains with her husband ; if displeased at any time, she returns to her own home.

It is considered that the husband of a young girl should not be over sixteen years of age or so. But it often happens that a youth of sixteen marries a young girl of eight or nine years of age ; and they do live together. The earliest age at which they become mothers is from fourteen to sixteen. Children are not very numerous in a family.

Polygamy is common, a man taking as many as four wives, all married as above : there is no fixed limit. Polyandry is never practised. But a brother-in-law may take the widow. If a husband wishes to get rid of his wife before she has borne children, he may take her back to her parents ; and if she also wishes to be freed from him, his money (the 22 fanams) will be returned to him. But if she was unwilling to part with the man, this money is not returned. If another man afterwards desires to have her, he pays the parents the 22 fanams, and they repay the first husband. No ceremony whatever is observed on this re-marriage.

Adultery and disputes arising from jealousy are not very prevalent, perhaps because a change is so easily effected. Discontented parties can separate and leave at once ; the women are also so poor, badly-fed and hard-worked, that there is less incentive to evil. The Pulayars are spoken of as less licentious than Pariahs. If adultery is committed they would be excluded from their caste privileges. They also worship spirits called Kannimar or virgins, apparently the ghosts of girls who have died unmarried, who are supposed to punish this crime. In case it is committed, the injured husband will beat his wife and her paramour. Or, he invites the chief men of the caste (on which occasions many will assemble), and makes his complaint before them. Then both the guilty parties are tied, and beaten with rattans by his brother-in-law, or by persons employed for the occasion. Fines are resorted to, generally 12 fanams, paid by the adulterer, and spent on arrack for all who were assembled to adjudicate. No money is paid to the injured husband.

Pregnancy.—The ceremony called *Vayittu pongàli* is observed in the seventh month. It is an offering to Tottiya or Bhagaván, the sun. New pots are procured and brought to the centre of the courtyard, and rice boiled in them. Some rice is taken out of the pot while on the fire, and shown or presented to the sun. It is waved three times, then put back into the pot; afterwards distributed to the persons invited. There is no dance on this occasion.

Then a pot is brought full of water, the mouth tied tightly with a cloth and a plantain leaf, and the pot put upside down. The priest repeats some mantrams while the pregnant woman stands on the top of the inverted water-pot: it will not break. At the four corners of the yard, four plantain stems are fixed like posts, and connected with strings, which the woman cuts with a knife after getting down from off the pot. At the foot of the four plantain stems are placed four cocoa-nuts; the husband goes with a bill-hook and splits them. Then they feast on the rice, of which the woman also partakes, and all return to their homes.

Sickness.—Pulayars are subject to many ailments arising from their privations, and the nature of their employment. Standing at times in the rice swamps with their feet in water or mud and the head uncovered produces headache, rheumatism and fever. From their uncleanly habits they are afflicted with skin diseases, inflammation of the eyes, ulcers, and leprosy. Bad food, strong drinks and tobacco-chewing also injure them. From the beginning of any sickness they, like many other castes, consider it dangerous to wash or bathe; and this, of itself, often aggravates disease.

They are both careless and ignorant in the treatment of the sick. Wives or husbands are often abandoned to the care of their parents when ill. They have no professional doctors amongst them; and no knowledge of medicines even so simple as castor oil. A mixture of salt and chillies is sometimes used. The Sudra masters give some medicines; and would sometimes on an emergency, visit their slaves, purifying themselves afterwards. When physicians of other castes are applied to they charge very heavily, such as on account of *tottukuli*, "bathing after having touched" a patient of this class, 3 fanams; for feeling the pulse, a few fanams and a basket of parched rice; all must be paid in advance, besides offerings of fowls, rice, &c., to various demons. For all diseases both medicines and incantations are resorted to.

Every ailment is attributed to the agency of some demon or other whom it is the business of the *pújári*, or priest, to discover. He is acquainted with the proper *mantrams* or incantations, and has an iron rattle, called *kokkara*, by the sound of which he divines. "It will be revealed to him by a kind of inspiration or possession which demon it is that has caused the sickness; and he will declare who it is, and what is to be done in the particular case."

The kokkara is formed of a plate of iron turned into a tube, the edges strongly serrated and not closely united. It is about nine inches in length and one and a half in diameter. From it hangs a chain and an iron pin, or spike, which is rubbed along the dentate edges of the iron cylinder, making

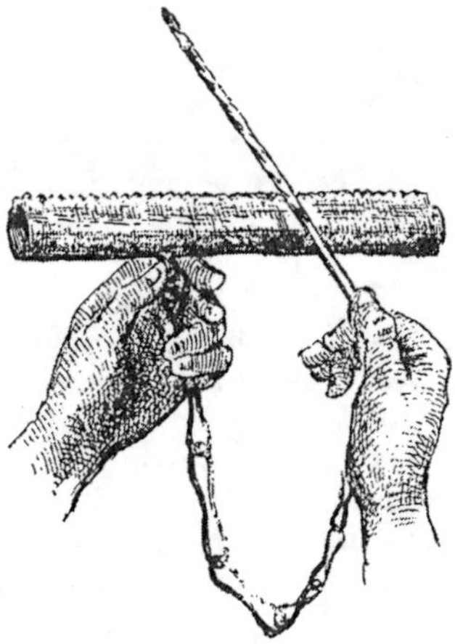

IRON MUSICAL INSTRUMENT.

a horrid grating noise. This instrument is used by sorcerers amongst Pariahs, Védars and Kuravars, but it seems more especially to belong to Pulayars. It is used in seeking demoniac possession, in exorcising demons, in divination and in cases of sickness. The instrument costs from three-quarters to one rupee, and is made by the ordinary blacksmith.

When a youth wishes to learn this black art, he goes to some one accomplished in it, and presents a para of paddy, three fanams in money, seven cocoanuts, and two chuckrams' worth of betel leaf. A feast is also given to his relatives, costing, say twenty-five fanams. He learns for about a week the names of all the demons and the charms with which the teacher is acquainted. When fully instructed, he receives from the teacher a kokkara and a cowry shell, and pays a further fee. It costs about 100 fanams to learn the business.

He is then called to cure patients, young and old, of various diseases by playing this instrument; and with the addition of a conch shell, a cocoanut and a cowry, he may make a reputation for himself and much gain by deceiving the people. All Pulayars honour and fear him; Sudras also employ him in various matters. When he goes to find omens for fortune-telling, he is paid one fanam; for casting out demons, three fanams and three edungalies of paddy; for rescuing a pregnant woman from a demon, seven fanams; for offering sacrifices, ten fanams and the flesh of the fowls slain and some toddy; and for destroying enemies or detecting robbers, twelve fanams.

In times of sickness, these dancers frighten the people by announcing the wrath of the demons, and the necessity of further propitiatory offerings in order to get rid of the disease. They also give sacred ashes to patients for their recovery.

When the priest is called to a house for a case of sickness, he generally comes in the evening, and is first entertained with food, toddy to drink, and betel to chew. He then prepares a tender cocoanut, the flower of the Areca palm, and some parched rice powdered—these he lays down and covers over with a young palm leaf. Bringing the sick person forward, the priest draws a circle with an iron pen or stylus round the patient, then sticks the stylus outside the circle. This is called "putting in fetters." and by this the demon is supposed to be arrested. The demon sometimes causes the patient to cry out, "Oh, I am in pain—he is beating me," and such like; but the patient does not know who it is that is afflicting him. Sometimes the priest will make the demon speak. The sick man makes a vow, which is to be fulfilled in due course, promising sheep, rice, flowers, palm leaf, and arrack. All such vows are paid at their annual festivals in February or March.

Or, on visiting the sick house, a rice fan or sieve, containing three betel leaves with areca nuts, three nári of paddy, Ocimum flowers, sacred ashes, and the conch and cowry shells, is laid in the yard; sitting before this fan and facing the sun, the officiator begins to worship the demons. While doing so, he holds the shells in his hand, and turns to the four points. After noticing some omen, he takes the kokkara and sounds it, chanting the names of terrible demons, such as Mallan, Karunkáli, Kottu-tamburan, Ayiravilli, The Five Virgins; and repeating incantations. This is varied with dancing also.

The performer plays on the iron instrument, sometimes from evening till noon of the next day; and it is no wonder that the nerves of the tortured patient are unstrung by a whole night's incessant grating of this harsh file. The sick person is often terrified into confession of some sin (possibly in the case of hysteric females a purely imaginary one), when a fine of, say three fanams, is imposed, and at once spent for toddy, which is drunk by the assembled party.

If death unexpectedly occurs, he consoles the bereaved, and warns them that their offerings to the spirits have been insufficient.

Sometimes affliction is supposed to be brought on by the enmity of others who have got incantations written on palm-leaf or potsherds, and buried in the earth near the house, or by the side of the well. Another sorcerer will be called to find out and counteract such evil charms, for which he digs, destroying them when found. Of course, this pretence affords great opportunity for imposition.

Death.—When just on the point of death they give some rice water conjee, "because the soul is leaving." As soon as death takes place, the family set up a cry; hearing this, the relatives, both male and female, come to the house. Lamentation is made in various terms, such as "You are dead, are you not? There is no one left us now. This is our misery. We have no father now to help us. Precious father! you did us such and such benefits. O demon! you have very quickly taken his life. If you had not called him away, we should have given you fine gifts. We have now lost both our expenditure (in the sickness) and our friend. O, Udaya Tamburán (Possessor-God), thou gavest him birth, and now hast taken him again." Sometimes comfort is offered to the bereaved, such as "Why should you weep—what can be done? It is God who has taken him away. Though you weep and cry, he will not return." The influence of Christian teaching as to the existence and unity of God seems apparent in some of these statements.

The body is washed by the near relatives, men for men and women for women. Cocoanut oil and turmeric are rubbed over the corpse, and it is covered with a white cloth. Women are buried with all their ornaments on. Men wear ear-rings and finger rings, and these are left on after death.

Váykkari, "rice for the mouth," is a pinch of raw rice put into the mouth of the corpse. In some higher castes a coin also is put into the mouth, as was done by the ancient Romans. If a priest dies, the body is bathed and oiled; all his devil-dancing ornaments, head-dress, &c., are put on, but removed again before burial.

Bodies are buried in their own gardens, or if they had no land, in some retired place belonging to their employers. Those who are better off are buried in a room in their own house, at a depth of about four feet. The grave is levelled and smeared with cow dung; no bad smell is observed to come from the grave. This is done through affection to the deceased; still it is rare, and no women are so buried. It is not priests merely, but wealthy and esteemed persons who are buried in this way; the relatives are not careful to avoid treading on the grave. "The soul does reside there—this is what is desired. The spirit is called *vádha*, or familiar, and will not harm the survivors, but watch over their interests and protect them from disease and danger. Propitiatory offerings are made to it occasionally of anything they eat; and the ghost can be set on their enemies. If neglected or displeased it haunts and troubles the household."

The corpse is taken to the side of the grave, and incantations and prayers made there. It is carried by the sons and nephews and others, on a frame, and covered with a cloth. A small quantity of paddy is brought, and whispering over this an incantation (the names of demons, &c.), it is cast into the grave. The pújari, or priest, then goes round the grave three times, without drumming or singing on this occasion. The corpse being put in, the grave is filled up, and the relatives throw in three handfuls of earth. At the four corners of the grave a few grains of rice are placed, and a little pebble laid over this with mantrams, "to prevent jackals from disturbing, and to hinder the spirit from molesting people." The grave is dug north and south, the head placed to the north. The grave will be preserved, and no cultivation made over it.

On the seventh day, the priest goes to the grave and lifts a handful of earth, as other castes gather up the burnt bones, makes a rude image of the dead man, and brings it near the house. It is not brought into the yard, but to a place cleared for it at some distance from the house, to avoid pollution. Then turmeric, flour, &c., are put on it to prepare it for the spirit's reception. Now he rattles the kokkara, spins the conch, and invokes the deceased by name to enter the image; from thence it passes into the priest, and from him into a cloth which a man standing beside him holds out like a sheet. While possessed by the spirit the priest dances; when he ceases, he puts the spirit into the cloth and holds it there.

The image is no further used. Both men now go to the water, they bathe and dip the cloth in water, then return into the house, holding the cloth folded up, which they put on a plaited palm leaf, placing around it offerings of rice, toddy, arrack, and betel-leaf. The conch is again spun round to ascertain whether the offerings have been accepted. If the spira of the conch points towards the spirit in the cloth, the offering has been accepted. They simply spin on till they obtain a favourable omen of complacency, and again until they obtain permission to eat. They then go into the yard with the cloth, mix a little turmeric with water and with oil, and sprinkle the cloth, thus representing the anointing of the spirit as the body had been anointed. After the food (*annam*) has been presented to the spirit, the priest repeats mantrams to retain the spirit in the house. It is then supposed to have left the cloth, which is taken into the yard and opened. No further Sraddha or funeral ceremony is performed.

The conch shell is used by sorcerers near Cottayam to spin round in order to ascertain from which of the eight directions the evil spirit has come, and caused any given case of affliction.

The spirits of deceased relatives are called *Chávu*, "the dead." They are seen in dreams, especially by near relations, who repeat such dreams in the morning, telling that they saw and spoke with the deceased. The souls of women and children, even of still-born infants, are existent. "Many of these ancient spirits are now great gods." A man will continue to worship the spirit of his own father, and of his deceased wife.

Superstitions and Worship.—As will be evident from the preceding observations, the worship practised by the Pulayars is simply that of demons and evil spirits, or of deceased ancestors, who must be propitiated by offerings of such things as will please them. Images are not used in the South, but small ones of brass, a few inches in height, are not uncommon in North Travancore. They represent both males and females, and are called *préthain*, or ghost, equivalent to chávu. A case is mentioned in which the image of a murdered slave was made and worshipped by the murderer, to appease the spirit of his victim. The spirits are supposed to be displeased if the people receive instruction in Christianity. A woman said, "Our domestic demon troubles us whenever we hear your Bible read, therefore we do not wish to become Christians." Another said that a demon was residing in his hut, and begged the teacher to come and pray in his dwelling, that the evil spirit might take his flight. The sorcerers and devil dancers also hinder the people from Christian instruction, lest their profits should be gone. Some of the priests are dreaded even by the higher castes, as exercising great influence in the spirit world, whether to set their familiars to destroy, or to restrain them from injury by magic arts. They are consequently employed by Sudras and Shánárs for casting out devils and counteracting enchantments.

To avoid the malignance of these demons, various plans are adopted. Some wear rolls of palm leaf tied round the neck, to prevent the demons approaching or annoying them. Baskets are hung up in rice fields, containing peace offerings. Wherever there is a grove or dense forest, adoration is paid to Mádan, Káli, &c., supposed to reside there, and sacrifices are occasionally offered. Special efforts to please their demons occupy all the leisure enjoyed from rice cultivation between the close of November and the beginning of April, when the dancers go about the slave huts, collecting money to provide parched rice, fowls, and ardent spirits for offerings.

Gardens and cultivation will be protected from the blight of the evil eye by hanging up earthen pots with spots of lime daubed over them. If a good cloth is worn when going out, sickness is supposed to result from the evil eye of jealousy.

These poor people are also deceived by Hindu mendicants of other castes to secure some money from them. One came and uttered mantrams over a young cocoanut, which he gave to a woman who had no milk for her babe.

Their chief deities are Mádan and the Five Pándus. "These are greater than the Sun, but of course Udaya Tamburan (the Possessor-God) is greater than all" they now say. Last come the deceased ancestors, or Chávus. Pulayars have no temples built by or belonging to themselves, but chiefly attend the Sudras' temples as far as permitted. Temporary places of worship are formed by trees planted in a square, one at each corner—such trees as Odina odier, Silk cotton, Rottlera and Erythrina. On these a platform of cocoanut wood or common sticks is erected, and upon this a frame or cage of cocoanut leaves, as the special residence or shrine *pro tempore* of the demon. At the foot of the trees is a representation of the cobra. Several little shrines of this kind are put up for the habitation of several demons, the Chávus or Ghosts and the Virgins, once a year; and offerings are made of rice, grain, parched rice, and flowers. A fowl is decapitated and the blood sprinkled over the shrine; the flesh is afterwards eaten by the worshippers.

For devil-dancing there is a special dress and ornaments.

Any one may become a priest by practice, but the profession is often, as might be expected, hereditary. The head-dress is a helmet of basket-work with red cords hanging down from either side. A cotton scarf is worn round the waist, and bells tied on the legs. In one hand an old sword is held, in the other a bell. At first the dancer goes round slowly, then greatly quickens his motion. He stamps heavily on the ground with the feet alternately, trembling and greatly agitated.

On one occasion in March I had the opportunity of witnessing a little of their dancing at Trevandrum during the prevalence of small-pox, when similar scenes were enacted generally through the country. They had been engaged in this festival all night, and the noise of their drumming and cheering was still heard in the early morning. The scrub and weeds had been cleared off a raised bank by the side of the rice-fields, and a kind of temporary altar, as above described, made on the stem of a tree cut off at the height of ten or twelve feet. On this was a small platform with a rude ladder leading up to it, and offerings laid upon it. At the base of this frail structure stood two or three painted boards, one of them the figure of the cobra's hood very clearly represented. At one side was a shed for the accommodation of the people, and at the other side a miniature house, about two feet high, which was supposed to be the residence of the demon, and in which offerings of cocoanuts and other things were placed. Women were beating rice for the feast; others selling provisions; altogether about a hundred people were then present.

Some of the principal officiators were adorned with fringes of young palm leaves tied round the waist, and with the usual brass bells around the ankles and calves of the legs. Several had plaited bundles of palm leaves to represent horses, on which they pretended to gallop round the altar, whipping the horses and shouting. A fire was alight, and they galloped through and over this until it was extinguished. On such occasions dancing and singing are sometimes carried on for several days with great enjoyment and enthusiasm.

In the North a curious "club dance" is practised at night, by the light of a large fire. The dancers, men with clubs a foot long, one in each hand, go in concentric circles in different directions, and meeting each other very prettily strike each other's clubs, keeping time to the songs they sing—now bending to catch the blow made towards the feet and then rising to ward off or meet one directed towards the head.

Attendance at Hindu Temples.—It has been remarked that the servile castes, have, in various parts of South India, special privileges granted them on particular festivities, whether as treats in relaxation from sore toil, bribes to keep them submissive under oppression, or as vestiges of a higher position in former times, when they were masters of the land before the arrival of the Aryans.

Captain Mackenzie, in the "Indian Antiquary" for March, 1873, thinks that the Holiars of Mysore, now despised and outcast, once held the foremost place in the village circle, having been the first to establish villages there. A Holiar is even now generally the priest to the village goddess, and, as such, on annual offerings takes precedence of Brahmans. At Mailkota, and at Bailur, Holiars have the right of entering the temple on three days in the year specially set apart for them. He considers that it proves that the Holiars were the first to take possession of the soil, that the Kulwadi, or village henchman, a Holiar, receives fees from the friends of any who die—"they buy from him the ground for the dead."

In Travancore, nothing of this kind is observed, but on festival days the Pulayars and other low castes are permitted some games and a little nearer approach than usual to some pagodas, as at Pareychaley, &c. At Ochira, on the great sham-fight, slaves are permitted to join and give and receive blows equally with Náyars. Wooden swords and shields are used. At Kumáranallúr annual feast of slaves, Sudras come from Bhagavathi's temple with little beaten-gold images of the goddess for sale. The slaves buy and offer them to the deity; the same image being sold over and over again, and each time offered by the buyer to the goddess.

At the Neduvengaud Temple, where two or three thousand people, mostly Sudras and Ilavars, attend for the annual festival in March, one third of the whole are Pariahs, Kuravars, Védars, Kánikárs, and Pulayars, who come from all parts around. They bring with them wooden models of cows neatly hung over and covered, in imitation of shaggy hair, with ears of rice. Many of these images are brought, each with a separate procession from its own place. The headmen are finely dressed with clothes stained purple at the edge. The image is borne on a bambu frame, accompanied by a drum, and men and women in procession—the latter wearing quantities of beads, such as several strings of red, then several of white; or strings of beads and then a row of brass ornaments like rupees—and all uttering the *kurava* cry. These images are carried round the temple, and all amuse themselves for the day.

Oaths and Ordeals.—They swear by the Sun, raising the hand towards the sun—or by some temple—saying, "By this deity, I did not do so." "By the Sun, I did not." "If I speak falsely, may my eyes perish, or my head be struck off by lightning," or, "let me be cut off by cholera or small-pox;" or, "let me not live more than forty-one days."

If falsely accused of adultery, an oath is taken, or the following ordeal:—A new pot is procured, in which some cow-dung is mixed up with water, then made to boil thoroughly. Into this the man dips his hand, stirs it three times round in the water, and lifts out some of the cowdung which he lays on a plantain leaf. Before the pot is placed, the priest utters some imprecations on the man if guilty. If the hand is burnt, he is guilty—if not burnt, innocent. In case of other faults than adultery, he will make oath at some devil temple.

Once when a theft of rice occurred, the loser went to a temple of Lakshmi, belonging to Sudras, and standing afar off as required, laid down three fanams as an offering, praying aloud to the deity, "Oh, hear my complaint!" The priest comes out and takes up the money; then the deity is expected to punish the thief. If the thief afterwards suffers from sickness, he will make the usual inquiries and be informed—"So and so made vows against you." The temple priest is not able by his charms to discover who it was that committed the theft.

Good Manners.—In presence of an elder brother, a younger brother cannot sit down. Before a father, grown-up daughters should not sit; and sons sit on a somewhat lower level. Little children sit anywhere. Nephews and nieces must not sit on the same level with the maternal uncle, nor the common people with a Head Pulayar. There is one of these in each Proverty, formerly appointed by the Sirkar, now by the people. A woman cannot sit at all in the presence of her son-in-law, and *vice versâ*. These two cannot approach one another nearer than about twenty feet. This rule sometimes causes little difficulties when converts first begin to attend Christian worship. We have seen the son-in-law climb into the prayer-house over the wall at the farthest point from where the mother-in-law was sitting; but this absurd regulation is soon dropped as useless and inconvenient.

Slavery and Work.—All castes, Brahmans, Sudras, Ilavars, and Shánárs possessed slaves. Yet Pulayars have of late years since their emancipation, and perhaps in rare cases previously, had some little property in cattle, or land purchased or reclaimed by their own labours. They still regard themselves and speak as being slaves, but those who have opportunity to break off the old connection are free. Many prefer their former situation when at all favourable, to independence and self-help.

When they work in the rice-fields, women now receive daily one edungaly of paddy; men, one and a half, also four armfuls of straw and rice (or perhaps only two) from each field for watching the crops throughout the year. For residence, a small bit of land is allotted. The trees in this belong to the master, but the Pulayar enjoys the produce while he lives there. When not required by his master, he is at liberty to work elsewhere, or for himself. Actual work for the master occupies about three months in the year, and watching, three months. There is little to do in the hot season, say March, after the February rice crop has been garnered. In April, rice nurseries are prepared, enclosures repaired, and manuring and ploughing attended to. In the middle of May the rice is sown and transplanted; in June, weeding occupies till the end of that month. There is then little field work for two months till August when the second harvest begins.

While some masters treated their slaves with consideration, others greatly oppressed them. If a cow gave them milk they must take it to the house of the master. When bought and sold, the agreement specified "tie and beat, but do not destroy either legs or eyes." For faults or crimes they were cruelly confined in stocks or cages, and beaten. For not attending work very early in the morning, they were tied up and flogged severely. Awful cruelties were sometimes perpetrated. Cases are known in which slaves have been blinded by lime cast into their eyes. The teeth of one were extracted by his master as a punishment for eating his sugar cane. A poor woman has been known, after severe torture and beating, to kill her own child in order to accuse her master of the murder and get revenge. Even the Syrian Christians were sometimes most cruel in their treatment of their slaves. Rev. H. Baker, *fils*, was acquainted with a case in which a slave ran away from his master, but afterwards returned with presents, begging forgiveness. He was beaten severely, covered with hot ashes, and starved till he died. It cost the unworthy master, however, five hundred rupees in bribes "to settle the trouble."

Slaves were not only bought and sold outright, but also mortgaged like lands. Female slaves were valued at double price, on account of the "produce"—the children—half of which went to the seller and half to the purchaser. Lieut. Conner says in Report of Survey, 1820, "Husband and wife sometimes serve different persons, but more frequently the same. The females of this class are given in usufruct, scarcely ever in complete possession: the eldest male child belongs to the master of the father: the rest of the family remain with the mother while young, but being the property of her owner, revert to him when of an age to be useful; and she follows in the event of her becoming a widow."

In 1852, before emancipation, the Rev. George Matthan wrote that the price of a slave was usually Rs. 6, but in Mallapalli, Rs. 18. The children were the property of the mother's owner. Being paid in kind and at the lowest possible rate, they were able to obtain only the coarsest support of life. Lying, stealing, and drunkenness were common among them.

CHAPTER IV.

VÉḌARS.

THOUGH the caste name means "hunter," these people are in a condition very similar to that of the Pulayars, living in jungle clearings, or working in the rice fields, and formerly sold and bought as slaves. Their usages, worship, and superstitions greatly resemble those of the Pulayars. They are in deep poverty, very timid, and destitute of temporal comfort and conveniences. They have to wander about in seasons of scarcity in search of wild yams, which they boil and eat on the spot, and are thorough gluttons, eating all they can get at any time, then suffering want for days. Women are filthy in their habits, the sick are uncared for, and mortality amongst the children is great. Polygamy is common, as men are not required to provide for the support of their wives. But some who have been converted to Christianity show wonderful and rapid improvement in moral character, civilization, and diligence.

CHAPTER V.

KURAVARS.

THE Kuravars, or Coravars, appear to be identical in race with the Kurumber, Kurubar or Korawa caste in Madras and Mysore and on the slopes of the Neilgherries, and closely allied to the Vḗdar, or Bedur, hunting caste. The Kuravars in Travancore are mostly found in the Quilon district, and thence northwards. This tribe once formed a State of considerable power in Madras and Mysore, where their descendants are now musicians, snake charmers, basket-makers, cultivators, or robbers. Small bodies of them were driven into the jungles of Travancore, where they have sunk in civilization and fallen into the position of predial slaves. They, are, however, higher in the caste system than Pulayars, Pariahs, and Védars. There are four principal sub-divisions of this caste, one of which is called **Kákkei**, or "Crow" Kuravars, because they are said to eat crows, vultures, alligators, and such like, though they will not touch beef. These, however, are very few, and chiefly mendicants, ear-borers, soothsayers, gymnasts, or thieves. Their dress is like that of the Tamilians.

Others are called **Kunda**, "low or mean" Kuravars; and are in fact slaves (though legally emancipated). They are not allowed to approach the higher classes in markets, or to enter their houses; and were formerly sold from one owner to another. They perform various agricultural labours; and receive payment in kind or in money. They imitate the Náyar custom of marriage, that is, a mere temporary union, technically called "presenting a cloth and living together." The husband, however, continues to pay for the wife to her uncle in rice, &c., as long as he retains her. Those now under Christian instruction are called Malayám Kuravars. Their religion is the aboriginal worship of demons as Mádan, Bhadrakáli, and others; in groves or small temples; without images, or with rude stones to represent the spirit.

A party of "**Hill Védars**" came to visit Mr. Baker, and spoke with peculiar words and in a curious tone, rendering it very difficult to converse with them. Their women had immense necklaces of beads, pieces of lead, and brass; one had a broad chain of brass round her neck. These people were coal-black, and many quite curly-headed.

CHAPTER VI.

THE HILL TRIBES.

VARIOUS tribes of wild, but inoffensive mountaineers, occupy the higher hills and the mountains of Travancore, finding a rather precarious living by migratory agriculture, hunting, and the spontaneous products of the forests. The Hill men proper number close upon 12,000; and Ulláḍars, a hunting caste, 2,829. The Véḍars are scarçely mountaineers, being found rather at the foot of the hills, and in a social condition very similar to that of the Pulayars. These hill people are most numerous in Neyáttankara district, where fully a fourth of their whole number are found: the others are scattered over the mountains north and south of this centre.

These remarkable people are very rude and primitive in manners, and are generally regarded as the aborigines of the country. Bishop Caldwell, however, considers that they are not, like the Tudas of the Neilgherries, the surviving representatives of the earliest inhabitants of the plains, but, like the hill tribes of the Pulneys, the descendants of some Hinduised low-country people who were driven to the hills by oppression, or who voluntarily migrated thither.

THE KÁNIKÁRS.—The tribes living towards the south of Travancore are most usually designated by this term, while those in the north are more commonly called Mala Arayans. There are differences between these two classes, probably arising not from variety of origin but from their isolation on separate mountains or ranges which present physical obstacles to close or continued intercourse.

Kánikáran means "hereditary proprietor of land," thus recognizing their ancient rights over the forest lands. They are sometimes spoken of as *Vélanmár*, "spearmen," a cognomen which they disclaim, and which seems rather inappropriate, unless it has been suggested by the staff or pike which is always carried. They are also called Malei Arasars in Tamil, Mala Arayars in Malayáḷam, derived from *arachan*, chief, or more distantly from *rája*, king. The term means "hill kings" or chiefs, and has nothing to do with "Aryan," as applied to the Sanskrit people.

The Káṇikárs are generally very short in stature and meagre in appearance, from their active habits and scanty food. Some have markedly negroid features. The men go almost naked, having only a small strip of cloth round the loins. Men and women alike grow the hair long and tie it up in a knot behind, like the Cingalese. A few men of the better grade imitate the Sudra mode of wearing the hair. Their clothing and habits are generally uncleanly.

The women are rather better clad, and are very shy of strangers. They wear bracelets of iron or brass, and load the neck with countless strings of red beads or shells: leaden rings are also worn in the lobe of the ear.

The men always carry a cane basket slung upon their shoulders like a knapsack, containing a few necessary utensils, or used for bringing home the food or other articles which they may secure. They also carry a long staff, a heavy knife or billhook stuck in the waistcloth, and sometimes a bow and arrows.

The Kánikárs live together in little clans, each hamlet under the patriarchal rule of a headman (*Múṭṭukáṇi*, the "stem" or principal Kánikáran), who is but one of themselves, but has great influence and authority over all his people. Their dwellings are very small, but neatly made of bambus and the elephant reed (Melocanna Rheedii), the leaves and stems being interwoven for walls as well as roof. Besides the huts on the ground, a number of booths are built on trees with large branches, a platform being made of sticks, and the hut built on this in order to be out of the way of mischievous elephants, tigers, &c. Access is obtained by a ladder or a single long bambu with the side shoots cut off on either side at a distance of a few inches.

These wandering husbandmen cut down a patch of forest, burn and clear it, and sow a crop, with little or no tillage. After cultivating this plot for two or three years, it is exhausted, and they move off in search of fertile land for a fresh field for operations, though not to great distances. They grow rice and millet, tapioca and sweet potatoes, as is done in the low country. This mode of cultivation yields a larger return for the same amount of labour than permanent plough husbandry, but is highly destructive of valuable forest lands. Their migrant habits arise partly from laziness: it is easier to cut down and burn new forest than to rear cattle, plant trees, manure land, and build houses. They, therefore, prefer this savage life, but should be encouraged to settle if possible: only by such means can they be reclaimed to civilization and education, as has been done farther north.

From their intimate acquaintance with the forests and hills, the Kánikárs can readily point out the places haunted by wild beasts, which they recognize by the smell, either to warn travellers against danger, or to guide sportsmen to their game. They strike fire by the friction of dry wood. A peg of the wood of Isora corylifolia (or of bambu) is taken and inserted in a small reed which is rapidly revolved on another piece of the same wood, this being the best for the purpose: in a few minutes smoke is evolved, then fire, which is caught in tinder contained in a small joint of bambu, and can then easily be preserved or carried about.

Though thus familiar, from ages of experience, with the ways of the forest, these poor people are not gifted with even an ordinary amount of knowledge, not one of them being able to read or write, except very recently a few in Pareychaley Mission district, who have learnt to read a little and to sing Christian lyrics. They can never tell their own ages, and if asked, sometimes make absurd guesses. They are unable to count a hundred; over ten they lay down a pebble for each ten. They knot fibres of various climbing plants to express their wants. At Purattimalei twenty years ago, only one had seen a white man before; none had ever travelled to a greater distance from home than twenty miles.

In the south they speak Tamil, and Malayálam further north, but pronouncing very badly, as *víchi* for *víthi.* Words strange to the people of the coast, or archaic, are intermingled with their speech, as "*kálá*" (*kaláyi*, second cultivation of a rice field), for a place where they have remained for two years; "*kurumá*" (*kurumba*) a child; "*yengachi*" where? for "*yewide*," and *pátti* (a fold), or *wádi* (an enclosure, entrenchment) for house; with other oddities in talk, which it requires some time to become familiar with. They are said to pay homage to the Maharajah occasionally, when they address him without the customary honorifics, their boorish ways being good naturedly excused on the ground of their ignorance, and furnishing rather subject of amusement. The very large fruited "bambu plantain," which produces but few fruits in a branch and those of great size, they used to bring as presents on such occasions. I formerly had difficulty in persuading them to part with a sucker of this curious plantain, as they fancied it must be reserved for the use of the Rajah alone.

The Kánikárs are much imposed upon and overcharged in the purchase of beads, cloth, and ornaments, by the Muhammadan and other dealers; by the itinerant blacksmith, who comes round to repair their billhooks ; and the goldsmith, who gives but little gold and much brass, and squeezes a good price somehow out of them, giving long credit and taking double when the harvest is reaped.

They ask large pay of the European planters, partly because they do not care to work at all unless under such inducement; partly, perhaps, from ignorance of the value of money and the difficulty of obtaining it, as formerly they never saw such a thing.

The hillmen will not eat with Shánárs or Ilavars, or still lower castes, but will take food cooked by Sudras. They do not eat the wild ox or buffalo, nor the grey or Hanuman monkey, but only the black species. They gather wild honey in the clefts of rocks and on branches of trees, and bring it home, or for sale, in joints of bambu. Being great smokers of tobacco, which they grow for their own consumption, they stop work frequently when employed on estates in weeding or clearing, to indulge in a smoke.

Till recently, none possessed wealth in coin, only hatchets, billhooks, knives, hoes, and other tools. Their traps for the wild boar and tiger are made with rough timber supported on a spring which falls and lets down the whole weight upon the animal's back. They have no weapons, but are very ingenious at wickerwork of bambu, rattan, and reed. I have seen a bridge over a river, perhaps a hundred feet wide, constructed by them of such materials, over which a pony could pass. Their circumstances have greatly improved of late wherever coffee estates have been opened and worked; but those who are unwilling to take work are driven farther into the hills in search of fresh lands. "The fate of the hill-kings, says Mr. Honiss, is rather sad. For ages past they have boasted of being the undisputed lords of the primeval forests. The elephant and tiger were their only foes; but with snares and traps they could hold their own against these enemies. But they could not resist the onward march of a superior race. The planter approaches them in a peaceable way, offering wages for their hire, but demanding as his right the land he has purchased. The proud men of the woods decline to herd with coolies, and work like common people. As soon as the planter's axe is heard, the hill kings pack their traps and desert their homes to establish themselves in another valley. In this way they have been driven from hill to hill and from valley to valley, until some have found now a safe resting place in the dense jungles of the lowlands of Travancore. If the planter wishes to penetrate some unexplored jungle, or cut a path in some out-of-the-way place, the hill men are ready to assist, and it is the universal testimony that they are more faithful to their engagements than their more civilized brethren from the plains."

Though reckoned amongst the low castes in the Census and in vernacular works, the Kánikárs are somewhat superior in several respects, and are by no means regarded with the abhorrence felt towards the Pulayars and others. Being credited with the possession of considerable influence over their local demons, other castes are afraid to offend them.

Marriage Customs.—The lowest age for marriage of girls is seven, for boys sixteen. Girls sometimes remain unmarried till near sixteen, "because no bridegroom has offered."

A youth desirous of marrying a girl visits her uncle, accompanied by four of his relatives who make the proposal. If agreed upon, the marriage day is at once fixed, and guests are invited by both parties by presenting betel and spices. On his arrival at the marriage house, the bridegroom presents a cloth to the bride's mother, which is called *amma vídu mundu*—"mother's house-cloth," and five and a half fanams to her uncle if she has become marriageable; if otherwise, seven and a half fanams. The bride is then brought into the marriage shed amongst the company assembled. A *táli*, worth four chuckrams, is handed to the bridegroom, who after adoring the Sun with it in his hand, holds it near the bride's neck, and his sister standing behind ties it on. He also hands over a cloth to his sister, who puts it on the bride. The headman offers some "advice" to the husband as to the management of his wife, beginning his rule with mild measures and proceeding to extremities only by degrees as required. The heads of his discourse are said to be as follows:—

1. *Cholli kodu*—Teach by words.
2. *Nulli kodu*—Teach by pinching—slight punishments.
3. *Talli kodu*—Teach by blows. Next,
4. *Taḷḷi kodu*—Cast her away (at last, if she will not obey!)

On that day a feast is held at the bride's house, and on the following day at the house of the husband. The richer families spend 100 fanams on the feast, while the poor simply entertain their guests with betel-nut to chew and Indian hemp to smoke.

The dowry consists generally of mattocks, axe, a large chopping knife, brass cups, earthen vessels, and such like. Having no landed property, no dowry of this kind can be given. If there be anything to inherit, the nephew is the heir.

The ceremony practised on the occasion of pregnancy is called *vayaru pongala*, when boiled rice is offered to the Sun. First, they mould an image of Ganesha, and setting it in a suitable place, boil the rice. To this they add for an offering *aval*, or flattened rice, parched rice, cakes, plantain fruits, young cocoa-nuts, and tender leaves of the same palm, with the flower of the Areca palm. The headman then commences dancing and repeating mantrams. He waves the offerings to the Sun.

The name is given to a child when it is able to sit on the ground, say at the age of three or four months. The usual names are very much the same as those used by other people —Parappankáni, Sáttan, Eiyan, Mádappan, Vikkiran; and for women—Eechi, Valli, Kannammei, Púmálei, Parappi. They were willing to tell us the names of their wives.

On first giving rice to a child, a feast is held, and an offering presented to the jungle demons.

Sickness and Death.—When any one takes ill the headman is at once consulted; he visits the sick and orders two drumming and singing ceremonies to be performed. A whole night is spent in dancing, singing, drumming, and prayer for the recovery of the patient. The offerings consist of tapioca, flour, and cocoanuts, along with the articles previously mentioned. After some time, the headman, with manifestations of demoniac possession, reveals whether the sufferer will die or not. If the former, he repeats a mantram (*kudumi vettu mantram*, formula on cutting off the topknot), and cuts off the sick man's kudumi. This being a sign of approaching death, the relatives and others pay their last visits to the sick.

After death, a mixture of ganjá (hemp), raw rice, and cocoanut is put into the mouth of the corpse by the son and nephews; and it is buried at some distance from their abode, mantrams being repeated over the body. Occasionally one is cremated. The relatives bathe before returning home, and cannot take any of the produce of their lands till the death pollution is removed, fearing that wild beasts will attack them or destroy their crops. To this end a small shed is built outside their clearing on the third day, three measures of rice are boiled and placed in a cup or on a plantain leaf inside the shed; then all bathe again and return home. On the seventh day all this is repeated, the old shed being pulled down and a new one put up. On returning to their dwelling, they sprinkle cow dung on their houses and in the yard, which finally removes the defilement. People in better circumstances make a feast of curry and rice for all present.

Ceremonies with reference to Cultivation.—When intending to clear some land, the headman is invited; three edungaly measures of rice and six cocoanuts are presented to him. These he takes to a suitable plot of forest-land, makes an offering, and first clears a small portion with his own hand; then the others follow. These offerings are repeated at the burning of the felled timber, and the sowing of the seed, plantain fruits and other articles being added. On the first appearance of the ear, they spend two nights in drumming, singing, and repeating mantrams at the field, putting up a *tattu*, or platform, on four sticks as a shrine for the spirits, where they offer raw rice, tender cocoanuts, flowers, &c.

At harvest-time, a sufficient quantity of rice being beaten, sweetmeats are prepared, and cocoanuts, plantain fruits, and flowers added to these for a general offering to the various spirits, such as Ayiravilli, "he of a thousand bows;" Mádan Tamburán, "the Cow-like Lord;" Mallan Tamburán, "the Giant Lord;" Mátthándan Pey, "the Sun Demon;" Púcha Mallan Pey, "the Cat Giant Demon;" Athirakodi Pey, "the Boundary Flag Demon," and a great many others whom they regard as deities. They wait upon the headman for the manifestation of the gods, then devour the offerings.

These demons are supposed to be peculiar to the hills, to reside in large trees, and rule the wild beasts, restraining them from mischief. No images or sacred stones are used, but a small stone may be taken when required as an idol or fetish.

The Kánikárs have not much idea of the soul or immortality. When asked, they say, "Who can tell?" Some with whom we conversed said they knew nothing of a hell, or of the wicked going there. Some of their superstitions are connected with the serpent; for example, a vein in a certain granite rock is said to have been caused by a snake creeping over it before it hardened.

Some days are lucky, as Monday for sowing seed, Wednesday for building, Friday for reaping. They observe two days in the year as fasts, the dates of which they learn from Muhammadans or Hindus, who come to them with rice or other articles for sale.

These wild men are usually ranked above the more civilized Hindus of the plains in point of morals. Though rude, hardy, and courageous, they are inoffensive, and are regarded as somewhat truthful, honest, chaste, and hospitable. Men may stay in their villages as long as they like, but must be very reserved and careful respecting the women. It is said that formerly individuals amongst them guilty of adultery were punished with immediate death. Some, however, have two wives if they can get both wives to agree together. We have met with individuals who scarcely seemed to understand the distinction between good and evil.

The great vice of these mountain men is drunkenness, through the almost universal prevalence of which they are constantly in distress. It is cruel and wrong to offer them strong drinks.

Some of our preachers on a tour came upon a large number of them assembled with jars of arrack, &c., to offer to their deities, and to drink. The headman was intoxicated, and while the Christians were speaking, he shouted, "Children, make a pile of wood at once to burn these fellows. They are come from the white men to take us to their company and make us eat beef." So the preachers had to make their escape.

When the Christian religion is recommended to them, they reply that if they embraced it, the jungle-demons would be offended, and send elephants and other wild beasts to kill them, and destroy their cultivations. "Why, then," it was asked, "do not the Europeans suffer, who cut down the forests?" to which they answered, "As the white men worship a mighty God, the demons take their flight from their presence." Jungle fever also is attributed to the agency of these deities, and they remove from a place where it prevails. Some altogether refused to hear our exhortations. When they see books in the hands of the Christian teachers, they will say, "Do you come to destroy us by bringing the wrath of the demons upon us?" One woman said, "I have only two children; do not kill them by teaching them your Vedam."

The Muhammadans, dreading the loss of their influence and opportunities for cheating these simple people, endeavour to hinder them from receiving instruction, even in reading, by saying, "These people want to make you all Christians, then the devils will desert you so that you shall become the prey of wild beasts. If you learn letters the English will carry you away to foreign lands in ships."

Efforts have from time to time been made by the Mission for their benefit, especially in Pareychaley and Trevandrum districts, but the deadly fever of the hills has sometimes proved fatal, or prostrated the catechists employed, and but little success has been met with. The hillmen are now often addressed by the catechists of the Cooly Mission labouring amongst the Coffee Estates.

Mr. Emlyn writes:—"The spirits so much feared in the plain, are not supposed to concern themselves with the moral conduct of men; all they are thought to care about is to be honoured with pujah, sacrifices, and offerings. The divinities of the hills are believed to have a moral law. It is a pity their prophets have said nothing against drinking. Drink is the curse of the Kánikárs. Their belief, too, that learning to read is a religious act, a sort of initiatory step to another religion, and, therefore, displeasing to their gods, is another serious evil.

Coffee planting in this country seems as if largely intended, in the Providence of God, for the good of this hill tribe. In the plantations Kánikárs and Christians meet and work together, and some of the latter are not backward in showing what the Lord has done for them in spiritual as well as in temporal things, and they urge their companions to accept the same blessings. In these plantations, too, catechists, and occasionally missionaries can speak with as many Kánikárs as take employment there, and staying there at night, can spend the day in preaching in the unhealthy valleys below.

These people have already learnt one or two valuable lessons. One is, that the spirits they worship have no power over Christians from Europe and the plains. When Europeans and native Christians began planting on the hills, some of the Kánikárs went to their priests, and in the most solemn and religious manner got awful curses pronounced on their new neighbours. All were to be utterly destroyed unless they went away. This was done repeatedly, but nothing happened. Some of the priests now declare that it is in vain to curse Christians, or, as they call them, 'the people that have books.' Another lesson they have learnt is that Christianity is a civilizing and an elevating religion, and a good religion for this life generally. The people that live nearest the abodes of the Kánikárs are Pariahs and Puliahs, our converts from these castes, and their Sudra masters. The hillmen despise the Pariahs and Puliahs, but they see that our converts from these castes have wonderfully improved since becoming Christians—some of them even to become superior to themselves. A few more lessons learnt, and He who is the Truth will, we trust, be welcomed as their Teacher and Saviour."

THE MALA ARAYANS.—In treating of these people we cannot do better than make extracts from the valuable account given by Rev. H. Baker, junr., in a pamphlet entitled "The Hill Arrians," published in 1862. Mr. Baker was very intimately acquainted with the Arayans, and was one of their most distinguished benefactors—the apostle and father of the Christian converts whom he was privileged to gather from this tribe. We shall add to that first published monograph, further observations by himself and others, rearrange, and bring up the whole to the present date.

The majority of the hill tribes are divided into small wandering bodies, living for a few months in a particular spot, and then deserting it for another as soon as their scanty crop of grain is reaped. The Mala Arayans, however, have their fixed villages, and reside generally on the western slopes of the higher range of mountains or their spurs. Their villages consist of houses scattered all over the steep hill sides, like birds' nests perched among the rocks. They are often lovely spots, in a ravine not accessible to elephants, near to some gushing rivulet falling over granite rocks, and surrounded by gigantic trees and palms, rarely at a less elevation than two or three thousand feet above the sea. Many of their houses are good substantial erections of wood and stone, built by workmen from the plains, and after the fashion common to the Western Coast; but in many cases they prefer temporary huts of mud, bambu, and grass-thatch, as the survivors often dislike living in a dwelling in which the head of the family has

HILL ARAYANS' HUTS IN TREES.

died. Small huts are also built in trees for watching and security from wild beasts.

"The Arayans are for the most part short in stature, and not very long-lived. But the feverishness of the climate in the districts they inhabit is enough to account for any physical degeneracy of race. They are as fair as the high-caste Hindus, the women frequently beautiful, proving that the aborigines of India were not black from race peculiarities, but only sometimes black through circumstances."—(Collins.)

Those who live on the Melkávu range being near large Romo-Syrian villages are more civilized, perhaps, than other Arayans.

By the Government officials they are called "Mala Vélans," and are considered to rank in caste above all mechanics, and equal to Muhammadans and Jews. Sudras do not deem themselves polluted by contact with these respectable and independent people, while they keep Chógans at a distance for fear of defilement. The Chógans, however, consider themselves superior to the Arayans. The more degraded Malei Arasars in the south, who speak Tamil, are not allowed by them to be of the same race.

The Arayans are some of them rich, being large cultivators of the hill slopes, which they clear of jungle in the dry season, sowing during the rains. This gives them abundance of rice. Little terraces are cut out on the steep ascents to prevent elephants from getting at them, and some protection is obtained by high and strong fences piled up of wood from the trees that have been felled. Every man, however, has to watch with loaded guns during seed-time and harvest, to protect the crops from elephants, deer, and other animals, as well as from swarms of birds which destroy the crops, and tigers and leopards which kill the cattle. They are also frequently exposed to danger of drowning in the swollen torrents during the monsoon, to falls from trees and precipices which they climb to procure fruits and honey, and to the occasional ravages of small-pox and other diseases. The headman of one village is considered very wealthy, his annual crops yielding him ten or twelve thousand parahs (say four or five thousand bushels) of paddy, besides other grain, pulses and roots.

They will not often work for hire, and are very averse to carry loads. All their produce is carried in baskets, which are slung on the shoulders; and every son has his own room in the family house, into which no one intrudes excepting himself and the wife. There is a general store for provisions for the family, which is provided by all in common: but each individual has, in addition his own cultivation and store, to provide for his private wants. The collection of old coins, jewels, and other valuables, hoarded up by some is very great. They dispose of their hill produce at the markets in the plains. They are free and somewhat intelligent in their manners, more truthful and generally moral in their habits than people of the plains. They are great hunters of the wild beasts and game which abound in their hills, and relate a tradition giving them special permission to eat the black monkey. From this they are called by the low country people *kurangu tinni*, "monkey eaters." Though sometimes spoken of as an inferior race by the Hindus, yet we generally find them looked upon as beings in alliance with some powerful demonolatry; and presents are abundantly bestowed in order to prevent their curses producing ill-effects. Náyars often deprecate in no measured terms prognostics of evil uttered by a hill-man, without reference to his caste or tribe. Doubtless the defenceless low castes have found it tend to shield them from worse oppression to make pretensions to spiritual powers of this kind.

As a rule, the names of individuals among this hill tribe are not Hindu; they severally signify some peculiarity, as Kannan—"the eyed one;" Pottan—"the deaf one;" Thadian —"the fat one," for men: and for females, Madura—"the sweet one;" Shangam, and also Ponna, "the golden one;" Chakra—"the sugar one." Where the people are under the influence of the Náyars, there only we meet with names from the Shastras. The language is Malayálam, with several words, however, not known on the coast. Only in three Arayan villages does the custom of Nepotism hold, and there because the Zemindar has compelled them to do so; but still they have outwitted him by making it obligatory on cousins to marry. In all other Arayan settlements, children invariably inherit their father's property.

At all Arayan feasts, particularly weddings, husbands and wives eat off the same plantain-leaf, sitting side by side; this shows their relationship. After thus eating together the bridegroom ties the *táli* on the bride's neck, and a collection is made for the happy couple, which is concluded by the bride taking possession of any brass cooking vessels or gold ornaments in the house, saying, "This is my father's:" then her husband appropriates them. The marriage rite is held as sacred and indissoluble.

A child, when a month old, is seated in the father's lap and fed with a little sweetened rice; the omission of this ceremony implies it to be illegitimate. The maternal grandfather, and other near relatives repeat the ceremony. The birth of each child renders the mother impure for a month, when she must reside out of the village, and cannot cook, or go near the springs, or enter the provision grounds, or touch any implement or vessel. She generally lives in a hut in a tree. The father also is impure for a week and must not eat rice; but, like the mother, must live on roasted roots and water. A funeral prevents the family from entering their cultivation for a week.

The Arayans bury their dead; consequently there are many ancient tumuli in these hills, evidently graves of chiefs, showing just the same fragments of pottery, brass figures, iron weapons, &c., as are found in other similar places. These tumuli are often surrounded with long splintered pieces of granite, from eight to twelve or fifteen feet in length, set up on end, with sacrificial altars and other remains, evidently centuries old. Numerous vaults too, called Pándi Kuri, are seen in all their hills. They stand north and south, the circular opening being to the south; a round stone is fitted to this aperture, with another acting as a long lever, to prevent its falling out; the sides, as also the stones of the top and bottom, are single slabs. To this day the Arayans make similar little cells of pieces of stone, the whole forming a box a few inches square; and on the death of a member of any family, the spirit is supposed to pass, as the body is being buried, into a brass or silver image, which is shut into this vault; if the parties are very poor, an oblong smooth stone suffices. A few offerings of milk, rice, toddy, and ghee are made, a torch lighted and extinguished, the figure placed inside the cell and the covering stone hastily placed on; then all leave. On the anniversary, similar offerings being made, the stone is lifted off, and again hastily closed. The spirit is thus supposed to be enclosed; no one ventures to touch the cell at any other time.

The objects of Arayan worship are the spirits of their ancestors, or certain local demons supposed to reside in rocks or peaks and having influence only over particular villages, or families. The religious services rendered to these are intended to deprecate anger rather than to seek benefits; but in no case is lust to be gratified, or wickedness practised, as pleasing to these deities.

The woodcut on the following page represents one of their effigies of ancestors. It is a brass image about three inches in height, the back of the head hollow, the hands holding a club and a gun. This represents a demonized man of wicked character, who lived about a century ago. He is said to have beaten his wife to death with a club, wherefore the people joined to break his skull, and he became a malignant demon. Another image carried an umbrella and staff and had a milder countenance—this was a good demon. One such image is kept in each family, in which the spirit is supposed actually to reside. They were also put into the little square chambers described above.

Rev. W. J. Richards, of Cottayam, has favoured me with the following history, which throws much light upon this curious superstition:—

"Tálanáni was a priest or oracle-revealer of the hunting deity, Ayappan, whose chief shrine is in Savarimala, a hill among the Travancore Ghāts. The duty of Tálanáni was to deck himself out, as already described in this book, in his sword, bangles, beads, &c., and highly frenzied with excitement and strong drink, dance in a convulsive horrid fashion before his idols, and reveal in uneathly shrieks what the god had decreed on any particular matter. He belonged to the Hill Arayan village of Eruma-pára (the rock of the she-buffalo), some eight or nine from Mélkávu, and was most devoted to his idolatry, and rather remarkable in his peculiar way of showing his zeal. When the pilgrims from his village used to go to Savarimala—a pilgrimage which is alway, for fear of the tigers and other wild beasts, performed in companies of forty or fifty—our hero would give out that he was not going, and yet when they

IMAGE WORSHIPPED BY ARAYANS.

reached the shrine of their devotions, there before them was the sorcerer, so that he was both famous among his fellows and favoured of the gods. Now, while things were in this way, Tálanáni was killed by the neighbouring Chógans during one of his drunken bouts, and the murderers, burying his body in the depths of the jungle, thought that their crime would never be found out; but the tigers—Ayappan's dogs—in respect to so true a friend of their master, scratched open the grave, and, removing the corpse, laid it on the ground. The wild elephants found the body, and reverently took it where friends might discover it, and a plague of small-pox having attacked the Chogáns, another oracle declared it was sent by Sástávu (the Travancore hill boundary god, called also Cháttan or Sáttan) in anger at the crime that had been committed; and that the evil would not abate until the murderers made an image of the dead priest and worshipped it. This they did, placing it in a grave, and in a little temple no bigger than a small dog kennel. The image itself is about four inches high, of bronze. The heir of Tálanáni became priest and beneficiary of the new shrine, which was rich in offerings of arrack, parched rice, and meat vowed by the Arayans when they sallied out on hunting expeditions. All the descendants of Tálanáni are Christians, the results of the Rev. Henry Baker's work. The last heir who was in possession of the idol, sword, bangle, beads, and wand of the sorcerer, handed them over to the Rev. W. J. Richards in 1881, when he had charge for a time of Mélkávu."

Lamps to the memory of their ancestors were kept burning in little huts, and at stones used to represent the spirits of their ancestors. At one spot, where the genii were supposed to reside, there was a fragment of granite well oiled, and surrounded by a great number of extinguished torches. A most fearful demon was said to reside in a hollow tree, which had been worshipped by thousands of families. They did not know the precise hole in which the symbol was to be found; when discovered, it looked like the hilt of an old sword. One deity was said by the priest of a certain hill to have placed three curious looking rocks as resting-places for himself on his journeys to the peak; but he could not answer the objection, "How could a god want to rest, or how was it he could not place his seat quite upright, or in the pleasant shade of a grove?" Cocoanuts are offered to famous demons residing in certain hills. It has been observed that in cases of sickness sometimes Arayans will make offerings to a Hindu god, and that they attend the great feasts occasionally; but in no case do they believe that they are under any obligation to do so, their own spirits being considered fully equal to the Hindu gods.

Each village has its priest, who, when required, calls on the "Hill" (*mala*), which means the demon resident there, or the *Prétham*, ghost. If he gets the afflatus, he acts in the usual way, yelling and screaming out the answers sought. The devil-dancer wears the kudumi, and has a belt, bangles, and other implements; and invokes the demons in cases of sickness.

They have some sacred groves, where they will not fire a gun or speak above a breath; they have certain signs also to be observed when fixing on land for cultivation or the site of a house, but no other elaborate religious rites. In choosing a piece of ground for cultivation, before cutting the jungle they take five strips of bark of equal length, and knot all the ends together, holding them in the left hand by the middle. If all, when tied, form a perfect circle the omen is lucky, and the position in which the cord falls on the ground is carefully noted by the bystanders.

The Arayans draw toddy from two wild palms of the hills, and much arrack is taken to them from the low country; drunken fits are common, but though their fights are sometimes desperate, the filthy language commonly used by Hindus is never heard. Drunkenness is their besetting sin, and makes the middle-aged look older than they really are; while the young men, from exercise in the clear mountain air, have a healthy look. They grow tobacco, steep it twelve hours in a running stream, dry, and pound it. Instead of areca nut, they chew the bark of a tree.

These mountain men were in former times terribly fleeced and oppressed by their rulers, and by powerful neighbours. The Sirkar required each individual to furnish a certain quantity of wax and wild honey and firewood for temples without remuneration; also to assist in catching elephants. They were otherwise free even from paying land-tax. The Kanikal people, though freemen, paid head money for themselves and all males who had died within the previous ten years, besides the usual land-tax and ground rents and taxes on fruit trees; and were besides fleeced by the local petty officers. The services required furnished occasion for continual annoyance and exactions, men being seized by the officials to carry cardamoms from the hills to the boats without pay; and if they hid themselves, as was natural, the women were caught, beaten, locked up, kept exposed to the sun and the pouring rain, and all sorts of indignities were inflicted. They also had to complain of some of their cows being killed, others stolen by the tax gatherers, so far from the central authority; and worse than all, some had been beaten and expelled from lands which their forefathers' sweat had bedewed for years untold. The Arayans of Todupuley, it is said, are still much oppressed by their Muhammadan neighbours.

The Puniáttu Rajah, who ruled over those at Mundapalli, made them pay head-money—two chuckrams a head monthly as soon as they were able to work—and a similar sum as "presence money," besides certain quotas of fruit and vegetables, and feudal service. They were also forced to lend money if they possessed any, and to bring leaves and other articles without any pretext of paying them, and that for days. The men of these villages were thus placed in a worse condition than the slaves. This petty Rajah used to give a silver-headed cane to the principal hillman, who was then called Perumban, "cane-man."

Among these wild out most interesting tribes the late Rev. Henry Baker, junr., began, about 1849, a good work of evangelizing and civilizing, which he carried on in the teeth of many difficulties and perils which would have discouraged a less resolute man, travelling on foot by the jungle tracks, crossing bridgeless streams, climbing the hills to their romantic settlements, and once spending nights in a hut in a great tree for protection from the wild elephants. Great opposition was experienced from the heathen, especially in the Puniáttu Rajah's country. The inquirers were beaten by some of the Rajah's servants, made to stand in water up to their very necks "in order to wash Christianity out of them;" kept in stocks for days, chillies rubbed in their eyes, and their heads tied up in bags and in loosened head cloths filled with the large black ground-ants and red tree-ants.

Mr. Baker was privileged to baptize many hundreds of the Arayans, instructing them and forming them into congregations. This good work is still cared for by other missionaries, and is likely to extend. There are now about 2,000 Arayan Christians in congregations, situated chiefly north of Puniáttu and around Mundakayam, all within a radius of thirty-six miles from Cottayam—an imperishable memorial of Henry Baker and his indefatigable labours. At Mélkávu a church has been substantially built of stone on a site about 2,000 feet above the sea-level. The Christians still suffer persecution from rich Muhammadans and Náyars in the neighbourhood, who fear the loss of their gains if the hillmen are taught to read, and from the Sirkar's underlings, who try to obtain money on false pretences. The need of trained agents is now much felt for the guidance and growth of these new churches. Very recently the inhabitants of two hills near Mélkávu have expressed their desire to be instructed, and asked for teachers. Thus is "the wilderness made glad, and the parched desert become like a garden of the Lord."

Several other tribes dwell in the hills, as ULLADARS, a true jungle tribe of wild and timid savages, whose subsistence and life are miserable and pitiful. They are without settled villages and civilized clothing, wandering within certain boundaries prescribed to each division, living a few months in one spot till the crop of ragi is reaped, then decamping to another place more likely to be productive of wild roots. They subsist chiefly on wild yams, arrowroot, and other esculents, which they find in the jungle, and for the grubbing up of which they are generally armed with a long pointed staff. They also further enjoy the fruits of the chase, and are adepts in the use of the bow and arrow. The arrow they use has an iron spear-head, and an Ulladan has been known to cut a wriggling cobra in half at the first shot. When armed with guns they make excellent sportsmen.* They were claimed as the property of celebrated hill temples, or great proprietors, who exacted service of them, and sometimes sold their services to Nairs, Syrians, and others. A few Ulladars in the low country say that they or their fathers were stolen in childhood and brought down as slaves.

A small number of URÁLIS wander over the Todupuley hills, building their huts on trees like the Arayans. They entertain a singular aversion to buffaloes, whose approach they anxiously avoid; and are expert in the use of the bow. Urális and Ullådans are said to intermarry. The former, originally slaves, were employed by their Nair masters in cultivating rice on the lower slopes of the hills; they afterwards migrated to the high lands, changing their quarters annually, and obtaining good

ULLADAN.

crops of rice from forest clearings. They are first-rate guides, and some of them particularly useful in carrying heavy loads. From the practice of polyandry, they are, like the Tudas on the Neilgherries, fast diminishing in numbers.

These tribes generally consider themselves superior to the Palayars and Pariahs.

The MANNANS are also a wandering people, little, strange-looking, mountain-men, hardy, and very black, speaking bad Tamil, much employed by the Sirkar to collect cardamoms, keep watch, &c. They rarely cultivate anything but ragi.

* Collins' "Missionary Enterprise in the East."

There is also a hunter caste called PULAYARS, which Mr. Baker considers to be nearly the same as the Urális, except that their speech is Tamil. He also met with a few miserable beings calling themselves HILL PANDARAM, without clothing, implements, or huts of any kind, living in holes, rocks, or trees. They bring wax, ivory, and other produce to the Arayans, and get salt from them. They dig roots, snare the ibex of the hills, and jungle fowls, eat rats and snakes, and even crocodiles found in the pools amongst the hill streams. They were perfectly naked and filthy, and very timid. They spoke Malayálam in a curious tone, and said that twenty-two of their party had been devoured by tigers within two monsoons.

These jungle tribes have generally the same rules and notions respecting women, property, demonology, &c., as the Arayans, and look upon the people of the plains as immigrants to the country. The Sirkar recognized headmen among the Mannans and Arayans, and gave them swords and other insignia, still preserved among them.

CHAPTER VII.

PARIAHS.

THESE are more numerous in the South, where they are also found less reduced in social status, and their usages resemble those of the Tamil Pariahs. They profess to have been once free and powerful. The flesh of cattle left dead by the roadside is their perquisite, and it is their partaking of this food that excites the abhorrence of ordinary Hindus, who venerate the cow. The Pariahs are employed chiefly in field labour. Zealous devil-worshippers and dancers, they make great pretensions to sorcery and magical powers.

About Trevandrum the people of this caste are rather strongly built and bold. They live in hamlets, and eat the putrid flesh of dead cattle, tigers, &c. As with the Sudras, nephews are the heirs. Their girls are married when very young—for mere form—by their cousins, but when grown up are selected by others, who "give cloth." Instances occur both of polygamy and polyandry. The females are rather fair and licentious. They rub turmeric on their faces and bodies, and wear numerous heavy ornaments.

The Pariahs are employed by Sudras and Shánárs for casting out devils and counteracting enchantments. A Christian convert of this caste, who had been a devil dancer, being asked concerning his former practices, replied that they were mere tricks to obtain money.

In North Travancore, their condition seems at the lowest, as they enter farther into the Malayálam country, and have had fewer opportunities of escape from their caste degradation and bitter servitude.

CHAPTER VIII.

ILAVARS.

THESE are a branch of a great and widespread race of people that occupies South Tinnevelly, Travancore, and the Malabar coast as far as the Tulu country. In the far south on both coasts they are known as Shánárs; in Central Travancore as Ilavars; from Quilon to Paravoor, Chógans; in Malabar, as far as Calicut, they are called Teers, or Tíyars; and still farther north Billavars, which appears to be a slightly altered form of Ilavar.

Ilavar, or Eeloover, is derived from Ilam, Ceylon, whence they are said to have immigrated into Malabar, bringing the cocoanut tree along with them.

"The general and natural course of migration would doubtless be from the mainland to the island; but there may occasionally have been reflex waves of migration, even in the earliest times, as there certainly were later on, traces of which survive in the existence in Tinnevelly and the western coast, of castes whose traditions, and even in some instances whose names, connect them with Ceylon." (Caldwell.)

A few are found in Sivagási district in Tinnevelly, where they are called Pándi Ilavars, or Panikkars—distillers of arrack—also in Travancore, from Továla to Velavenkodu. These generally obey the Makkatáyam law of inheritance like the Shánárs and Tamil people, but they are Malayális in dress, language, and customs.

In the census of Travancore. the Ilavars are classified with Paravans, Noolians, Thandáns, and Shánárs, as all "slightly modified forms of the same order of the Hindu community." The Ilavars proper, however, number 383,017; if Shánárs and others of similar standing are added, there are over five lacs, or nearly a fourth of the entire population. Shertala is the stronghold of the Ilavars, as half a lac of them reside in that Tálook. Some of their community are among the most respectable ryots in the State. All speak Malayálam, while the Shánárs are Tamilians.

In Travancore there are several sub-divisions of the caste, which are respectively held in various social and local estimation. Sometimes the terms by which the higher castes are accustomed to denote them differ from those which they use of one another; and offence may be given by appellations, which are regarded as nick-names. The Pándi, or Tamil Ilavars, have already been mentioned; sometimes they call themselves Pattanam varikár. The Páchotti, or Páchili Ilavars, are found between Kovelam and Quilon—the Chevannár or Shánár Ilavars, South of Quilon to Anjengo—the Pula Ilavars, very numerous from Neondakara to Cochin, appear to be simply Chógans. Tandáns, Panikkans, and Válans are also Ilavars.

Titles of Honour.—The "Chánnán" amongst the Chevannár Ilavars is the one who conducts marriages and presides at all important ceremonies, for which he receives presents of tobacco, &c. He is the head-man of the village, and the office is hereditary from uncle to nephews.

Panikkar (artificer, an honorific applied to different classes) is used chiefly in the north from Káyenkulam, more particularly to denote a priest of this caste.

The *Illam,* "house or lineage," is a curious classification amongst this caste, purely Hindu and copied, apparently from the Brahmanic *gotras.* It may be traced also amongst the Pulayars and the Mukkuvars (the latter are said to be immigrants from Ceylon, and are probably allied to the Ilavars). Persons who belong to the same illam are accounted as brothers and sisters, and may not intermarry, for this would be regarded as incest. These illams, they allege, continue the same from generation to generation; new ones are not established, nor do the old ones die out, while of course the actual blood relationship between the families of an illam is becoming more and more distant. The illam is counted through the mother. It is an instance of the law of exogamy—marriage prohibited within the clan. "It must be remembered," says Sir A. C. Lyall, "that in all pure Hindu society, the law which regulates the degrees within which marriage is interdicted proceeds upon the theory that between agnatic relatives connubium is impossible. And as by an equally universal law no legitimate marriage can take place between members of two entirely different castes or tribes, we have thus each member of Hindu society ranged by a law of intermarriage, first as belonging to an outer group, within which he *must* marry; and secondly, belonging to an inner group of agnatic kinsfolk, among whom he must *not* marry."

Amongst the Ilavars this rule is purposeless and very troublesome, sometimes proving quite a check on desirable marriages; even after becoming Christians the prejudice clings to them.

At Mayanádu, a few miles south of Quilon, of which we have particulars, the illams are stated to be Chóli, Múttu, Mathinádu, and Mádambi, the origin of each of which is traced to Veerabhadran marrying wives of various castes. The Ilavars there regard themselves as belonging to the second and third of the above illams, and each takes wives from the other illam only. Those of the Mádambi illam, they say, are numerous about Trevandrum and Neyáttankara, and are said to intermarry amongst themselves sometimes. Múttu appears to mean the "stem" or principal line; Mathinádu to be merely Mayanádu, the name of the locality; and Mádambi, the "baron's" servants.

When marriages take place at Mayanádu between persons of the Múttu and Mayanádu illams, the headman of each is paid five fanams for conducting the ceremony. They also receive a bundle of betel leaves when the *pulikuli* ceremony takes place on pregnancy; and at the *tirandukuli* ceremony, on the arrival at maturity of a girl. Various other marks of respect are paid them.

The Múttillam comprises but one class, who are also called Náyan Shánán. There are four subdivisions in the Mayánádu illam, viz., Senior Shánán, Junior Shánán, and Ayanthi and Kannankara Shánán, names of places. They say that the title of Chánnán was obtained from their former rulers by paying a fee to them.

At the temple of "The Five Lords" in Mayanádu (probably the Five Pándu Brothers), a festival is conducted in April for five days by the headmen of the five sub-divisions of illams last mentioned, during which the five nieces or heiresses of these headmen are allowed to carry lamps and walk round the idols inside the temple, while other women can only perambulate on the outside.

The special **occupation** of the Ilavars is the culture of the cocoanut palm, and the manufacture from it of toddy and ardent spirits, described in another chapter. They are also general agriculturists; some are weavers and boatmen, and a few are petty traders, teachers, priests, doctors, and such like. They are a pleasant looking, intelligent, and respectable people, the highest of the so-called low-castes, but very bigoted in their superstitions, and strongly attached to their caste usages and high pretensions. At Vakkam men are sometimes supported by their wives, who earn a living by trade. The land in that village is divided into neat little square plots of half an acre, or an acre, each planted with cocoanut trees, and having a neat thatched cottage in the centre.

Customs.—The ceremony called *Pulikudi*, "tamarind drinking," is observed in the seventh month of pregnancy. For her delivery the woman is put in a separate room and attended by the midwife. If the infant is a male, the assembled women make the *kurava* cry; if a female, they strike the earth with the midrib of a cocoanut leaf to remove the fear of demons. The infant is immediately washed, and *totturekka* ceremony performed as follows:—A little palm sugar and some onion are mixed in water, and a few drops of this given to the infant by some relative or friend whose excellences, it is supposed, will be acquired by the child. Some give the water of a young cocoanut—others rub a little gold into powder on a stone, mix with water and administer this.

The parents note the exact time of birth as well as they can by the length of their shadow or otherwise, and apply to the astrologer for a horoscope. Regarding the house as polluted by the occurrence, the husband cannot eat food in it for ten days, but goes elsewhere to eat. On the seventh day, pollution is removed by a ceremony performed by the barber woman. She breaks a cocoanut and scrapes it into fine flakes, which she throws about the house.

Women of well-to-do families only go out of the compound on the 28th, or the 40th day, but poorer people go abroad on the seventh. On the eleventh day after the confinement, food is given to the women who had attended on that occasion.

The name is given to the child on the twenty-eighth day. Names are selected by lot, or sometimes the father settles it. Names of deities are usually chosen. On the day the name is given, offerings of boiled rice are made to the god whose name is taken, and a feast is given; an ornamental chain of silver or gold is put on the waist of a boy and a kind of *táli* on the neck of a girl. Poor people only tie a cotton cord on the waist.

The first rice is given to the infant when six months old, with some ceremony. When the first tooth appears, a kind of sweetmeat called *pallada* is made of rice, sugar, and cocoanut, and given to the relatives. On the child's birthday rich parents give alms to the poor, or food to a number of children of their own caste.

Thoughtful parents send their children to school at the age of five or six. Education is begun with the following ceremony:—An edungaly of rice is placed on a smooth floor or plate, and a lamp and a náli measure containing rice, cocoanut, and flowers of Ixora and Jasmine laid close by. The teacher, holding the boy's right hand, makes him to write on the rice the word Hari (Vishnu). The rice is given to the teacher, who then writes on a palm leaf a word of praise to the deities and the first sixteen letters, and at the end of the leaf "Hari;" this he gives to the pupil, receiving from him in return some chuckrams as a present. When the boy becomes able to read short words, *náráyam edukka*, "taking the iron pen" is the next step. The teacher writes a line on a palm leaf and hands it to the pupil along with the iron pen, receiving again a present of one or two fanams in a betel leaf. Some parents present beaten rice and plantain fruits to all the children in the school.

Ornaments for girls are made in various forms, as, a leaf of gold or silver tied on the waist, a gold chain round the neck, silver and gold bracelets, a *takka*, or large cylinder for the ears, which last is not worn by those who have become mothers. Some families have large quantities of jewels, which they keep in a box and bring out on special occasions.

Marriage.—Ilavar girls are all married in infancy as a mere form or custom, at various ages, from one to nine. If not so married, the neighbours reproach the parents for their neglect, and exclude them from social privileges. The person who marries a girl in infancy does not afterwards live with her—often it is a near relative who is the nominal bridegroom.

A month before the solemnization of the nuptials, betel and tobacco are sent as a preliminary invitation to the heads of the community as well as to the maternal uncles of the couple, who are immediately consulted about the erection of a *pandal* or marriage-shed. The materials having been provided and an auspicious day named by the headman, they assemble and erect the shed. The finishing touches of this work, as trellis, steps, windows, arches, and ornaments, are afterwards given by degrees. In the south-west corner of the pandal, a platform of stones is made, white-washed, adorned with flowers, and covered with a canopy of red, white and coloured cloths, upon which are fastened lotus flowers and leaves of *Ficus religiosa* cut in paper. A stool is also placed there covered with silk, upon which caskets, looking-glasses, swords, &c., are placed. A plank is also arranged in the pandal north and south, covered with clean cloth.

To save expense and trouble, several girls are usually married at one time. They are taken to the river to bathe, dress, and put on their ornaments. On returning they are accompanied by the barber-women of their caste, who sing marriage songs, and by men, women, and children of their own people, shouting, blowing snake-horns, and the "five kinds" of music. At the entrance of the pandal the noisy display is stopped, and the eldest of the brides is prepared for marriage ; her face is veiled and she is carried by one of her cousins and seated on the decorated platform, while the other brides are seated upon the boards, having their heads covered with white and red cloths. On the left side of each girl is laid a plantain leaf, and on this a nári measure, an edungaly measure made of the wood of *Alstonia scholaris*, and filled with paddy, a brass vessel containing an edungaly of rice, and a clean cloth folded, on which half a cocoanut, containing a little oil and a wick, is placed. A brass lamp is also lit and laid close to each leaf, in addition to silver rings (worth one fanam each) tied with thread.

The barber-woman now places a betel leaf beneath the left elbow of each girl, takes up the ring, and thrice begs permission of the principal men and women, "Shall I tie the bracelet?" Permission being given she binds it on.

Here it may be observed that the barber-women bathe, put on their ornaments, and go to the marriage shed on the day previous to the wedding, where they keep up singing until the hour fixed for the marriage on the following day. On this occasion, the mother of each bride presents a red cloth, while other females present make them gifts of common cloth and money.

Again, the brides' uncles employ the brothers of the girls who are to be married to furnish a memorandum of the names and birthdays of the brides, with a parcel of betel-nut and tobacco, to the respective bridegrooms' maternal uncles, by whose permission the bridegrooms retire to some place at a considerable distance, where they have their hair partly cropped or shaved. After bathing and daubing sandalwood paste over the body in stripes, they put gold bracelets on the wrists and gold beads round the neck, and tie a gold tissue on the red cloth which covers the muslin on the head. They also dress in a white thick cloth, over which is worn a thin muslin, also a gold or silver belt with similarly mounted writing style and penknife. These ornaments are hired for the occasion if not possessed by the family. This is a common practice amongst all castes.

The bridegrooms return to the marriage house in procession with shouting, trumpeting, the five kinds of drums, playing with swords, and other athletic feats. Arriving at the entrance of the pandal, they make a present of four or five bundles of betel to the workmen who erected it. The astrologer then comes forward and announces that the appointed and auspicious hour has arrived. Instantly the bridegroom of the eldest girl, already sitting on the elevated platform, is taken in and seated by her side, while the other bridegrooms are seated on boards or planks in the shed. The bride sits on the left of her bridegroom. As soon as all are seated, the barber-woman, holding in her hand the *táli* of the girl who is about to be married, and declaring the astral days and the names of the spouses, begs leave of the male and female relatives of the bride, thrice repeating the words, "Shall I take advantage of the lucky hour?" Permission being granted, she hands over the *minnu* or *táli* to the bridegroom, who then ties it on the neck of the girl. Afterwards the mothers of the newly-married couples put into the hands of each bridegroom ten chuckrams, while other guests throw into a brass plate various sums, from five to ten fanams each. A list is then made of the names of the contributors, and the amounts paid in. The barber woman takes, as her fee, one fanam from each bridegroom, and leaves the remainder of the money to the bride's maternal uncle, who counts and takes care of it.

The married couple remain at this house for a week, and are amused with various athletic performances, which they reward with appropriate presents. On the seventh day, the ring tied up by the barber woman is taken off—the wedding is over, and the bride's party give to the mock bridegroom 25 fanams and a bunch of plantain fruits, with five edungalies of rice and a suit of cloth, and conduct him back to his home.

When girls thus married in childhood attain maturity, they are usually chosen as wives by a relative who is willing to do so. Then they are sent to his house with the money contributed to each during their first marriage, and in addition, ornaments, brass vessels, cows and she buffaloes, or any other presents her parents may wish to give.

Death and Burial.—In sickness, sorcerers are consulted, who divine that a certain demon is provoked, and must be pacified by offerings of rice, flowers, fowls, &c. For rendering this service he is paid. Vows are also made to various deities. Sacred ashes are sometimes thrown on the patient, with the promise that he shall recover.

The ceremonies after death vary according to the means and circumstances of the parties. Notice being at once given to relatives and neighbours, both men and women visit the remains. The body is washed and laid on a cot looking north and south. Before washing the dead, the Tandán is sent for, who constructs a shed of cocoanut palm leaves in the yard; the corpse is laid there immediately after washing, and the *váykkari*, or "putting of rice into the mouth" performed. The barber takes some paddy, beats it free from the husk, mixes with it some scraped cocoanut and keeps the mixture ready in a cup. He presides over the ceremony. The children, nephews, and other relatives of the deceased, come forward one by one, and each puts a small pinch of the mixture into the mouth of the corpse. Afterwards the nephews and others put new cloths on the body, which cloths, together with the earrings, &c., of the dead, become the perquisites of the barber himself. While the vaykkari ceremony is being performed, offerings are laid in the shed, and the relatives cry and mourn. The offerings consist of a nári measure of paddy, flowers, and tender cocoanuts. A lamp is also kept burning. This shed remains for seven days, during which time there is daily mourning. The body is buried, either wrapped in mats, or enclosed in a coffin. But if the deceased had been distinguished for wealth, social position, or great age, the remains are burnt.

The grave is generally dug in the compound, and on the south side of the house. Relatives alone bear the body to the grave. They carry it seven or eight times round the grave before lowering and burying it. Afterwards a tender cocoanut is placed at each end of the grave, and some green leaves on it lengthways. A cocoanut tree is also planted on the spot, which is afterwards called "the burning ground cocoa-tree." If the corpse has been burnt, a lamp is kept burning at each end of the grave, instead of the young cocoanuts.

On the sixteenth day is the *pulakuli* or "purification" ceremony, when the caste people are invited, and comparatively large sums spent by wealthy Ilavars on sumptuous entertainments. Bundles of betel-leaf are presented to the principal guests on leaving, and they are thanked for their attendance. To indicate that the "pollution" is over, the barber sprinkles milk in the house.

We may here observe that the barber attends in various ways. At feasts, for instance, it is his office to remove the plantain leaves which have served the guests as plates. Should he publicly refuse to take away the leaf, it is considered a most bitter and degrading insult.

The graves of virgins dying young are used as places for worship, some tree, such as *pálá* (Alstonia scholaris) being planted over the grave, and a lamp kept burning. Pregnant women dying are supposed to become demons, and are, therefore taken for burial to some distant and lonely jungle, and mantrams repeated over the grave to prevent their spirits from returning to injure people. Those who die of fever are supposed to become Maruthás, and are buried inside the house, mantrams being said over them also, to hinder their attacking the survivors. This miserable superstition is common amongst all classes, and the grief of a bereaved husband is often sorely aggravated by the thought that the future destiny of the beloved wife is that of an evil spirit, and that he should have to hear continually stories of her making frightful appearances and possessing others.

The nepotistic law of inheritance is, to a considerable extent, followed by this caste. Those in the far south being more closely connected with the Tamil people, their children inherit.

Amongst the Ilavars in Trevandrum district, a curious attempt is made to unite both systems of inheritance, half the property acquired by a man after his marriage and during the lifetime of his wife going to the issue of such marriage, and half to the man's nepotistic heirs. In a case decided by the Sadr Court, in 1872, the daughter of an Ilavan claimed her share in the moveable and immovable property of her deceased father, and to have a sale made by him while alive declared null and void to the extent of her share. As there was another similar heir, the Court awarded the claimant a half share, and to this extent the sale was invalidated. Their rules are thus stated by G. Kerala Varmman Tirumulpád :—

"If one marries and 'gives cloth' to an Ilavatti (fem.), and has issue, of the property acquired by him and her from the time of the union, one-tenth is deducted for the husband's labour or individual profit; of the remainder, half goes to the woman and her children, and half to the husband and his heirs (*anandaravans*).

"The property which an Ilavan had inherited or earned before his marriage devolves solely to his anandaravans, not to his children.

"If an Ilavatti has continued to live with her husband, and she has no issue, or her children die before obtaining any share of the property, when the husband dies possessing property earned by both, his heirs and she must mutually agree, or the caste-men decide what is fair for her support; and the husband's heir takes the remainder."

Demon worship, especially that of Bhadrakáli, a female demon described as a mixture of mischief and cruelty, is the customary cultus of this caste, with sacrifices and offerings and devil-dancing like the Shánárs. Shástávu, and Veerabhadran are also venerated, and the ghosts of ancestors. Groves of trees stand near the temples, and serpent images are common, these creatures being accounted favourites of Káli. They carry their superstitions and fear of the demons into every department and incident of life. In some temples and ceremonies, as at Paroor, Sárkarei, &c., they closely associate with the Sudras.

The Ilavar temples are generally low, thatched buildings, with front porch, a good deal of wooden railing and carving about them, an enclosure wall and a grove or a few trees, such as Ficus religiosa, Plumieria, and Bassia.

At the Ilavar temple near Chákki, in the outskirts of Trevandrum, represented in the illustration, the goddess Bhadrakáli is represented as a female seated on an image, having two wings, gilt and covered with serpents. Twice a year fowls and sheep are sacrificed by an Ilavan priest, and offerings of grain, fruit, and flowers are presented. The side-piercing ceremony is also performed here.

ILAVARS' TEMPLE AT CHAKKI.

A temple at Mangalattukónam, about ten miles south of Trevandrum, at which I witnessed the celebration of the annual festival on the day following Meena Bharani, in March or April, may be taken as a fair example of the whole. In connection with this temple may be seen a peculiar wooden pillar and small shrine at the top, somewhat like a pigeon-house. This is called a *tani maram*, and is a kind of altar, or residence, for the demon Mádan, resembling the temporary shrines on sticks or platforms erected by the Pulayars. On it are carvings of many-headed serpents, &c., and a projecting lamp for oil.

For the festival, the ground around the temple was cleared of weeds, the outhouses and sheds decorated with flowers, and on the *tani maram* were placed two bunches of plantains—at its foot a number of devil-dancing sticks. Close by were five or six framework shrines, constructed of soft palm leaves and pith of plantain tree, and ornamented with flowers. These were supposed to be the residence of some minor powers, and in them were placed, towards night, offerings of flowers, rice, plantains, cocoanuts, and blood.

The Ilavars who assemble for the festival wear the marks of Siva, a dot and horizontal lines on the forehead, and three horizontal lines of yellow turmeric on the chest. They begin to gather at the temple from noon, and return home at night. Over five hundred persons attend on this occasion—formerly many more came. The festival lasts for five days. Some of the neighbouring Sudras and Shánárs also attend, and some

Pulayars, who pay one chuckram for two shots of firework guns in fulfilment of their vows. Offerings here are generally made in return for relief from sickness or trouble of some kind. The *pújári*, or priest, is an Ilavan, who receives donations of money, rice, &c.

A kind of mild hook-swinging ceremony is practised. On the occasion referred to, four boys, about fifteen or sixteen years of age, were brought. They must partly fast for five days previously on plain rice and vegetable curry, and are induced to consent to the operation, partly by superstitious fear, and partly

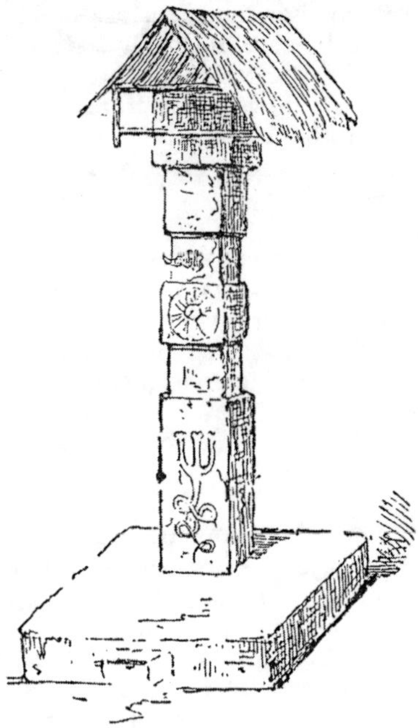

DEMON SHRINE, OR TANI MARAM, AT MANGALATTUKONAM.

by bribes. On the one hand they are threatened with worse danger if they do not fulfil the vows made by their parents to the *dévi;* on the other hand, if obedient, they receive presents of fine clothes and money.

Dressed in handsome cloths and turbans, and adorned with golden bracelets and armlets, and garlands of flowers, the poor boys are brought to present a little of their blood to the sanguinary goddess. Three times they march round the temple; then an iron is run through the muscles of each side, and small rattans inserted through the wounds. Four men seize the ends of the canes, and all go round again in procession, with music and singing and clapping of hands, five or seven times, according to their endurance, till quite exhausted.

The pújári now dresses in a red cloth, with tinsel border, like a Brahman, takes the dancing-club in hand, and dances before the demon. Cocks are sacrificed, water being first poured upon the head; when the bird shakes itself, the head is cut off and the blood poured round the temple. Rice is boiled in one of the sheds in a new pot, and taken home with the fowls by the people for a feast in the house.

At Mayanádu, the Bhagavathi of the small temple belonging to the Ilavars, is regarded as the sister of the one worshipped in the larger temple used by the Sudras, and served by a Brahman priest; and the cars of the latter are brought annually to the Ilavars' temple, and around it three times before returning to their own temple. At the Ilavars' temple the same night, the women boil rice in new earthen pots, and the men offer sheep and fowls in sacrifice.

In further illustration of the strange superstitious practices of this tribe, two more incidents may be mentioned.

An Ilavatti, whose child was unwell, went to consult an astrologer, who informed her that the disease was caused by the spirit of the child's deceased grandmother. For its removal he would perform various incantations, for which he required the following, viz.:—Water from seven wells, dung from five cow-sheds, a larva of the myrmeleon, a crab, a frog, a green snake, a virál fish, parched rice, *ada* cake, cocoanut, chilli, and green palm leaves.

An Ilavan, who had for some time been under Christian instruction, was led away by a brother, who informed him that if he built a small temple for the worship of Nína Mádan and offered sacrifices, he should find a large copper vessel full of gold coins hid underground and under the charge of this demon. The foolish man did so, and dug to the depth of eighteen feet, but did not find a single cash. Now the lying brother avers that the demon will not be satisfied unless a human sacrifice is offered, which, of course, is impossible.

Ilavar converts form a proportion of the congregations under the care of the London Missionary Society. Through the labours of the Church Missionary Society, also, in the north, some thousands of the CHOGANS have been converted to Christianity; this work commencing about thirty years ago. Various little difficulties arose from the peculiar laws of marriage (or rather concubinage) and inheritance observed by the Chógans. Some of the daughters of the converts were claimed and taken away by their uncles as the legal guardians: heathen nephews also made complaints that their Christian uncles had gone mad! Generally the difficulty was met by the Christians at once dividing their property equally between children and nephews.

The heathen relatives also attempted to remove the children, or prohibit their baptism, on the ground that, according to Travancore law, a father has no right to his own children among Hindus below Brahmans. The right of Christian converts to

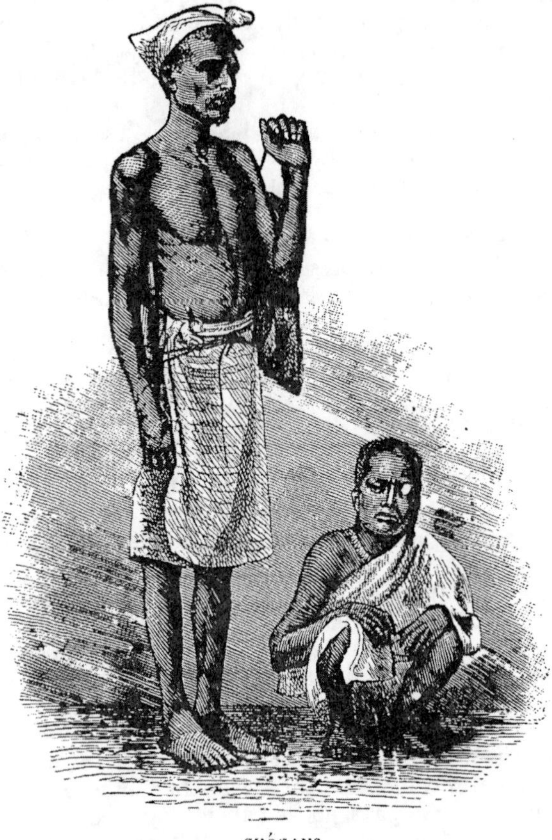

CHÓGANS.

walk on the high road and enter public markets and streets was also discussed, the Brahmans and Náyars objecting to this, but the point was at last carried, as mentioned in our chapter on Caste.

Yet such is the corrupting influence of caste prejudice, that it was equally necessary to warn a few of these Christian converts against attempting to carry out the same unjust and cruel prejudices against Pulayar Christians. In 1877, some of the latter wished to attend the church at Arpukara near Cottayam, but the Chógan Christians appealed against this to the Bishop of Madras on the ground that they would lose some employment and advantages in their work for Náyars if they were obliged to mingle with Pulayars every Sunday, and threatening to secede if they were obliged to do so. An admirable reply was given by the Bishop, explaining the spiritual principles of the gospel, the duty of brotherly kindness to the long-despised Pulayars, and the impossibility of Christianity adapting itself to heathenism; at the same time, enjoining the Pulayars to attend divine worship clean in person and dress, in order that no reasonable cause of offence should be given. The Chógans were displeased, and held worship separately for a time; but being judiciously advised, they returned by degrees, and all goes on well now.

Chógans sometimes have a few stones around a tree in the front of the house to represent the spirits of their ancestors, and perform certain ceremonies in their honour every year.

VÁLANS are the most degraded branch of this tribe in Travancore, whose social condition demands special consideration and improvement. They are found at Shertala, Vaikkam, Paravúr, and other places on the banks of the great back-waters in the north. They are sometimes called "fishing Arayans," though not very appropriately, seeing that they have no connection with the Hill Arayans, their headman only being called *arayan*, or chieftain. Through ages of oppression by the native rulers these unfortunate people are virtually in a state of slavery, out of which it is impossible for them to redeem themselves, being unalterably bound by the system of government impressment for forced labour to their present residences, employments, and status. They are commonly regarded as lower than Ilavars and Chógans, but their manners and customs and laws of inheritance show them to be of the same origin.

The Válans have no fields or lands of their own, but like Pulayars and Kuravars build their wretched huts on the lands of the Náyars or Chógans, so that they may be dispossessed at any moment. Their food is scanty, and never includes eggs, milk, or rice cakes. Their dress is unclean and poor, the children going quite naked, and often suffering from indigestion, worms, and other diseases; while the parents are so ignorant that they do not even know the use of such a simple remedy as castor oil. They fear also to go to the Sirkar hospitals, which, indeed, are scarcely for the low castes. Very few have learnt to read, and those only in Christian schools.

Through extreme poverty their women do not, like Ilavar females, wear ornaments of gold. Their usual dress is the waist cloth and a small cloth on the shoulders, not covering the breast.

When the Válans converse with high caste people, they must use the old terms of humiliation and self-depreciation. Too many of them waste their earnings on drink. They "give cloth" for concubinage, and, therefore, change their partners often, like other such castes.

The men fish only in the backwaters, not in the sea, using large nets which catch the fish at the ebb and flow of the tide as it affects the lagoons, and raising the nets nightly to gather the fish. The most they get at a haul is eight or ten chuckrams' worth. The nets are made of cotton thread, and repaired by themselves, one being the work of two or three months, and lasting for three years. Their tradition to account for this employment is that while Paraméswara and Párvathi were crossing a brook, a ring which the former wore fell into the water. From the thigh of his wife the god created a man, who went into the water and brought up the ring. This man and his descendants thus became a race who make their living by labouring in the water. Sometimes they do a little cultivation, and the women eke out a livelihood by spinning coir yarn, buying the green husks from the farmers.

They have a few small temples of Bhagavathi, in which Válans officiate. They dread demons, some of whom, as "Water Giant" and "Up to the Skies," seize people maliciously. Some are driven by their oppression into the Roman Catholic or Syrian communities.

Those who live at Tannírmugham Customs Station have to be ready at a moment's call to examine boats passing, in order to detect opium or other smuggling. If the peons are sleeping, or at their food, boatmen must just wait. The Válans are also employed for rowing the boats of government officials, for which they receive the usual hire—six cash per man per mile.

Their headman is called Arayan, and has a sword of honour presented by the Rajah. He lives at Chembil. When the Maharajah travels by water, it is the business of the Arayan to collect his people in snake boats for the procession in front of and behind the royal cabin boat. On such occasions the rowers are provided with food from the Ootooperahs, but of course cannot enter; they eat at a distance. The headman has an allowance from the Sirkar. While rowing, the Válans sing portions of the Rámáyana in Malayálam, keeping time very well. They are great at boat-racing.

One class amongst these people are called MARAKKÁNS: their

employment is similar; but Válans do not take food from a Marakkán's house, and the two never intermarry.

Large numbers of these Válans are impressed by the Sirkar for the purpose of guarding the custom houses, salt warehouses, and excise stations; and rowing the canoes of the superintendents, inspectors, and peons whenever they go out on duty by water. Though the number daily required may be but one or two hundreds, yet the pressure affects the whole class, as each man has to serve a certain number of days by rotation, and each village is indented on for its quota. The apology usually made for this is that these people enjoy free the right of fishing in the backwaters. But this indulgence is free in every part of the country, and the poor Válans have been so long and so effectually crushed down and hindered from agricultural pursuits, that they are now entirely dependent on their fishing and daily labour.

This system of forced labour is as oppressive as it is injurious to the industry of the poorer classes, and is of little real benefit to the State. The work indispensably required should be done by regular paid rowers and watchmen, and by the government servants to whom it legitimately belongs; and the Sirkars have now abundant means at their disposal for this reform. It only needs more consideration for the sufferings of the poor, and an awakening to a sense of the great injustice perpetrated on this class. We trust that this much-needed reform will be carried out during the reign of the present Maharajah: it is rather surprising that it has not been effected long ago.

CHAPTER IX.

SHÁNÁRS.

THE Shánárs of South Travancore are identical with those of Tinnevelly, who have been so well described by Dr. Caldwell in his monograph published in 1850. Their domestic usages, however, have not hitherto, we believe, been detailed.

The cultivation of the palmyra palm-tree is practised by this interesting race, from which many converts have been made to Christianity. The palmyra yields a sweet sap, from which sugar is obtained; as it is from the sap of many other palms, the sugar-cane, beetroot, and the maple-tree. The sap flows from the unexpanded flowering stem, which comes out at the very top of the tall, mastlike, branchless palm; and to collect the sap the tree must be climbed at least twice daily. With marvellous agility the climber ascends, just like a monkey, clasping the tree with hands and feet, assisted only by a loop of fibre, seen in the illustration, laid on the man's head, as his hands are fully occupied. This loop is placed around the feet to hold them together, and enable the toes to grasp the stem more firmly. The crutch-like staff being laid against the tree, the first step upwards is taken upon it. The hands being required for climbing, the vessels are tied to the waist-cloth. The uppermost vessel is a basket made of the spathe of the palm, and this holds the smaller apparatus—a brush, a little lime to prevent the over-rapid fermentation of the juice, and so forth. Besides the staff, the climber holds a pair of wooden pincers for crushing the flower stem slightly, and a knife to trim it daily, in order to make the sap flow freely. The next is a basket or bucket of palm leaf, plaited double, to hold the juice and carry it down to the bottom of the tree; and the lowest is an earthen pot, holding about a quart, which is suspended to the bleeding flower-stem to catch the sap. The climber's wife boils the sweet juice into sugar, which she takes to the market for sale.

The work of palmyra-climbing is very laborious, and demands great strength of muscle, incessant practice, and caution to avoid dangerous falls. The more prosperous owners of palm groves rent out the trees, or hire climbers to do the work for them. A hundred palmyras are said to suffice for the support of two families by their produce of sap, sugar, coarse fruits, leaves, fibre, and timber.

Birth.—On such occasions they put margosa leaves (Azadirachta Indica) in the eaves of the house, and keep a lamp lit in the room all night. This is done for sixteen days.

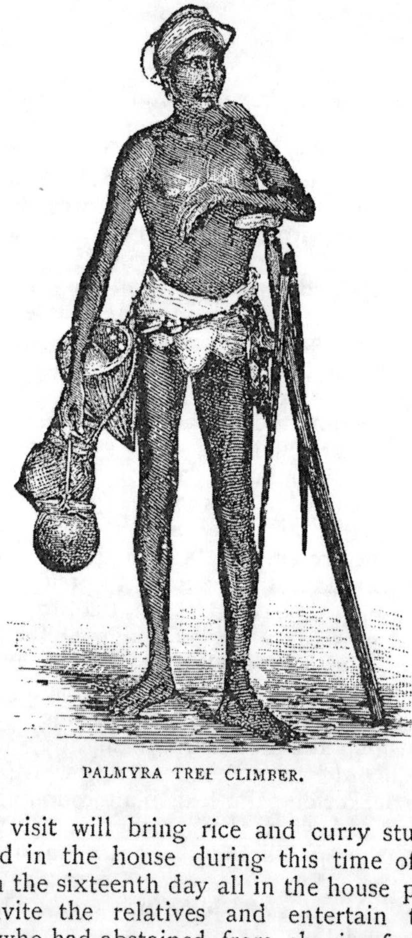

PALMYRA TREE CLIMBER.

Relatives who visit will bring rice and curry stuffs, but not partake of food in the house during this time of ceremonial pollution. On the sixteenth day all in the house put on clean cloths, and invite the relatives and entertain them. The husband also, who had abstained from shaving from the time he first knew of his wife's pregnancy, has the whole body shaven from head to foot, and bathes.

When the child's head is first shaved, the barber pours some milk into a brass plate and shows it to the relatives sitting near the child—then they put some chuckrams in the plate as a present to the barber; the parents also give him either some money or a palmyra tree, the produce of which he enjoys so long as the tree stands.

The ears of children of both sexes are pierced, but those of boys are not enlarged. The ears of female children are bored at the age of about six months, and the hole barbarously enlarged—first by means of twisted cotton or elastic rolls of palm leaf, then by leaden rings, added one after another till the opening in the lobe of the ear is extended sufficiently to contain a large cylinder of wood or of gold. Girls in running, are sometimes obliged to hold up the ears with their hands, lest the lobe should break with the weight of the leaden rings; and a cruel husband in anger, or a robber grasping at the golden jewels, is sometimes known to tear the ear-lobe, which has then to be repaired by the native physician, tying it up again until fully re-united and healed. The umbilical cord, being dried in the roof and preserved, and the first hair shaven off the head, are enclosed in a small silver tube and tied round the neck with other ornaments, to ward off the attacks of demons.

When the whole of the hair of the head has grown to such a length as to be tied in a knot, a feast is given to the boy's maternal uncle, who brings a head-cloth, ties four chuckrams in a corner of it, and binds it on the head of the boy.

Betrothal.—After the relatives of a youth have understood that the guardians of a girl will consent to give her in marriage, the former go and confirm the agreement by partaking of food in the house of the latter, and fix the date for bringing the *parisa* money or donation by the bridegroom to the bride, before proceeding to the house for marriage, along with fruits, fish, and other things. After this is done the bride's people return the visit. An auspicious day for the marriage being fixed, rice-cakes are made, and a little paddy boiled and beaten, and reserved without a single grain being taken from it, until the marriage day.

Erecting Pandal.—On the day of the wedding a green palmyra-tree is cut, and nine posts are set up in the courtyard of the house. The first post is called "south-west post;" a measure full of paddy, four chuckrams, betel, and areca-nut being laid down, the post is set up with drumming, whooping, and rejoicing. Then the other posts are fixed and the roof erected. The measure of paddy and other things along with a pot of boiled rice, will go to the headman of the village. Food is supplied to the guests. The bridegroom fasts on the day previous to the marriage, but on this day he is shaven from head to foot, and is supplied with food made from the rice auspiciously prepared some time before.

The barber marks the bridegroom's forehead, puts on him the marriage cloth and gold ornament, and brings him into the pandal, where his maternal uncle will be fed with milk and fruits. The uncle then sitting on a low seat near the banyan-wood post and next to the "Brahma," or middle post, a basket of rice, a cloth, cocoanut, plantain, and betel leaf will be laid before him. The bridegroom, too, brings the bride's *táli* and cloth and jewels in a wedding basket of special form called *péré petti*, which the uncle returns into his hands, blessing him, and tying four chuckrams in a corner of his head-cloth. The bridegroom hands the basket, which contains a smaller one for the *táli*, to his sister, who carries it along.

SHÁNÁR'S WEDDING BASKET.

This marriage basket is of considerable significance in the ceremony, and is used by all the *makkalvari* or true marriage castes, Brahmans, Shánárs, Vellálars, Chetties, Barbers, Pariahs, &c., with some diversities in the form of the basket and the details of its use. Pariahs were permitted only to have a single coverless basket in which the wedding cloth would be seen; now being free, they naturally imitate other people.

The Brahman basket has several divisions for rice, betel, saffron, two of their gods, *Sivalingam* and *Táli kirámam* (an egg-like idol), in two of the little divisions, with the cloth in the centre and the táli in another small basket.

Shánárs and similar castes used the kind of basket plaited of palmyra-leaf represented in the engraving. The chief wedding cloth costs from Rs. 10 to Rs. 30 or more; some use cheaper coloured cloths, or common calico, according to their means. In all marriage baskets there is a smaller one, which contains the táli, along with which they always put three grains of rice and the points of three betel-leaves, without which, they say, the táli would have to fast. There are also placed in the basket some measures of rice, one or more cocoanuts, seven areca nuts, seven betel leaves, &c., which are to be given to the relatives of the bride. Some castes also keep in it a small vessel of oil.

The marriage basket must be carried only by a sister of the bridegroom—if not his own sister she must at least be a cousin. She carries the wedding-cloth in the basket for clothing the bride, as will be described presently.

Among the fisher caste the custom differs very much. The marriage basket and cloth and táli are provided by the bride or her family, because in that caste husbands are bought by females for so many fanams, and should live in the wife's village or house. The baskets, &c., are, therefore, sent on the wedding day from the bride's house to the sister of her bridegroom.

Amongst Sudras, being nepotists,* the custom is quite different; they have no marriage basket. Their girls go through a make-believe marriage ceremony in their childhood. On the marriage day, when the nominal husband leaves his house, his sister puts the cloth in a large brass plate *kankálam*, commonly used by wealthy natives for eating food. She holds the plate in her left hand and a lighted lamp in her right. That cloth is called *mantra kodi*—"charm cloth." (Holding a light near the marriage basket is customary amongst all castes except Pariahs and Pulayars. The higher classes, and rich heathen Shánárs, carry it all the way.) The Náyar táli is made in the bride's house at the expense of her family, costing from three fanams to any sum they may wish to expend. But whatever they may spend on this, the bridegroom pays only one fanam for it; as soon as this is paid, the goldsmith puts the táli in a small wooden or horn box, and it is given to the sister of the bridegroom.

In the Shánár marriage procession, the bridegroom, if possible, rides on horseback, or is carried in a palankeen, holding a cocoanut and a sword in his hands. Before starting for

* See Chapter XVII.

the bride's house he bows to his parents. All along the way cocoanuts are broken, tom-toms beaten, playing, fencing, and fireworks go on. When nearing the bride's house, they are met from thence with drums, and the bride's brothers place a garland of flowers on the neck of the bridegroom. They rub sandal-powder on his forehead, seat him in the place prepared, and offer a slight refreshment of jaggery and water, betel-leaf and areca nut, to his company. After a few minutes' rest, his sister, accompanied by some women, enters the bride's room with the basket and the little vessel of oil. There the bride will be holding two rolls of betel-leaf in her hand, which are taken by her bridegroom's sister. Then oil is poured on the bride's head three times (if heathens, prepared saffron is added). After that the bridegroom's sister invests her with the marriage cloth and jewels brought in the basket. Her parents also receive money for the fees of washerman, barber, drummer, and other assistants, seven fanams for the village goddess, and five fanams for the village people. The bridegroom's sister receives, besides the betel-leaf and nut, some money for her aid to the bride.

After the bridegroom has come into the marriage shed, the girl's female relatives cover the mouth of a large new pot with their hands; and the bride's mother brings twenty-one measures of paddy and puts into the pot.

Tying the Táli.—The marriage badge is a gold bead on a string: the bridegroom holds it on the bride's neck, and his sister ties it securely. Both persons standing on the marriage board, or plank, the bride's father causes the man to hold the woman's right hand. Then a rice-mortar, in which some cotton-seeds and oil are put and set on fire, is carried by the bridegroom's brother thrice around the Brahma post, the bride and bridegroom following. This completes the marriage.

Both persons are then seated on the board, and a little oil, with a few chuckrams in it, is given into the hand of the husband; this he touches thrice with his fingers, and sprinkles on his wife's head—she does the same to him. After this, both are clothed with a long cloth, supplied by the washerman, and bathe. Then both are fed from the auspicious rice; the remainder, together with a large quantity of boiled rice and cakes, is used by the relatives. A little lime and turmeric are mixed, waved thrice round the heads of husband and wife, and thrown away. The bride, paying due obeisance, transfers all the things she brought from her father's house to the hand of her mother-in-law, who puts a bracelet on, and bids her bow to the salt-vessels, &c. They all eat together, and return to the bride's house, where also they are entertained.

The following curious estimate of the expenditure in both houses in a Christian marriage of this caste on a respectable scale, is furnished by a native friend intimately and practically acquainted with these matters. It is calculated in *fanams* = value the seventh of a rupee.

	Fs.
Tobacco brought by the agents of the bridegroom on going to ask the consent of the bride's parents	1
Feast on receiving these men	6
Tobacco given by the bridegroom's party to the bride's on settling the *achi panam*, "mother's money"	3
Feast on this occasion, at the bride's house	5
Tobacco brought by the bridegroom's party to the bride's house when paying the *achi panam*	15
Paid on same day by bridegroom's family as a sign that both are now connected	41
For the bride's jewels, from both parties	464
Feast at bride's house on same day	70
Pillapani, jewels given to the bride by her relatives	121
Feast at the bride's house when writing application for marriage licence	5
Tobacco brought by the bridegroom's party	2
Erecting marriage pandals, both parties	95
Betel, &c., distributed to guests as invitation	80
Feast at the bride's house to those who bring the provisions from the bridegroom's house	18
Marriage feast, both parties:— rice, fs. 425; cocoanuts, fs. 45; plantains, fs. 115; salt, tamarinds, and curry stuffs, fs. 35; vegetables, fs. 32	652
Oil	30
Páyasam, or pudding of rice, milk, jaggery, cinnamon, ginger, and cumin seed	54
Pappadam cakes to eat with curry	14
Alms for Pandárams, Kuravars, &c.	15
Hire of horse, carriage, &c.	14
Hire of gold chains, silver waistbelt, turbans, bracelets, for dressing bridegroom and bride's brother	15
Cloths for the bride and bridegroom's uncles	70
Cloths and jewels brought by the man for his bride	140
Drumming, shooting guns, singing, &c.	146
Given to the bridegroom by the bride's father when giving her hand to him	7
Váthilida (door) money to the bride's mother-in-law	41
Presents of rings, ear-rings, money, &c., by their relatives to the young couple when bidding farewell	210

	Fs.
Cow, brass vessels, &c., dowry given to the bride by her father	160
Given to the bridegroom and his brothers in visiting the bride's house	40
Feast to them, the same day	35
Marriage fees, &c.	19
Washerman and barber	6
	Fs. 2,594
	= Rs. 370½

Pongalpánei.—New pot to boil rice for the Pongal feast. From the day of marriage the woman's parents supply cloth, washerman's hire, and other expenses to their daughter. Early in January they give notice of this feast to their daughter, and, accompanied by other relatives, visit her, taking with them some money, rice—raw and boiled—tobacco, betel, &c., with pots from three to eleven in number.

At other festivals they invite their daughter and son-in-law to a feast. She is presented also with a spinning-wheel. From her marriage till the first child is born, all her expenditure is supplied from her father's house, where, also, her first confinement should take place. The parents come in good time to take her home. All these expenses are considered as part of the dowry.

Burial.—When one dies, the body is covered with cloth, and the barber is sent to call the relatives and others, who come and make a great cry; then proceed to prepare the bier and fetch water. They go with beating of tom-toms to the river or tank, walking upon cloth spread by the washerman all the way, the relatives holding a long cloth carried above their heads, with a pitcher for the ceremony on the head of the son of the deceased. This is filled with water, adorned with garlands of flowers, and placed near the dead body, which is then shaved, rubbed with oil, and bathed with the water brought by the villagers, clothed with a new cloth, and incense burned before it. A small hole is made in the side of the vessel which the son carried; and the water which gushes out is received in a brass cup containing some cotton-seeds, cocoanut blossoms, turmeric, &c.; the cup is then carried round the corpse. Then the nieces and near relatives weep and beat on their chests, and the women put rice and chuckrams into the mouth. While carrying the coffin to the grave, the mourners again walk on cloth spread along. The coffin is carried thrice round the grave, and the son breaks the pitcher of water at the foot of the body. The males then put rice and money into the mouth, and bury the body in a sitting posture. The barber, washerman, drummer, and other attendants are then paid, the mourners return to the house, where they are sprinkled with salt water, and spend the night in fasting, except that they may take some peas, cocoanut, or betel.

The next day all the rooms cf the dwelling are purified with cow-dung, and the people mourn and burn incense. Mourning is continued till the sixteenth day. On the grave, palm-blossoms, tobacco, rice, and fruits are offered by a barber and a pandáram. A small bier is prepared in which some of these articles are put ; it is carried to the sea-shore, cut to pieces, and thrown into the sea. A burning wick, with a little flour on a plate, is also sent afloat on the waves. Boiled rice is also placed near the grave, the conch-shell blown, and a cactus, or banyan, or palmyra palm planted for a memorial.

The **Devil worship**, zealously practised by these people, is minutely described in "Land of Charity," pp. 189-226. The

BELL MUSIC USED IN DEMON WORSHIP.

accompanying illustration represents the bell music used by them. A bow, seven or eight feet long, is fitted with a cord of strong leather, on which are strung a number of bells. The singers sit down on the floor with the bow before them, and strike on the cord with short sticks made for the purpose ; four or five do this in turn. This is a regular study ; when lads have finished a course of training, they are considered worthy to sing in the pagodas, and other places, where they get a handsome fee.

CHAPTER X.

POTTERS.

THE Kusavars, or potters, are found, as might be expected, scattered generally throughout the country, evidently attracted to each locality by the nature of the soil and the extent of the demand for earthen vessels. They eschew, however, the sandy district of Sherttala and the wild mountainous regions of Meenachel and Todupuley.

There is a very large and steady demand amongst the poorer classes for earthenware, as it is constantly used for household purposes, and readily breaks, the quality being inferior. If supposed to be ceremonially defiled, earthen vessels are broken; and for religious rites, in which the boiling of rice is almost always included, new pots must be used. The potters manufacture small drinking cups and larger cooking vessels, small oil lamps, and other household utensils, large round water-pots, and great jars for storing rice, tiles for roofing houses, and clay idols and images of various kinds. In the South they are specially busy in making pots for the climbers during the palmyra season.

There are in Travancore two classes of potters—Tamil and Malayálam. The Tamil potters are called **Pándi Vélans.** They wear the sacred cord, and their women the *táli* and conch on their necks. The marriage ceremony lasts for seven days; re-marriage of widows is strictly prohibited; so also is polygamy.

The larger body are called **Malayám Vélans.** Their usages resemble those of the Nairs. The women wear thick cotton cords round the neck, and other ornaments as Sudra women do. "Giving cloth" is customary, both partners separating when they please, and forming other unions. A man's property, however, goes to his own children among both divisions of potters.

The Kusavars work diligently, men, women, and children from four or five years of age assisting. Fair earnings are made, but the potters do not seem to be provident. The men dig the clay; then all unite to carry it to the place where the wheel is fixed, where it is softened and tempered and put on the wheel by men. The wheel is horizontal, and is generally spun round

Potters at Work.

by a woman, the man dexterously moulding and shaping it with his hands, the simple impetus serving for the formation of the vessel.

A batch of pots is put in the kiln once in a couple of months or so. Fuel being laid in the bottom, the pots are arranged over it, and the kiln is covered with earth to exclude the air and to keep in the vapour. While the pottery is in the furnace, worship is paid to a demon called Chúla Mádan, who they fear, if not propitiated, will break it. On the third day the ware is taken out; and *if* but a minimum of loss has been sustained in the firing, these worldly-wise artificers present thank-offerings to the demon, such as a coin, rice, cakes, fowls, or a goat. They also make offerings of boiled rice to the sun.

The women and girls carry large loads of pottery on their heads, secured with ropes, to the markets for sale.

These people are held in some repute as sorcerers. One saw an aged potter making incantations before a crowd of others on behalf of a sick Ṣhánár child. The man had raw rice laid on a plantain leaf, some betel-nut and tobacco, and a medicinal root to be tied round the child's waist with a thread. He was complaining, however, that the offerings were inadequate.

Some potters enjoy free grants of lands from the Government for supplying the pagodas with idol gods and images of horses. They sometimes boast of their dignity as manufacturers of the gods that other men worship.

Annually new clay images are conveyed in procession to pagodas, with great reverence and display, from the potter's house: "This, said one of them, is done for the honour of the god, instead of sacrificing a child."

CHAPTER XI.

PANDÁRAMS.

THESE are a Tamil Sudra caste, never engaging in manual labour, but usually subsisting upon alms as religious mendicants. They wander about singing songs and begging, sometimes officiating as priests. They are Púrva Saivas, and worship

PANDARAM DEVOTEE.

Supramanian as their patron deity, also Ganesha and the Siva-lingam. Some of them are intelligent and clever.

Their marriage ceremonies and rules resemble those of the Tamilians. Th^a body is buried in a sitting posture, and facing the north.

CHAPTER XII.

MALAYÁLAM SUDRAS.

"THIS is the most numerous class of the Hindu community. There are numerous sub-divisions among them, and sometimes the distinctions are so nice and capricious that the men and women of one house will not eat meals prepared by the members of another, nor sit for eating together in the same row, though they do not object to eat in the presence of those others, or sit with them in different rows. The members of this community are sometimes called Nairs (Náyars), which is a title of distinction, and cannot be indiscriminately applied to all the classes among them. The principal sub-divisions included under this head are thirty-four." (Census Report.)

The Sudras are generally a cleanly and respectable people, residing in their own houses, on the banks of the rice fields which they own, and cultivate by the aid of the low caste labourers. Many are employed in the service of government, and some of the poorest of them are day labourers; but scarcely any are engaged in trade or shopkeeping. They are a home-keeping people: rarely do native-born Malayális visit other countries.

Their strange laws of marriage and inheritance being fully discussed in the chapter on Nepotism, a few notes on domestic manners will here suffice.

Malayalam Sudras are careful to pay much respect to aged relatives. Nephews will not sit down in the presence of their uncles, but stand with the left arm crossed on the breast and the right hand over the mouth; or, at least, sit on a lower seat or level. Sudras meeting Brahmans adore them, folding both hands together; the Brahman, in return confers his blessing by holding the left hand to the chest and closing the fingers.

Friends are invited to a feast, not by sending betel-leaf, as the low castes do, but by going in person. Guests are first served with water to wash the hands and face; then different kinds of curries, rice, fruits, sweetmeats, and salt are served on plantain leaves. The leaves used for plates by officials and influential men are removed by maid-servants: other persons carry out their own. Usually the first polite inquiry concerning health is—"How is it that you are so much reduced?"

Men are not accustomed to cover the body above the waist; so also females when in the house, but when going out they cover the bosom with a piece of light white cloth, which is sometimes a costly article, having a border of gold thread. They wear many ornaments, and the hair done up in a kind of chignon on the *left* side of the head.* Women are fond of swinging while they sing songs; dancing and plays are much liked.

SUDRA LADY.

On a journey, wealthy people are attended by men-servants carrying a brass betel-box, drinking vessel, fan, and provisions. Before partaking of a meal, they always bathe and put sacred ashes on the forehead: some also repeat the praises of Rama. They eat from brass or earthen vessels, sitting on the ground: after eating, the place is swept and purified with cow-dung. At some special feasts women are first served, then the men, the food being distributed by men. Some wealthy Sudras employ Brahmans to cook for them at feasts, according to the Brahman mode: food cooked by them may be eaten by all classes. Sudras do not eat beef, but mutton, poultry, &c.

* It is rather amusing to find that a humorous suggestion made in the "Land of Charity," in allusion to the various absurd fashions of chignons in England some ten years ago, has been taken by a native writer as a serious recommendation of the adoption of the Malayáli custom by more civilized nations.

Their barber women, having some experience, officiate as midwives. If a male child is born, they utter the *kurava* cry; if a female, they beat on the ground three times. The name is given on the twenty-seventh day, with offerings to Ganésha. The mother sits down with the child, and whispers the name chosen by the father in its ear; then the midwife takes the child, and calls the name aloud before all assembled. At six months old the "first rice" is given with due ceremonial; also, on a girl's attaining maturity a festival is held for four days. The *táli* marriage and the "giving of cloth" are described in the chapter on Nepotism.

In the seventh month of pregnancy the *pulikudi*, "tamarind drinking," ceremony is held. The woman is sent to her parents' house, and on an appointed day the husband takes, according to his means, rice, cocoanuts, plantains, and seven pots full of sweetmeats to her house for offerings, called *pongála*. On that day rice is offered in seven pots. Afterwards the woman goes to the house of one of her cousins, and brings a plant of the tamarind tree, and some plants of *Sida retusa* and *Achyranthes aspera* in a pot to the front yard of the house where she is to be delivered. She stands on a piece of plank facing the Sun; and a Márán takes the juice of some leaves of the *pinaru* (a gamboge tree, *Garcinia Roxburghii*) and of the Sida, which he gives into the hand of one of the woman's cousins. The woman takes this acid juice in her mouth, and spits seven times. Some of the offerings are given to the Márán.

Sudras have no priests but Brahmans. Some, however, begin to entertain and to show great aversion to Brahmans on account of their profession of superiority, and probably really superior force of intellect. This dislike seems rather on the increase, amounting at times to bitterness and jealousy.

Some classes of Sudras, who may eat together, do not intermarry.

"The Nair's house almost invariably faces the east, which long-established custom and superstitious belief enjoin. Every house has in addition to the *púmukham*, or building over the gateway used for more public purposes, a *tekkathu*, "southern shed," which is generally dedicated to the presiding deity of the house, and is kept neat and clean, and without any furniture or household utensils, except a brass lamp which is lighted up every evening. The place is looked upon with reverence by the inmates of the house, who do not enter it except after purifying themselves by a bath, which is generally done by dipping into cold water. The Brahman visitor of the family retires to the *tekkathu* for purposes of meals and drink. The spacious open yard enclosed by this cluster of buildings, so useful for drying paddy, grain, peas, and other annual stores, is kept scrupulously neat, the floor having been first hardened and made smooth by a solution of cow-dung and charcoal, which is often repeated during the hot weather. The master of the house, most probably an old Proverty accountant or a pensioned Tahsildar, not noted for over-scrupulousness while in office, but now in affluent circumstances and respectable old age, sits in the *púmukham*, or porch-house, chewing away the tender betel and the narcotic tobacco, or beguiling the hours of the afternoon with anecdotes of his early prowess, achievements, and successes; while the religious books of his family, the time-honoured Rámáyana and Mahábhárata, alternately engage and exact his time and attention."*

* Census Report, p. 123.

CHAPTER XIII.

THE ROYAL FAMILY.

THE royal family of Travancore are certainly an ancient dynasty, exercising sway for some centuries, originally over a very confined territory, which was occasionally increased by conquest or otherwise, so as at one time to include the southern portion of Tinnevelly, and within the last century and a half to comprise the whole of the present principality. Around such a race of rulers cluster many traditions, histories, and loyal sentiments, the particulars of which can with difficulty be gathered by Europeans, because the law of caste pollution makes Hindu domestic life inaccessible to strangers. Curious customs, religious and social, have also arisen from precedents once formed in the course of time and of events. It is scarcely correct to speak of them as a single family, as it is evident from historical records that the reigning family has often died out from lack of direct heirs, which it has been remarked is singularly often the case in Hindu families of the higher classes; and has been recruited by adoptions—usually from the allied line of Mávelikara, but formerly, it is said, even from so great a distance as Kólattiri, near Cannanore.

There are several families of petty Rajahs in Travancore allied to the Maharajahs, the principal of whom is the Mávelikara family, from whom adoption of princesses is usually made, and with whom therefore close relations of friendship subsist. The present Ránees were selected from this family in 1858. It is said that the Mávelikara line was itself perpetuated in ancient times from Travancore, mutual adoptions thus producing intimate union between the two houses.

Besides the various noble families known as Rajahs, another class are found called "COIL TAMBURÁNS," or "Lords of the Temple." These are usually regarded as Kshatriyas; and from their ranks are chosen the consorts of the princesses of the realm. Several families of this class reside in the northern part of the State. The men "give cloth" to Sudra females, while the women are united to Nambúri Brahmans.

The accompanying illustration is a portrait of a gentleman of this caste.

National Ensign.—As various nations have adopted particular plants or animals as their emblems, such as the rose for England, and the dragon for China, so Travancore has adopted the conch shell, and for coat-of-arms, within the last few years, two elephants rampant and a Sanskrit motto, meaning "Charity is our household divinity." The conch shell is also one of the emblems of Vishnu, and is used in temples for blowing as a horn.

Birth and Education.—In prospect of the birth of a prince, the mother is put apart in a separate building, where she is attended by female servants and midwives. The English

COIL TAMBURAN.

physician is also kept in attendance, to be ready in case of need. On the sixteenth day the lady bathes, and returns to her residence.

In the sixth month rice is given to the infant for the first time, on which occasion all the relatives attend.

The education of the young princes in vernacular languages, and for a long time past in English also, has always been carefully attended to; and several princes have developed a considerable taste for literature, of which the present Maharajah is a distinguished example.

Investiture of Sacred Thread.—This is done early in the sixteenth year of the young prince, when he comes of age. The ceremony is called *Upanayana*—investiture with the sacred cord, or *Tirumadampu*—a royal pupil having completed his studies.

Europeans sometimes speak of it as a "marriage," from a mistranslation of the word *Kalyána*, which literally means "joy," and is applied to various occasions of special rejoicing. It is one of the twelve purificatory rites, which are supposed to purify a man from the taint of sin derived from his parents, and which are enjoined, with certain variations, on all the twice-born classes. The cord, however, is worn not only by those classes, but also by all the Kammálars or artificer castes, and even by Pariahs on particular occasions.

This ceremony is usually performed about the time of the Pongal, as an auspicious period for this or for marriage. The ceremonies are announced by a salute of 21 guns; and last for nearly a week, during which the young prince is not at liberty to go about freely, but is under strict religious rules as to food and observances. The ceremony, being rather of a domestic character, is performed in one of the palaces inside the fort. Multitudes of Brahmans and visitors assemble, clad in holiday attire, and the fort is full of noise and excitement. The Alvancheri high-priest presides, and the Brahmans are liberally fed, as upon all great occasions, and charities distributed to them at the Palace. The native troops of the Nair Brigade, with the band, attend every morning to do the honours. Salutes of cannon and fireworks are fired repeatedly. Music and plays fill up the day, and feasting and dances the night. On the fifth day the Mahârajah circumambulates the Fort in full procession, visiting the Temple and the palace of the youth's mother.

At the close of the ceremonies the Rajah usually entertains his European friends to dinner in a magnificent temporary shed erected for the occasion, and sumptuously fitted with furniture, lamps, pictures, and cloth and tinsel decorations in Indian style. The young Prince, in whose honour all is performed, cannot even attend the dinner, on account of ceremonial pollution, but he and the ladies of the family sit in a side room which looks into the dining-hall to enjoy the festive scene. The whole is closed with fireworks, burning of blue lights, and other illuminations.

From this time the young prince has a separate staff and residence and monthly allowance, and is very much at liberty to select his own friends, and to live as may please himself. The ceremonies cost about Rs. 18,000.

After the investiture with the cord, the young prince is required to pay a visit to Attingal, in order to offer homage at the domestic shrine there.

Marriage.—The Maharajah, as head of the family, decides whom the young princes or princesses should marry. The union is that common to the Nairs, not like that of Brahmans, except that an *Ammachi*, or wife of a Rajah, if put away or widowed, is not allowed to marry any other man. The connection may, according to theory, be dissolved by either party; but an ammachi would not be likely to do so; and now public opinion is so valued that the union is usually steadfast.

Little is heard of this ceremony amongst outsiders, because it is really not an important one like a Hindu marriage. "The ammachi is not a member of the royal household, and is in nowise associated with the royal court. She has neither official nor social position at Court, and cannot even be seen in public with the ruler whose wife she is. Her issue occupy the same position as herself, and the law of Malabar excludes them from all claims to public recognition."

Náyars usually go to the lady chosen, give the cloth, and take her home, or reside with her at her brother's house. In the case of the royal family, a number of splendid cloths are sent, and she is brought to the palace of her consort. But, unlike other Sudra unions, the Ammachi, having once been married to a Rajah, is required to remain single all the remainder of her days; and is shut up and guarded in her own residence. Hence it is not all parents that are willing to give their daughters on these terms. The bereaved lady is comfortably provided for by endowment during the life of the husband, and pension after his decease. Precisely similar is the custom in China, where, on the death of an emperor, his women are removed to a portion of the palace, in which they are shut up for the remainder of their lives.

The *Tangachis*, or daughters of the Rajah, who, like sons, have no titles of rank, are first married in childhood by a Tirmulpád; when one attains to maturity "cloth is given" by some one who takes her to wife.

The nieces, who, like nephews, have the titles of Highness and Ránee (fem. of Rajah) are married when young to Coil Tamburáns, who afterwards live with them so long as both parties are mutually content. It is not necessary that the same person who nominally married the lady in childhood should actually consort with her in maturity. The princess can choose for herself, and if one consort dies, another is called in.

Pulikudi, or "Tamarind drinking" ceremony. When a Hindu wife has reached the seventh month of her first pregnancy, this festival is celebrated on her behalf. A bower, formed of the leaves and flowers of the cocoanut tree, is constructed in the courtyard of her dwelling, when all her female relatives and friends assemble by invitation of the husband, who sends them betel leaf and other things. First, a rice offering, called *pongal*, is made on a plantain leaf. Along with the rice there may be some figs, sugar, and butter. This offering is made to ensure the protection of the young mother from all dangers during this period. Next, a cocoanut is broken and presented as an offering to Ganésha. Sitting in the centre of her bower, a garland of flowers is hung round the neck of the woman ; and a dish of water, in which saffron and lime are dissolved, is placed before her. To frighten away the evil demons, to whose malice females in these circumstances are supposed to be peculiarly exposed ; all the women present take up the dish and wave it backwards and forwards three times before the woman's face. A wooden vessel is then brought containing some milk, with gold and silver coins, which she holds in her hand. Taking a piece of gold or silver, the women place it between her shoulders, invoking the aid of the goddess Lakshmi for a safe delivery in due course. Having put some cloth on a tamarind tree, they walk round it ; and, on returning to the house, the woman is to taste or drink some juice pressed out of tamarind leaves.

Order of Succession.—The nearest heir to the throne is usually the Rajah's next younger brother, or the eldest son of his sister. Should the nephew be older than the brother, the senior is the heir. The heir apparent is called Eliya, or "junior" Rajah ; and the next heirs First, Second, Third Princes, and so on. When one dies, the next takes the vacant title, so that the Third Prince will become Second, then First, then Eliya Rajah. These changes of title are rather puzzling to outsiders, as young princes grow older, and older ones are removed by the hand of death. Native designations, however, are permanent, being taken from the star under which each prince was born. As the succession is continued through *sisters'* sons, it is not, as amongst Brahmanical Hindus, males who are adopted in case of need, but females, as sisters to existing heirs, and their sons will succeed. Should there be no sons, or only infants, the mother rules during the minority.

The sons of the Rajah, who are called *Tambi*—younger brother—reside with him in his palace during their youth, and are provided for while the father is alive, as are their mothers also, by gifts of estates, houses, or money, which they thenceforth enjoy as private property.

Accession to the Musnud, or Throne.—During the eleven days of mourning for the deceased Rajah, the new king lives a life of seclusion, attends to the funeral ceremonies and mourning, and receives expressions of sympathy in his bereavement, and of submission to himself as the incoming ruler. On the second day after the obsequies, all the officers of state visit his palace, in mourning attire, to condole with the young Rajah. And on the sixth day, the native officers of the brigade visit the new ruler, when each offers a present of a piece of silk cloth. The new king is not, however, proclaimed for thirteen days; but, by order of the British Resident, the usual guard of honour sent to the Maharajah attends upon the Prince in the meantime. Until formally installed, he is addressed by his previous title.

A new governor-general having arrived in India in the interregnum between the death of the late, and the accession of the present Maharajah, the usual official intimation had to be addressed to the Ranee. The letter was in English, accompanied by a translation in Persian, beautifully written on paper powdered with silver, and enclosed in a rich satin bag, covered with white net.

The days of mourning for the deceased ruler being ended, purification is made on the twelfth day; and on the thirteenth day the new Rajah visits the pagoda of Patmanábhan for the native ceremonial answering to a coronation. The whole kingdom having been bestowed by Rajah Martándah Vurmah on this deity, in 1750, in perpetual endowment, the crown can only be received from him through the Brahmans. The ceremony is called *padiyéttam*, "receiving of subsistence allowance," and is the clearest possible acknowledgment of entire subservience to the god and his only representatives, the priests. The Ránees being regarded as the custodians of the keys of the temple while the god is absent from it at the Aráttu procession, receive for this service a small allowance of rice; the new Rajah likewise attends the temple for his instructions, and allowances of food and clothing, and for investment with office, and with the first of his official titles, *Sree Patmanábha Dausa*, "the servant, or slave, of the holy Patmanábhan."

The royal house of Orissa in like manner, "has for centuries performed menial offices before the image of Jagannath; and, as the sweeper caste is the lowest in the Hindu commonwealth, so the kings of Orissa have reached the climax of religious humility in their most cherished title of 'Hereditary Sweeper of Jagannath.'"—(Hunter's "Orissa," p. 115.)

Ascending the temple steps with due acts of homage to the presiding deity, the Maharajah receives from him an allowance of rice and cloth, in token of administering the kingdom as his tenant and vicegerent. The head-accountant of the temple reads from the ritual the rules originally prescribed for observance on the accession of a new sovereign. Offerings are then presented, and various acts of adoration performed, such as *pradakshina*, circumambulating the pagoda, and *sáshtángam*, prostration of the whole body. The Maharajah is anointed (*abhishégam*) with consecrated water, and the whole is concluded by the high priest handing to His Highness the sword of state and the belt (which are supposed to belong to Patmanábhan, and have been kept in the temple from the demise of the late king), the *prasádam* (sandal-wood powder given from the temple as a mark of the god's favour), the ration of a cocoanut, and 1½ *edungalys*, of rice, which the Rajah has boiled, and eats. The eight Yógakár (Brahmans who are the members of the ruling council of the temple) give the *neet*, or "grant" of the regal office. On receiving the sword, the Maharajah says, "I will keep this sword until the uncle who has gone to Mecca returns." Finally, marching round the pagoda, he returns to take possession of the palace and to sign his first order. This, in the case of the present sovereign, was a grant of an additional five thousand rupees per annum for the repairs of temples, which caused a profound sensation throughout the country in favour of idolatry. So, also, on the arrival of the new Dewán, his first official act was to sign an order for the punctual feeding of the Brahmans.

On the day of the native installation, special *pújas* and offerings for the Rajah's health and prosperity are made at the temple in the fort, and at all other pagodas throughout the kingdom. European officials and friends now congratulate him on his accession.

As soon as convenient, a Durbar, or "levee" is held for the public recognition and installation by the British Government. Till this comes off, there is a sort of interregnum, the reign of each Rajah being officially dated from this day. The old Audience Hall in the fort is still preferred, on account of its historical associations, to the Durbar Hall in the new public buildings. The British sepoys from Quilon, with their English officers, are invited to be present, and all Europeans resident in the country; while multitudes of the native population flock into the capital for a holiday, to witness the pageant and join in the general rejoicings. The houses are gaily decorated with floral arches and fruiting stems of the plantain; and festoons of foliage, bright-coloured flowers, and palm-leaf ornaments are strung across the roads from tree to tree.

The Durbar Hall is a long, narrow, upper room, handsomely furnished with carpets, sofas, large mirrors and lamps, paintings of former Rajahs and distinguished British officers, and other furniture in Western style. Outside, in the great square, the troops are drawn up under arms in imposing array; the state elephants, richly caparisoned, and with bells about their necks, bear costly howdahs, though rarely, or never used for riding purposes; and crowds of the people assemble in honour of the occasion.

The royal party, officers, and retinue being in readiness a little beforehand, the British Resident is received on his arrival, with the usual salute from the artillery and troops, takes the Maharajah's arm, and is placed on a seat immediately on his right. The Commanding Officer of the Nair Brigade, who also bears Her Majesty's commission, sits on the other side; and the Princes and English officials or guests, with their respective wives, take their seats on either side of the room, the whole forming a brilliant and impressive scene.

The ivory throne at the head of the hall is adorned with cushions, shield, and weapons, and a glittering canopy supported on pillars of silver. Beside it stand the Prime Minister and favoured officers in appropriate costume.

The Maharajah is now placed upon the throne by the Resident and the Commanding Officer, when the Resident also presents the insignia of sovereignty—what may be called the Crown—a plumed and jewelled turban worn by each ruler in succession, with drooping feathers of birds of Paradise, aigrette of diamonds and emeralds, and two large pendent pearls. The new Rajah, in turn, resigning the turban that appertains to the heir apparent, hands it over to the next heir, who thus becomes Eliya Rajah. It cannot but be deeply touching to those who may have known and entertained personal affection for the ruler so recently departed, to witness his crown thus solemnly handed over to his successor. A Proclamation by the Governor of Madras is then read, proclaiming the new king, and "requiring and directing all the subjects of the Travancore Sirkar to acknowledge and obey His Highness as their Maharajah and sovereign."

The reading of this proclamation is followed by a royal salute and a *feu de joie*. A translation of the same in Malayálam, accompanied by a proclamation from the new ruler, is read to the people outside, the Rajah, Resident, and assembled company standing in the long verandah in front of the Hall; another salute being fired, a number of unfortunate criminal convicts, corresponding to the years of the Maharajah's age, and previously selected as the fittest objects of his clemency, are liberated down below from their chains to commemorate the auspicious day. Throughout the ceremonial, the company politely rise and stand whenever His Highness does so, or sit when he does. After further congratulations, a speech by the Rajah expressing his sentiments on the occasion, and the principles on which he intends to govern, is read. On the installation of the present Maharajah, this was a most remarkable document, such, it was observed, as few of the native Princes of India could prepare or deliver. Another royal salute, and the assemblage is dismissed with distribution of garlands and bouquets of jasmine flowers, and the fragrant leaves of the Artemisia; rose water is sprinkled, and each visitor shakes hands with the Maharajah on retiring.

After this Durbar, attended by Europeans and the representatives of the British Government, is over, the Rajah resumes his seat on the *musnud;* and another levee is held for the reception of the native officers of position in the service of the State, who have all been ordered in from their posts throughout the country in order to pay homage by offering the usual tribute of money, each according to his rank and grade. The amount formerly presented was one-tenth of a month's salary —now a much smaller sum.

About 3 o'clock P.M. the Rajah goes in public procession for *pattana pradésam,* "entering the city," in his state palankeen, every one but himself marching on foot; even a little son will walk holding on by a corner of the royal palankeen for assistance. They go round the principal streets of the Fort, escorted by the Bodyguard and Brigade, and attended by the Dewán and native officials, and a vast concourse of the people. All being obliged to walk, and no umbrellas allowed by etiquette to the highest or the feeblest, this is a very exhausting ceremony in the hot sun. A royal salute and three volleys of musketry are fired on His Highness appearing after his return on the upper terrace of the palace. Provisions are afterwards distributed to the Brahmans under the superintendence of the sepoys out of uniform.

In the evening a State dinner is given at the Residency; and next day, the Maharajah honours the British Resident with a visit, coming in full procession of cavalry and led horses, Brigade brass bands and native musicians with strange flutes and other instruments, the State elephants and carriages, attendants strewing green leaves on the ground, the sword and emblems of State, and two curious gold stands for a kind of incense sticks always borne burning before the Rajah in State procession.

Visits to Attingal.—This is a village and palace situated on the bank of the river about five miles inland from Anjengo, the revenues of which, with the surrounding district, comprising four Athigárams, form the private patrimony of the Ranees. This district is called Sree Bhágam, or "the sacred portion," and is administered by the princesses through their káriakár or manager. They reside here at least once a year, for a time, for change of air, river bathing, and boating, and worship at their tutelar shrine. It is said that Attingal was selected as a residence for the Travancore Ranees in M.E. 480 (A.D. 1305), when pagodas were erected to their guardian goddess, Bhagavathi or Durga. In the earliest periods of the English factory at Anjengo, contracts for pepper were all made with the Ranee of

Attingal. Cantervisscher says, "Attingal is the name of the maternal house of the Rajah of Travancore who rules over the country lying between Tengapatnam and Paroor, three leagues south of Quilon." And from the account which he gives of the massacre of a hundred and forty English there, in 1721, in revenge for cruelties which had been practised on a Brahman priest, it would seem as if the Queen of Attingal then possessed a sovereign power distinct from that of the Rajah of Travancore. According to tradition, this power was surrendered by the reigning princess in 1740, when the arm of a strong man was felt necessary to reduce the petty chiefs to one master.

Attingal is still visited by the Maharajah as an ancient and honoured residence of the family. He goes about the same time in January of each year, to begin the reaping of the rice harvest, and to make offerings of the firstfruits; and is accompanied by the Dewán and a military escort. Some notes of the royal visit in 1881, will best supply definite information regarding the observances.

The Maharajah arrived at the landing place in the afternoon of 20th January, and proceeded to the palace in procession, in the royal palankeen, accompanied by his officers, sepoys, and band. After walking to bathe in the river, and going out in a boat a short distance, he went in procession to the Pagoda, where the festival is celebrated, at the time prescribed by the astrologer as auspicious.

Previous to the arrival of the Rajah, the Pótti Brahmans themselves conduct preliminary rites as follows:—The golden image of Bhagavathi is decorated with silk cloth, bright flowers, sandal paste, &c., and having been placed on the back of an elephant and held by a priest, it is conducted four times round the pagoda. There are never less than four elephants at the procession; on this occasion there were eight, on the tallest of which the idol is carried. During the procession a splendid silk umbrella is held over the head of the image by a Brahman. The cortége is accompanied by drumming and music, fireworks, cheering of women and shouting; and the goddess is again placed in the temple. After this, two or three people of a caste called *ponnara panikkar* draw a sketch of Ganesha on the ground in front of the temple, with powders of various colours, such as rice, charcoal, red ochre, dried leaves of the acacia, turmeric and lime. The priest then offers to this figure plantain fruits, parched rice, cakes, sugar, ghee, and cocoanut water. These offerings are afterwards given to those who have drawn the picture; and they obliterate it again with further accompaniment of music. The place is then swept, and sprinkled with cow-dung by Sudra women; and the priest places there an altar adorned with silk cloth. He then takes the sword which is placed before the goddess in the temple, brings it with music to the altar, on which he fixes it upright. Then he offers worship to the sword, presenting flowers, sacred water, and sandalwood.

All this being in readiness some days previously, the Rajah comes in procession, wearing no covering on the head or chest, but only the cloth round the waist, and carrying a sword in his hand. With great pomp and solemn reverence, he approaches the sword upon the altar, and stands before it. The priest now brings a measure of raw rice in a vessel, which he lays in front of the sword. The Maharajah lifts this with his own hand, and gives it back to the priest. The latter then scoops up some of the rice in a hollow conch shell, pours a little three times on the top of the sword, and thrice on the head of the image in the temple: the remainder of the rice in the conch shell he puts on the head of the Rajah. This is called *abhishégam*—anointing or consecration. It is also called, "Putting rice on the threshing-floor." It may be compared with the old western custom of throwing rice onthe bride and bridegroom; and with the Malabar rite in the coronation of Rajahs—a Brahman taking some rice in his hand from a silver dish, and dropping it slowly on the crown of the Rajah three times while proclaiming his titles.

During this performance the firing of guns and crackers, drumming and music, the *kurava* cheer and shouting are continued. His Highness still standing before the sword, the priest enters the temple, brings the garlands of flowers and the sandalwood from the goddess, and presents these in a golden vessel to the king. He receives the gifts, which are called *Bhagavathi prasádam*, with much humility, and is at liberty to return to the palace.

This festival is celebrated annually from 1st to 10th Magaram (say 13th to 22nd January), but the Rajah attends only on the ninth day after the sword has been placed and worshipped. It appears to correspond to some extent with the ordinary Pongal or "boiled rice feast," seeking prosperity throughout the year.

Birthday Rejoicings.—The Maharajah's birthday, according to native calculations, is celebrated on dates varying considerably in each year, whether in accordance with the astrologer's determination of lucky days, or at the period when the natal star attains its position.

On the first birthday after his accession a ceremony, called *Tirumudi kalasam* or purification, is performed in the great pagoda by pouring holy water on the Maharajah's head, a royal salute being at the same time fired. A series of religious ceremonies having been solemnized within the palace, he sets out in grand procession, adorned with his finest jewelry of diamonds and emeralds, to go through the main streets of the fort in the state palankeen, headed by the cavalry, the band playing a lively march, and the infantry under its English officers following in two columns. In front of the palankeen walk the Dewán, the judges, and peishcars, and the palace and other officials. Slowly moving round the fort, His Highness visits all the principal pagodas inside and outside the fort. At each he alights to drop in his offerings at their shrines. The procession is over by ten o'clock; and then commence the festivities, closing with *sarváni* or peace offerings to the Brahmans, who have also been feasted for days before, and small donations to some other castes. The more intelligent Sudras are beginning to exclaim against this incessant feeding and feeing of idle and profitless Brahmans from public funds to which the Sudra taxpayers so largely contribute, to meet which feeling the present Maharajah thoughtfully included the Nair officials, subordinates, and pupils in his hospitality—a sensible arrangement unheard of before. Dinners are also given at the Residency, and an entertainment by the Dewán to the native officials at his residence in the fort.

On this day the Maharajah breakfasts with all the family—a privilege accorded once a year to each prince on his birthday.

Another procession to the temple at Shástamangalam, in the suburbs of Trevandrum, is undertaken, usually about a week after this, with full procession of horses, elephants, peons, ensigns and banners, officials and soldiery, the Rajah riding in his great Car of State, ornamented with flowers, and drawn by six horses. (See engraving.) The English officers accompany the procession part of the way: it then proceeds to the temple, where offerings are made, and coins are thrown to the assembled multitude.

Daily Life.—The Maharajah is an early riser, and goes first to bathe, visits the temple for private devotions, then takes a drive to his country house, where visitors are commonly received between seven and eight o'clock. Returning to the palace, he bathes again, and partakes of breakfast in Hindu fashion at nine or ten o'clock.

Animal food is not used, and Brahmanical customs in several respects have been adopted. Though not absolutely bound, they are as particular in diet as Brahmans; as also are various high Sudra families. Rice and a great variety of curries, bread and cakes, tea and coffee, sweetmeats and fruit, are the ordinary diet. Pure water is brought every morning, under a guard,

MAHARAJAH'S STATE CARRIAGE.

from the river at Karamana. When invited to dinner with Europeans, no food can be eaten with them, but His Highness sits at table, and engages in polite conversation with his nearest neighbours.

The day is occupied with public business, receiving officials and hearing their reports, consulting on affairs of State, signing orders, &c. On particular days audience is given to the Dewán, the judges, and heads of departments, who present their respective reports. After seeing the Rajah on Monday, the Dewán visits the Resident on Tuesday to convey or receive any communication. Other officials are received as may be convenient; and presents of gold bangles, valuable rings, and other tokens of favour are sometimes given to deserving officers.

In the afternoon or evening, the late Maharajah was accustomed to hear the Sastries read the Hindu religious works for an hour, and to converse with them. Another drive is taken in the cool of the evening. Petitioners often place themselves at prominent points of the road, hoping to remind their royal master of their applications or needs.

At 8 or 9 o'clock, supper is taken; and on special occasions nautches or plays fill up some more time. Rajah Bhagyodya Martándah Vurmah was remarkable for his attention to religious duties. "Every day," says Mr. P. S. Menon, "the Maharajah spent no less than three hours in the morning and evening in prayers and devotions, which often interfered with His Highness taking his meals at the proper time. There was scarcely a day on which the Maharajah took his breakfast before 1 P.M., and supped earlier than twelve in the night; and on certain particular days of fasting, or on the occasion of any other ceremonies, he would not swallow even a drop of water during the day, and would take his meals only at night after all the ceremonies were over." These lengthened hours of attendance at devotions, and also at theatrical representations, of which he was very fond, with the consequent irregularity of retiring to sleep, probably affected the Rajah's health, and tended to shorten his life.

While at home and at ease, and on the most solemn religious occasions, all dress in the simplest possible fashion—a mere cotton cloth wound around the waist and a cap or turban on the head. They pleasantly call this undress their "uniform," apparently on the principle that they are "when unadorned, adorned the most." Fine robes and valuable jewelry are reserved for great occasions and for appearance in portraiture.

Dogs are not kept, nor the chase engaged in, though there appears to be a relic of former hunting expeditions in the *palli vettu* ceremony.

The amusements of the Court are pretty fully detailed in Mr. Shungoony Menon's "History." English books and illustrated papers are procured and read. Occasional tours are made through various parts of the land, for change of air, restoration to health, or pilgrimage to temples. In long journeys to Madras or Benares, the ladies may accompany their husbands or uncles, and a great retinue of hundreds of persons, including the family gods, and the priests, who need some precautions to avoid pollution. Once a golden casket containing the tutelary idols was missing for some time, and only recovered by the police after much expense and anxiety.

The members of the royal family pay their devoirs to the head of it from time to time. The strictest attention is always required to etiquette and respectful bearing, a humble salutation being given on entering the presence, and no inferior presuming to sit before the sovereign till invited to do so by word or sign.

Pleasant intercourse is maintained with Europeans of position by attending their garden parties, or meeting them at the military band in the public gardens. The Maharajah pays visits only to the Resident or distinguished visitors to the capital; but the princes visit more freely; and all receive visits of courtesy, appointments for which must always be made beforehand. They correspond in English in the usual style of polite society. English officials and friends write notes of congratulation and good wishes to the Rajah on his birthday, and he addresses such notes to them on our New Year's day.

The Ranees lead a secluded life in the bosom of their own families, rarely appearing in public. They did so, however, in Travancore, in June, 1881, on the investiture of the Senior Ranee with the Imperial Order of the Crown of India, and at Madras in February, 1883, on the investiture of the Maharajah with the Order of the Star of India. They are often visited by English ladies, and sometimes even gentlemen. They are not allowed to leave the kingdom without special permission, but travel in company with their consorts to various palaces and visit noted temples such as Vaikkam, Tiruvattár, &c. Both royal ladies are educated in English as well as the vernaculars; and are accomplished in music, needle-work, &c.

Court Etiquette may be described as simply the ordinary regulations of caste, carried out in all their details and to the fullest extent. Shoes are laid off by natives before entering the presence; the chest must be uncovered; and the head covered with a cloth or turban. Umbrellas must be lowered before royalty. Native officials and subjects meeting the royal carriage must stop and get out and stand, make a low obei-

RANEE AND CHILDREN
(*From an old Painting.*)

sance raising both hands and performing the curious twiddlings, or closing and extending of the fingers, which is the Malabar salutation to Rajahs. On obtaining an audience, presents of fruits, cloth, or money are offered by subjects. In the presence, all stand with the left hand on the breast and the right hand covering the mouth lest the breath should pollute the king or other superior. So also at Parisnath Jain temple, a low-caste man carries in the incense and musical instruments with a broad bandage tied over his nose and mouth, in order that his breath might not pollute the idols. And in China it was formerly customary for the officers of the Court to hold cloves in the mouth before addressing the sovereign, in order that their breath might have an agreeable odour.

A special language of a highly artificial and conventional character is used of the royal person, property, and actions, ordinary terms being forbidden. The palace occupied by the prince is called *bhajanapura*—"worship building;" the royal food, "nectar;" a birth, an "incarnation;" and a birthday, a "holy day;" a death, "leaving the country," or, "going to the heaven of Vishnu, *Vaikuntha;*" travelling, *erunnellu* or procession; and the word *palli*, church, or *tiru*, sacred, is applied to almost everything connected with the king.

The Maharajah cannot in the vernacular be spoken of as "he," but at least "the Maharajah themselves;" and is personally addressed as *ponnu tamburán*, literally "golden god," but perhaps implying not much more at present than "precious lord"—*Tiru manassu*—the "sacred mind," is also incessantly used. None dare say *nyán*, "I," but "*adiyén*," "your slave" or servant.

Proper names are never uttered, but the various members of the royal family are spoken of in the third person by the star under which they respectively were born—as the *Viságha* or the *Múlam* Prince; or by descriptive epithets, as the Senior or Junior Rajah, the Great, or Little, Coil Tamburan; and so forth.

On the decease of a Maharajah, the *literati* compose poems and elegies in language of the highest Sanskrit style, quite incomprehensible to ordinary people.

As no subject can be seated in the presence of the Rajah, the coachman has to stand up while driving him out in the carriage. Formerly when a series of lectures was commenced, at which the Prince kindly consented to preside, serious difficulty was at first experienced from the highest officials being compelled to stand with others during the whole time, but afterwards His Highness kindly gave a special permission to sit; to avoid entire reversal of recognized etiquette he himself, when delivering addresses, now sits to allow the hearers to do the same.

Tulábháram and Hiranya Garbham Ceremonies.—The extraordinary ceremonies called *Tulábhάram,* "Scale Weighing," and *Hiranya Garbham* "Golden Womb," each performed once in the life-time of each Rajah, have been fully described in "Land of Charity," pp. 169–175; and further reference to them will be found in the review of the "History of Travancore" in the present volume, Chapter XXXV.

For the "Scale Weighing," the Maharajah is seated on one scale of an ornamental balance, with his sword and shield; and in the other scale his weight is heaped in gold coins having the name of the god inscribed thereon, which are afterwards distributed to the Brahmans in various proportions according to their dignity and claims. The weight of gold for this costs about £12,000 and additional expenditure, say, £4,000 besides. One king performed this ceremony a second time in silver at the end of his reign.

The "Hiranya Garbham" ceremony is performed in a large golden vessel or tub with a cover of gold, an engraving of which with the accompanying priests, officials and guards in procession, forms the frontispiece of this book. Inside the vessel is placed a mixture of "the five products of the cow." After many preparatory rites the Maharajah enters the golden tub, the cover is put on, he bathes and offers prayers inside for ten minutes while the assembled priests continue praying and chanting hymns. After coming out, he is again crowned by the chief priest and is supposed to be advanced in caste purity, and religious privilege, as well as full authorization to reign over his people.

This golden vessel is also cut up and distributed amongst the Brahmans. The ceremony costs the State about £14,000.

Bhadradípam Ceremony.—One of the principal religious ceremonies in which the Rajah himself takes a principal part, is the *Bhadradípam,* or "Lamp of Good Fortune." After the wars for the subjection of the petty Rajahs and neighbouring principalities, in which much blood was shed, and that often without just cause, Rajah Bála Martándah Vurmah appears to have been somewhat pricked in conscience (as our own fierce but superstitious barons were in similar circumstances in the dark ages), and he set about inquiring what could be done to expiate these sins, secure general prosperity, the destruction of his remaining enemies, and the conciliation of the conquered peoples. Consulting learned Brahmans from various parts of the country, they recommended the Bhadradípam and Murajapam ceremonies. Bartolomeo falls into error in referring the "Golden Cow ceremony" to this origin, instead of the Bhadradípam.

This festival is a kind of sun worship, like the Pongal of the

Tamils, which occurs at the same time, and in which offerings of boiled rice are made to the sun. It is performed at the two *ayanas*, or solstices of the year, calculated by the Hindus as occurring about 12th January and 14th July. It was first celebrated in M.E. 919 (A.D. 1744), and the first Murajapam six years afterwards.

The Bhadradípam chiefly consists in the priests transferring, by means of mantrams or invocations, the spirit of the Sun to sacred lamps. The five lamps are lighted on 1st Magaram (13th January). After seven days of prayers and offerings are made, Brahmans are feasted, and special donations made to them. This is repeated on 1st Karkadagam (15th July). The Trevandrum *Sívéli*, or circumambulation of the temple with the images, is made on the previous evening. At these times the Rajah is secluded and fasting, and unable to receive European visitors. Presents of money are still made by the Sirkar to leading Brahmans at Kidangúr, as a peace-offering to compensate for the crime of killing Brahmans in the last century.

Every twelfth Bhadradípam is preceded by the Murajapam, which thus occurs once in six years. The last took place in November and December, 1881. It is a special and extraordinary observance of the Bhadradípam, and is supposed to compensate for any defect during the preceding six years. The three Vedas (Rig, Yajur, and Sáma) are recited in rotation in the great temple once in eight days. This recitation is thus repeated seven times during the fifty-six days continuance of the festival. About 3,000 Brahmans are feasted all this time at the expense of the Sirkar. The fifty-sixth, or concluding day, is called Lakshadeepam, or "Hundred thousand Lamps," when innumerable lights are lit in the evening. For further notes, see "Land of Charity," p. 167.

The Worship of the Sword.—The great Hindu festival, called Dasara, or "The Ten Days," occurring about the end of September or the beginning of October, is known in Northern India as Durga Pújah, and in Travancore by the terms *Púja Weippu* and *Eduppu*, which means literally "setting worship" and "removing worship." This is rather of the character of a domestic festival, when all families adore the instruments, tools, and implements by which they gain their livelihood—the plough of the farmer, the hammer and chisels of the artisan, the barber his razor, the tailor his needle, the writer his pen, teachers and scholars their books, the soldier his sword, shield, and gun, and so forth. Women heap together their baskets, the pestle and mortar with which they clean the rice, and other household implements, and worship them. The worship of the sword appears to have descended from the ancient Scythians, and is practised especially by the martial tribes of India. Among the Mahrattas the cannon are praised, invoked, and propitiated. These instruments are adored as so many deities, to whom the Hindus present their supplications, and offerings of incense, flowers, fruit, and rice, that they would continue propitious, and still furnish them with the means of living.

A British officer, who seemed not to have fully considered the moral aspect of his action, informed me that he and many others are accustomed to hand over their swords to the sepoys for this festival, with a contribution towards the expenses. Enlightened natives, on the other hand, plead that they only join in this absurd worship through fear of giving offence to their elders.

In this Púja, several deities are worshipped, especially Saraswathi, the wife of Brahma, and goddess of music and letters; and Durga, Párvathi, or Bhagavathi, formerly propitiated with human sacrifices and offerings of blood.

To honour this festival with their presence, two of the ancient deities of the royal family, kept in temples which belong to their ancient territory, are brought to Trevandrum. "They must needs be borne because they cannot go." The Maharajah himself goes to Attingal to present his offerings; but the images of Kumáraswámi of Kumárakoil, near Palpanábhapuram, and of Saraswathi, are brought to the capital in solemn procession, carried on a great litter or wooden frame, by forty or fifty bearers of good caste, bedecked with flowers, and escorted by a company of the Nair Brigade, temple women cheering and shouting, magistrates, and some of the people. The image of Kumáraswámi, or Supramanyan, son of Siva (the same as Shástávu, or Iyenár, and virtually a species of demon worship, as in Tinnevelly—probably the religion of the aboriginal inhabitants, including the Sudras) is in the form of a human figure riding on a horse, all in silver.

But Kumáraswámi, they say, married one wife of the Kuravan, and another of the Pariah caste. He is, therefore, supposed to have lost caste, and is not allowed entrance into the pagoda of Patmanábhan, but made to reside in a temple outside the fort, called Ariya Cháley, and taken for the Púja Eduppu to a Mandapam, or Stone Pillared Hall at Pújapura, in the suburbs of Trevandrum. They also say that his two wives are on bad terms with one another, and ready to proceed to blows. Yet Kuravars, and other low castes, are driven out of the road on the procession day lest they should pollute the god who married into their castes!

The presence of this god for the feast costs the native Government over four hundred rupees annually, besides travelling expenses. The god is supposed to receive this fee on account of his difficult task in crossing three great rivers, at Kulitory, Neyáttankara, and Karamana. After the close of the ceremonies, the images return to the South in state, escorted as before.

On the first of the Ten Days the flag is hoisted in the temple on the golden flagstaff, and dancing and other amusements are kept up during the whole night. On the second day the Púja Weippu is held in the palace itself, in honour of the goddess Saraswathi. During the ten days the Maharajah remains partially secluded, and is obliged to fast for the last two or three days. Splendid feasts are given to the Brahmans during the whole time.

The ninth day is called *Maha navami*, "the great Ninth," being celebrated on the ninth day of the increasing moon, which is also a grand night in Bengal. Then the implements are collected, and placed on altars for adoration. The next day, Púja Eduppu, they are removed, and the celebration ends. On this day the grandest pageant of the year is exhibited—an imposing State procession from the Fort to Pújapura, for a ceremony called *palli véttu*, or *náyáttu*, "royal hunting." In other parts of India it is not unusual for Hindu kings to move a short way out of town or camp on this day, to a sacred tree planted for the occasion, and adored in order to secure a propitious time for undertaking various enterprises, especially hunting and warlike expeditions. The *palli véttu* seems to be a relic of such expeditions formerly conducted in Travancore.

In the afternoon the Rajah sets out, under a royal salute, in procession in his magnificent royal car of state, glittering with gold and perfumed with scents and flowers, drawn by six large white horses, preceded by the State elephants, one bearing the national standard, the Nair Brigade with the band playing lively airs, the bodyguard, and the officers and native musicians of the palace. Behind the car move the carriages of the princes, the Dewán, peishcars, and judges—then the sástries, songsters, and other native officials.

The houses in the streets traversed by the procession are profusely decorated with garlands of flowers, bunches of plantain fruits, flags, and various devices. On some gates are arches with the motto, "Long live His Highness the Maharajah," and the streets were lined with crowds of people—men, women, and children in holiday attire hurry from all quarters to Pújapura. Even the poor Pulayars come out in clean or yellow-stained cloths, but have great difficulty in getting along without touching any others in the crowd, where the roads are narrow and enclosed with walls on either side.

The people seem to meet one another, and chat in an unusually friendly and good-humoured way. Near the open plateau at Pújapura a very lively scene is presented. It is a stirring sight to witness the dense moving mass of soldiers, elephants, carriages, and men coming up; and everywhere as the car passes a low obeisance is made by the people, which is acknowledged by a courteous bow from their Sovereign.

Before the procession arrives, various ceremonies are gone through by the Brahman priest of Kumáraswámi, who accompanied the image from the south. It is placed on its carriage in a small enclosed space added to the Mandapam. A square pedestal of stone also stands in front of the building, on which are planted some green branches of a tree and a plaintain stalk in fruit, garnished with the blossom of the palm, and festoons of flowers. At the foot of these is laid a large soft cocoanut, with one end of the husk sliced off to shoot into; also a brass pot of consecrated water, a bell to call the attention of the god, and a lamp blazing the whole time. The priest puts some sacred grass between his fingers, sprinkles holy water, and puts flowers one by one on the cocoanut, muttering *mantrams*, or prayers. All this is repeated several times.

A little before reaching the Mandapam, the party alight and proceed on foot. The military forming a cordon around them to secure a clear open space, they stand till Kumáraswámi is lifted on the shoulders of his bearers and carried round the stone pedestal several times. This is called *pradakshina*, or circumambulation, and in it the right side is kept towards the person or object to be honoured. The idol is then set down on one side, and the priest takes a large bow in his hand: he first shoots three arrows cautiously into the cocoanut, then the Maharajah comes forward and receives the royal bow, a small and highly decorated one, with light, steel-headed arrows, which he quietly and carefully shoots into the cocoanut, standing quite close to avoid the ill-luck of missing.* The booming of another salute, followed by three volleys of musketry, announces the accomplishment of this exploit.

The god is again carried to the Mandapam, where His Highness and the princes enter, witness the burning of incense and camphor, and present each a number of coins and a few yards of silk to the god. They come out again in a few minutes, and pass to the adjoining palace for a brief interval of rest.

As soon as the Maharajah retires, a scramble ensues for the flowers, fruit, and leaves on the pedestal, which are immediately torn away and carried off. Sir J. Malcolm speaks of a similar

* The accompanying engraving is a copy of an oil painting in the palace, representing this ceremony performed about the end of the last century.

RAJAH AND ATTENDANTS AT HUNTING CEREMONY.

ceremony by the Mahratta Peishwa, who plucks some leaves from a sacred tree, and from a field a stalk of grain. The whole crowd then fire off arms, pluck in like manner, and carry the leaves and grain home with joy.

Songs of praise are chanted, and dancing performed before the idol by the temple women, led by an old Brahman whom they surround in a circle. But neither reverence nor pious awe is exhibited, and the tumult of the crowd is distracting. The dancing is, like most idolatrous worship, a mere play—a subject of laughter amongst the dancing women and attendants—the spectators, at the same time, pushing and fighting to get a good place for seeing, and the Sepoys almost striking with their muskets to maintain some order. When the singing has ceased, these decorations also are torn away by the crowd.

The procession returns after dark to the fort, where it receives a final salute, and the Púja Eduppu closes.

Throughout the country in all public offices and schools this holiday is more or less kept. In schools it is considered essential to prosperity for the coming year; and a teacher who cannot himself attend to it, hands his books to a neighbour, and gets them back next day, paying in return a suitable fee for the accommodation. A portion of the schoolroom is screened off with leaves as a kind of sanctuary, and beautified with flowers, plantain stems, and ornaments plaited of the white soft leaf of the palm. On a chair inside, covered with fine silk cloth, are placed the books to be worshipped. A Brahman is called to perform the service, for which he receives a fee of, at least, three quarters of a rupee.

Sickness, Death, and Funeral Ceremonies.—In case of illness famous native doctors are applied to for treatment, as well as the services of the English Court physician. Difficulties arise from the conflict of Hindu and caste usages with the particular diet or drugs that may be prescribed according to European medical science. Frequently a fair and sufficient trial is not given to European skill and medicines.

Travelling for change of air and scene, and for pleasant bathing, is commonly resorted to with advantage. This is turned into, or combined with, a pilgrimage to shrines and sacred places, to which sometimes an improvement in health is attributed rather than to the fresh air and exercise, and the hopefulness inspired by the effort. One prince expended more than his income on gifts to the deities and temples in seeking to ward off death, and spent all his time in repeating "Rama, Rama," employing a person to count the number of repetitions.

Further superstitious measures are tried. The *prasádam*, or oblations of food consecrated by dedication to the idol, and brought from the temple of Patmanábhan, are expected to exert a healing power. Special praises of the gods, sacrifices to conquer death, vows to noted temples, and other rites are performed by Brahman priests. Many Brahmans are fed with the most delicious articles of food, and endowed with liberal gifts.

Should sickness be prolonged and distressing, and appear to be mortal, it is supposed that the sins of the invalid hinder his peaceful departure. And, in any case, the burden of sin and the need of a sin-bearer cannot but be felt.

The *Alingana Dánam*—"Embrace Gift" is now made, a most touching ceremony, which bears some resemblance to the Jewish institution of the scapegoat. A holy Brahman is found who is willing to undertake this responsibility in consideration of a large sum of money, rupees ten thousand; he is brought in, and after the performance of certain ceremonies by the Brahmans, closely embraces the dying man, and says, O King! I undertake to bear all your sins and diseases. May Your Highness live long and reign happily." Thereby assuming the sins of the sufferer, the man is sent away from the country and never more allowed to return.

Gifts of cows are also made to Brahmans to ensure the support of a cow in crossing the river of death. *Gómúlya Dánam*, or "Gift to purchase cows," is a present of 45 fanams each, given in money, instead of the actual animals, to a thousand Brahmans, this being equal to the gift of a thousand cows. Sudras, when ill, sometimes offer a cow, with silver decorations on the horns, to Brahmans for atonement of sin and recovery of health.

The worship of cows, especially at the time of death, is a favourite one with the Hindus. Baka Bhai, widow of the last Rajah of Nagpore, spent twelve hours daily in the adoration of cows, the Ocimum plant (*tulasi*), the Sun, and her idols. When her end was at hand, five cows were introduced into the room where she lay, in order to be bestowed on Brahmans. The gift of the animal was accompanied by a further donation in money; and as one after another they passed onward from the bedside, they were supposed to help the dying woman forward on her way to heaven. Among the last acts of her life, was to call for a cow, and having fallen at its feet, as far as her now fast waning strength would allow her, she offered it grass to eat, and addressed it by the venerated name of mother.

When death is imminent, *Kála Dánam*, or the "Death Gift," is made. A buffalo is brought; it is covered with valuable cloths, the neck and horns decked with jewels, and a little fire in a pot tied under its belly, but without touching it. A

Brahman is called, who receives four paras of sesamum seed and a few rupees, and is then mounted on the buffalo and sent away.

The dying person is laid on the ground upon soil brought from Attingal, a last farewell taken of the members of the family, and disposition made of personal effects. Words of consolation and kind advices are also addressed, and reconciliations effected. All the rites and donations are completed; the sacred oblations of the household deity brought from the pagoda, and applied to the eyes and forehead; and a Brahman repeats some mantrams in the ears of the expiring Rajah.

The women connected with the palace, assembled in expectation of the solemn event, stand in two lines, ready to commence mourning. Immediately that death occurs, they begin a terrible wail, beating their breasts and unloosing their long hair. The cry is heard outside, and hundreds of women join in concert.

Trumpeters are instantly sent round, whether it be day or night, to call in the whole of the Nair Brigade, and the barrack bell is also rung. At dead of night, as on the last occasion, the melancholy sounds of the death horn are sadly impressive.

The household being polluted by the occurrence of death, none can partake of food till the remains are disposed of. The body is therefore washed, rubbed with sacred ashes, and at once prepared for cremation. The funeral pile is quickly erected in a small yard outside the fort, the fuel of mango, with some cedar and sandalwood, being in readiness beforehand. A shed ornamented with flowers is put up to protect the pile from rain, and sufficiently high to be out of reach of the fire. The body is lavishly decked with bracelets, necklaces, and ear-rings of plain gold (no precious stones being allowed), all of which are burnt along with it, the melted gold becoming the perquisite of the priest and others. The body is also wrapped in a silk cloth and girdle bestowed by Patmanábhaswámi on his servant the king, as he also is accustomed to give the sere cloth for burial to his dependants. This cloth is brought from the temple in procession with music.

Placed in the State palankeen, the mortal remains are closely covered up, the palankeen also being overspread with a rich silken pall, and decked with garlands of jasmine and other flowers. It is taken out of the palace through a breach in the wall, made for the purpose, to avoid pollution of the gate, and afterwards built up again so that the departed spirit may not return through the gate to trouble the survivors. On the starting of the mournful procession, and during its progress, minute guns are fired, one for each year of age of the departed prince.

The funeral procession much resembles that on the occasion of the Aráttu, or bathing of the god, and starts within a few hours after the decease. It is headed by the Maharajah's body guard on foot, bareheaded, and leading their horses, followed by the band, with drums muffled and colours draped in black. The bandmen march bareheaded, playing the Dead March; the Brigade also bareheaded, their muskets reversed and flags furled; the English officers on foot in full uniform with strips of crape. Behind the band walk the great Officers of State, then the Eliya Rajah who is to succeed, next the Princes in order. Behind these comes the palankeen with the royal remains borne by a caste called *Pounders*. It is surrounded by the domestics and favourite followers, and by hundreds of Sudra women, with their hair dishevelled, wearing but a single cloth around the waist, and filling the air with their loud weeping and lamentations. All are in similar undress; even in the heaviest showers not an umbrella is permitted, so that the risk is sometimes great to delicate constitutions from standing two or three hours in rain during the cremation. A vast multitude of men, women, and children, of various castes and creeds, follow the funeral procession to the burning ground, but only the princes and chief officials are allowed to enter it. The ceremonies are performed under the direction of the Brahmans.

Underneath the high outer shed, a small inner canopy immediately over the pile is very handsomely decorated with flowers, plantain trees, young cocoanuts, palmyra nuts, and many other ornaments. The fuel is piled on planks, and a mattrass placed on the top. The remains are laid in the centre—the head southwards, the feet to the north, and completely covered with sandal-wood. As soon as the body reaches the place, it is borne round the pile three times, then placed on the pyre, and three volleys of musketry fired—the last salute to departed royalty. Then the brothers and nephews put a little rice and money in the mouth, and break the pots of water according to custom. Two lights are placed at the head and at the feet, and kept burning for five days and nights.

Before lighting the pile, a *mantram* is repeated, giving the elements of the body to the five elements—the eye to the sun, the breath to the wind, the limbs to the earth, the water, and the plants whence they had been derived. In accordance with the theory that each element must have a portion of the body at dissolution, it usually expires on the earth, is washed with water, burnt with fire, to set free the spiritual element from the superincumbent clay and complete the regenerative process;

and the ashes are, in some cases, scattered in the air, in others buried in the earth, or thrown into the rivers or the sea.

Fire is applied to the pile by several of the nearest relatives, the chief mourners, who hold the torch behind their backs, reverently looking away from the remains. The military and band are now permitted to depart, but the princes and high officials remain for two or three hours till the body is consumed. Fuel is added, and oil and butter poured on, with fragrant substances, till the body is fairly reduced to ashes. Then more oil and ghee are supplied in order to raise the flame so as to ignite the sheds and their decorations. At intervals the mourning women utter a loud wail all in unison.

The bereaved family now return to their palaces, bathe, and continue in deep mourning for eleven days, the pile being left to smoulder under charge of a guard of about fourteen sepoys, till the fire dies out in a day or two.

After the funeral is over, Brahmans flock in and receive gratuities of three or four fanams each.

A notification is at once issued by the Dewán announcing the demise, the consequent closing of all public offices and institutions, and suspension of all business for three days, and other customary marks of mourning. All shops are closed and work dropped throughout the kingdom. Umbrellas also are not allowed to enter the fort. For eleven days the palace women and all Nairs have to go mourning with hair loose and without wearing new cloths or rubbing sacred ashes. For the same period, mourning is observed by the Nair Brigade, the men shaving off their moustaches and hair, excepting the *kudumi*, which hangs loose, and going about bareheaded, without their turbans.

In Alleppey, as soon as the sad intelligence is known, the Commercial Agent orders all the shops in the town to be closed, and the national standard hoisted half mast from the flagstaff.

Barbosa, writing early in the 16th century of the death of the kings of Malabar, says (p. 107)—

"After having burned him, all shave themselves from head to foot, excepting the eyelashes, from the prince, the heir of the throne, to the smallest child of the kingdom; and they also clean their teeth, and universally leave off eating betel for thirteen days from that time; and if in this period they find any one who eats it, his lips are cut off by the executioner."

For a full year it is forbidden to celebrate marriages, or other occasions, with the usual music or display.

It is customary to give a chuckram to each Sirkar official present at the burning, which he is supposed to place in the mouth of the deceased. The surviving relatives, therefore, for some days after, always enclose a chuckram in letters to officials whom they may have occasion to address.

After the cremation, the royal palankeen is again brought, morning and evening, for five days in procession to the burning ground, accompanied by a Brahman priest, sepoys, and attendants, and mourning women, who cry as before. It is carried round the ashes thrice, and then returns.

On the fifth day, by which time relatives who live at a distance will have arrived, the new prince goes as before, bareheaded and barefooted, and wearing only a single cloth, in procession with music, wailing women, &c., to collect the ashes and the remains of bones still unconsumed. After a Brahman called the *Kakkáttu Pótti* has performed certain ceremonies, the bones are gathered, and part placed in a pot to be sent to the Ganges at Benares in charge of a Brahman, who receives two thousand rupees for this service, and is also regarded as degrading himself by such an office. The remainder is put with many ceremonies in another urn, and buried under a jack tree in some compound in the neighbourhood. Over this grave is placed a stone with the name and age of the deceased ; and the owners of the garden receive for the perpetual guardianship of the tomb a daily grant of two measures of rice, and half a *nári* of cocoanut oil for constantly burning at night in a lamp over the grave.

The ashes of junior members of the royal family are buried at the burning place, and a jack tree planted over each.

The melted gold is divided into three or four parts, and distributed to the officiating priest, the temple, the palankeen bearers, and the mourning women.

On the twelfth day *Punyáham,* or cleansing from pollution, is celebrated by the Pótties, after which the new ruler can take possession. Into a quantity of water in a vessel they throw sacred flowers, then prayers are recited ; the holy water is sprinkled over the person and house to be purified. Presents are again made to Brahmans.

Sixteen days after the cremation the **Sráddha,** or oblation to the manes for the repose of the soul, is celebrated, and this is continued daily in the palace itself for some time. It consists in the offering of *pindams,* or rice balls, and oblations of water to the deceased ancestors and the gods, with the feeding of Brahmans required in all ceremonies. The Sráddha is explained by Prof. Monier Williams to the following effect :—

The Hindus fancy that a man has three bodies ; and sometimes the attempt is made to puzzle Christian preachers by catechising them on this point. The first is the *sthúla sarîra,* or gross body, which is burned ; but the soul quits with the *linga sarira*, or subtile body, sometimes described as the size of the thumb, and hovering near the former. The departed spirit has now no real body capable of enjoying or suffering anything, so that it is restless, uncomfortable, and impure. If funeral rites are not performed, it may become a foul, wandering ghost, disposed to take revenge for its misery on all living creatures by malignant acts.

The object of the Sráddha is to soothe the troubled spirit by libations of consecrated water, and to furnish it with an intermediate body, by which alone it can obtain *gathi*, or progress onward to other births, and ultimate emancipation. The first pinda offered endows it with the rudiments or basis of a body; the next day another pinda supplies limbs, and so on. When the soul receives a complete body it becomes a *pitri* (ancestor), and is held to be a *deva* or deity, and practically worshipped as such in the Sráddha ceremonies, which continue to accelerate its progress onwards to a temporary heaven, and then through various stages of bliss to final union with the Supreme.*

As the new sovereign cannot, through press of official duties, observe all the mourning ceremonial, it is customary for the next heir, the Eliya Rajah. to conduct these: he willingly remains in mourning and unshaven for the twelve months, during which the Sráddhas are frequently repeated.

On the first anniversary of the Maharajah's death, and commencing some days before that date, the *Tirumásam*, or annual Sráddha is observed. Many thousands of people are then amply fed, and largesses freely distributed for four days amongst the Brahmans, the first day at the rate of one rupee each, on succeeding days one fanam each, and five rupees per head to Nambúri Brahmans. The royal party and suite visit in procession the temple of Parasu Ráma at Tiruvellam, near Trevandrum, where further rites are performed, and gifts presented to Brahmans. The Eliya Rajah is now relieved from mourning observances. The temple at Neyáttankara is also visited in state, and offerings presented there.

Sráddhas are repeated annually as long as there are relatives to take an interest in the ancestors and remember the anniversary of their deaths. At Palpanábhapuram and Suchindram, a ceremony of long-standing usage is annually observed in grand style—the feeding of some hundreds of Nambúri Brahmans for the good of the departed spirits of some Rajahs of bygone days.

A palace in which the sovereign dies is left vacant, and preserved, with all its furniture and contents intact for one or two generations before it is again opened and re-occupied; as in

* "Indian Antiquary," July, 1876.

Central Africa, everything belonging to the deceased king is preserved with the greatest reverence. Care is taken, if possible, that younger members of the house die in some unoccupied palace that can conveniently be spared from ordinary use.

CHAPTER XIV.

NAMBÚRI BRAHMANS.

THE laws of this remarkable people respecting marriage and inheritance being fully discussed in the chapter on Nepotism, we have only room here to add a curious glimpse of their inner life given in the Census Report (p. 214) by an official, who, as a Brahman, though of another class, could obtain admittance to

NAMBURI BRAHMAN.

their dwellings. The accompanying engraving is from a photograph of a priest in the temple at Trevandrum.

"The women are guarded with more than Moslem jealousy: even brothers and sisters are separated at an early age. When the Nambúri lady goes to worship the village god or visit a neighbour, a Náir maid, who accompanies her, commands the retirement of all the males on the road, while the lady moves all shrouded in cloth, with a mighty umbrella, which protects her from the gaze of profane eyes. At home they are simple in their habits, dressing, like Nair women, up to the waist. The way in which the cloth is worn is slightly different with them, one end of the cloth being passed between the legs in addition to covering all round, while with the Nair women, the cloth is simply wrapped round the waist. They are not extravagant on the score of their ornaments. A necklace consisting of a number of gold coins, through the eyes of which a silk cord is passed, constitutes the most important of the set: gold bangles, and in the case of the poor silver and metallic ones, nearly exhaust the list. The males wear only a cloth, like all other Travancoreans, with the usual complements of a waist string, an under-cloth and a scarf used as an upper-cloth.

When the Nambúri eats alone, the wife generally serves him; but if strangers are invited, the master of the house, or one of the younger members in it, serves them, when the wife sends on the dishes from within the kitchen, where only the husband could go.

The Nambúri's hospitality and charity are proverbial. The Brahman guest in the family is most kindly treated; and in spite of the uncouth manners and queer conversation which he may meet with, he is certain to carry away the happiest recollections of the *Illam* (Nambúri's house). On entering the gate of the extensive property, in the midst of which is situated the palatial mansion with its suburban buildings severally dedicated for the household god, the younger members of the family, the cutcherry of the proverty officers, and for the weary Brahman traveller, the visitor is received by the lord of the manor, who, in his native simplicity, inquires whether he has bathed, without any further ado about the health or other concerns of his guest. If the answer is in the negative, he himself leads the guest to the bathing tank, with its cool shed and refreshing waters, most politely inquiring if oil and cleansing materials are required—all the time innocently gaping at the dress, the walk, the arrangement of the hair, the moustaches on the face, the absence of the scarf-cloth, and the conventional waist-string and under-cloth, while the stranger, accustomed to more formal society, smarts with shyness at the gaze of his host. The Nambúri must be asked to leave the bath for a short time before he can be expected to go.

The visitor is next led into the Illam, and asked to sit before the leaf spread out, not where the inmates generally eat, but in one of the outer rooms: the inevitable thought occurs that you are treated like an outcast. Even the ghee and dhall (peas) eating propensities of the visitor are attended to, though these are carefully eschewed and even disliked by the Nambúri in his own meals. Before serving rice, the Nambúri inquires whether the morning prayers are over, which he thinks improbable on account of the speed with which the visitor has returned from the tank ; and feels a conscientious but unexpressed hatred of the light manner in which religious observances are regarded by the Brahmans of the other coast. The feeding of Brahman travellers is not, however, a rare business with the Nambúri, and he is often a victim of indebtedness caused by the ruinously expensive character of the marriage of his daughters, and by his unbounded hospitality."

CHAPTER XV.

MUHAMMADANS.

THE total population of this class numbers close upon 140,000, scattered all over the country, most thickly near the coast, but very few in Yéttumánúr and Cottayam districts, where they form less than one per cent. of the inhabitants. With few exceptions, they have no acquaintance with Hindustani, but speak the vernacular of the country in which they live. The Hindustani speaking families come from North India, and comprise, in all, 2,844 persons.

Most of the men wear only the ordinary native waist-cloth; and for full-dress a cotton jacket or long coat. They are fond of coloured handkerchiefs and cloths, and often carry about with them a China paper umbrella. A skull-cap is to some extent a distinctive mark, as joining their religion is usually called "putting on the cap." The beard is worn, not shaven like the Hindus.

Women dress in the ordinary Malayálam cloth and jacket and upper-cloth, as is well shown in the accompanying copy of a native drawing. Foreign Muhammadans retain their own respective national costumes. The features of the latter are, of course, Arabic or Jewish, while those of most of the native Mussulmans are Indian. Islamites in creed, they are almost Hindus in person.

In the census Muhammadans are divided into seven classes, of which three are insignificant in numbers in Travancore, viz.:—Two or three thousand MOGHULS, who should be descendants of the Tartar chiefs who followed Tamerlane into India; six or seven hundred ARABS, who came over as horse-dealers, traders, &c.; and over eight hundred SHEIKS (or Shaikhs), who profess to be the descendants of the immediate friends and followers of Muhammad, though the title (which means "an old man," especially one who has authority and respect) is given to any one who is learned and clever. Besides these, there are some fifteen thousand persons belonging to other minor sub-divisions.

Of the four principal classes, the first are PATHANS (*Pattanis*) or Afghans, adventurers and settlers of that nation, chiefly descendants of sepoys retained by the Rajahs of Travancore. They number over three thousand, and are generally poor and unimportant.

SYEDS are descendants of the prophet through Ali and Fatima his favourite daughter. Yet, mingled with other blood, they marry whatever women they choose, but do not give their females to others. Those who so classify themselves number over six thousand.

LUBBAYS (Labi or Lebbe) are about 18,000 in number. The term is of doubtful origin. Some trace it to the Arabic *labek*,

MUHAMMADANS.

"may it please you," used by servants to their masters. Many of these reside in Trevandrum and on the coast southwards. They speak chiefly Tamil, and are of mercantile habits. They are of mixed parentage, being descendants of Arabs and natives. But the proportion of Arabic blood is exceedingly small; they are but a mongrel breed of circumcised Hindus. From various words in use amongst them, and ornaments worn in South Travancore, some suppose that a large proportion of them were formerly Shánárs converted, not recently, but centuries ago. Bishop Caldwell says, "Muhammadan Arabs seem to have settled first on the Malabar Coast in the ninth century, and thence to have spread to the eastern coast and Ceylon. Their principal settlement on the eastern coast is Káyalpattanam in Tinnevelly. Heathen Arabs, that is, the

Sabæans of Southern Arabia, frequented the coasts of India long before, following the lead of the Greeks. The mixed race consisting of the descendants of those Arab merchants are called Mápillas on the western coast, Lebbies on the eastern. By the Tamil people they are generally styled *Tulukkar* (Turks) or *Jonagar* (Yavanas ?). Their ordinary title is *Māraikān* or Marakán, a word which means steersman, implying that they were first known as sailors, which doubtless is correct."*

Méttan, a term of respect used to these people, appears to be the Mahratta "*mehtar*," a common designation for a hereditary village officer, or the head of a business or a caste, who used to exercise considerable authority over the others. It was once a title of honour given by the Rajah to the chief Muhammadan at Powár and others: now every man is politely called Méttan.

The TULUKKANS should scarcely be classed as distinct from the preceding, being also the descendants of Arab immigrants by the Indian women, but more closely connected with those on the East Coast. The great body of the Mussulmans of Travancore, say over 110,000, come under this head.

Here, as in British India, the Muhammadans stand low in education and attainments. Of the two classes last-mentioned, about eight and a half per cent, of the males, but only eighty-four females in all, can read and write. They have little taste for education, scarcely a single school or publication of their own, and few who learn English. In this Hindu State there are no nobles amongst them. In Government service 384 persons are employed, chiefly Tulukkans and Pattánis, mostly in the humble position of peons or policemen. About a fifth of the whole body are cultivators; one-fifth traders; a tenth are labourers; a few are weavers, men of property, &c. Though rather stubborn and troublesome, they are persevering and industrious. Females are not allowed to enter a place of worship, of which restriction we have known some complain in view of the liberty of Christian women; but they are not secluded as in some parts of British India.

The better class of Muhammadans are extremely polite and hospitable. In Alleppey the houses of the Cutchmen are large and roomy, but close and dirty. On entering the archway leading to the courtyard in order to pay a visit to such, the old and hale householder may generally be seen sitting tailor fashion, and propped up with pillows. If word is sent beforehand, the visitor is honourably received. Two men appear with bottles of rosewater who completely drench him, his hands are filled with

"Political History of Tinnevelly," p. 36.

cardamoms and cloves, and on rising to take leave, a bottle of otto of roses is put into his hand as a parting gift.

They, of course, avoid pork and other forbidden food, but may eat beef if it be killed with the requisite ceremonies. They are very loose in their moral principles and in their attendance at mosques and observance of religious rites, yet superstitious and even heathenish in common life, and bigoted against all others, though they understand very little of their own religion and do not care to learn more. The ignorance of their youth even in their teens is sometimes remarkably dense, of which an amusing instance is given by Mr. Yesudian. In examining a new class in the Tamil First Book and endeavouring to test their general knowledge, he questioned them as to the various points of difference between, say, an ox and a dog, and then said, "You have told me that the tail of an ox is useful in driving away the flies that annoy it—would it not be a desirable thing if we likewise were provided with tails?" This they all answered in the affirmative. Then he required them to tell, one by one, what number of tails they would like to have. The first boy said he would like to have one tail; the second boy, two tails; the third boy, three; and the fourth, as if desirous of excelling them all, said he would have four tails. On this the whole school burst into loud laughter. Then the fifth boy said with some hesitation, "we do not require a tail;" and some of the silk weaver boys said, "we have hands instead." On being interrogated as to the reason for their giving such ridiculous answers, they said it was because they had not previously learnt anything of letters.

Circumcision they call *márga kalyánam*, "religious rejoicing;" it is performed on children of five to eight years of age according as money is available for the feast. It is not done in infancy, "lest it should grieve them—a little older, they know what it is." Children think the rite an honour and submit. The barber operates. Several boys are generally circumcised at one time and in one house, with prayers by the Lebbe, all the neighbours being invited, and spending the night without sleeping, at watch over the children, feasting, talking, singing songs, and playing games. Feasting and rejoicings are continued for a week.

Wedding processions are conducted with as much display, and the festivities continued as long as can be managed. The bridegroom is richly dressed and adorned, and the accompanying party join in a chant as they proceed. Some marry their children in infancy, which is contrary to their law.

As might be expected from the views and practice of Islam and the Malayálam examples around them, the Muhammadans are very dissolute and sensual. Not many, however, can afford to keep more than one wife. Divorce is not infrequent. The wife must first be warned, then may be beaten, then put away for a few days; then finally divorced by repeating the *tallàh*, or formula for the occasion. After two months she is at liberty to marry *another* person.

The Muhammadan **law of inheritance** is extremely difficult and intricate, but rarely claimed to its fullest extent in Travancore. Indeed, they seem to have little knowledge of their own laws of inheritance, frequently talking of the "undivided family," and other Hindu customs and rules which they are familiar with, and look upon as applicable to themselves as a matter of course.

When suffering from **sickness**, the patient is not only treated with medicines for his recovery, but is given holy water, over which the Tangal or priest has repeated texts and prayers. If death seems near, his face is turned towards Mecca, he repeats the creed, and the 36th chapter of the Koran is repeated for the consolation of the dying man.

At death, the eyes are closed by the attendants, and the legs stretched and tied together with a band of cloth. Relatives are immediately informed, and friends flock in to the funeral, which is conducted as soon as they can arrange. The Lebbe is sent for and the bier brought, the attendants served with betel-nut, and the body bathed and dressed for removal to the cemetery adjoining each mosque. The remains of widows are always clothed in white; those of wives whose husbands survive, in red cloths of silk and other materials.

To follow a bier on foot to the grave is an obligation incumbent on good Mussulmans. During the funeral procession from the house to the burial-ground, the Lebbe repeats certain plaintive songs, the others joining in at intervals repeating the *kalima* or creed. The body is not carried inside the mosque, but taken near it, and the prayers repeated. Coffins are never used; the corpse being only wrapped in cloths and laid on mats. After the prayers, it is lowered into the grave, and each puts in seven clods of earth, repeating a text in the Koran, cap. 112. "We created you of earth, and we return you to the earth. We shall raise you out of the earth on the day of resurrection." The grave is dug north and south, and the body buried with the face towards Mecca; poor people place two stones at the ends, while the rich erect tombs and monuments, or a canopy of cloth over the grave.

After the funeral all return to the house of mourning, chew betel, and then go home. For forty days after the interment, a lamp is kept burning day and night. On the second day fruits and flowers of various kinds are made ready at the house; and the Lebbe and others again attend, when the priest performs other ceremonies, takes the articles to the burial-ground, and again repeats texts and prayers for the remission of the sins of the deceased. This over, all the articles are distributed amongst those present. On the tenth, and on the fortieth days, feasts are made for the friends; and special ceremonies performed at the expiration of twelve months after the death, all doubtless imitated from the Hindu *sráddha.*

Here are a few **notes of a fishing village, Vilinjam,** a few miles south of Trevandrum, inhabited both by Roman Catholics and Muhammadans—the one class at the north end, the other at the south of the village. They are not mutually hostile, but do not go out to fish in the same boats. The Mussulmans are divided into two classes, whom they call merchants and *marakáns* or Lubbays—the last inferior. These two do not intermarry, but they attend the mosque together, and are buried alike, close by the mosque. The marakáns will eat food from their superiors, but not *vice versa.* They are probably pure native proselytes from the Mukkuvar and other castes. None however, have recently been converted to Islam here.

These fisher people marry early, boys at the age of ten or twelve; girls at seven to ten, but occasionally remaining unmarried many years longer, if a suitable husband does not appear. Lucky days are sought for marriage and other engagements.

They do not go out to fish on Fridays, but attend the mosque, though not very regularly, where the Lebbe reads the Koran from a palm-leaf manuscript. The mosque is built on a prominent point of land, and wholly of stone, as are some wayside rest-houses, with three spikes on the top, like some Hindu temples. They assert that it was not built by human hands, but by persons sent by the prophet. The children are excessively rude and ignorant, shouting at a European traveller, "White man! go from the mosque!" and other impertinences. They go out to fish with the fathers from a very early age.

The men do not carry fish to market, but sell to the merchants of dried fish, who export to Colombo. Some days they take nothing: then must run in debt to the merchants, or want. Their houses are wretched huts, put up on the sands in the shade of a few cocoa-nut trees, and formed entirely of leaves, as they cannot procure clay for walls. The graves are neglected, and the remains sometimes shockingly exposed to view.

The two great religious divisions of Islam are SUNNIS and SHIAHS. Of the latter, who admit tradition only when verified by any of the twelve Imáms, there are none in Trevandrum.

They mourn the martyrdom of Hassan and Hossein, the women abstaining for ten days from betel, flesh-meat, and other luxuries, leaving off their ornaments and coloured cloths, and wearing only black in token of mourning. They offer prayer with unclasped hands. *Shiáh* is literally "a follower," *i.e.*, of Ali, the son-in-law of Muhammad, and, in the opinion of his followers, the lawful successor to the Khalifat.

The Sunnis (from *sunnat*, the record of those sayings and acts of Muhammad which oral tradition had at first preserved) recognizing the lawful succession of the first four Khalifs, are the great body of the Mussulmans, and are again subdivided into four sects, named after four eminent orthodox Imams or Doctors of the Law, who decided questions regarding which Muhammad had given no explicit direction. These are :—

1. Hanífa, born A.H. 80. He admitted very few traditions as authoritative in his system, which claims to be a logical development from the Koran, and permits the right of private judgment. The Pattánis are of this sect, and their tenets generally prevail throughout India.

2. Málik, born A.H. 93, founded his system on the "customs of Medina." He arranged and systematized the traditions current there, and formed a historical and traditional system of jurisprudence rigidly embracing the whole sphere of life. His tenets are not known to prevail in India.

3. Shafií, born A.H. 150. An eclectic system from the works of the two previous Imams, and requiring a considerable number of traditions in proof of any single point. In offering prayer they put the hands on the breast or shoulder, the thumbs touching the lobes of the ear. His doctrines have some currency along the sea-coast; the Calicut Mussulmans belong to this sect.

4. Ibn Hanbal, born A.H. 164, professed excessive veneration for the Koran as uncreated and eternal. There are none of this sect in India.

Of WAHABIS there are but a few, chiefly men from Sind, very zealous against the use of tobacco, opium, &c., but attending the usual mosques.

Proselytes are called *Maula Islam*. Cases of conversion are very rare in Trevandrum, but more common in Alleppey and Cochin. Children are sometimes purchased or picked up, and educated in Islam. They cut off the *kudumi* at once, as heathenish, and because they think an outward mark is needed. Yet a few wear it for temporal profit, as for example, sepoys in the Brigade. There are five special commandments imposed upon all, viz :—

1. To learn the *Kalima* (a "word," or speech, the confession

of faith), and repeat it. "There is no god but God, and Muhammad is the Apostle of God."

2. To pray five times a day.

3. To fast in the month of Ramzán, the ninth Muhammadan month, during which eating, drinking, and any sensual gratification is interdicted between dawn and the appearance of the stars.

The preceding ordinances are for all, the next for the wealthy:—

4. To give five per cent. of income to charity.

5. To go on a pilgrimage to Mecca.

Priests and Religious Teachers.—Of the regular *moulavi* (a learned man, teacher, expounder of Muhammadan law) there are few, if any, in Travancore. Officers are retained under this title at the principal law courts at Trevandrum, Alleppey, &c., to administer oaths to Mussulman witnesses. This is done by making them take a Koran in their hands, or place it on the head, then making solemn affirmation in set form that they will speak the truth.

Sometimes, they say, a peer or saint may visit the country, or a Moulvi may come round and preach, but such visits must be rare.

The local priests are called *Tangal*, a common Malayálam honorific, meaning "they themselves." These are supposed to to be Syeds, and exercise considerable influence; they have no regular training for this office—any one who has learnt, and can conduct the prayers acceptably, may become accustomed to it by degrees, and be popularly recognized. The Tangal of Powár travels about as a great man in a palankeen, sometimes as far as to Colachel, the people of each place where he is invited, in order to conduct special ceremonies, bearing the expense of bringing him to the locality.

Under a Tangal are several Lebbes, one in each mosque, who conducts the worship, kills sheep for food with due ceremonial, and conducts marriages. He is appointed by the people, and paid by fees and presents.

Friday (*jumá*) is the day of public prayer. In the mosques there are no sermons, no common prayer, and no singing. At the principal mosques no public service is held except there be forty persons present, exclusive of strangers, slaves, and the deformed. The Lebbe repeats some portion of the Koran in Arabic, but without explaining it, as he does not know the meaning himself. At least three texts must be repeated, taken from any part of the sacred volume. All stand while this is repeated, and follow the action of the Lebbe in ritual as he stands, bows, prostrates himself, or sits down. The common explanation of these acts is that man should praise the Creator as head of the creation, and on behalf of all—standing like a tree, stooping like quadrupeds, prostrate like reptiles, and sitting like mountains and hills.

They should attend the mosque five times a day for prayer, but this is never done. When the time of prayer comes, men pray wherever they are. Women should pray in their houses five times daily, but not when unclean.

The mosques in Travancore number 335 in all. There is a remarkable one at Tiruvánkodu, the ancient capital. It is usually called Malukku Muthaliár's Mosque, this being supposed to be the name of an Arab buried on the site before the building was erected, whose tomb—a low brick-built structure—is now enclosed within the building. Strangers are not allowed to enter.

The tradition is that, a Rajah of Travancore, then residing at Keralapuram, near Takkaly, heard a sound like the muezzin's call to prayer, and gave orders for the erection of this mosque; hearing also the blowing of the conch shell in another direction, he built the temple of Mádévan. In digging the foundations, the remains of a human being were discovered, and the same night a person appeared in a dream to one of the principal parties, and said, "I am Malukku Muthaliár."

The courtyard is large, and surrounded by a high brick wall, like some Brahman temples, with a porch-house surmounting the front entrance. Within is a deep tank, square, with fine stone steps on the four sides leading down to the water. The mosque itself is remarkable as being built entirely of granite, like some Hindu temples. The eastern end is used as a porch for the accommodation of the people before engaging in worship, and has a pent roof of stone, with stone rafters. A door leads into the body of the building, which has a flat roof, all of stone, and is fifty-nine feet in length and twenty-five feet wide; the stones for cross beams must therefore each be about thirty feet in length.

At the western end of the mosque there is a kind of pulpit or platform, called *mimber*, used by the Lebbe while officiating. It is built of brick and plaster, bare of railing, but with a flight of steps for ascending.

An old inscription on another tombstone is indistinct, but is read by some as dated *M.E. 179*, which would be over eight centuries ago, but the letters seem of much later date. This mosque is maintained and lighted daily from the produce of a garden granted free of tax by the Rajah, who is said to have built the mosque; from fees on marriage dowries at one-tenth (not always paid now-a-days), and on trade, at a quarter per cent. of the capital expended; and from the collections made at the annual festival, amounting to some eight hundred rupees. On the anniversaries of the death of honoured individuals, rice is brought to the courtyard by the relatives, and distributed to the poor.

The chief festival at this place is held about April, and is called *Sandanakudam*, "vessel of sandal-wood." A silver pitcher is filled with the powder of this fragrant wood, and brought from the old mosque to the new one, borne by the priest in an open palankeen, in full procession, torches burning, banners waving, and music and shouts of "Allah, Allah," concluding with fireworks. People from as far as Quilon visit this celebrated temple.

The *Muharram* ("sacred, or prohibited," being the first month in their year, in which it was held unlawful to make war) is observed about November or December. It has gradually assumed the appearance of a scene of amusement and merry-making, while the religious principles on which it used to be observed—in commemoration of the tragic fate of Hassan and Hossein—are fast melting away. Pretty *tábúts*, or biers, are made of coloured paper or tinsel, something like a mausoleum in the Saracenic style of architecture, and carried in procession on the shoulders of men, with drum and fife, beating of tom-toms, masquerading, and other mummeries. Some of the company are painted with yellow and brown stripes, frightful red mouth, and bloody jaws, to represent tigers, holding rattles in the hand, the long tail supported by a friend, looking frightful enough to women and children. These go about demanding money from the people. A feast is also prepared, and the *Fatiha* repeated in the name of Hossein, and over the graves of friends.

The Mussulmans are accustomed to speak of Islam as the "Fourth Veda," or Religion, alluding to Adam, Abraham, and Jesus Christ as previous prophets with a divine mission, each bearing new laws and revelations, which superseded all that had been delivered by their predecessors; Muhammad being the the last and greatest of the prophets, the final authoritative organ of the divine will. Sometimes, however, Christianity is referred to as the "Fifth Religion." They are very fond of the illustration that, as of these four—milk, butter-milk, curd, and butter—the last is the best and most valuable and durable, so their religion, "the Fourth," is superior to all that preceded it. Still they admit the excellence of the Christian faith in some respects, occasionally purchasing and reading with pleasure the Pentateuch, the Proverbs of Solomon Nabi, or prophet, and even the Gospels. They admit the divine mission of Jesus, and

His authority as a prophet of God, and assert that His birth was glorious, that He did not die as commonly believed, but that He still lives in a mountain near Jerusalem; and they say that He was endowed with miraculous powers of which Muhammad was destitute—yet that Jesus was inferior to their prophet. Some believe that Jesus is now in the fourth heaven, and will come again to destroy antichrist.

"We also," say they, "are *Vedakar* (people of a book religion); we have Allah and Muhammad." They strongly object to the image worship of Romanists. One of these was found engaged in discussion with a Mussulman, and insisting that Muhammad was wrong in not allowing females to attend the mosque for worship. The other retorted upon his opponent respecting their worship of images, and the dispute was referred to a colporteur who then came up, for his opinion. He thought both were in error on the points in question.

They are for the most part strongly prejudiced against Christianity; a few read books published by Islamites against it; and without making any serious inquiry, they urge blasphemous objections, and abuse and insult the Christian preachers. "How," they ask, "could the Saviour of the world be put to death on a cross?" The miraculous birth of Jesus Christ is to them a standing difficulty. We have known some refuse even water to drink to a European, because he was a Christian.

Yet they are far from any correct acquaintance with their own religion, or any intelligent submission to its principles and precepts.

In country parts we have asked them who was Muhammad, and why they believed in him, but they could give no answer. Such repeat scarcely any prayers morning or evening, nor attend to other prescribed duties; they have no zeal for their religion or its propagation, and are full of heathen and caste superstitions. There is a decided tendency to deify Muhammad and even to confound him with the heathen gods and to speak favourably of their power. "Vishnu and Muhammad are the same," said one, "Muhammad is an Avatar of Vishnu." "Muhammad was created," says another, "before the world was, and was consulted by the Supreme Being respecting the creation of the world." They speak of the prophet coming down from heaven, when prayed to, and restoring children to life.

The ignorant often thus assert that Muhammad was before the creation. This arises from a text in the Koran, or a tradition, "I have created thee from my light and by thy light I have created the world. If I had not created thee, I should not have created the world," meaning, the world is created for thee. A bright light, they assert, shone on Adam's forehead, and was transmitted down to Abdullah and Muhammad his son.

Many superstitious notions and practices prevail amongst them. Pattánis make a hand of gold or silver, "because Hossein's hand was cut off in battle," which they take to the Karamana river and bathe. "During the prevalence of cholera in 1875, the conduct of the Muhammadans who occupy the northern portion of the Tittuvilei village, was deplorable. For they stubbornly refused to take medicine, on the plea that their Koran prescribes no remedy for cholera; and sacrificed cocks, goats, and even young bulls, tumultously calling upon evil spirits whom they considered to be the cause of the plague, to abandon their dwellings and to repair to those of the heathens or Christians. When this proved ineffectual, the males of the village joined together, and bawled out simultaneously a prayer which means something like the following :—

"Allah is Allah—no other Allah.
"Muhammad is the prophet of Allah.
"Save, O Allah!
"Save, O Allah!"

This they commenced every night at nine or ten o'clock, and continued till they felt exhausted by the depth of their outcry, to and fro, along their several streets. The effect was awfully distressing, as it struck with a panic the heart of every person in the neighbourhood. The obstinacy of the deluded Mussulmans brought on them no trifling loss; for about one-fifteenth of their entire number was swept away by the plague."

So ignorant and heathenish are the Muhammadans of Travancore, that they are pronounced by those of the East Coast "worthless." They do not allow people of other castes or religions to eat with them. Few go to Mecca on pilgrimage. Sickness is attributed to the agency of demons, wherefore some secretly send gifts to the devil temples; many attend the idol procession at Aráttu. Many give their children in marriage in infancy. Though forbidden to sell arrack or opium, some do this secretly. As education is low, so crime, it is admitted, is excessive amongst them. Little moral discipline is exercised, though they may be excluded from the mosque, and others may refuse to speak or hold intercourse with them or give them fire, for adultery with heathen women, for disobedience, or drunkenness.

CHAPTER XVI.

THE SYRIAN CHRISTIANS.

THESE very interesting people are well described, and an admirable and exhaustive history of their Church given in Whitehouse's "Lingerings of Light in a Dark Land." To this a few general remarks may be added, with some account of their domestic manners and customs, which have not hitherto

SYRIAN CHRISTIANS.

been described. For part of the latter I am indebted to an able paper written at my suggestion by Mr. M. Matthew, B.L.

Birth.—A horoscope is generally procured immediately on the occurrence of a birth, from the Kanián, or astrologer, one of whom resides in each village, of course knows the families well, and can make shrewd guesses as to the future. For this custom the apology is made that it is "convenient for preserving the date as a register;" but it is happily dropping out of use.

Names are taken from Scripture, chiefly the New Testament, and many of them considerably altered in the course of ages from the original Syriac form, so as to be hardly recognizable. Peter, for instance, has come to be Poonén; Joshua, Kóshi; Paul, Peili; Zechariah, Tarien; Alexander, Chándy; and John, Lohanan.

Baptism.—The children are accompanied by sponsors. The water for baptism is first consecrated, the infant placed in the stone font, and water lifted up in the hand of the priest and

SYRIAN PRIEST (CATTANAR) AND BISHOP (METRAN).

poured or rubbed over the whole body of the child, which is also anointed with holy oil on the forehead, ears, chest, hands, and feet, both before and after the baptism. "There are a good many ceremonies besides the simple baptism—the exorcism of evil spirits; a strange plan of mixing warm and cold water with the assertion that 'John mixed water for baptism and Christ sanctified it, went down into it, and was baptized;' and an investiture of the baptized person with the priest's girdle and a crown, of which the latter is removed by the priest seven days after the baptism, with a prayer that the child may receive instead of it a crown of glory. The doctrine of regeneration in baptism is strongly stated." (Bishop Cotton.) A "baptismal feast" is usually held afterwards.

At a year old, "the giving of rice," is observed. For this occasion the maternal grandparents supply a string of ornaments. For a male child, the largest ornament is a gold cross—for a female, a golden ducat or other coin. Parents take great pride in having many and costly ornaments tied round the neck of the child. But this exposes the little ones to danger from the cupidity of thieves. An ornament consisting of a tiger's claw set in gold, curiously carved, is worn round the waist of children for good luck.

Boys when young wear these golden ornaments, but they are removed as they grow older. The Syrian girls are very fond of ornaments, wearing armlets, gold rings on the right hand; and in the upper part of the ear, in the southern parts of the country a golden *takka*, or cylinder, like the Sudra women. These earrings are the only ornaments retained after marriage. The ears of girls are bored, but not those of men, whereas among Hindus both males and females have the ears pierced.

At about four years old, the alphabet is learnt. A brass vessel full of rice is taken to the teacher. A lamp being lit, the teacher holds the right hand of the child and makes him write a letter or two on the rice, which afterwards, along with a few chuckrams, some tobacco and betel-nuts, is presented to the teacher. On beginning to use the pen, a present is given to the teacher, and a feast to the whole school, consisting of parched corn, plantains, cocoanuts, and jaggery, distributed by the monitors. The lessons chiefly consist of grammar and poetry, Syrian prayers and songs in Malayálam, which is at present the vernacular of these people, and Scripture stories, all written on palm-leaves and committed to memory. Boys and girls are taught alike, as long as girls attend school, generally until married.

Food.—There are no prejudices against any particular kind of food. Beef is ordinarily not procurable, therefore not eaten. Rice and curry is a favourite dish. The Syrians eat sitting on the ground, on a mat or piece of plank. Brass vessels are used to contain the food, and on important occasions plantain leaves. The right hand only is used in eating.

Marriage.—Few or none remain unmarried, except the higher orders of priests. A girl is never left unmarried, and only the very poorest have been known to wait till the age, say, of twenty-two. Even a deaf, or dumb, or blind girl must get married, because girls receive no share of the parent's property, only marriage dowries. Some fifty years ago, eight thousand chuckrams (Rs. 285) was considered a large dowry—at present such a sum is insufficient, as much as a thousand rupees being sometimes given. The dowry is supposed to be equal to one-third of the property of the bridegroom's father. Should the husband die, the dowry is returned to the widow; in case of her early death, it goes to her relatives.

Re-marriage of widows is conducted in the early morning before daylight, as a somewhat shameful thing. Hence the possibility of such a fraud as was committed by a priest about ten years ago, who substituted a niece of his own, a young widow with several children, instead of the bride promised to a certain man. The officiating priest was not in the secret, but on coming to the light at the door after the ceremony the sexton recognized the woman, and the deceived bridegroom took to his heels and fled to the Metrán to complain. Of course, this was no valid marriage. Second marriages are thus allowed without the usual display, while third and fourth marriages are severely reprobated.

The minimum age of marriage is ten for a boy and seven for a girl, though such early and scandalous marriages are contrary to the ancient canons of the church, and apparently from a recent decision of the Sadr Court, contrary to the law of Travancore. In Christian marriage, it was decided, the free and reasonable consent of both parties is absolutely indispensable, therefore a marriage performed between such mere infants is null and void; and to this point the attention of the Syrian community was invited. Yet a Syrian marriage, it is said, was recently solemnized between a boy of eleven years of age and a girl of nine, the children of educated and influential people. The usual ages are respectively sixteen or eighteen, and twelve. Never is a youth supposed to wed a girl older than himself—girls are always professedly but twelve before marriage, and strange to say, some are eighteen within two years after! Unfortunately there are no registers of births or deaths kept in the churches. The young man may have no means for supporting a wife: then his parents must provide.

Intermarriage between blood relations on either side is prohibited to the seventh generation, which stringent rule interposes unnecessary difficulty in the way of finding suitable wives. They never intermarry with converts from inferior castes. Generations must pass before even high-caste converts get rid of the reproach of idolatry.

Wooing is not customary, nor are love-letters written: all is arranged by the parents alone. Often the parties have never seen each other until they meet in the church. The girl's family are first to make proposals. It is a common saying that young men, whatever be their age, will find a wife at pleasure, but if girls are not married young, suitable husbands will not easily be found.

M

The fortunes of the young couple are usually cast from their ages and horoscopes. There is a "book of fate" in the hands of the clergy for this purpose.

Much useless expenditure is incurred on weddings for the hire of conveyances, jewels, umbrellas, and musicians and feasting for days. The marriage expenses are roughly estimated at half the dowry. Both parties meet in the bride's house to arrange the dowry and date of marriage. The dowry may consist of ornaments, lands, or money. Eight days before the wedding, the parents of the girl send a deputation to the house of the boy's father with the money for the dowry: it is contained in a purse carefully tied and received without counting, but should the contents prove, in the meantime, to be less than the sum agreed on, the boy does not come to the church.

The banns are published a week before the wedding, and only once. Marriages are always, except amongst a few of the reformed churches, celebrated on Sundays, and forbidden on all

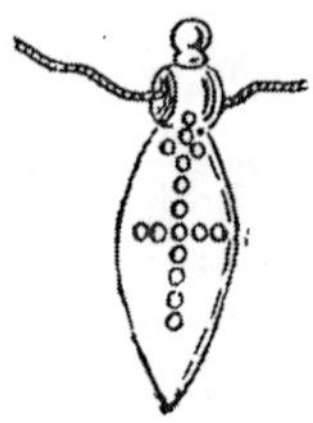

SYRIAN MARRIAGE BADGE, ENLARGED.

fast days. The bride and bridegroom must attend the public service immediately before being married, else a fine is imposed. The bride never enters the church before the bridegroom: should she happen to arrive before him, she waits in some house in the vicinity. Her dress is a white cloth with red stripe down the front; or a coloured cloth, and a jacket worked with yellow silk on the sides and round the neck: a light muslin is thrown over the head as a veil. She is generally laden with borrowed jewels and strings of gold coin hung round the neck.

The bridegroom wears a splendid robe and turban, heavy gold bracelets on the arms, and a large golden cross on the breast; sometimes a silver girdle encircles his waist. They do not use the ring but a *táli*, a bit of gold with the figure of a cross strung on a piece of cord, which the bridegroom ties round the woman's neck, and which she always retains.

"The *táli* or marriage badge (like our wedding-ring) which every woman wears while her husband lives, proclaims her at once and everywhere as a married woman, and as having a protector. It also ensures her attention and respect, where a woman without the *táli* might receive neither." ("Every Day Life," p. 102.)

Both are required to fast on the day of marriage till the ceremony is over, generally in the afternoon. This appears to be a Hindu custom. In return for this abstinence they have the peculiar privilege of sitting in the church during divine service, while others stand. And when returned to the bridegroom's house, they are seated for the time on an equality with the Cattanars. Only after all the guests have feasted may the married couple partake of food. Some, indeed, is offered them in church, immediately after the marriage, but it is generally declined, or only a handful accepted—even this the bride cannot do unless the husband has first taken a little.

Returning from the church, the newly-married couple do not enter the house till the ceremony called *nellum nírum* "rice and water," is over. A female relative meets them in front of the house, with a lamp in her left hand (even in broad daylight, which is one of the privileges of the Syrians in Travancore), and some paddy powdered and mixed in a vessel with water in her right hand. With this she makes a spot on the forehead, first of the husband, then of the wife, who makes obeisance in acknowledgment. To omit this would be regarded as dooming the parties to poverty. The attendants then conduct the young couple into the house amid the exciting shouts of men and women, the men crying *nada*, "march," and the women making the *kurava* cry, a shrill sound produced by the vibration of the tongue between the lips and teeth. This is much used at Hindu weddings, devil-dancing, and so forth. The wedded pair enter the house and are seated on a plank curiously adorned with patterns of rice flour mixed with water, and surrounded by circles of the same substance.

The feasting now begins, the guests sitting in rows parallel to each other. All the men are seated on mats by themselves, and are served first. The women are seated inside. The men take rank according to seniority and the antiquity of their pedigree. The position of greatest honour is marked by two pieces of cloth, one black, the other of some dark colour, put in a place visible from all parts of the pandal. If an upstart, or a convert from Hinduism, however wealthy, takes his seat on these, irony is poured on him by the younger men till he is glad to vacate the seat.

A man having a head-cloth tied on his head stands in the marriage *pandal* holding a basket full of tobacco, areca nuts, and betel leaf for chewing. Thrice he begs permission of the company to present the basket, which being accorded, it is laid before the principal persons. Others with similar baskets, and a little lime, and spittoons, enter and supply the guests. A short time is spent in chewing betel. After going out to cleanse their mouths and returning to their respective seats, the large leaves of the plantain, which are used as plates, are laid before each. The Syrians enjoy the peculiar privilege of folding up the end of the leaf!

Salt is put upon the righthand side of the leaf, then rice upon the leaf, and around the rice various curries of fish, fowl, and vegetables. Afterwards milk curd is brought to each leaf, and sugar, plantains, curd, and rice are mixed together and eaten. The sign of being satisfied is to close the fingers, which is noticed by the attendants. When all have made this sign, the question is formally put, "Have all closed their fingers?" and an affirmative answer is given. Afterwards all leave the pandal to wash their hands, tobacco is again distributed, and they go home.

On the second night of the wedding, small and great unite in merriment and joy, dance and song. Women amuse themselves by repeating all the songs they have ever learnt. Men and women come to the pandal splendidly attired, glittering with gold and silver jewellery. The young couple are placed in the centre of the pandal, four pieces of cloth are presented by the bridegroom to his mother-in-law, uncle, grandmother, and father respectively. Each embraces the bridegroom; the most respectable men and women in the company embrace the bride, the men first and women afterwards. Dancing, singing, and cheering are kept up till daybreak, when the company quietly disperses, to meet again in the evening. Only men dance. The bride's relatives supply the guests with *churutti*, a sweetmeat in shape like a conical roll, thought indispensable at Syrian weddings, and peculiar to that people.

The next evening is also spent in dancing and singing. One of the bride's relatives acts the part of mother-in-law to the bridegroom. She is bound to supply him with rice, and to superintend the cleaning of the marriage chamber. On the fourth night of the wedding, the fictitious mother-in-law stands at the door of their room, which has been purposely closed, and anxiously requests that it be opened. The attendants dictate various conditions, to which she assents. She knocks at the door with songs full of fine promises. "Open the door, my son and daughter. I will give you a cow and a calf to provide milk to drink—a servant to attend upon you, a brass cup for the children's rice—a basin to wash your hands," and so forth, exhausting the catalogue of domestic utensils, earnestly beseeching and knocking till the attendants report that the son-in-law is pleased, and orders the door to be opened for her entrance.

Other plays and jests are performed amongst the friends, in which several days after the wedding are spent. Parents, relatives, and visitors freely intermingle and rejoice together. The greatest happiness of Syrian parents is to see all their sons and daughters married during their own lifetime.

Laws of Inheritance.—Property devolves to legitimate children alike by first or second marriage, sons inheriting the bulk of the property in equal shares; daughters can claim only dowry, and are, therefore, not responsible for debts on the estate. The father cannot quite disinherit any of his children, but may, while alive, distribute his property to them by gift in any reasonable manner or proportion that he pleases.

If there are no sons, all goes to the daughters, or brothers, or next heirs—if no near relatives, to the Church. Persons without children may bequeath all their property to the Church, but this is not allowed if they have children. A widow with a family may enjoy her late husband's property till her sons come of age; if she re-marries, nothing is given her.

Burial.—The body is carried in procession on a bier to the church, decently covered with white cloths, the hands crossed, and only the face exposed. Chanting a psalm on the way, the Cattanar, or priest, precedes the corpse with a cross, umbrella, &c., the male friends and relatives following.

The body is laid in the porch of the Church, with the face towards the east, and a lamp and a cross at the head, where prayers are read. It is then re-wrapped with additional strips of cloth, the priest's fees are paid, the body is placed in the grave, and the funeral service completed. Consecrated water is sprinkled on the corpse, and both it and the grave are incensed. All present turn eastward, and offer intercession for the departed. Then the priest first throws in a little earth, the people follow, and the grave is filled up.

Some are buried inside the church, for which a large fee is required, or in a kind of skeleton church or "cemetery," erected and consecrated for the purpose. Metráns are always buried near the altar. Rarely are monuments erected; on the contrary, the remains are often treated irreverently, being thrown out on the next occasion when the grave is required, and cast into a great pit in a corner of the churchyard.

Fasting for the dead is kept, like the Hindus, for a whole year, by a member of the family of the deceased, during which time he who fasts is to abstain from meat and from shaving.

Amongst the southernmost churches, the Syrians have been largely awakened and enlightened through the influence chiefly of the Church Missionary Society, who have laboured directly amongst them, and the London Missionary Society in the Quilon district. In some churches the public service is conducted almost wholly in the vernacular, and the gospel is preached. About fifty of their churches are more or less reformed; but the future of this movement greatly depends on the result of the lawsuits going on for some years past, as to the legal rights of the Patriarch of Antioch, and Metráns appointed by him, who desire to maintain the old state of things. Farther north, little improvement is discernible—there is no preaching or teaching of the people, no effort for the ingathering of the heathen. When urged to go out to read and exhort at least on a Sunday afternoon, they said that after con-

REV. K. KOSHI, C.M.S.

fession they must not even speak to a Hindu, or answer when called! Caste rules are observed by them towards their inferiors, and applied to them by Sudras and Brahmans. Immorality, it appears, is not inconsiderable in amount; opium eating, intemperance, and quarrelling not uncommon. There is no discipline in the churches, as the priests are dependent on the fees received for sacred offices; and some of themselves are blameworthy. Sorcerers are sometimes secretly consulted, especially in cases of epileptic disease, and offerings made to propitiate demons.

It is chiefly these who swell the proportion of crime amongst Christians to an undue extent by their smuggling tobacco and cardamoms, in which they seem to take the lead, and which they, perhaps, regard as venial sins.

The Syrians appear to be in the lowest condition in the northern and mountainous districts in Múváttupulay direction, where the Mission has, as yet, been able to do very little. Between Cottayam and Trichoor, a distance of about 70 miles, a great field for Christian labour lies open, for which the Alwaye Itineracy has been established. At Múváttupulay and Todupulay there are large numbers of Syrians, poor, hard-working, and kind people, renting lands from the Nambúri landlords, for which they pay four or five times the seed sown, and cultivating areca palms and the fruits, roots, and grains on which they live. They have no Scriptures or other books, and few schools. Nor is there a Sirkar District school at either of the two district towns just mentioned. The priests conduct service and go off to their houses; sometimes indeed there is no one to hold worship in the churches. The surrounding population have very little idea as to what God the Syrians worship, or how.

The ignorance and spiritual darkness of these poor nominal Christians is very great. On a tour in that quarter not long ago to see the country, I very carefully and cautiously examined those whom I met, or stayed with, as to their knowledge of Christian truth. It was heart-rending to learn of the criminal indifference and negligence of the priests, and to find old men and young quite ignorant, not only of the Scriptures, which they never read nor hear read, but even as to who Jesus Christ was. "I know nothing of it" said an old man with whom I conversed. A youth with handsome open countenance could not tell what kind of person or character Jesus Christ was—whether a Brahman, a government officer, a carpenter, or what! He "could not say." One could hardly credit that such ignorance was possible; but a native friend, who accompanied me, also repeated the queries in various forms to make sure that they were understood, and both of us used their Syriac terms. The old man could mumble over the creed, but did not know the meaning. "What then do you go to church for?" "To do the appointed things, and worship the cross. The priest shows us God." But he could not tell why the cross was worshipped. Another said he went to worship the Apostle Paul, but did not know who he was, or what he did. "Why are you baptized?" "For the religion and for the soul; to make me a Mapillay," were the answers. "Why do you attend the holy communion?" "Because it is the custom. We are told to do it, but do not know the reason why." "Is it the same as eating your rice?" "Oh no, something quite different, but I do not know what." Scarcely any knew who the first man was, and such like things. I found that the Syrians were beneath the Roman Catholics of the neighbourhood, both in knowledge and in morals.

The accompanying engraving of the carved stone-work on the doorway of the Syrian church at Kotárakara is copied from a sketch made on the spot, and shows their usual style of ornamentation—the cross, angels, &c.; and what rather sur-

DOORWAY OF SYRIAN CHURCH.

prised me at first, the cock beside the cross. I asked a man what this meant, and he told me it was the cock which the *Angel Gabriel* heard crow! He meant the Apostle Peter. Then he related some foolish story respecting the armed figures on the posts of the door. It is a solid and neat piece of stone-work.

CHAPTER XVII.

NEPOTISM.

THE indigenous inhabitants of the Malabar Coast may be referred to three principal classes—Brahmans, Náyars, and the various Low castes. For some four or five hundred miles along the coast northward from Cape Comorin, the mass of the population speak Malayálam, and have strange customs and characteristic laws of their own. Having been driven by subsequent waves of immigration to the very extremity of India, and being both protected and hedged in by the great range of the Western Ghauts running nearly parallel with the coast at an average distance of some fifty miles, these races retain very primitive and semi-civilized usages and peculiar practices. Amongst these may be named polyandry, polygamy, and nepotism in domestic economy; demon-worship and Brahmanism in religion; and the institute of caste in its most rigid form.

The law of Nepotism—by which relationship is traced obliquely, only through the female line, so that not one's own but the sister's children are regarded as the nearest heirs—can only be understood, and its origin investigated, by first examining the marriage and inheritance laws of the Malayálam Brahmans, or Nambúris, and those of the Malayálam Sudras, or Náyars, both of which are inseparably connected and interdependent.

The Nambúris and other Malayálam Brahmans are the special priests of the Malabar Coast, and are regarded as most sacred. None of them reside in South Travancore, which is only visited by them from time to time for the celebration of religious festivals and ceremonies for the kings and temples. They are extensive landowners, often possessed of much wealth. The family property is owned and enjoyed in common by all the members of the family; and to preserve this intact for the general welfare and protection, a kind of law of entail is observed. In order that the family property may descend undivided, the eldest son alone is permitted to marry, the younger sons being only provided with subsistence, and obliged to form temporary connections with Sudra and other females of inferior caste, who abide in their own ancestral dwellings, with whom, however, these Brahmans cannot, on account of caste, eat food, and whose children, being by Hindu law, of necessity illegitimate, can only be supported by, and inherit property from, their mothers' brothers.

The law by which property descends to heirs of the body is called **Makkatáyam**, or "children's inheritance"; that law by which the nephews of Náyars are their heirs is called **Marumakkatáyam**, the term *marumakkal* being used for nephews, or sometimes for son-in-laws, from *maru*, "to dwell or fondle"—those who reside with one, and are affectionately treated as his own children.

The following summary of the laws of the Malayálam Brahmans, relating to marriage and inheritance, is taken, in substance, from a native work by G. Kerala Varmman Tirumulpád, one of a class who profess to be Kshatriyas, and who usually consort with the royal family of Travancore:—

"Parasu Ráman ordained that only the eldest son in a Malayálam Brahman family should marry. How then are the younger sons to attain heaven without children to perform the necessary ceremonies on their behalf? Manu says: 'If there be several brothers, the sons of one brother can perform ceremonies for all, so the sons of the eldest brother may do among the Nambúris.'

"If the eldest son be without issue, he may marry one or two additional wives; but the younger brothers must not marry. The wives, so long as they do not disagree, live together in the same house. If the eldest brother still have no children, or die without issue, the next in succession may marry, and so on.

"Though the wife be alive, and have children, yet if the Brahman is unable to meet the expense of giving his sisters or daughters in marriage, he may, in exchange, take one or two additional females, as wives, from the family to whom he gives wives. Thus accounts will be balanced. Yet, however many wives he may have, only one among their children can marry; and that according to seniority of birth, not of the mother's marriage.

"If in a poor family there be four or five virgins, the eldest son in another family cannot, according to Dharmma Sástra, marry more than three of them in exchange, but may consent to one or two of his younger brothers marrying; but should the younger brother have issue before the elder, the order of seniority of such issue shall not be that of the fathers, but of the children themselves.

"The general rule is that girls should be married before arriving at maturity. But as only one man in a family is at liberty to marry, available husbands are scarce and women plentiful, so it is customary to marry after maturity; and many women are left to live and die in celibacy. Widows are never permitted to re-marry. Marriage of a female after puberty involves the payment of a considerable dowry to the husband.

"Should a Malayálam Brahman die without issue or relatives, leaving a widow and an unmarried daughter only, the widow may cause another Brahman to perform the funeral mourning and oblations for her late husband, and may, in order to continue the family, give him her daughter and the whole of the property.

"If an elder brother die, leaving only an unmarried daughter, the next younger brother should marry to perpetuate the family. The orphan daughter is not to be given in marriage with the whole of the property, but merely with a fair portion.

"Division of family property is forbidden among these, and is not practised. The eldest brother is to see that no loss is suffered by the family; the younger brothers are to remain unmarried, to aid the increase of the family estate as much as possible, and to honour and obey the elder like a father. The eldest alone has authority over the family and the property; the younger sons have merely daily subsistence (for which they may sue at law), and the property can never be divided.

"But if the family be numerous, and one brother wishes to separate and live apart, the *káranavan* (elder brother or manager of the united family) should give him a share sufficient for food and clothing, &c., or may make a regular allowance for this.

"Those who can claim support from the common fund are—(1) all the males of the family; (2) their wives; (3) their virgin daughters and sisters; (4) widows—and this for the last two classes only while residing in the house."

Sudras or Chetries have sometimes to pay heavily for engagements with men of higher caste to consort with their families. The nieces of the Cochin Rajahs, whose male children succeed to the throne, form such morganatic alliances with the Nambúris, who, however, lose to some extent in caste, and forfeit all ancestral privileges; and, becoming dependent on their new connections, receive in compensation large marriage portions and separate establishments at the palace. The nieces or sisters of the Travancore royal family intermarry with Chetries only, and this seems to be the sole reason why the Cochin Rajahs are admitted to be superior caste to those of Travancore: the former manage to procure Nambúri Brahmans as consorts; the latter only Chetries of the class called Coil Tamburán.

The Malayálam Sudras, of whom the better class are called NAYARS (or lords), are the bulk of the respectable population—the landholders, farmers, soldiers, officials, and rulers of the country. There seems reason to believe that the whole of the kings of Malabar also, notwithstanding the pretensions set up for them of late by their dependents, belong to the same great body, and are homogeneous with the mass of the people—if, indeed, the so-called Brahmans and Kshatriyas of the Western Coast are not also of identical origin.

Náyar customs admit of no real marriage—nothing, in fact, that can rightly be called marriage, the trivial bond being dissolvable with a word at the will and pleasure of either partner. Such a temporary association, or concubinage, even if it should be continued till death, as it sometimes is (the people being often better than their laws), cannot in any proper sense be dignified by the sacred name of marriage, though in such cases the union may have much of the effect of marriage through the mutual affection and fidelity of the parties.

The females of a wealthy Náyar family, especially where there is but one sister, are visited at their own homes by Brahman paramours, or by persons of their own caste; and their children are reared up in the same house, and inherit from their mothers' brothers, as the fathers have nothing of their own to give them. Females of poorer and less fashionable families go to reside with partners of their own caste, so long as they agree together, or permanently: the average duration of such unions happily is increasing through the spread of civilization and enlightenment.

There is, indeed, a ceremony called "marriage," which is performed in the infancy or childhood of every Sudra girl; but it is the merest pretence—never consummated as a marriage, and conferring no connubial claims or obligations on the nominal bridegroom, who has thenceforth no further connection, but rather serving to set the girl at liberty, as soon as she arrives at maturity, to form temporary associations, or to change them as she pleases.

The Malayálam Sudra laws are as follows:—

Sudra women usually marry in their own caste, but sometimes are married by men of higher caste. But the mere ceremony of marriage does not make her a wife, unless the same man should also "give cloth" and cohabit with her. The trifling ceremony of "giving cloth" is rarely omitted in any case of cohabitation. It is not now usual for a woman to enter into such concubinage with several men at one time, except she resides with several who are brothers. Nor can she ever associate with a man of lower caste. In no case can an inferior male have intercourse with a female of superior class.

Their children have no claim to inherit from the father. The nearest heirs of a Sudra man are his mother, brothers, sisters, and sisters' children. The woman's property goes first to her children, male and female.

The Náyar family is undivided, and by theory the ancestral property is impartible, though it sometimes is divided by consent of all the members, and this should be more and more allowed and approved of for the advancement of the country and the welfare of society. The family property is enjoyed by all in common as a kind of commonwealth or civil family, administered by a *káranavan*, or head of the family—either the maternal uncle, or the eldest brother. The common property is vested in him as executive officer or trustee, but without power to make arbitrary alienation. He is authorised to alienate it only to meet necessities, in order to save the family from greater loss, or for some such similar purpose. The theory is that the unanimous consent of every co-proprietor is required to each valid act of the *káranavan*, because each member claims, not through another, but through himself. This would make the transaction of business well-nigh impossible, but for various legal rules; as, for example, it is presumed that every act is done by him for the good of the family, and the negative must be proved by a complainant, which is difficult. A transfer of land by a single member is quite invalid: at least one other member of the family must sign the document, and in fact all should do so.

Each member of the *Tarawád*, "household," is legally entitled only to subsistence, and the acquisitions of each merge in the common fund, excepting movables and jewels individually acquired by gift or otherwise.

A man's sister's son, and a woman's own son, as their respective nearest blood relatives, perform (if their age permits) the funeral rites on their decease, and observe mourning, remaining one year without shaving or cutting the hair.

Should a Náyar woman, after bearing a son to a man, reject the latter, he having presented to her some property, then bear children to another man and receive some property from him also, the whole property is common to her and her children. But if the grant was made in the name of particular children, it is theirs individually.

The Náyar **ceremony called "marriage"** is celebrated as follows:—

Every girl must somehow get married with the *táli* (marriage badge, a small gold ornament threaded on a cotton cord), before the age of eleven, to avoid reproach from friends and neighbours. In case of need, a sword may even be made to represent a bridegroom. The ceremony may be performed for nine or ten girls at one time. The *pandal*, or marriage shed, is built and decorated in special style for the more distinguished families. On the day previous to the marriage there is an observance called "changing of clothes," when the brides are brought into the shed, clothed with new clothes and gorgeously adorned. Some relative usually acts as bridegroom, for which he receives a present of money; or a Malayálam Brahman is invited for the purpose. An astrologer having previously determined the auspicious hour for the marriage, and the agreement of the bridegroom's natal star with that of the bride, the former is met in procession, his feet are washed by the bride's brothers, to each of whom he presents a piece of cloth, and he is then seated along with the bride on a board covered with cloth, the *manavadei*, or marriage-altar. Then the *márán*, or drummer, places a light in the front yard along with a measure containing paddy, some cocoanuts, flowers, betel, &c., and the cousins of both bride and groom sing a bridal song. At the propitious moment the *táli* is tied. If the make-believe bridegroom be a Brahman, one will suffice for all, and he ties the *táli*, beginning from the eldest girl to the youngest in due order. Often there is one boy for each girl. Finally the Brahman washes his hands in expiation of the sin against caste, and in token that he has nothing further to do with the brides, receives his dues according to the number of girls, and goes off. The ordinary officiating bridegroom receives at the end of the ceremonies two pieces of new cloth. During the ceremony the musicians play, and the women present make a curious cry called *kurava*.

In a Sudra "marriage" recently witnessed in South Travancore, a *manavadei* was put in the centre of the pandal, the bride and bridegroom were seated upon it, and a Brahman guru was performing the ceremonies. Near the manavadei stood a small image of Pilleiyar, made of cow-dung, ornamented with garlands, and before it was placed some boiled rice, a measure full of rice, and a light. A silk towel was spread on the ground, and a grinding-stone laid upon it, which was taken and first given into the hands of the father and mother of the bride, who gave it into the hands of the bride, and she again into the hands of the bridegroom. He having this on his hands, they both came round the *manavadei* three times, then laid it on the same silk towel. After this the bridegroom put the *táli* on the neck of the bride, while the Brahman priest was uttering some mantrams. Then the couple were led into the house.

Four days are spent in feasting and merriment; then a ceremony called "bathing" is observed, at which the *máráns* must be present, as well as the relatives. On the fourth day, the bride and bridegroom go to a river in procession with music to bathe, and ceremonies are performed the same as on the first day.

At any time subsequently, the girl may "receive cloth" from any suitable man, and consort with him. There is no fixed rule that the person who "married" her must not "give cloth" to the same girl, and this sometimes happens, but not very frequently. The girl continues to reside with her brother, or in a house built or given by her relatives, and the husband may be sent off at any time. The person who "married" the mother is called by the children "*appan*," the actual father "*achan*."

The ceremony called "giving a cloth," or agreement for concubinage, is also performed in the presence of relatives and neighbours, at an appointed time, usually in the night. The girl is set, with the young man, on a mat on the ground, the emblems called *lingam* and *yoni* being marked in front. A valuable cloth being offered by the youth, the girl asks her uncle, "Shall I receive it?" "Yes." The same question is put to the mother, who also gives her consent. A cheaper cloth is given to the woman's father, mother, sister, brother, and other near relatives.

Rev. J. Abbs, in his "Twenty-two Years in Travancore," gives the following narrative, related to him by a Sudran, which well illustrates the subject in hand:—"Being a tall, handsome man of respectable family, although poor, I was engaged several years ago by two rich men of my own caste to be the husband of their sister. As they did not wish to give me a dowry, or to let their sister leave them, it was agreed that I should have a monthly allowance, go whenever I pleased to see my wife, and when at the house of her brothers, eat in common with the males of the family. This I expected would be permanent. But a few days ago, when I went to the house, I was told by the elder brother that I could not be admitted, as another husband had been chosen for his sister. Her brothers have taken the two children to train them up as the heirs of the family property."

The Ilavars, or cocoa-palm cultivators, who are the highest representatives of the Malayálam low castes, also perform a sham marriage in the infancy of the girl, generally by a near relation: when she is grown up she "receives a cloth," and goes to live with some man of her own caste. Like Sudras, they may separate at any time; but it is proper to call in four respectable men of their caste to see that accounts are duly settled, and to write a deed of separation. Ancestral property, or that acquired by the man before his taking a woman, goes wholly to the children of his sister, not to his own; but property earned by both during the continuance of the union is divided—half to the wife and children, and half to the sisters' children. Some other castes have a similar custom.

On review of these singular laws and usages it will be observed that—

(1) They materially deviate from orthodox Hindu law, and are, in fact, quite opposed to it. They are recognized and administered by the British Indian Courts as a distinct and separate code. According to Hindu law the marriage bond is permanent, and of most sacred obligation—so much so, that the widow can never re-marry, being considered as still virtually a part of her deceased husband. Christian missionaries regard the marriage of Brahmans, Shánárs, and others, as perfectly valid, being a life-long contract, of legal force; but those who have only "given a cloth," and may, therefore, at any moment separate from one another, are required to be re-married in Christian form. Amongst Hindus, children inherit equally, after deducting the widow's share; or, if there be no children, the father succeeds, or the mother. The Malayálam Brahman system may be characterized as "primogeniture run mad." Hindu marriage is monogamous; but Nambúri Brahmans practise polygamy up to the number of seven wives; and Náyars, Ilavars, and others occasionally practise polyandry—that is, a woman will reside with two or more brothers who are unable or unwilling to support a wife for each, as concubine to all. Amongst Hindus, the family property is owned by the members of the family individually in shares, not by the family as a corporation. But in the *Marumakkatáyam* family it is otherwise. Brahmans cannot even adopt a sister's son, or any child whose mother they could not have married; while Malayális ignore their own children, and value their nephews as sons and heirs. By Hindu law, only men and women of the same caste can intermarry. But in Malabar by far the greater number of the Brahman men, as will be obvious, are obliged to cohabit with females of some inferior caste, while the offspring of Sudra women may have either Sudras, Chetries, or Brahmans as fathers; and *no distinction of caste is made from the circumstance of the father's caste.* Those descended from Brahman fathers are simply Sudras like others, and merge with-

out distinction into the caste. Even in the case of the royal families, who can afford always to have Brahmans or Chetries as consorts for their females, their children marry ordinary Náyar women, and fall into the mass of that caste, with no more distinction than the very natural one of having been descended from royal blood. "The king's sons," remarked Forbes, "whether by his wives or concubines, have no privileges annexed to their royal descent; neither are they by birth entitled to any importance in the government."

Under the circumstances described, no widowhood is possible to Marumakkatáya women, while the Hindu widow is for ever incapable of re-marriage. The marked contrariety between the two usages appears in a celebrated case which occurred in 1872, and which still remains a serious blot on the civilization of Travancore. An Iyengár Brahman nobly and courageously gave in marriage again a young virgin daughter who had been left nominally a widow by the death of her betrothed. The father was formally excommunicated from the temple and from the society of his fellow-castemen, and the temple was cleansed at great expense and with solemn ceremonies from the pollution supposed to have been caused by his having entered it after the re-marriage; while on the other hand, about the same time the consort of one of the royal ladies having deceased, a cousin of his was quietly called in soon afterwards to fill his place, with the trifling observance of "giving a cloth."

(2) These regulations are all astutely planned for the exclusive interests of the Malayálam Brahmans, as indeed everything in the State is supposed to be devoted to the enjoyment of this very small minority of the population. They are free from tax on land and from capital punishment; about one-fifth of the annual income of the State is expended on religious entertainments and ceremonies, chiefly for their benefit. Of course the Brahmans of the present day are not the authors of these laws; but they maintain and enforce them, and are prepared to resist any measures of reform. The preface of the native work on this subject, already quoted, says:—

"As Malabar is but a small country, and other countries are extensive, should no exact account of these laws be prepared for the guidance of foreign priests, they may be found fault with, and fall into contempt. And it might come to pass that even Malayális, without sufficient information, might say, Such and such are the traditions and customs of our land, but all men object to them, therefore it will be better for us to adopt the usages of other countries; and thus they may, without fearing to sin, reject the ancient customs and observances prescribed by Parasu Ráman and others."

N

The whole is placed on religious, or rather superstitious grounds. "Parasu Ráman ordained it." This personage may be altogether mythical, or may have been the leader of some immigration of Brahmans into Malabar. Whether the Brahman colonists found such aboriginal laws in operation, and adopted and maintained them for their own convenience and aggrandizement, or whether the present Malayálam Brahmans represent simply the highest class of the primitive inhabitants, raised to this position in imitation of the orthodox Hindu system, by circumstances or by popular vote, it is not easy to discover. But it is clear that they have endeavoured to make the Sudras not only in theory, but in fact, their social slaves, and wicked threats are used to some classes if they do not place their females at the disposal of the Brahmans. G. K. Varmman says.—

"Műttathus marry females of their own caste; but they only perform the customary ceremony, while Brahmans cohabit with them and beget children. Should men of their own caste dare to approach them, it is like incest with a mother—there is no atonement possible for them—and such progeny are sacrilegious!"

No wonder that these and other statements in the same book formed the ground of a complaint in the Courts of Travancore, the decision in which is understood to have been, that they did not constitute a personal libel, but mere historical statements, the accuracy or untruthfulness of which was simply a question for literary debate.

(3) Such loose customs respecting marriage are only suited to semi-civilised races, whose ideas of the sacred bond have not risen much above that of the association of the lower animals. These usages are not far dissevered from promiscuous intercourse of the sexes, or free love. Friar Jordanus, who resided at Quilon, and wrote his description of the Wonders of the East some five centuries and a half ago, assigns as the reason for the nepotistic law the following:—

"In this India, never do even the legitimate sons of great kings, or princes, or barons, inherit the goods of their parents, but only the sons of their sisters; for they say that they have no surety that those are their own sons; but 'tis not so with the sister, for whatever man may be the father, they are certain that the offspring is of their sister, and is consequently thus truly of their blood."

In a note on the above, Colonel Yule says that this remarkable custom of inheritance exists, or has existed, also in Canara; among the aborigines of Hispaniola and tribes of New Granada and Bogota; among negro tribes of the Niger; among certain sections of the Malays of Sumatra ; in the royal family of Tipura and among the Kasias of the Sylhet mountains (both east of Bengal) ; in a district of Ceylon adjoining Bintenne ; in Madagascar ; in the Fiji Islands ; and among the Hurons and Natchez of North America.

(4) This peculiar patriarchal and primitive system seems to suggest that both the Brahmans and Sudras of the Malabar Coast are of homogeneous descent, and of a primeval Turanian race. It appeared to W. Taylor that "the Náyars are the descendants of the aboriginal inhabitants of Kérala, who probably were brought into some measure of civilization by the colonist Brahmans, yet retaining so much of their own manners as to be a people, inclusive of mixed tribes, very different from genuine Hindus. There are traces of resemblance between their customs and those of the Maravars ; and there is little doubt that they were aboriginally portions of one homogeneous, but excessively barbarous people. The Maravars have peculiar customs contrary to those of the Hindus, particularly the frequency of remarrying allowed to the women, either upon voluntary separation from their husbands, or at their death." Dr. Gundert defines the Náyars as the "Sudras of Kérala, raised to the rank of Kshatriyas by their intimate connection with the Brahmans." Thus the so-called Kshatriyas or Chetries of Malabar may be but the higher classes among the Sudras ; indeed, from their usages and history this would appear to be the case. And as it is known that the original partitions of caste early broke down, so that it is difficult to find pure Brahmans or Kshatriyas anywhere, more especially in the south of India, the popular traditions may embody some fragment of truth regarding the transformation of fishermen into Brahmans by Parasuráman investing them with the sacred thread. Dr. W. W. Hunter remarks that the Brahmans throughout India are of two classes—more ancient settlers, and aboriginal superior natives raised, as tradition generally asserts, to this rank. The Namburis, for example, are said to originate from fishermen : they follow different customs from the orthodox caste, allow only the eldest male to marry, practise polygamy, and their ideas of marriage closely resemble those of the aboriginal Náyars. But in spite of their descent from a low caste fisher-tribe and semi-aboriginal customs, they make high claims, and despise other Brahmans. ("Orissa," vol. i. p. 254.)

It will be evident, from the preceding remarks, that under the Marumakkatáyam system of law there is a marked absence of the peculiar advantages and benefits of true marriage, and of family privileges which men highly and justly prize. Virtuous love and the noblest affections, parental rights and domestic order, the obligation to protect wife and children as the weakest party, the right of men and women to domestic felicity, all are more or less ignored ; and this violation of the Divine law carries with it its own punishment, in the promotion of family dissension and of sensuality in various forms.

As to the **evils and inconveniences of nepotism**—

(1) Polygamy, with its accompanying demoralisation and cares, is prescribed to the eldest son of Malayálam Brahmans in order to offspring, in place of the happy marriage of the sons to one wife each.

(2) The revolting system of polyandry is not rare among Sudras, Carpenters, Ilavars, and other Marumakkal castes, and has been thought by some to have been the origin of these laws. But they rather appear to be traceable to the Brahman prohibition of marriage to all but eldest sons.

Rarely is there ever felt such strong and elevated affection in these cases that the brothers quarrel, or are jealous about possession of the common partner ; on the contrary, we have known an elder brother offended because the younger, on becoming a Christian, very properly took a wife to himself.

(3) The natural relationship and reciprocal love of parents and children are interfered with, and perverted by this pernicious law. It is somewhat odd that notwithstanding the introduction and spread of enlightenment among the higher classes in Travancore, so far as to lead to the preparation and publication of interesting native works, some are yet found who are not ashamed to defend this distortion of the law of nature and of God, and to represent the love and relationship of the father as something merely conventional and legal, rather than natural : just as some tribes ludicrously go to the opposite extreme of obliging the mother to rise, and the father to go to bed with the new-born babe.

"The reckoning of blood relationship," says G. K. Varmman, "through the mother is more natural than through the male parent : the latter is rather by a legal rule. Among animals the mother alone cares for the progeny. Amongst men we find by experience that commonly the mother has more affection for the children, the father a little less. But as mankind are rational beings, besides that the father has some parental affection (by nature), he cherishes it also by obligation to law, and on account of the children performing funeral ceremonies for him and inheriting his property. And we see amongst Nepotists greater affection, arising from reason, towards sisters' sons, who are not their own children, and merely by law their heirs and mourners."

Here the love and care and discipline of the father are systematically absent. And if children do not know, or scarcely know, their own fathers, how can they love them? Should there be a natural longing for the love of the father, it cannot be gratified. I have known a fine Sudra youth bitterly lament that his own father, a Brahman, cared nothing for him; and, in fact, the father could not, under any circumstances, eat with him, nor touch him without ceremonial pollution. If in any case we do find the same affection entertained for nephews as for children, it is but a forcing of nature, there being no other way of preserving the unity of the household and family property. Mr. Abbs remarks: "I have often been astonished to observe how natural affection is perverted and transferred by these customs. It was common for a man to have his nephews living in his house and attending to his affairs as sons would have done, while his own children would be with their mother's family at a distance—seldom, if ever, having communion with their father. A Nair came to me one morning and told me very unconcernedly that his wife had died on the preceding day. He was married again in less than three months. In about a twelvemonth afterwards, he came to me weeping bitterly, and told me that he had lost one of his nephews by death, and could not, therefore, attend to his usual vocation for a day or two. I asked him how it was that he grieved so much for his nephew and so little for his conjugal partner; he said that he considered his own sorrow more according to nature, as, being a rich man, when his wife died he could easily obtain another, but, having lost his nephew, he might live to see his estate fall into decay by neglect."

(4) The security of the marriage bond is affected. Indeed, there is no recognized form of marriage by which a Náyar man and woman could bind one another, even if they wished, for life. A poor man engaged as husband by a wealthy family may be sent off at a moment's notice, without wife or child, beggared in the domestic charities as well as in purse: sometimes for failing to send a present on festival days, or on other trivial pretexts, he is discarded. Or his partner may be seduced away from him by a richer or younger man, and he left heart-broken and desolate. Still less has a woman any assurance that she will not be deserted in her advancing years, when her need is greatest, though she had been maintained while young and fair. We have known a Sudra, hard to satisfy, and of an imperious temper, who had eleven women, one after another. A Sudra woman may be dismissed with a word, "Go, leave the house," and another may be brought into her place next day. Concubines are frequently changed before having children, or even after bearing several children to one man.

(5) Much misery and heart-burning are caused to the victims of this social tyranny, the youngest sons of Brahmans being pro-

hibited honourable marriage with persons of their own class, and forced to form illegitimate connections with strangers, and the larger proportion of Brahman women mercilessly doomed, notwithstanding the high estimation in which the Hindus hold marriage, to perpetual celibacy, with all its risks and privations. Many of these females live and die unmarried: yet, strange to say, the corpse undergoes all the ceremonies of marriage. To prevent their falling into unchastity, they are closely shut up and guarded. Occasionally they do fall, and then are irrevocably expelled from family, friends, and society. In such case they must join the lower castes, to whom they were formerly sold as slaves and concubines, or go over to the Roman Catholic or Syrian Christians, uniting with some one in marriage. And before a case of this kind is decided by a committee of the heads of the Brahman caste, the expense of the investigation is sometimes so great as to ruin the family.

(6) It is evident that sensuality and lust are fostered and encouraged by such usages. The union of the sexes is viewed in the lowest and most degrading light, and the whole country becomes saturated with immorality and vice. Castes which have the institute of marriage, as Shánárs and others, are tempted to adopt more or less of these rules; and some branches of these castes have become so corrupted. Individuals of some castes are allowed to form connections with Sudra females which are to them irregular, but which they attempt to justify by pleading the Náyar usages; and many cases of prostitution occur, even among the respectable classes.

(7) Community of property naturally tends to discourage individual activity, personal exertion, and independence of spirit. The expenditure of a large family thus united may be less than if divided into several separate families, but the aggregate income would be much larger, and the peace and comfort enjoyed by the latter plan would be incomparably greater. Misery, idleness, ignorance, and poverty follow from these laws; life is wasted in listless inactivity. Such a home is "no true home, but rather a sort of family club, where all the male members of the household take their meals together. Employed or unemployed, active or indolent, he and his may live here and take their share with the rest as long as there is property enough, or employment enough, among them all to keep things going."

Sir H. S. Maine observes: "Where people are living in a state of Arcadian simplicity, without the desire or the possibility of advancement, the family system is a very sound one, as it prevents properties being split up, and enables a number of persons to be supported with a maximum of comfort on the minimum of means. But as soon as society begins to dash ahead, then the effect of the corporate union is deadening in the direct ratio of its strictness. Who will work with full energy when the benefit of his labour goes not solely, nor even chiefly, to himself? Who will work at all when some one else is working for him? Ingenuity could not contrive a more effectual plan for damping the spirit of the industrious, and extinguishing the spirit of the idle. It makes the best member of the family a slave, that the others may be sloths."

(8) Though some large Náyar families are known to live in peace and unity, the tendency of the law of nepotism is to promote family dissensions and discord. The Marumakkatáyam system of law is in itself intricate and complicated, and is one of the most difficult to administer in Travancore, because of the cheating to which it gives rise. A junior member of the family pretends that he owes a sum of money to a friend, with whom he is in collusion, and whom he gets to file a suit against him for the sum, in the hope of somehow squeezing it out of the *Tarawád* property. Or, money is lent to one who seems, from all outward appearance, to be the actual manager of the family, till it is discovered long afterwards that he is not in this position. Complaints are frequent against the *káranavan* that he is dissipating the common fund; he is provoked, and sometimes becomes really indifferent to the general welfare. Since many individuals in each caste, sometimes even two brothers, bear the same name, a member of the *Tarawád* may have the same name as his *káranavan*. He asserts that it is his own name that appears in the deeds and legal documents; and may thus succeed in gaining possession of property.

A man may be left with several sisters, all of whose children are dependent solely upon him. On the other hand, there may be two or more uncles responsible for the support and training of the children of one sister, and disputing among themselves as to the share of expenditure devolving upon each. Amongst the Ilavars and others, the temporary wife sometimes secretly accumulates property in anticipation of being left unprovided for by the death of her husband; or she obtains, by clever management from him while he lives some gift of property.

The sons might, of course, be quite content to inherit from the uncle, and to profit by this law if he be more wealthy than the father; but cases have occurred in which the sons felt sorely aggrieved by their unnatural exclusion, and desired a change of the usage. A century and a half ago, two of the sons of a recently deceased Rajah of Travancore were slain by the new king, because they demanded the right of succession to the throne instead of their cousin, the nephew of the deceased.

There are, it is true, one or two incidental advantages of this system; or rather, we should say, there are certain evils of the orthodox Hindu social system which it is impossible to unite with the nepotistic *régime*. For instance, Malayálam Brahman girls are not married till after puberty; and Sudra girls, though nominally married, are usually left free till the same period, when they enjoy more or less freedom of choice in the selection of their temporary partners. From this curious law of succession, the sister, being the mother of the heirs, becomes a person of great importance; daughters are longed for, and sons treated as of less account. The whole arrangement tends to give Náyar women (though not Brahmanis) much influence, and admits of their being to some extent educated (1·19 per cent. of their number), and saves them from the sad privations of Brahmanical widowhood. But it will be observed that it is all for the pleasure of the Brahmans; and the same benefits would accompany any just or rational marriage law. The end should be attained by other means. No mercy is shown to the Brahman women: the men only have the whole world (down to a certain grade) cast at their feet. The only hope of continued subsistence and increased comfort to the dense and ever multiplying population of India consists in the adoption of prudential restraints on improvident and early marriages irrespective of the means of subsistence; but the plan adopted by the Malayálam Brahmans only removes the burden of providing for their progeny from the shoulders of this small but influential and wealthy community (10,762, or a half per cent. of the total population) to those of the more numerous and sturdy Sudra caste (440,932 = 19·1 per cent.).

Some of the more enlightened and educated Náyars are now beginning to realise their degradation, and to rebel against the Brahmanical tyranny, and absurd and demoralising laws under which they are placed. The Nánjinád Vellálars have addressed petitions to the Maharajah, praying to legalise their reversion to the law of nature instead of nepotism. This may easily be done if all agree. Nepotism is felt by a considerable number of Sudras to be a special grievance because a man's own acquisitions, as well as the ancestral property, devolve to nephews; and only during his own life can he bestow anything on his sons. Even this is difficult of accomplishment. Many intend to do so, but go on procrastinating till it is too late. Ilavars have not such a grievance, as half of a man's own earnings goes by law to the children. Many Sudras would like a change, but it is impossible, they say, "unless the Maharajah commanded it, and led the way." It is not easy to see how the native Government could make such a change before public opinion is ripe for it and demands it. Division of property and individual ownership might, however, at once be allowed, as throughout British India; and the clear head of Sir Madava Row many a year ago discerned the necessity for this. In his Administration Report for *M.E. 1050* he says: "It is evident that some effective legislative action is required without delay in certain directions. For instance, it has to be declared lawful for any member of a Malayáli (native) family to insist upon a division of common property so far as he or she is individually concerned, if he or she wishes to separate. Not that such a law would be generally acted upon at once: the feeling in favour of relatives living together in an undivided state of property is too strong to yield to reason in the present generation. But it is obviously the province of Government to see that a general feeling of the kind does not operate as an instrument of tyranny over individuals." We fear this enlightened intention has dropped almost entirely out of sight, and that the tendency of more recent action has been rather to rivet more tightly the chains of this barbarous system of law.

But the Government has no authority whatever over the social usages of Brahmans. A good deal of controversy has taken place on the subject in the public prints, and a society for the reform of the Malabar laws of marriage (and inheritance) has been formed at Calicut by the leaders of the Náyar community, especially those educated in English.

Besides being opposed by orthodox Hindus and Muhammadans, this system of laws also forms an obstacle in the way of the spread of Christianity. Civil rights are lost by the change of religion. R. Moothookristna Naidoo says, in his work on the subject: "Females who will not obey their *káranavan*, and who apostatise to other religions, lose all right both to subsistence and inheritance from the family property." A *káranavan* is also removed should he break caste by joining another religion. Christian fathers have been exposed to the interposition, in violation of natural rights, of the authority of the maternal uncle of their children to the extent of withdrawing them from their own control, and of preventing them from being received with the parents into the Christian community. The paternal right of converts to Christianity, who may have children at the time of their conversion, ought to be fully secured to them, notwithstanding anything to the contrary which may have obtained in the caste or people to whom they previously belonged.

Converts to Christianity in Travancore are liable also to be deprived of inheritable property on account of their change of religion. In some instances, as appears from the decrees of the old Appeal Court, Christians have been thus deprived of their property, though in other cases property has been awarded to Christians which belonged to their ancestors, or relatives who were not Christians. And in a recent case, where an Ilavan convert to Christianity has long individually enjoyed property derived from ancestors, and paid tax for it separately in his own name, which, therefore, he devolved by will to his children, the decision of the Lower Court in favour of the will has been reversed by the High Court, on the ground that ancestral property *can never be divided*, and, therefore, a share in it cannot be willed away to children, or others than the nephews. Such a decision is prohibitory of all reform in the future, and scarcely in consonance with the altered habit of the people, which no longer entirely ignores the paternal relation. Objectionable laws and customs are sometimes brought into prominence, sanctioned and perpetuated by judicial recognition. "There are cases," says Lyall, "in which the action of law courts, in stereotyping and enforcing invariably customs that were naturally very elastic and varying, tend to check the natural modifications according to circumstances, the sloughing off of decayed forms." The law should be adopted in Travancore which was passed by the late East India Company in 1850 (Act XXI), that no one should suffer by loss of property, or in any way, on account of a change in religion. In one case, that of a Hindu dying without heirs, except such as have become converts to a different religion, the Sirkar has relinquished its claim to escheat, and permits the property to descend to the natural heirs independently of religious considerations (Procl. No. 90 of 1869). But where there are Hindu heirs, converts still lose their rights.

An additional difficulty is also cast in the way of Christian converts, who had formerly belonged to distinct castes, intermarrying, as the domestic usages and the laws of inheritance vary so widely. So in regard to Christians seeking to adopt the law of nature and of Scripture, in leaving their property to their own children by will. By the law of British India this may be done; but there is some uncertainty as to whether it is yet allowed in native States or not. It is of great importance to future progress that this right be granted. Property might easily be divided according to existing customs of Marumakkatáyam which are occasionally applied, and each might then enjoy in future his individual estate, and hand it down to his children, like other Hindus, by will; or, if intestate, in accordance with the provisions of the Indian Succession Act of 1865, with any modifications that might seem demanded by the circumstances.

Some effective form of marriage, instead of "cloth giving," might also be settled on, and left to the option of individuals desiring to adopt it, which would no doubt come into repute in course of time with the more intelligent and well-disposed Náyars. It is said that some such Act has already been drafted in Malabar, intended for proposal to the Madras Government.

Any hasty or ill-considered attempt at change or legislative reform could not but cause infinite confusion. The facts should first be made accurately known, and a more enlightened public opinion created by free ventilation of the question. But it is obvious that great difficulty would be found in altering, even for the better, the law of inheritance obtaining amongst a million or two of people, most of whom are possessed of some property. One singular advantage of the monarchic form of government is the avoidance, by the law of hereditary succession, of disputes as to succession, and of discussion as to the personal merits of candidates for power. An attempt to change the nepotistic law would naturally and reasonably aggrieve the next legal and expectant heirs according to the present system. It so happens, however, that while in the Cochin State, which is but a small kingdom, with a population of only three-quarters of a million, no less than twenty-two princes are heirs expectant to the throne, and form a heavy burden on the public for maintenance in idleness and luxury; in Travancore, the only other, and much more important, State in which the nepotistic law carries with it royal power, there are but four princes still to reign, and no possibility of more, except by adoption. The family, in fact, judged by their nepotistic law, has come to an end, as there are no sisters alive of any of the present heirs, to continue the nepotistic line. Indeed, all but the next heir are themselves the sons of ladies adopted some twenty-five years ago for the purpose of continuing the succession. As these princesses have no daughters, the dynasty is again near to extinction after the present four princes shall have had their turn, unless the children of the present Maharajah, or of future sovereigns, are taken into account. It happens, therefore, that it would be easy to alter the Travancore succession by the simple plan of adopting no more females into the family: no one would be personally aggrieved or injured, and sons or heirs of the body might succeed thenceforward. There is no need to manufacture factitious heirs when there are natural ones. Who knows whether the next fifty years may not bring round such general enlightenment, or such a spread of true Christianity amongst the higher classes (which we look upon as the only true remedy for all social disorder), as to admit of the possibility of even this reform?

CHAPTER XVIII.

THE KUDUMI, OR HINDU TUFT OF HAIR.

THE propriety, or otherwise, of Native Christians retaining the *kudumi*, or top-knot of hair worn by Hindus, has for the last twenty years been greatly discussed amongst missionaries in South India, and upon it opinions are seriously divided. To aid those who wish to arrive at a right conclusion on the subject, we purpose to lay before them our notes and experience for the consideration of all interested. The moot point is—Whether is the wearing of the *kudumi* a national and respectable usage—a mere fashion depending on personal taste, and therefore to be included in the category of things absolutely indifferent to the Christian believer—or a badge of Hinduism—of religious significance, and consequently to be rejected by those who profess to follow the Lord Jesus Christ? This question is in many respects similar to and affiliated with, that of Hindu caste, the identity of which with social rank, or its un-Christian and heathenish character, was long debated; and judgment in it is now given almost unanimously by evangelical missionaries *against* the observance of caste. Hindu caste and the kudumi appear to be closely associated. Those who retain the former invariably retain also the latter; and sometimes but a half-hearted opposition is given to caste by those who defend the use of the kudumi.

The scale for and against the kudumi has vibrated variously at various times. In the early stages of Protestant missions, the matter appears to have excited but little attention, being swallowed up in the more comprehensive and burning question of caste and its evils. Yet when a mission was evangelical, and its founders careful, the kudumi was generally objected to and discarded. In the Church Mission in North Travancore, it was naturally laid aside from the first, the clear and united testimony of the ancient Syrian Christian Church, the Roman Catholics, and the Muhammadans having guided the English missionaries to a sound decision. In the London Mission in

Travancore, little attention appears to have been paid to the subject; but the Rev. J. C. Thompson, who arrived in 1827, was one who took a zealous interest in it. Mr. Abbs from 1837 required the relinquishment of the kudumi by all communicants and mission agents. Mr. Cox also bore testimony that "the greatest care has always been taken not only to remove every mark of caste and heathenism, as the kudumi, &c., but also to root out every lurking remnant of those evils;" and Mr. Baylis wrote of the Neyoor District under his care—"By degrees I got all the agents and church members to leave off the kudumi, and then never admitted or baptized with it; and it became customary to leave it off in Nagercoil District." But within the last dozen years a change has gradually taken place. Though the missionaries, we think, generally dislike the top-knot, they do not seem to feel it their duty, or perhaps quite practicable, to insist on its entire abandonment.

In Tinnevelly, definite action was taken respecting caste and the kudumi in 1846, as described by the late Rev. J. Thomas in the following terms. "When in the year 1846, the Committee of the C. M. S. determined upon presenting to the Bishop for ordination several of their catechists, they resolved that caste should be entirely relinquished by the candidates, and that the kudumi should also be removed. Mr. Thomas went to Madras in company with Mr. Pettitt to confer with the Committee on the subject. At that time there were several members who from their knowledge of Hindu customs and literature were thoroughly competent to deal with such a subject. We found on our return to Tinnevelly, that there was no hesitation on the part of the candidates to comply with the Committee's resolutions. The Rev. J. Devasagayam had been in holy orders for many years previously, and had never worn the kudumi."

The learned Bishop Caldwell, however, wrote in 1867 a pamphlet on the other side of the question, regarding the top-knot as merely a national fashion, and as rather a mark of civilisation, refinement, and adornment, than as possessing any particular religious import, and now the kudumi is allowed to a very large extent in the missions of the C. M. S., as well as in those of the Propagation Society.

The light in which the top-knot is regarded in some other parts of India is fairly stated by Mr. Thomas in the same paper. "Throughout the whole of India, all Protestant missionaries of every denomination (except indeed the old German Missionaries of Tranquebar and Tanjore, with their successors in the Tamil Mission field) have been led, and no doubt after much anxious inquiry, to insist upon the removal of the kudumi at baptism, as a sign of sincerity. Such is, I believe, the uniform custom in

Bengal—on the Western Coast among the German Evangelical Missionaries—and at Masulipatam by missionaries of the C. M. S.; and we may be well assured that the missionaries of North India, whose knowledge of Sanskrit literature is a necessary qualification to their usefulness in that part of the country, must have made themselves thoroughly acquainted with all the adjuncts of the kudumi question before deciding that it ought to be removed by their converts. We may also feel satisfied that a man of Mr. Noble's stamp at Masulipatam, having Mr. Sharkey as his coadjutor, would not lightly require a sacrifice on the part of his converts which was not indispensably necessary. To the Brahman, the removal of the kudumi and string is considered as equivalent to death; and yet his Brahman converts at baptism willingly gave up the string and kudumi, with the conviction that this was imperatively necessary to prove that they fully and entirely renounced heathenism, and willingly took up the cross to follow Christ." ("Ind. Evan. Review," April, 1876.)

In the vigorous Arcot Mission of the Dutch Reformed Church, the views held on this question are thus described by Dr. Jared Scudder: "With reference to the kudumi, my own opinions are very clear and definite. I believe it to be a distinctive mark of heathenism. I am thankful to say that in our Mission we have never baptized a kudumi, and I hope we never shall. . . . We have, from the first, enforced excision of the tuft, it being a principle with us that the kudumi must fall before baptism; and once off, it does not often grow again. . . . I am persuaded that it is a badge of heathenism. Some time ago, a learned Brahman in one district was asked what would be the effect of the removal of the kudumi. 'When the kudumi goes, Brahmanhood goes,' was his significant reply. Judging from personal observation and conference with others, I feel pretty sure that no missionary, however tolerant he may be of the kudumi in practice, likes his native ministers and catechists to wear it." (Bang. Conf. Report, Vol. I. p. 316.)

To similar purport are the words of Dr. E. Scudder of the same Mission. "The view we have held from the origin of our Mission is that the kudumi is one of the strongest links in the chain of religious superstition and caste feeling. Our people, therefore, all excise it when they join us. Very little objection is made to this, and their heads certainly present a more civilized and Christian aspect when the European mode of wearing the hair is substituted. Whether an evil or not in itself considered, the kudumi is certainly productive of discord and mischief in its relations to the Church of Christ. Formerly it was regarded as heathenish by the majority of Christians, and the applicant for church membership was required to excise it before admission. Now there appears to be a disposition to ignore it.—There is much confusion, and not unfrequent heart-burnings, among the Christians of different societies. The advocates of the tuft are not willing to abandon it, even when they enter communities where the opposite practice prevails; and hence the latter are made to feel more forcibly their singularity."

In Mysore, the kudumi is cut off by the Wesleyan Missionaries. Rev. W. Burgess, of Madras, considers that "this practice in its origin is undoubtedly heathenish, and had a religious significance; though not clear in his own mind that it is now thus to be regarded."

Rev. B. Rice, L.M.S., Bangalore, thinks it is, "if not a mark of heathenism, at least of caste, and a disposition to fraternize as much as possible with the ways of the Hindu world."

"In the Telugu country," says Rev. F. W. N. Alexander, "the kudumi is not known anywhere. It is a universal opinion that it is completely heathenish, and we should set our faces against it." Mr. Hay, of Vizagapatam, says: "The change is so great in embracing Christianity that all caste ideas are completely given up. The Hindu kudumi is given up, and the hair worn in some other way." So also the late Mr. Beynon, of Bellary: "Kudumi and other caste and heathen customs have never been allowed amongst our Christians." Rev. J. H. Walton also writes: "We discussed the subject in Bellary; and after consulting the opinions, not only of influential native Christians, but also of leading orthodox Hindus, we considered that the tuft of hair was so intimately associated with heathen practices, so much an evidence of worldliness in those Christians who wore it, and so diametrically opposed to the apostolic doctrine contained in the 11th chapter of the first Epistle to the Corinthians, that it was desirable to disuse the custom among the members of our churches."

Rev. J. B. Graeter, of Mangalore, points out that in Lev. 19, 27, the practice is condemned, though the passage may not literally refer to the kudumi.

Rev. P. Rajahgopaul, of Madras, remarks, "Most of our pupils were of caste families; and when a man became a true believer, and wished to enter the Christian Church, at once the kudumi went, and there was no more trouble about caste." And Dr. James Glasgow, of Guzerat, informs us: "The top-knot is voluntarily cut off by converts of the Irish Presbyterian Mission; if they did not do so, the Missionaries would insist upon its relinquishment."

In order to form a correct judgment upon the question before us, it is essential to note **the position of the kudumi in the system of Hinduism**, and also the light in which it is regarded in the present day. On these considerations necessarily depends its practical treatment in the Christian Church. Now it is an undoubted fact that the *kudumi* (called also *caula*, *chonti*, *shendie*, &c.) is one of the most important observances of Hinduism. The remarks of Professor Monier Williams in his useful "Manual of Hinduism" (pp. 59-60) seem to us abundantly sufficient to set the whole matter at rest. He says:—

"As an unmarried student, the young Brahman was to reside with his preceptor until he had gained a thorough knowledge of the three Vedas. He was to go through twelve 'Sanskaras,' or purificatory rites, which purify a man from the taint of sin derived from his parents, and which are enjoined, with certain variations, on all the three first classes alike. They are as follows:—

1. Garbha dhána, ceremony on conception; 2. Punsavana, on the first indication of a living male's conception; 3. Simanton nayan, arranging the parting of the mother's hair in the fourth, sixth, or eighth month of pregnancy; 4. Jata karman, touching an infant's tongue with honey and ghí thrice at birth; 5. Náma karana, giving a name on the tenth or twelfth day after birth; 6. Nishkramana, taking out the child in the fourth month to see the sun; 7. Annaprásana, feeding it with rice between the fifth and eight month; 8. C'úda karman, or c'aula, *tonsure of the hair, except one lock on the crown of the head*, in the third year; 9. Upanayana, induction into the order of a 'twiceborn' man by investiture with the sacred cord; 10. Kesánta, cutting off the hair, performed on a Brahman in his sixteenth year, on a Kshatriya in his twenty-second, on a Vaisya in his twenty-fourth; 11. Samávartana, solemn return home after completing a course of study with a preceptor; 12. Viváha, marriage, which completes the purification and regeneration of the 'twiceborn.'

Of the above rites—1, 2, 3, and 10 are little observed. The other eight are more worthy of attention; 8 and 9 are of *considerable legal importance*, even in the present day, and 7 is still practised; 7 and 12 are said to be the only rites allowed Sudras; and the 12th, viváha, marriage, is a religious duty incumbent on all persons alike."

To the same effect writes Dr. John Wilson, of Bombay, in his work on "Indian Caste" (p. 15): "Caste has its marks, and signs, and symbols, and symbolical acts, as well as its laws and customs; and very great stress is laid by it on their constant exhibition. The grand index of Hinduism is *the tuft of hair* on the crown of the head—called in Sanskrit *chúda* or *shikha*, in Maratti *shendi*, in Bengali *tika*, and in Tamil *kudumi*—which is left there on the performance of the sacrament of tonsure on the first or third year after birth in the case of the three first classes of Hindus. In consequence of this mark Hinduism is popularly known as the *shendi-dharma*, or religion of the shendi."

Until the kudumi is worn, the Brahman child is but a Sudra, and every Shastri attests the religious character of this symbol; and this is as expressive to-day as it ever was. Balfour, in the "Encyclopædia of India," defines the *chonti* or *kudumi* as "*among Hindus*, a tuft of hair left unshaved on the top of the head."

For some of the actual **present-day uses** of this heathen badge see a very instructive essay by a native Christian—Mr. V. Samuel, of Nagercoil—published in the *Indian Evangelical Review* for October, 1876. He shows that the kudumi is in Travancore fully saturated with superstition, and inseparably associated with Hinduism and caste. On the sixteenth day after the birth of a child, the father bathes, and, taking a few drops of water from his wet kudumi, pours them into the child's mouth: then, for the first time, he sees and handles the child. When the child's head is first shaved, the barber is invited, incense is offered to the image of Pilleiyar, and the shaving of the greater part of the hair is done by the barber, the remainder by a Brahman with certain mantrams. The last portion of the hair is enclosed in a silver case and tied around the waist of the child as an amulet. On the child's first going to school the teacher touches him by the kudumi, divides it into three parts, and after having plaited them together at the crown of the head, worships it.

The chief use of the tuft, however, is to perform the funeral ceremony necessary for the salvation of the father. "In order to quench the hell fire, the son must uncover the sacred portion of his head by shaving off the Kudumi, put upon it a new pot full of water, that it may attract from it the virtue of quenching the hell fire, and walk with it three times around the deceased parent, each time cutting a new hole in the pot, that the water may spout out as he walks along. The third time he must break the pot at the head of the bed of the deceased, and pour a few drops of this sacred water into the mouth of the parent, as the parent formerly did to the son. The cutting off the kudumi on the occasion of the death of the parent, is not regarded as a sign of sorrow, but is considered an essential requisite for performing the funeral ceremony which is absolutely necessary for the eternal welfare of the deceased parent.

No one but the heir of the deceased cuts off the kudumi, and that at no other time but on the occasion of the parent's death. A father may lose a dozen children, but he never thinks of shaving his kudumi as a sign of sorrow. A man may have six sons, of whom only the eldest cuts off his kudumi on the occasion of death." Is not this literally "making baldness between the eyes for the dead"? (Deut. xiv. 1.)

With this we may compare the classical custom of cutting off the hair and devoting it to a deceased father, or as an offering to appease the infernal gods. In the Choephoræ of Æschylus, Orestes at the tomb of his murdered father says:

> ——— Thou dread shade
> At whose high tomb I bow, shade of my father!
> Hear me, O hear! To thee *these crisped locks*,
> Once sacred to the nurture-giving stream of Inachus,
> In the anguish of my soul *I now devote.*

Compare also the curious custom of the Buddhist priests in China, who have small round bald spots on the head, increasing in number with their rank in the priesthood. They take a small candle, or some such combustible, and set it on fire on the head till it burns down to the flesh, leaving a bald spot. This is done again when the next step in the priesthood is obtained—therefore, a purely religious badge.

Quotations are given from commentators on Lev. xix. 27, from which the following sentences may be extracted:—"This kind of coiffure had a *highly idolatrous meaning*, and it was adopted with some slight variation by almost all idolaters in ancient times."———"The Gentiles cut their hair for the worship of devils or idols, to whom young men used to consecrate their hair, as Homer, Plutarch, and many others write. God would not have his people agree with idolaters, neither in their idolatries, nor in excessive mourning, no, nor so much as in the appearance and outward significations or *expressions thereof.*"

From these and other considerations, the essayist with great reason asks, "Is not this reason quite sufficient for the Christians of the present time to cut off their kudumi, especially in the infant state of the native church, when they should be taught, not only to keep themselves aloof from superstitions, but also to show their aversion by acting quite contrary to them?"

In deciding the question before us, it is not the historical or traditional origin of the kudumi that is of primary importance, but the actual feeling of the Hindu mind upon the subject—the associations connected with the kudumi, or any other custom—and the influence which the observance or abandonment of the practice is seen to exercise upon converts to Christianity. There are some questions, too, that are settled by a kind of spiritual instinct, rather than by logical reasoning alone, or specific texts of Scripture. We generally find that when men become decided on the subject of personal religion, card playing, dancing, and theatres, and in India, the tomtom used in demon worship, flaunting processions, and wasteful and extravagant display at weddings, are given up, and people of evangelical views and earnest piety are fairly well agreed on these matters. There is greater care to live separated from the world, and to avoid everything that leads the heart away from God. In consulting with native Christians as to the propriety of permitting or discouraging various doubtful native customs, we have often found them saying, "this, or that, must be allowed to the new Christians, else they will be dissatisfied or leave us; but the mission agents do not approve of it, and ought not to practise it." The relinquishment of the kudumi by the native clergy of Tinnevelley doubtless had its rise in some such feeling, that though it may be allowable to the common people, yet the clergy are expected to be very much their superiors in the strict avoidance of whatever is of doubtful propriety. Even were we to take the lowest ground, that the kudumi is to be classed with gold ornaments and fine clothes, we think that the excessive pride, the intense love of the world, and the characteristic weakness for vain display before heathen neighbours, and passion for paltry fame exhibited by many Hindus, need correction; and that it is thoroughly in accordance with the spirit of the admonitions of Scripture to renounce the kudumi.

Even granting that it *were lawful* for native Christians to wear the tuft, we have no hesitation in saying that in Travancore and Malabar, at least, it is, in the Scriptural sense, highly *expedient* for the sake of others to relinquish it. There the Syrian Christians, Roman Catholics, and Muhammadans have left it off on the ground that it is a badge of heathenism, which it certainly is to all intents and purposes in that part of India. It is not right to shock the feelings of other Christians by retaining such a mark of Hinduism. Not long ago a native missionary from the Tamil country was itinerating amongst the Syrian Christians. Lodging in one of their houses, his servant, who wore the kudumi, entered the kitchen to prepare some food. The women of the house, seeing the tuft of hair, cried out, "A heathen has come in here!" and fled in dismay. The missionary, who himself did not wear the kudumi, had to explain, with much shame, that his attendant was not a heathen, but a Christian.

There can be no doubt that the kudumi is *associated in the minds of Hindus* with the profession of Hinduism, and with heathen ceremonies and ideas, and that, therefore, it should be given up by native converts, so as to separate them completely, as far as this goes, from heathen influences. Of course our readers will understand that only that particular mode of cutting the hair, so as to leave a central tuft, which *has a special significance* among Hindus (as the blue ribbon has amongst temperance reformers), is objectionable, and that the hair may be freely worn in any European fashion, or shaved off periodically as most Hindus prefer, or in any other form which *has not this special significance.* Without the queue a Hindu cannot perform the appointed ceremonies, nor retain his caste standing, although certain curious and anomalous exceptions to this rule have been pointed out.

In the theistic Tamil poem, Siva Vákyam, the kudumi is opposed along with other Hindu practices, as in the familiar quotation:—

"The four Vedas, the sacrificial Kusa grass, the kudumi, the ascetic's staff which Brahmans carry—when (you were) born, were the Brahman's cord and the kudumi born with you?"

Fully a century ago, Father Bartolomeo remarked that "when a Brahman by his own fault has forfeited his cord, *or his tuft of hair,* he loses all his privileges, and can no longer discharge any of the sacerdotal functions." (Voyage, p. 298.)

The relinquishment of the kudumi has, therefore, a far greater influence in separating Christians from heathenism, and distinguishing them on all occasions as Christians, and so reminding them and others of their obligations to act consistently under circumstances of temptation, than some would be inclined to give it credit for. It will be found that by far the greatest number of thoroughly *earnest* and sincere Hindu converts acknowledge that they ought to give up this custom. Take, as an instance, the following sentences in the autobiography of a convert to Christianity applying for baptism in Madras in 1853. He says, "As in the last assault they laid hold of the hair of my head (kudumi) I had that removed. This *effectually severed my connection with Hindus,* for without the hair as it is commonly worn, I could not maintain my position among them. It is one of the marks of Hindu idolatry, and removing it has effectually cut me off from them." The rejection of the tuft is thus a proof of sincerity, an invariable and noticeable mark of having fully relinquished heathenism and caste. The Rev. J. D. Thomas, of Madras, remarks that he noticed some time after the baptism of a convert that he had discarded the kudumi, and asked why he had done so, though it had not been insisted on by the missionary as an essential for baptism. The convert replied that his friends did not believe he was baptized because he had not removed it, and therefore to convince them of the fact, he had voluntarily cut it off. (*Madras C. M. Record,* June, 1880.)

Candidates for baptism sometimes beg the missionary to allow them to retain the kudumi in order to lessen, as they fancy, the mockery and annoyances which they shall have to endure from heathen relatives. In cases where this concession has been made we have sometimes found that the application was but an index to the general state of mind of the individuals —that they had never thoroughly broken with heathenism, nor heartily placed themselves on a level with their Christian brethren. It is extremely doubtful, too, whether the yielding in this one item of usage would, on the whole, lessen the trials of a convert; and sure we are, that to require them to surrender without reservation, and at once, say before baptism, *all* that is inconsistent with the Christian profession is truest kindness in the end, and much preferable even for their own comfort. Those who manifest thorough decision of character will meet really less annoyance from others. The heathen relatives or employers will have less hope of success in the endeavour to turn back a thorough-going, earnest convert; and will sooner cease their useless efforts than in cases where timidity or hesitation is shown.

Generally, native Christians who wish to retain the kudumi profess to think it a trifling matter, of no importance whatever—simply for personal adornment, or a concession to popular usage; yet in some instances, when tested, they would rather be outside of the visible church and its privileges than yield the point. The only individual instances I have met with, in twenty years, in which persistent refusal to part with the tuft of hair was maintained, were three. One was that of a Government Apothecary, educated and brought up amongst Christians on the Eastern coast, by whom the kudumi is worn and caste distinctions zealously observed. On asking him to conform to our rules in the matter of the top-knot and of partaking of food with other respectable Christians, he refused, on the ground that he was accustomed to visit and enter the houses of heathens, where the absence of this mark would lead to a less favourable reception. Now his wearing or lacking the kudumi does not at present connote his caste or rank, as it is worn by all castes, but he found it a convenience to be *mistaken for a Hindu*, or *not identified as a Christian*, in his professional attendance upon heathen patients. This spirit, or that which leads a "caste Christian" to determine that *under no circumstances will he ever taste food* from the hands of native Christians of lower caste than himself, however respectable in character or office, or from Europeans, cannot belong to one "born of God."

Another case was that of a Christian teacher in a Travancore Government school, who had Hindus and others in his class. He dressed in a particular mode in imitation of the higher castes, and retained the kudumi, as he himself acknowledged, for reasons similar to the above. The third case was somewhat of the same character.

In a lamentable instance of the total apostacy of a youth who had been well educated in English for mission service, and who afterwards wished to pass for a caste Hindu, he not only took a heathen name but assumed the kudumi also. In Damaun, in the Bombay Presidency, a large number of Roman Catholic Christian Kolies, being alarmed by an epidemic of cholera in 1821, abandoned Christianity and supplicated Devy and other deities. "They discontinued all intercourse with their Christian brethren and *resumed the custom* of wearing the *sandhy*, or tuft of hair on the crown of the head." (*Madras Jour. Lit. Sci.*, January, 1837.)

The absence of the kudumi, usually somewhat disadvantageous in Travancore as being a sign of association with Christians known to be of humble birth, has been in troublous times highly inconvenient and even dangerous; and occasionally quite the contrary. The Hindu officials of the Native Government regard the tuft as a distinct mark of heathenism, and its absence as one proof of the actual profession of Christianity. In former times, when people were seized for Government service on Sundays, or for work for the temples, Christians were often exempted on the spot on showing that they had no kudumi. Again, in a certain district a persecution of the poor Christians was begun by a Tahsildar and Sudra landowners, exasperated by the rapid spread of Christianity and the elevation of the low castes. False charges were laid against the Christians, and the Tahsildar sent his peons to seize *as Christians* all whom he found *without the tuft.* During the "uppercloth" disturbances in 1858, "some of the Sudras collected mobs of men with whom they frequented the daily markets, watching both for the Christian men and women, examining the heads of the former to ascertain whether they had cut off the kudumi, or lock of hair which is a mark of heathenism, and to assault them if by its absence they were found to be professors of Christianity."

From the preceding remarks and illustrations, it will be evident that the kudumi is not such a trifle as it might appear at the first glance to be. Some may think it a great descent from the delightful and elevating topic of Infinite Mercy in the conversion of a human soul to advise upon the subject of hair dressing! Yet an inspired Apostle more than once delivered judgment in addressing converts from heathenism, respecting the covering of the head, the length of the hair, and mode of dressing it, and other apparently trifling points. When such usages have a religious bearing or signification they become matters of conscience. No true-hearted soldier will be ashamed of the colours of his regiment, but rather glory in them. It is remarkable that the kudumi is only permitted where there are large bodies of nominal Christians, whom it may be sometimes difficult to retain under strict discipline. As the "adherents" of our various Missions, unbaptized or non-communicants, become more numerous and more powerful by their contributions for the support of native agency, and thus less amenable to judicious control, is there not danger of their demanding indulgence in caste and kudumi, in doubtful or heathenish ceremonies at marriages, in worldly display and immunity from Church discipline, and thereby swamping the more spiritual element? This tendency should be met with sagacious prevision. Only the spiritual conversion to God of all our people, and their growth in grace, will correct all errors and remove all that savours of heathenism, and on this blessed work our best energies should be concentrated; but it may be helpful, meantime, to understand the true nature of indigenous customs, and the light in which they should be regarded by Christian missionaries; and this is what I have attempted to show with reference to the kudumi.

CHAPTER XIX.

FEMALE LIFE.

IN illustrating the social condition of women in Travancore, it may be convenient to present a somewhat general outline, speaking sometimes of one caste, or class, or status, sometimes of another, as there are so many classes, with corresponding diversities of manners, customs, habits, food, titles, marriage laws, religion, property, and rank in society.

As to **Dress**, each caste has its own distinctive style of dress and ornaments, forbidden by law and custom to others, the infringement of which prohibition has sometimes led to riots, lawsuits, and special legislation; and greatly varying in shape, pattern, and mode of wearing. Brahman, Mussulman, and Christian women wear jackets of different styles. The Roman Catholic fisherwomen, instead of jackets, tie a long cloth across the bosom.

Women, as well as men, generally wear around the waist and tucked in at the ends, a single calico cloth, two or three yards in length: a smaller one is sometimes put on the shoulders. Sudra women commonly wear a large waist-cloth, and a thin muslin "upper-cloth" over the shoulders and chest; while most of the poor habitually go uncovered from the waist upwards, the upper-cloth being formerly, and, perhaps, by the letter of the law, still forbidden to them. Poor people get only one set of cloths in the year, those of moderate means two sets, and the wealthy three or four in the year. Women are generally supplied with new cloths by their husbands at the Onam Festival, about September, and at Bharani, in March. Hence the proverbial reference to "the haste of the weaver on the approach of Onam," through the great demand for new cloth. If the customary presents be not given on those days, sometimes the women of the Sudra, barber, washerman, carpenter, and other concubinage castes, will forsake their men and go with others.

The pattern, make, and material of the ornaments of gold or silver, brass, wood, shell, or glass, worn on the head, ears, nose,

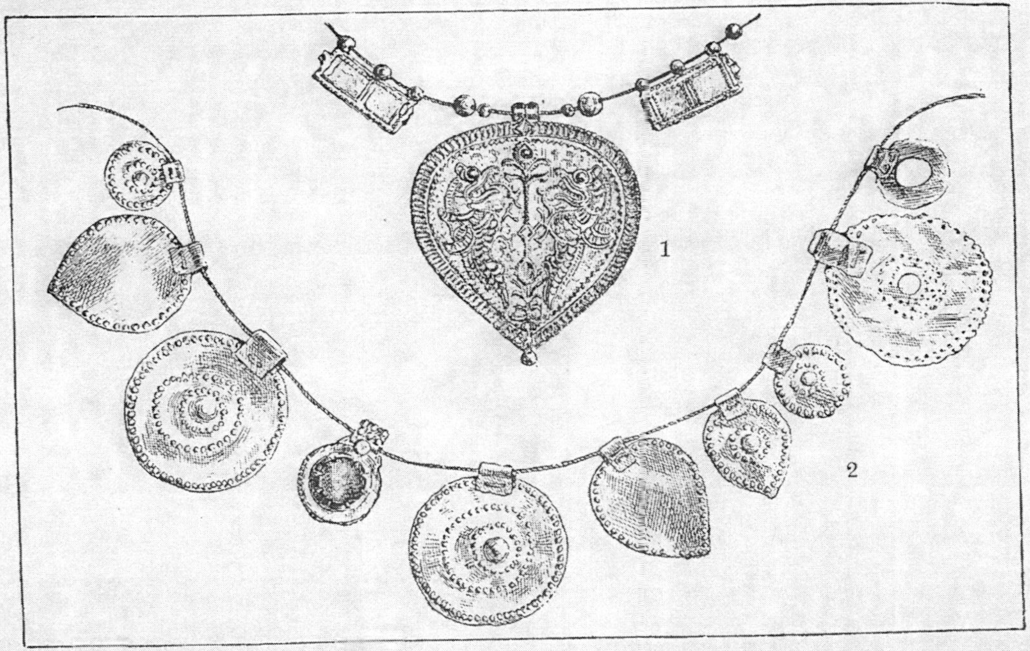

1. CHILD'S WAIST ORNAMENT

2. BRASS NECKLACE.

waist, legs or toes, also greatly vary; and only incessant training from infancy would enable one to understand the manners, mode of speech, and of acting in the most minute particulars, and on all occasions, great or small, appropriate to, and required of each caste. Even the most uncivilised and barbarous have their own code of etiquette to which they punctiliously and unswervingly adhere.

The principal jewels and ornaments worn by respectable females are the *takka*, a large cylinder of wood or gold, worn in the pierced and enlarged lobe of the ear; the *mani* and *minnu*, strung on a thick thread for the neck; rings of silver and gold worn on the toes; chains round the waist; nose rings amongst the Tamil women; necklaces, and bracelets. Ilavar women wear golden ornaments on the ears and neck, as many as they can manage to procure. On special occasions they also wear bangles on the wrists.

Employments.—Besides domestic duties in the house, and marketing, the poorer women must work for a living, as actively,

TOE RING.

often, as the men. Many are engaged in the lighter departments of field work, gathering leaves and cutting twigs for manure, carrying these to the fields, transplanting, weeding, reaping and threshing rice. Cooly women who live by their daily labour, commence work at seven in the morning, rest for an hour at noon, and leave off work at five in the evening; in the case of rice-field workers only at sunset. They carry home the provisions which they have earned; and, after the long labour of cooking, sometimes get supper only at eight or nine o'clock at night. Some are employed, especially Ottar women, for carrying mud in digging tanks, sand, mortar, and bricks in building, and earth and gravel for road-making.

Some carry produce to the markets for sale, as sugar, and salt, fish, and vegetables, and firewood. Many are obliged to aid their male relatives in their respective labours, the hill tribes in their cultivation, others in pottery, distilling and selling arrack, washing clothes, &c. The females of the oil-mongers are obliged to rise betimes for cooking and housework, as they have much to do in the daytime, drying the kernels of the cocoanut, laurel-nut, and other oil seeds, helping in the pressing and grinding of these, and disposing of the oil manufactured. The wives of goldsmiths, also, are often engaged throughout the day in spinning cotton thread, the Shánár females in boiling jaggery, and the Ilavars in distilling. A Malayálam proverb says, "When hammering the heated iron, the blacksmith and his

WOMAN GOING TO THE WELL.

wife are one." To eke out a humble maintenance, others also spin thread, make ropes of fibre, and do other light work. The Kuluvar women catch jackals and snakes, and other reptiles to eat. Pariah women plait mats of reeds, and make neat palm-leaf umbrellas: a few work in the fields.

Daily Life.—Women are the earliest risers of the family, being usually up by daybreak, sometimes earlier. High-caste women first sweep their houses and courtyards, both inner and outer, then go to the well or river to fetch the water required for the day.

In Travancore no one enjoys the convenience afforded in English towns by the water being conveyed through pipes to every house, so that the turning of a tap suffices for the domestic supply of water. Even pumps are very rarely in use, the wells being too deep, as may be judged from the length of the coir rope which the woman in the engraving carries in her hand. To draw up the water for filling her large earthen pot, she takes with her a light bucket, ingeniously formed from the fan-like leaf of the Palmyra palm. This fragile vessel does not last long, but is easily renewed in the south, where the palmyra grows in great abundance.

The earthen pot in which the water is brought home is almost globular in form, with a small mouth, and holds a considerable quantity. It must be set down with some care to avoid breaking it. Brass waterpots are used by those who can afford them. The work of drawing water and carrying it home is often toilsome, as a good quantity is required in a large household for use in cooking rice and other food, and for drinking and washing purposes.

In former times, caste regulations required low-caste females to carry the waterpot only on the head, not on the hip or side, as in the illustration. Wells belonging to Brahmans and other high castes are not open to those of inferior caste.

Excellent water is procured from wells, tanks, and rivers. Wells are often dug in the courtyard of the house to save time and trouble in going to a distance for water.

Before the drawing of the water in the early morning is finished, other members of the family have risen, whereupon the various apartments and verandahs are swept clean, then cleansed with a thick mixture of cow-dung and water (an emblem of purity, and universal disinfectant from ceremonial pollution), the raised verandahs being smeared over, and the courtyards sprinkled with it. Some flowers are also placed on the ground in front of the door, in honour of the Sun. When this is finished they wash their faces, hands and feet, clean the teeth, and put the "marks" on the forehead and chest, with the sacred ashes of cow-dung, or with powdered sandal-wood or turmeric. They then worship the rising sun, looking towards it, facing to the east; and the other gods, facing to the other quarters of the heavens; or repeat their prayers to the domestic idols, and cause their children who are over five years of age to do the same: the Christians gather round the family altar, and worship the true and living God.

While putting on the ashes, they are to meditate on their

guru's, or spiritual teacher's, name. A sloka, or verse, is in common use, to this effect—"He is blessed, who, in the morning, as soon as he rises from his bed, and has washed his feet and face, rubs the sacred ashes, meditating on his guru's feet, and lives here with prayer in the name of the guru." This used to be more strictly observed by all classes than at present.

After this, the domestic work of the day is begun, feeding and milking the cows, churning the milk previously boiled to make butter, cleaning their brass vessels, serving out a meal of cold rice with soured milk to the children, and sending them off to their respective duties, as ploughing, tending the cattle, or school. The men and boys generally take this light meal about seven o'clock, afterwards going to their work till nearly mid-day, when they get fresh cooked rice and curry. At Trevandrum, some women go to the pagodas, and buy for breakfast part of the rice which had been consecrated to the god.

If, however, the family means admit of providing a hot meal in the morning, the women busy themselves in cooking this, while the men go out for a while to bathe or to see friends, to arrange the work of the day, or to look over their crops and gardens. For a regular meal, whether morning, noon, or evening, they boil rice, prepare roots, vegetables, fish, peas, greens, and fruits; grind cocoanuts, pepper, and spices for curry, and add butter or oil. Some of the highest castes refrain from eating fish or flesh, but make up for this partly by the use of milk, butter, cakes, and fruits. The Brahman women especially are accomplished cooks; Ilavars, Syrians, and others are noted for making various kinds of cakes and sweetmeats.

Food is served out first to the men in brazen cups—these cups being filled with curry and rice by means of ladles or spoons made of cocoanut shells fixed on handles of bambu. Among the higher classes of the people plantain leaves are preferred to brazen cups, or even leaves of the banyan or other trees, pinned together with the stem of a grass. The females of the family generally wait upon the men until they have finished their meals. They use no tables or chairs or spoons, but sit on mats spread on the ground, with very little clothing, and eat with the hand, mixing the rice and the curry together. Afterwards the females take their food. Daily, after cooking operations are over, the women sit down near the cookroom to clean and polish the brass vessels in which the food is served, rubbing them with common wood-ashes or burnt husks of rice, or sometimes with finely powdered brick-dust.*

If cold rice has been used in the morning, the women soon

* Rev. J. Duthie, in "Juvenile Missionary Magazine" for 1870.

begin to prepare the dinner for noon. If a warm breakfast has been made, it may be over about ten or eleven o'clock, and in a little while the arduous and almost daily work of "rice beating" or pounding and cleaning must be begun.

The cheapest food in Travancore, except home-grown roots and fruits, is rice. Of this adults require about a pound and a half daily, and it costs something like a penny to a penny farthing per pound. Rice is not nearly so nourishing as wheat or oatmeal, and should be supplemented, as it usually is among vegetable feeders, with pease, milk, or butter. Numerous varieties are grown, and nice distinctions made of flavour and individual taste.

Rice can be purchased husked and ready for cooking, but most poor families are obliged to economise by purchasing it in the husk (when it is called *paddy*), and beating it clean with a heavy wooden pestle in a wooden or stone mortar. Cultivators, of course, must beat it for themselves, as there are no large mills to send it to. Soaked for a night, and partially boiled, the grain becomes soft, and is then dried in the sun, and beaten or threshed in the mortar till the outer husk or chaff comes off. Another beating removes the bran or dark outer skin of the rice; and a third makes it clean and white, as we see it in England.

This work is very heavy and exhausting to delicate women; it consumes much time every day, and requires severe bodily exertion. It is, therefore, more usual for two women to work together; in rich families coolies, or servants, are employed for it. All this is done in more civilized countries, and in Burmah, in large mills; and some small, cheap machines for domestic use are a great desideratum in Travancore, and would largely tend to better the position of women.

A flat fan is used for winnowing the grain from the husk or bran, which is given as food to fowls or cattle. The beaten rice comes to half in bulk, but two-thirds in weight, of the unhusked grain; and it again swells out to three times the original bulk in boiling. When properly boiled, the rice should be dry, each grain unbroken. It is sometimes parched in a pot on the fire till the grain swells nicely and bursts, called *pori*; or half boiled, bruised flat, and eaten, called *aval;* or ground into flour and baked into flat, heavy cakes. This grain will not, like wheat, make leavened bread, but good pancakes are made by adding toddy as yeast; these are often flavoured with sugar and butter.

Rice, the staple food of the people, is not commonly ground into flour, but boiled whole and eaten with curry—that is, highly spiced meat, fruit, or vegetables; other grains, as millet,

&c., are ground into flour, and boiled into a kind of porridge or pudding. Millstones being of granite, in so hot a climate the work of grinding is very heavy. The grain is poured into a hole in the centre of the upper stone, and the flour falls out on all sides from between the two stones into a cloth spread underneath. The work is lighter when two women work together; those in our picture might be mother and daughter.

Their dress is the Christian jacket, and the upper-cloth usually worn by native women. The armlet is of silver; and many ornaments are worn even by poor people. As there are no native banks, it is convenient to lay by savings in the form of jewellery, on which ready money can at any time be raised. The elder of these women wears a number of small gold rings

WOMEN GRINDING GRAIN.

encircling the ring of flesh into which the lobe of the ear has been drawn. The younger has, in addition, a flat gold pendant pinned to the upper part of the ear.

To return to the daily domestic duties—rice-beating is sometimes suspended at one or two o'clock for a few minutes to eat luncheon, and will be over by two or three in the afternoon. Then preparation of the evening meal—the most important of the day—shortly commences, similar to that of the forenoon, with the addition say of plantain fruits and *páyasam*, or sweet pudding of rice, sugar, and milk. The boiling of rice, going to the bazaar for fish, vegetables, and curry stuffs, grinding the last with a roller on a flat granite stone, and mixing and boiling the curry, may keep some busy until seven or eight, or even nine o'clock. The rich sometimes sup as late as ten or eleven at night, in which case, of course, they do not rise so early in the morning.

Amongst Christians, family worship is usually conducted the first thing in the morning, and before supper, at seven or eight o'clock at night.

The Indian women are not only the first to rise, but the last to retire to rest, taking supper after the men have done, and then washing and laying aside the vessels in due order. A woman may not unduly feel the pressure of house work when she lives with her husband's parents, for the mother-in-law and sister-in-law will help her, but when newly married and living separately with her husband, all this work is sometimes very trying.

The social circumstances and daily life of the poor low-caste or slave women, who are obliged to labour for their daily support, and sometimes have nothing to eat on any day on which they remain idle, present a direct contrast to the comfort of these just described, as might be expected from the condition of extreme and enforced degradation in which they have been so long kept, and the contempt and abhorrence with which they are universally regarded. Yet they are human as well as their superiors. They work hard, suffer much from sickness and often from want of food, and generally, like all slaves, also form evil habits of thieving, sensuality, drunkenness, and vice, which increase or produce disease and suffering.

Very early in the morning these women go with a pot or a leaf bucket to their masters, asking for food and instructions respecting the day's work. They are kept toiling in manuring, planting, or reaping through the day in the agricultural season, mostly with the blazing sun beating on the bare head, and the feet in mire or water, and return in the evening, fatigued and hungry, to their wretched huts to boil their rice and eat it with salt and pepper. The Pariahs eat the carcases of cows and other animals which have died of old age or disease, even when almost putrid. These are cut up for distribution by the females principally, and after partaking of this disgusting food, their odour is insufferable.

During the months of scarcity the Védar women go to the jungle, and dig up various kinds of wild yams and tubers with pointed sticks of wood which they always carry, and boil and eat these roots. The Pulayars, likewise, hunt for crabs, tiny fish, and snails, in the irrigation channels, eggs of red ants, the winged white ants, or anything else to fill the stomach and satisfy the cravings of hunger.

At night they sleep on the floor, or on a plaited cocoanut leaf or old mat. Dress, food, and dwellings, are alike uncleanly.

They rarely bathe or wash their bodies. Purchasing a cloth at harvest-time, it is worn till it falls to pieces. Their ornaments are bits of brass, glass beads, or shells. They are without the social amenities of life, not allowed to enter the markets or use the public roads without impediment, and were formerly bought and sold like cattle. They run into debt for strong drink, clearing off the debt with the grain earned during harvest. Their devil worship and ghost worship also spring from fear and abject superstition. Is it not surprising that the sufferings of these unfortunate and despised people do not move the hearts of their wealthy and educated countrymen, and that no Hindu practical philanthropist arises to labour for their regeneration and enlightenment?

Females of the higher castes are very cleanly in their habits, bathing daily in water, and rubbing the body with cocoanut or sesamum oil twice a month, usually on Fridays.

Seclusion of women is not so close or common as in other parts of India, except amongst the Nambúris and other castes next to Brahmans. The Ranees do not appear in public, but a happy innovation on this custom has more than once been made. An enlightened Brahman lady, from other parts of India, would be pleased to be able to go out here without covering the head with a veil, and would enjoy the greater freedom allowed. Still there is amongst respectable families much retirement and seclusion, which some are beginning to feel, complaining that they are "like parrots shut up in a cage."

The low estimation, and even contempt, in which women, as such, are too often regarded, appears in the laws by which a man's partner in life may be sent off at a moment's notice. The former salutation in Travancore was for a female to uncover the chest before a respectable man. Their grievance sometimes bursts out in such an exclamation as, "Better to be a clod than to have been born a woman!" A Hindu prayer is that the wife may have *seven* wise sons and *two* handsome daughters. Men are dejected when they hear of the birth of a daughter, according to the proverb, "Why do you sit as if a girl had been born at home?" Another proverb amusingly represents a grumbling father as foolishly complaining, "Through the incapacity of the midwife, the infant is a female!"

A counterfeit modesty is taught them, while true delicacy of speech and conduct are often absent. Should a man come to make inquiries at a house when the master is not at home, the woman does not reply to him direct, but addresses the door. In some castes a woman must not speak to male relatives, even cousins, who are in India called "brothers." The denial of education to females springs to a great extent from the fear that they would misuse such advantages and become unfitted for obedience and humble labour. The first question is not, "Can she read? can she do needlework? can she keep accounts?" Such things are secondary. But, "Can she cook rice? can she work well?"

Being without education, moral training, or real knowledge of the world, many women spend much time in gossiping with their friends on the most frivolous and profitless topics—dress and ornaments, which are their chief delight; their husbands and neighbours, and the scandal of the village; stories of devils, tigers, and so forth.

The wicked custom of child-marriage arises from distrust of female virtue, and sometimes naturally causes repugnance to live with the husband at all. The child-bride is all unconscious of the real meaning and obligations of the relation, although her girlish fancies have been continually directed to it. The veriest baby, when she cries in her cradle, is consoled by her grandmother with promises of marrying her to a good husband; but if the old lady is cross, the little darling is threatened to be married to a wicked husband. One day the grandmother of a little girl eight years old, who was learning at school, made the distressful complaint, "I have coaxed and scolded her alternately, and have even promised to marry her soon, but to no purpose. She does nought else but read her books and play."

The lot of the childless wife is deplorable. She meets not with the kind sympathy which would be reasonable, but her barrenness is blamed as a sin. Hence their continual resort to the temples and rites to seek the gift of offspring.

We can here only allude to the intolerable miseries of Hindu widows, of whom the late census shows that there are no fewer than 63,000 *under ten* years of age, and *fifteen and a half millions* between ten and twenty, all prohibited from marrying a second time. They are deprived of their ornaments —in which they so much delight—and of the use of coloured garments, and of their long hair, reproached as misfortunate, and cruelly debarred as accursed of the gods from assisting in domestic religious ceremonials. The too frequent results of this cruel treatment are immorality, suicide, and infanticide.

For newly-married persons to meet a widow anywhere, portends approaching calamity, therefore this is carefully guarded against and avoided. They are frequently required to fast: *ekádasí* is a day of close fast for all widows.

Yet, of course, women have great influence in social and domestic life. "Unlike their sisters in North India, the restraints imposed on them are few. They are not restricted to their own apartments, and the mother of each household occupies a dignified and honourable position. In the families of the Náyars she governs the whole house, often a large one consisting of from twenty to thirty persons, provides for the wants of each, settles all disputes, and rules even her grown-up sons, who never in public sit down in her presence, but stand humbly behind her chair.

Her duties are not light, for, besides buying, storing up and giving out food for so many mouths, she regulates the lives of the children, decides what schools they shall attend, how they shall dress, and what medicines they shall take when they are ill, their own mothers having no choice in anything that concerns them."

Though Travancore boasts of peculiar castes amongst whom widowhood is never possible (because the relation of wife does not, in truth, exist), and women hold a high place and are admitted to the benefits of education, it appears from the census that, after all, only a trifle over one per cent. of the Malayálam Sudra females can read and write, and but a little larger proportion of Brahman women; only 93 females of the hundreds of thousands of Ilavars, and not one amongst the heathen Pariahs, Pulayars, and other low castes. In the whole State only 3,452 females (from twelve years of age and upwards) are returned as able to read and write of all the Hindu castes; and only 86 Muhammadan females.

Ninety-eight out of a hundred females, therefore, even of the higher castes, are entirely uneducated. A Brahman gentleman was once asked, "What do you think a woman ought to know?" "She must know two things," was his reply; "first, she must know the way to the bazaar to buy necessaries for the house; and secondly, she must know the way from the bazaar home again!" A Munshi, also, when requested to instruct a class in our boarding-school in Tamil poetry and literature, stoutly objected at first, saying that if girls were instructed in such things, they would not make obedient wives, and, instancing the case of his own wife, who, he affirmed, could only count up to eight.

Women can, therefore, often scarcely speak correctly in their own language, indeed I believe they have some peculiar words or style of their own. I have heard a Brahman publicly state that he never yet heard a woman accurately pronounce the names of some of the well-known towns in Travancore. A Malayálam proverb says, "A travelled woman is like a garden trespassed by cattle."

Ignorant of moral duty and unawakened in conscience, most of the women do not know what sin is, as committed by themselves, not in a previous birth; and are surprised to be told that they have ever sinned against God. "I have never committed any sin," said one, "yet God took away my son."

The spiritual darkness and gross superstition of Hindu females are appalling. To them no light from heaven shines upon the mysteries of life, no solid ground of comfort is available under its sorrows and bereavements. In sickness, they murmur against God and his dealings with them, or attribute all their sufferings to the agency of malignant spirits or inexorable fate. An aged woman on the bed of lingering sickness was asked did she hope to be happy after death. "Happiness!" she exclaimed, "I am suffering in this way through my sins, for which God is making a play of me. Had I been free from sin I might have been permitted quietly to die. What I long for is death. What happiness do I require after death? Even my own children have become tired of me, and look upon me with aversion." Others say, "As we are suffering so much in this world, we are sure to obtain happiness in the next."

Those who die in childbed are supposed to be killed by demons, hence the offerings to evil spirits, and the sorcery continually resorted to on such occasions. In the South, branches of the margosa tree are used to prevent the entrance of the demons into houses where a birth has taken place. Tender mothers live in ceaseless terror of unknown spiritual agencies, to whom they attribute the infantile ailments or convulsions of their children. Their own dear ones are supposed under certain circumstances to become demons. An aged mother who had recently lost her son, a promising official, inquired, bitterly weeping, "Where will a man go who has died of small-pox? It is the opinion of our people that one who has died of this disease will remain unhappy and vagrant upon the earth as a *maruthá* demon. Can he go to heaven?"

Their whole life is made burdensome by superstitions, and vain terrors regarding lucky and unlucky times and actions and objects: these intrude even in the most common-place avocations. It is dangerous and foreboding to come out of doors when giving alms to beggars—to sweep the inner yard and remove the dust when it is dusk—to comb the hair at night—to sweep the house during the prevalence of small-pox, or to sweep the stable with the same broom as the house. To wear again a new cloth, part of which has got burnt, will prove fatal to her husband. To put on a new cloth on Saturday, or at night, is very inauspicious. If a woman happen to get ill after having been seen by others in full dress and ornamented with her jewels, she ascribes it to the blight of the evil eye of some one. A leprous Ilavar woman declared that the cause of her disease was when young her accidentally polluting a Brahman goddess.

Thenceforward she suffered from disease, "and I cannot afford, she added, valuable offerings to the goddess to propitiate her."

Not knowing where true consolation and refuge from their woes can be found, they can only try anything and everything that may be suggested to them—visiting temples, presenting gifts, prayers and vows, rubbing sacred ashes from the temple, repeating or hearing the *Pradósha Mahátmyam* and *Namaskára Japam*, which they deem highly beneficial, and so forth. Women are the chief inventors and upholders of all this superstition and folly, and they are also the principal sufferers from it.

Four women were met on their way to a temple to bathe and worship. On being accosted, they remarked that they were going for four several purposes. The first said, "I go in the hope of obtaining the blessing of a child"; another "In order to get rid of an ailment"; the third said, "When my child was sick, I vowed to offer worship there on his recovery." And the fourth said, "As I am now advanced in years, I am going there in order that my soul may be saved." A fairly typical picture this, of the common cases and petitions of the votaries at the sacred shrines.

Their best efforts, vows, pilgrimages, and gifts are often found to be in vain in respect of the temporal blessings for which alone idols are worshipped; and sore disappointment is experienced in the worship of gods that cannot hear or understand. "Just as I was arranging to pay a visit to the great temple at Vaikkam," said a Sudra woman, "my child took ill. I therefore thought it useless to travel so far. I perceive that the Vaikkam goddess is unable to save; if she were all-powerful, my child would not have fallen sick at such a time." "I expended," said another, "much money in offerings to noted demons on behalf of my daughter, and also made vows to Saint Xavier at Kottár; but none of them could deliver my daughter from death." A very wealthy Ilavar woman, whose only son, a fine youth, was attacked with small-pox, vowed that if he should recover from this she would put him in a scale, take an equal weight of gold, and fashion this into the form of a man to offer to the goddess Ammen. But he died on the ninth day. Their sorrows, truly, "are multiplied who hasten after another god."

A few more of their superstitious notions may be mentioned.

A girl born in the asterism Magam, and a boy born in that of Púrádam, are preferable for marriage.

Children born in April are unfortunate. Hence the custom of calling away females newly married from the house of the husbands in July to their parents' houses.

The falling of certain shadows, as of a woman who has given

birth to a still-born child, or lost her infant, the shadow of toads, &c., causes general emaciation of the body, if not immediate death.

"A mother who has a young baby will on no account take the baby of another in her arms, believing that, should she do so, her own child will pine away. If an elder child in a family has died, it will be said, whenever the younger one is ailing, 'Ah, the dead child is troubling it!' If an expectant mother walks across any grave, it is believed that her child, when born, will be a great sufferer. A mother whose baby has died, must not even touch the child of another until she has had another living child. A Christian teacher, who had lost her twin babies, refrained on one occasion from touching another's child, even to save it from a severe fall, because, although she herself knows better, she knew that the ignorant mother of that child would prefer its falling to its being touched by her. The cruelty that there is in this last restriction will be felt by all who know the yearning that a bereaved mother often has for all little children."

If an infant is observed to distort its limbs as if in pain, it is supposed to be under the pressure of some one who has stooped over it, to relieve which the mother places it with a nut-cracker on a winnowing fan, and shakes it three or four times.

Hindus never compliment one another on their beautiful and healthy appearance, for they think it bad manners to do so, and that this is the surest way to spoil everything you compliment them on. For instance, mothers never like any one to say, "What a fine child yours is," for they think people must be envious of them, and that saying such things will bring bad luck—the very opposite of the Christian sentiment, "I am quite well, thank God."

From the commencement of Mission work, both by the London Mission and the Church Mission, **female education** has been engaged in, and its benefits illustrated by examples of Christian females who have been trained in the Boarding and Village Schools. "The results that we are reaping to-day," says Mr. A. Spicer, one of the recent deputation to India, "and the rapid rate at which this work is growing in India, are in large measure owing to the work which our missionaries' wives have devoted to this department for years past." Now the strong prejudice against female education is slowly giving way, and the Hindus themselves have a few schools for caste girls. The royal family are also leading the way, and some desire for education of females is springing up. "You sometimes see people in the road walking about and hesitating which way to go," said one female to a Christian teacher, "that is just how I feel, and I want you to show me the way." "You are a happy woman," said a Sudra to our Bible woman, "for you have received a good education. Your children also are blessed, as they can read, write, and sing so nicely. Will you kindly take my daughters under your care, as I should like to see them as well trained as yourself." A Vellálar woman, thirty-six years of age, presented a quantity of lamp oil to our church in token of gratitude for having been taught to read. An encouraging number of adult females—Sudras, Brahmans, Muhammadans, and others, are learning to read at Nagercoil, Trevandrum, Cottayam, and elsewhere, under the superintendence of the missionary ladies,

GIRLS' SCHOOL AT NAGERCOIL.

and a very interesting work is going on amongst *adult* females, besides the *girls* learning in the Mission Schools—about 1,370 in the Church Mission, and 2,375 in the London Mission, of whom some are heathen children.

In the towns around Nagercoil, about 300 women are now receiving Zenana teaching, and three or four caste girls' schools are in operation. Very recently, at a school examination, a Bible woman who would have been classed as low-caste according to the Hindu system, brought with her about forty caste girls, whom she teaches in their houses, all respectable and well dressed, but diligently learning, and willing to sit down amongst Christian and low-caste children. Such a thing had never been seen there before.

"Several women who had learned with us," writes Mrs. Duthie, "have removed to neighbouring villages. These have excited others, and messages have been sent asking us to provide a Biblewoman to teach them. No doubt many of the women in the Zenanas are anxious only to learn to read, and may not have any great desire for the knowledge of the truth. Bible teaching, however, is the most prominent feature of the work, and not a few listen with attention and apparent interest to the lessons we try to teach them. In some cases we see even more than this, and are led to hope that the good seed has begun to take root, and is bearing some fruit. Heathen customs have been partially abandoned, and the general appearance and conduct of these women have much improved since we began our work amongst them. Amidst much that is depressing, it has been cheering to gather round us little groups of women and children able to read the Word of God, and to hear them repeat texts that they have learned, telling of a Saviour's love and power to save. Christian lyrics are sung by many of them, hymns are committed to memory, in various ways the truth is finding an entrance into these homes, and we pray that it may also reach many hearts."

Amongst Protestant Christians in South Travancore, fully one in six of the adult women can read and write (though a considerable proportion of them are direct converts from heathenism), and this can be proved from our lists of names, and might be expected from the great interest taken by the missionaries and their wives in this work. They are also taught to wear a decent native dress, to sing, to sew, and embroider, and work fine pillow-lace. Heathen women notice with admiration the marked difference in manners and speech of girls thus educated. Visitors passing through Nagercoil are greatly struck with their intelligence and accuracy in answering. So in Cottayam, the venerable Mrs. Baker, Senior, has for over sixty years been spared and privileged to educate generation after generation of girls in her valuable schools, and other ladies have laboured for various periods. The 46 female teachers in the London Mission are, of course, the pick of our Christian females (available to give time to such duties), and are diligent and devoted workers amongst their country-women. Many of the private members of the Church are faithful, loving, and earnest Christians, shining as lights in their own homes, visiting the sick, and conversing with the heathen women, to whom they make known the way of salvation.

CHAPTER XX.

AGRICULTURE.

MANUFACTURES being few and insignificant, agriculture is the principal industry of Travancore, one-third of the able-bodied population being engaged in it. Almost every one secures for himself a small area of land, sufficient at least for the site of a dwelling, and small garden around it. Indeed, in some parts of Malabar there are scarcely any compact towns, each house being separate, and situated in its own grounds. Agriculture is carried on with some measure of practical skill and success derived from lengthened experience, but with most primitive instruments, and needing much improvement as to manuring, rotation of crops, and the preparation of produce for the market. With a view to national progress in these respects, two students have been sent by the native Government to the Agricultural College at Madras, who, it is hoped, will be able on their return to introduce more scientific methods of husbandry. A beginning has also been made in holding Agricultural Exhibitions of cattle and produce, which may be expected, in time, to improve and encourage native agriculture.

The principal native agricultural products are rice, cocoa-nut, and other palms, and farinaceous roots for food, besides coffee, which is cultivated by European planters, with the aid of native labour. Fruit trees also are grown, more or less, by every one, and invariably planted as the beginning of an estate when waste land is cleared.

Rice is grown chiefly on irrigated or swamp land, though dry or "hill" rice is also grown wherever the soil is sufficiently rich to give a crop, and the rain sufficiently abundant to bring it to perfection. Most of the landed wealth of the country consists of rice or "paddy" lands, which vary greatly, however, in quality and produce, and consequently in value.

On account of the uncertain and varying character of the land and grain measures in use in various parts of the country, it is difficult to give exact estimates of cost and returns. The common measurement is the *para:* "100 paras of land" is the area which requires a hundred paras of seed sown. The para grain-measure itself differs throughout the country, but properly speaking, a para contains 920 cubic inches—a little over two-fifths of a bushel. The para land-measure is smaller for the valuable rice lands than for common dry or unirrigated land. In the case of government grants during the last fifty years, the para is taken at 4,000 square feet, which is a little over one-eleventh of an acre. The older estimate, applying to the greater portion of the rice lands in Travancore, is one-eighth of an acre = 5,445 square feet; but in the northern districts the para measures somewhat over this. For the present we shall assume the para to be equal to one-eighth of an acre.

The price of "paddy" lands varies according to the soil, facilities for irrigation, distance from the centres of population, and the returns they are capable of yielding. Some are worth only 30 rupees to 40 rupees per para; others cost up to 70 rupees (say, 24*l.* to 56*l.* per acre). The Government compensation for rice lands taken for public purposes is only 14 rupees per para. Land may be said to be worth generally about 15 years' purchase.

The proper soil for rice is found in valleys or plains irrigated by water-channels, often with a supply for the dry season in a tank at the head of the valley. The varieties of rice suited to different soils and seasons are numerous.

The produce of rice lands in Travancore ranges from so low as five-fold, and usually ten to fifteen-fold, up to thirty-fold occasionally. There is a popular complaint that the land is deteriorating, and the return less than in former days, which the old people ascribe to diminished attention to sacred rites and duties, but which appears to have some foundation in fact, and to arise from exhaustion of the soil through want of proper cultivation, sufficient manure, or regular fallows. Rice is a slow growing grain, of low nutritive value, and its cultivation prevents a rotation of crops. In the southern districts, where tillage is more careful, and manuring better attended to, and the sun hotter, the clouds and rainfall being less, the increase has sometimes been known to be forty-fold; but farmers think they are well off with fifteen-fold at each harvest—*i.e.*, twice in the year—and throughout the greater part of the country seven or eight-fold, or in the south twelve to fifteen-fold must be put down as the usual return. Of course, in unfavourable seasons the crop may be almost nothing. As it costs at least two paras of grain in wages to sow one para of seed, a return of at least three times the seed sown is necessary to repay expenditure. A ten-fold increase would be 80 paras, or 33 bushels, of "paddy," or rice in the husk. When cleaned of the husk, this is reduced to half the quantity—say 16 bushels—weighing on an average 64⅓ lbs. per bushel when raw. Old rice would be lighter, down to about 59 lbs. The produce, therefore, of an acre of good rice land may be averaged at 1,044 lbs.

Mr. Caird estimates that the present average produce of grain throughout India is below 10 bushels per acre. In a recent experiment at Saidapet Farm, near Madras, the average out-turn per acre was, grain 1,594 lbs., and straw 4,033 lbs.; but few of the native rice growers can show such results.

Paddy is usually sold at 12 chuckrams per para. The Government rate for commutation of taxes payable in kind is 7 chuckrams. When slightly boiled and beaten from the husk, the price is 32 chuckrams per para, or about Rs. 2¾ per bushel.

The total acreage of rice land under cultivation in Travancore is not exactly known, but a fresh survey and re-assessment are about to be undertaken. The survey of eighty years ago places it at about 400,000 acres; but since then much waste land has been brought under cultivation, and the total acreage cannot probably be taken at less than 500,000 acres. Whereas at the beginning of the century, Travancore exported large quantities of paddy and rice (in 1843 no less than 281,000 candies of 654 lbs. each), and imported but a small quantity, the case is now totally reversed—exports being only about Rs. 70,000 to Rs. 80,000 in value, and imports (duty free) having risen from 4½ lacs of rupees seven years ago to 9¾ lacs in 1881. The produce of the country is, therefore, not sufficient for home consumption at the present time. This arises not only from the diminished production already referred to and from increase of population, but also from the general improvement of the circumstances of the lower castes, who can now afford to eat more rice in place of, or in addition to, fruits and vegetables, coarse roots, and inferior grains.

Supposing the cultivated area of rice to be 500,000 acres, and the joint produce of the two crops fifteenfold, or 1,566 lbs. per acre; this divided amongst a population of 2½ millions would give 312 lbs. of rice per head per annum for consumption. Imported rice to the value of 10 lacs of rupees would give (at a chuckram per pound) 11 lbs. per head additional. The consumption in Ceylon of rice (and fine grain) is estimated at 5 bushels, or over 300 lbs. per head, besides fruits, vegetables, and roots; and in Burma, "where the peasantry have enough and to spare," 507 lbs. per head.

The quantity required for an adult living wholly upon rice is usually reckoned at 3 nári, about 1½ lbs. per day, or rather more. The Famine Commission compute that for a working adult male 1½ lbs. of flour or rice is sufficient, and for children, from half to a fourth of the quantity according to age. Twenty-six ozs. of rice daily is allowed in Trevandrum Gaol for labouring male prisoners.

The cultivation of the **Cocoanut** extends over the whole State, which has hence been facetiously called Cocoanut-core. At the survey of some forty-five years ago, the total number of these trees was 11 millions; and the increase since has been so great, much waste land having been planted with this valuable palm, that the present number cannot be estimated at less than 15 millions. These are almost invariably too closely planted to obtain full advantage of sun and air: but supposing they stood at the moderate distance of 20 feet apart (which is 109 to the acre) the area covered would amount to 137,000 acres.

The soils best suited for the cocoanut are the seashore, the banks and alluvium of rivers, and level lands exposed to the sea breeze; these conditions abound in Travancore. Inland, on the mountains, the cocoanut will grow, but not bear fruit, deteriorating as it recedes from the coast. The young plants generally require watering for the first two or three years, and must be protected from the inroads of cattle until they rise some feet above the ground. Ashes are applied as manure at the beginning of the wet season, and the ground opened about the roots of the trees, which come into bearing some eight or ten years after planting. To natives this is one of the most easily-managed and most remunerative products of the country —perhaps, as in the South Sea Islands, almost too easy for enforcing habits of industry and perseverance. They have but to put down the nuts and guard the trees, more or less, while attending to their other employments, and in due course a permanent and profitable plantation is created. Europeans, however, seldom attempt such an investment, and few who have done so have succeeded in it.

For new plantations, waste lands are usually taken up. Within the last twenty or thirty years much land, otherwise worthless, has been reclaimed along the sandy sea-coast, and many trees have been planted on either side of new roads opening up into the interior. To purchase a plantation, however, is a more costly undertaking. The value of such property, of course, varies greatly according to situation and productiveness. The price of 100 ordinary trees in the southern parts may be stated at about 400 rupees. These would produce, at a low estimate, say 2,400 nuts, value 34 rupees, annually. The produce of the tree is very much dependent on soil and climate. The average of good trees in full bearing has been stated at 120 nuts in the twelve months, while in low and sandy soils it will amount to 200, and in gravel or laterite, be under 60. Ripe cocoanuts are quoted in the Trevandrum market list at somewhat under 2 rupees per 100.

The kernels are dried into *copra* for the manufacture of cocoanut oil. The copra is largely exported to other parts of India, as well as the "coir" or fibre surrounding the husk, which is sent to Europe and America.

The annual value of the products of this palm exported—nuts, dried kernel or copra, oil, and fibre—amounts to 46 lacs of rupees, besides oil, nuts, timber, and leaves for home use. It has been estimated that 60,000,000 of nuts and 15,000 candies of oil are annually consumed in the country. The timber is not exported, but split up and used for rafters, and the leaves are in great demand for thatching.

The trees are sometimes tapped for a few months to procure the sweet juice, which, boiled while fresh, gives a palm sugar, and kept a day or two till it ferments and becomes toddy, a slightly intoxicating drink, somewhat like beer. The toddy also is distilled into arrack or native spirits.

Other palm-trees are also cultivated. Next to the cocoanut comes the **Palmyra,** which is grown only in the drier districts towards Cape Comorin. Farther north they appear to flourish fairly well when planted; but there are none of the class of people who climb and collect the produce of this palm, and the great rainfall would doubtless hinder such work; the tree, also, is of extremely slow growth, so that only rare specimens are found in those parts.

The palmyra, with its sweet sap and sugar, leaves, timber, and fruit, furnishes a living to a great number of the Shánár caste in Travancore, and in Tinnevelly. The number of trees in the former survey, was about 6,000,000. It is probable that no considerable increase has taken place since, as old trees are in demand for their timber, and the slow growth of this palm discourages planting. The export of jaggery, the sugar of this palm, has considerably increased of late, amounting in *M.E. 1056* to 50,741 cwts., valued at 180,000 rupees.

The beautiful **Areca** palm is planted in damp, clayey soil on the banks of tanks and rivers. Unlike the cocoanut it will thrive at a distance from the sea and on the hills. It is grown very largely in North Travancore, whence the nuts are carried to the South by Syrian and other traders. The trees will grow two or three feet apart. The areca begins to bear in five years,

OIL MILL.

and continues to produce for twenty-five years. The nuts are sold wholesale at six or eight chuckrams per thousand, and retail in Trevandrum at from eight to thirty-two for a chuckram, according to season and demand. Last year exports to other parts of India amounted to 3,866 candies, valued at nearly 5 lacs of rupees, say £50,000.

Roots, vegetables and fruits form a considerable proportion of the food of the population, especially of the poorest classes, who have little besides when rice is scarce or dear. The forest and hill people dig out wild, stringy yam-roots from the jungle as food in the hot season. Every native grows something, if he can, around his own dwelling for home use.

The principal cultivated root-crops are yams (*Dioscorea*) of various sorts, the small tubers of which are planted out in the beginning of the rainy season and dug again within a year. Some of these roots grow, under favourable circumstances, to a large size, up to four feet in length and one in diameter. Sweet potatoes, the root of a convolvulus, give good returns within three months after planting, and quantities of esculent arums (*Amorphophallus* and *Colocasia*) are grown in fields, furnishing a large supply of food.

Tapioca, introduced from South America, is now largely cultivated in Travancore, and admirably suited for still more extended use. As the price of rice has risen of late years, tapioca has become the more essential as an article of food. Within the last forty or fifty years, the growth of tapioca has rapidly spread; and now a large proportion of the population in the South live upon this root during the hot season. It will grow in any soil, and needs but little care except to preserve it from the depredations of cattle. After the roots are dug, the stem is cut into pieces about 4 inches long and planted some 3 feet apart, with a little ash or other manure. The root requires occasional weeding and earthing, and arrives at maturity in nine or ten months. Well boiled, it is eaten with fish curry. It is sometimes given to cattle. In a green state the root does not keep long, but it can be sliced and dried in the sun, or grated and made into farina. A field of this valuable and nutritious root is planted at but little cost; its yield is very large, and its cultivation highly profitable.

The produce has been estimated in Ceylon at 10 tons of green roots per acre: this weighs one-fourth when dried, and, if the dried roots gave half their weight of flour, it would amount to 2,800 lbs. per acre. With some care and attention any amount of the granulated flour might be prepared for home use and export; but, though this plant grows all around us, European residents find it more economical to send tc London for the prepared tapioca, as the people do not take the trouble to prepare it.

Arrow-root (*Curcuma angustifolia*) might be grown much more largely than at present. In an experiment with this root at Saidapet the produce was at the rate of 3,944 lbs. of tubers per acre, which would represent an outturn of one-eighth of that quantity of flour. The culture of this crop is very simple, so also is its preparation by reducing the tubers to pulp, mixing it with water, washing out the starch, and drying it in the sun. The flour could be sold profitably at 4 annas per pound. Last year 3,515 cwts. were exported, valued at 29,600 rupees.

Other culinary vegetables are Amaranthus, cucumber, brinjal, peas, &c. Fruits commonly grown are the jack, of which there are two or three million trees in the country, the guava, papaw, Anona, pine-apple, and plantains in great variety. The spices grown are pepper, ginger, turmeric and chillies. The exports of ginger amount to about 4 lacs of rupees; of tamarinds, 2 lacs; of turmeric, nearly 1 lac; of pepper 3 to 5 lacs; and of coffee, from 6 to 8 lacs. Good crops are often obtained from sesamum and horse gram, and much might be done in the production of fibres for cordage and papermaking.

"The size of farms is various; three or four hundred acres is an estate of considerable magnitude, which not two in a hundred will possess. The lesser farms do not exceed from seven to fourteen acres, and are often considerably smaller; indeed, taking the average as given in the Sirkar accounts, we should only have about two acres as the extent held by every farmer. A farmer with three hundred paras of paddy land, four hundred cocoanut trees, fifty areca, and twelve jack-trees, with vines yielding five or six tulams of pepper, will be in very easy circumstances; but scarcely twenty husbandmen in a hundred will have such a property; indeed, the lower classes rarely possess sufficient rice land on which to support their family; they trust, however, to the produce of their garden lands to make up the deficiency."

The following description of a Syrian Christian farming community near Quilon was furnished, in substance, by one of their priests:—

Though the Syrian Christians often complain of their poverty, they have fair houses, rice-fields, cattle and sheep, some of them possessing two or three native ponies. They are better off than formerly, and little oppression from government officials is now complained of. They cultivate rice for home use, reaping generally tenfold, of which a tenth is paid as tax to the Sirkar. Some will have rice to sell over and above what is required for domestic consumption. Then they have roots, plantains, and other fruits, &c., some of which are sold to boatmen and trading coolies, who carry their purchases to the town of Quilon for sale. Milk is procured from the cows. Sheep are occasionally sold at from 2 rupees to $3\frac{1}{2}$ rupees each —only the weakly or less valuable ones are killed and used as food.

A well-to-do Christian farmer may have twenty-five or thirty persons in his family, including sons with their wives and children. His annual income in money, derived from the sale of rice, sheep, cocoanuts, roots, and other produce, in addition to food of his own growth for all, may amount to from 500 rupees down to 50 rupees per annum. Out of this the purchase of clothing is almost the only expenditure in cash, excepting for marriages and festivals. The clothing may cost 70 rupees. The minimum expenditure here for marriage is 25 to 35 rupees, but sometimes extravagant sums are wasted in this way. There is not much hiding or hoarding of money in these days. The farmer invests his savings in additional paddy-land, which costs about 70 rupees per para, or less if the land be inferior or at some distance towards the hills.

A native friend supplies the following account of the life of a cultivator of the humblest class :—

A young man begins agriculture at the age of fifteen or so. Residing with his parents till the age of twenty, he may be able to save on his own account from 100 to 150 rupees, during this period. Then he gets married. After marriage, still diligently labouring, he may earn 65 rupees a year ; his expenditure will be 1 *fanam* ($\frac{1}{7}$ of a rupee) daily for food, and 40 fanams per year for clothing. Thus he may manage to save a few rupees a year. Then he builds a house and purchases some land. At the age of thirty he will be possessed of some property, and his annual income rises to 100 rupees, while his expenditure amounts to 70 rupees or 75 rupees.

The cultivator invests his savings in a lottery, to accumulate for the marriage expenses of his daughters. Then he may spend more than he has saved, and fall into debt and difficulties. But if his land be fertile and trees productive, he will recover ground again.

Taking the expenditure as 4 chuckrams ($3\frac{1}{2}$d.) a day, it may be apportioned as follows :—For rice, 1 chuckram ; salt, $\frac{1}{4}$ chuckram ; fish, $\frac{1}{2}$ chuckram ; cocoanut, $\frac{1}{4}$ chuckram ; curry spices, $\frac{1}{8}$ chuckram ; oil for light, $\frac{1}{8}$ chuckram ; tapioca roots, 1 chuckram, oil for the head, $\frac{1}{8}$ chuckram ; and the remaining $\frac{5}{8}$ chuckram for the noon meal, for which sweet potatoes, or peas, or jack, or mango fruits, or tender cocoanuts, or palm juice, or jaggery, are used. About 40 fanams will be required for cloths, washing, and barber's hire in the year. The annual expense for earthen pots will be 10 fanams; for mats, 3 fanams; for hospitality, 30 fanams; which, however, will be returned by others, as occasion offers.

The poorer class of cultivators generally go to their work at six o'clock in the morning, and return at the same hour in the evening. Only when the work is unusually difficult or pressing do they take solid refreshment at noon. They get food warm and abundant in the evening only.

CHAPTER XXI.

COFFEE CULTIVATION.

WITHIN the last twenty years, a new enterprise has sprung up, which has brought a considerable number of European settlers into the country, and covered the hills in some parts with careful cultivation, and a large, though migratory, native population. Where once the crouching tiger and lordly elephant, the panther and bear, the wild ox, sambhur and spotted deer freely roamed, there are now trim estates, neat bungalows, herds of cattle, and farm buildings, usually kept in firstrate order. Where formerly a score of Europeans assembled together on state occasions at the capital was a sight to remember, now a hundred may be seen at a public entertainment, or on the annual racecourse at Trevandrum. And though the planting interest is now struggling with serious difficulties and reverses, its influence on the social and economic condition of the country is a remarkable phenomenon of the age, worthy of attentive consideration.

The coffee plant was, perhaps two centuries or more since, introduced on the Western Coast by the Arabs, and in the early part of the present century cultivated in Travancore, some quantity even being exported. In the "Description of the Administrative System," by V. Kristno Row, we find that the export of this product in *M.E. 1018* (A.D. 1843), amounted to 155 candies = 910 cwt., on which a duty of 669 rupees was levied. This coffee would be grown by natives in the low country, and at a small altitude by Messrs. Binny & Co., of Madras, who, however, were unsuccessful with their plantations and afterwards sold them off. Further particulars of that period are not at present available.

Coffee was afresh introduced into Travancore, and extended to the Hills, about the year 1854, by Lt.-General Cullen, then British Resident. Procuring seeds from the Neilgherry Hills, he began a small experimental garden at Vélymalei, near Pulpanábapuram, at a height of about 1,800 feet. Here he cultivated nutmeg, cocoa, cloves, and other valuable plants; this garden still continues, and the acreage of coffee has of late been somewhat extended. Another small garden, of somewhat over two acres, was planted at Assambu, at a height of about 3,000 feet, which became the nucleus of a large estate, opened by the First Prince and Sir Madava Row, who jointly purchased the General's garden after his death. Experiments were also made by General Cullen with apples, New Zealand flax, and oranges, all of which failed, either through want of sufficient elevation, or through lack of care. Specimen trees of cypress, cedar, cloves, allspice, and the indigenous Assam tea, however, are now very healthy and flourishing. This portion of the Assambu Estate, now comprising about 12 acres in extent, is remarkable for the richness of the soil, being situated in a kind of basin, in which the soil washed down from the surrounding hills has collected for ages, and it has been known to give the enormous return of a ton per acre. The usual produce of this small plot is seven or eight cwts. per acre. The plants are now, of course, nearly thirty years old; some of the stems 13 inches in circumference.

Nearly fifty years ago a small estate had been commenced in the low country at Válrámpuram, near Trevandrum, by an East Indian. He planted his coffee in the shade of jack and other trees, and for many years made a considerable profit. The plantation has now nearly died out. But similar culture of coffee under fruit and garden trees is practised to a large extent in Trevandrum, Quilon, and elsewhere, and the produce is often a considerable help to the income of the native householder.

The first to enter upon the **professional culture of coffee** in the Travancore Hills was a native Christian, Mr. P. D. Devasagáim, of Assambu. This worthy man had been a teacher in the Mission Seminary at Nagercoil, but wishing to push his way in the world, he emigrated to Ceylon, at the same time generously supporting a teacher in his stead. He became a trustworthy and successful manager, and afterwards resolved to return and invest his savings in his native land. In 1859 he applied to the Dewán for a grant of 60 acres of forest land, which was granted after two years' delay and correspondence, demand being made at first for security to pay the taxes, as in the case of rice cultivation. Erecting a shed, in 1861, on a broad platform of rock in the Assambu Pass, he cut down the forest, drove off the wild beasts, and by the Divine blessing on a course of diligence and uprightness, now possesses a well-kept and profitable estate of 60 acres, producing in its earlier stage, before the appearance of leaf disease, about

400 cwt. of coffee, and now usually 160 cwt., half of the returns being net profit. Striking testimony to the worth and prosperity of this native planter was borne by H.H. the First Prince (now Maharajah) in a lecture delivered at Trevandrum:—

"Another example (of successful diligence) is that of Mr. P. D. Devasaháyam, of South Travancore. Born of very poor parents, at Nagercoil, and losing his father early, he was placed in the Mission Boarding School by the late Rev. C. Mault, and was there brought up and educated by him. When about eighteen years old, he was attached to the Mission as a catechist, with a monthly pay of five rupees. As such he continued for some years; but in 1844, at the instigation of a friend of his, who had just returned from a coffee planter in Ceylon with some little savings, he played the truant, and went over to that island in hope of large gain. At first he was employed as a conductor, on a salary of 20 rupees, under a coffee planter. He continued in Ceylon for about 20 years, during which he served several planters, and by his diligence and sterling honesty gave satisfaction to all. During the last few years he was employed in a large plantation, and drew 100 rupees per month. Being allowed a few months' leave every year, he was able to spend them in his native land, where, with his savings, he invested 2,000 rupees in a good house, and another 2,000 rupees in paddy lands. In 1858, he took it into his head to try coffee planting in the Assambu range of Hills. His hopes were strengthened by the sight of the coffee trees groaning under the weight of scarlet berries in the experimental garden of that keen and unwearied student of nature, the late General Cullen. In spite of very strong dissuasion from friends, he applied for land, obtained it, and at once seriously threw himself into the venture. Suffice it to say, that the results exceeded the fondest hopes. I have myself seen the Victoria Estate belonging to Mr. Devasaháyam, and I may say that it is one of the best chosen, best managed, best looking, and best paying coffee estates I have ever seen. In his neat, picturesque, and comfortable little *châlet*, with a coy little stream of crystal water near it, with every comfort which characterises a contented and cheerful homestead, with a bracing climate, with congenial and invigorating exercise in connection with his property, with the fruits of honest labour around him, with the sweet pleasure of having, ever and anon, silently contributed to a thousand little charities; without begging of any one, or crossing any one, and above all, with a clean conscience, Mr. Devasaháyam presents a model of life every way worthy of imitation in principle. I may add that myself and my partner have the good fortune of having secured Mr. Devasahāyam's agency to look after our property."

The pioneer of coffee culture on a large scale was the late Mr. John Grant, formerly of Ceylon, a gentleman in whom characteristic Scottish caution and kindliness were united with enterprise and indefatigable industry, and whose memory has been perpetuated by a hospital on the Hills, erected by public subscription; he was aided by two of his brothers. Mr. Grant received from the Sirkar a free grant of 500 acres of forest at Mahindragerry, north of Assambu; the planting of this estate was commenced in 1864, after a fourth of Mr. Devasagáim's estate had begun to bear. A total of nearly 800 acres was planted, and excellent pulping machinery, driven by a water wheel, introduced. Large crops have often been yielded by this estate—as much as 15 cwt. per acre on some plots of ten, twenty, or even fifty acres in extent. But, unfortunately, a fourth of the estate has had, of late years, to be abandoned, partly on account of the alarming spread and destructive ravages of leaf disease, but still more through fierce monsoon winds in the early part of the year blowing off the blossoms and preventing the growth of the tree. Another fourth seems to be slowly dying out through a disease affecting the roots, which has appeared both at Peermade and Assambu, and causes the whole tree to die off. Tea, cocoa, cinchona, and other products are now being introduced, and promise in time to prove remunerative.

On the Peermade range of Hills the first openings for coffee were made by Messrs. Baker and Munro, and General Stevenson, who obtained grants of forest land from the Sirkar for the experiment. Mr. Baker received a free grant of 500 acres, of which, however, 200 were grass land not available for coffee. The estate has been carefully managed, and is now of great value and giving good returns. Other estates also have prospered, but of late the ravages of leaf disease have been very trying. Tea is, therefore, being largely planted as a second resource, and so far, is doing well. From three to five cwts. of coffee has been the usual rate of produce per acre.

A planter who settled at Peermade with but small capital, but abundant energy and close application, accumulated within ten years a property of 250 acres of coffee planted land, worth say £10,000. From 20 acres of this estate he once gathered, in the second year, 18 cwt., and in the third year 120 cwt. of coffee; and from 150 acres, in 1876, about 400 cwt.

In 1862, when it appeared likely that this branch of agriculture would prove successful, a set of rules was drawn up by the Sirkar for grants of forest land, reserving valuable timber trees, such as blackwood and teak, and cardamom cultivations, and fixing an annual tax of three quarters of a rupee per acre; besides an export duty of five per cent., this to be remitted for the first five years on condition that a fourth of the land should be cleared and planted within the first three years.

Public attention having been widely attracted to the speculation, and several parties sometimes applying for the same tracts of waste land, indicating some amount of competition, the Sirkar established in 1865 a system of auction sales of the land, at an upset price of one rupee per acre, which continued till the last sale in October, 1874. At first there was little competition; but, in 1874 the upset price was raised to 10 rupees per acre.

The sale of these waste lands brought a considerable sum into the Government treasury. According to the State Administration report for 1874-5, the sales of land had produced over 3 lacs of rupees. Besides this, the annual tax of R. ¾ per acre on over 17,000 planted, and ultimately on the whole of the land taken up for coffee, ought to yield a good revenue. An export duty of 5 per cent. was imposed on coffee up till 1875, when it was dropped for a year or two, and afterwards re-imposed at 2½ per cent. on the tariff valuation of Rs. 20 per cent., at which rate it now remains.

It is impossible to trace year by year the precise **area actually under cultivation.** From the statistics for 1879, drawn up by the Dewán, it appears that the total extent of land sold amounted to 37,805 acres; and of this amount no less than 20,292 acres, though taken up with a view to coffee cultivation, were not then planted; and most of this is still in the same condition in consequence of want of capital, and the depression produced by leaf disease within the last ten years. The yield of mature plants was approximately estimated at from 336 lbs. down to 64 lbs. per acre, in various districts, the average of the whole being 192 lbs.

The following are the returns of crop exported for a few of the first and of the last years of the enterprise :—

1864	...	2,979 cwt.	value Rs.	59,644
1865	...	3,965 "	"	80,221
1867	...	9,655 "	"	211,542
1868	...	14,140 "	"	242,000
1877	...	50,000 "	"	990,058
1878	...	39,737 "	"	803,700
1879	...	18,781 "	"	374,600
1880	...	45,700 "	"	883,100
1881	...	29,611 "	"	599,400

The coffee estates in Travancore vary greatly in extent. The largest is Strathmore, comprising 2,800 acres, of which 1,500 are planted; and another is 600 acres, of which 500 are planted; and another 1,100 acres, of which 440 are under cultivation. Two or three hundred acres is a very usual size, and there are many smaller, down to native gardens of a few acres.

In 1879 it was stated that there were 121 regular coffee estates, and it is certain that but little increase has taken place since then, rather the contrary. The greatest proportion of mature plants is found in the southern estates, as the progress of the cultivation has been from the south northwards. The average elevation of the plantations is greater, however, in the north. The highest estate is in Velavengódu district, at an elevation of 3,900 feet; but there are only two estates there, which comprise unitedly 395 acres, and the out-turn of which for 1877–8 was the largest in the State, viz., 412 lbs. per acre of mature plants. The lowest estate is in Neduvengaud, altitude above the sea about 400 feet; and on this 154 lbs. per acre were gathered. The average produce for the whole in 1877–8 was about 276lbs. per acre of full-grown plants. Where the cost of cultivation is greatest, the out-turn also is greatest. In the two highest estates, mentioned above, the cost of cultivation was said to be Rs. 111 per acre.

Drought is often complained of in February and March, when rain is wanted to set the fruit. Coffee is a very precarious investment in Travancore, because the crop is entirely dependent upon rain at the blossoming season, and a few showers just at the right time make a difference of thousands of rupees to the planter. Violent and continuous rains in other months sometimes cause great injury to the plants, and carry away valuable soil. As compared with the estates in Ceylon, those in Travancore are very steep, the difference between top and bottom sometimes being over a thousand feet; they are thus greatly exposed to wash from heavy rains. The soil is, in general, a black or chocolate coloured loam, with a subsoil of red earth and decomposed granite; the quality much the same as in Ceylon—in some places very poor.

The profits made in the early stage of the coffee speculation, while the soil was unexhausted, the plants young and strong, and expenditure for manure not yet begun, and previous to the appearance of the leaf disease, were so tempting that nearly every one who possessed, or could borrow any capital, embarked in it. The "bumper crops" of 1869–70 and of 1871–2 added to the public eagerness. Those who had planted and sold out at such times made the most money, while those who just then invested came in for the bad times succeeding. The "coffee fever" spread, until at the last sale of land, in the latter part of

1874, wild competition sent up the price of land to an unprecedented extent. Hundreds of acres were purchased at rates varying from Rs. 10 to Rs. 57. Several small lots went up to Rs. 70. Two hundred and fifty acres were bought at Rs. 76; and some unfortunate native bid for 50 acres at Rs. 82, though he never got so far as to clear, or even pay for his purchase.

Many of the estates opened by natives were at by far too low an elevation, say from five to eight hundred feet, where there ought to have been two to four thousand feet of altitude, and consequently were subject to drought and premature exhaustion. Much of the land selected was unsuited to the growth and requirements of this plant, and the estates were often left weedy and neglected; the native planters were also generally less punctual and reliable paymasters than the Europeans. Many of these estates have since had to be abandoned, and great losses thereby incurred. But bad working had as much to do with the failure as the low elevation of the plantations. Native Christians who had saved money as conductors in Ceylon opened such estates, and their friends placing additional capital at their disposal, much loss was incurred. A trial of native probity and reputation was, at the same time, experienced, under which some lamentably sank.

Various entire estates, especially between Agastier and Assambu, and numerous inferior portions of others, have been **abandoned as unprofitable**, and are now returning to their original waste condition. Several causes of failure operated. One of the principal was the "leaf disease," which appears in brown or orange patches of fungus on the leaves, causing them to drop off, and injuring the fruit-bearing power of the plant. The fruits also were sometimes found empty of berry, or very light, the pulp only having been developed, while the external appearance led to large estimates of the produce that might be anticipated. Symptoms of the leaf disease were first noticed in Travancore in November, 1870. It appeared unmistakably in October, 1871, on several estates, but only became general after July, 1872; the other estates were completely stripped of leaves after the crop of that year. The disease first attacked a few individual trees, then patches; and finally the whole field suffered.

Bad management was also often a cause of failure after the time of the pioneers of the enterprise, who worked with a will. Lands were incautiously selected or carelessly planted, and extravagant expenditure incurred. Where a native might perhaps make a good living, an estate would not bear to be loaded with a monthly salary for a European superintendent; and there were instances in which some of these were not a credit to our country.

In various parts of the mountains strong winds, during the north-east monsoon, are the great enemy of the planter, smiting portions of the plantations so fiercely, that the trees could not grow, or are even blown down, and when in blossom the very flowers are blown off. Even trees for shade and shelter cannot be brought on in such localities. The wind is worse than in Ceylon, apparently because the Travancore Hills are a narrower range than the mountain region of that island—more like a backbone. If it blows fairly on an estate, the injury caused is less; but if sideways, and rushing through a gorge, it destroys all flower and fruit.

From these and other causes, some estates did not repay the expense of cultivation—in others, the crops were greatly lessened. Times were sadly changed. Where formerly two or three hundredweight of coffee per acre was expected even off two year old plants, or, at least, repayment of all expenses, there are now so many estates producing almost nothing that the whole average produce will not come to two cwts. per acre. A certain estate which cost Rs. 10,000 for up-keep in 1879, produced only eighty cwts. of coffee, value less than Rs. 4,000. Other estates only repay the annual expenditure. Some are quite abandoned after long and patient waiting and struggling in hope of better times. The total acreage thus abandoned we have not been able to discover; the subject is evidently too painful for free publication.

It is a sad sight to behold a ruined estate on which many thousands of rupees had been spent, and regarding which bright hopes had once been indulged. The plants, no longer pruned and trimmed, throw up thin, rod-like shoots, weeds and creepers flourish apace, and jungle shrubs spread and choke the neglected coffee. Among these the most conspicuous are ferns, *Lobelia gigantea*, *Knoxia corymbosa*, Melastoma, Elephant grass, Mussœnda, Clerodendron, and *Mœsa Indica*. Then jungle trees, as Macaranga, Conocarpus, Ficus, and the Bambu appear; though centuries must elapse ere the land returns to dense forest containing the same kind of trees, and of equal girth to those which had been felled to make room for the coffee.

In other parts of the East Indies, also, this branch of agriculture has suffered. The last crop on the Neilgherry Hills has been disappointing—much less than the estimates. In Ceylon, also, the late crop is complained of. Prices, too, have been considerably lowered of late through the large crops thrown into the market from Brazil, though this has hitherto been partly made up by the gain in exchange in bringing money from England to India.

Yet there are still, of course, some estates fairly prospering in Travancore, as evidenced by the export returns. Some small plots even yet produce nine cwts. per acre, and in one place a few acres give six to seven cwts. One estate is owned and managed by a gentleman of high intelligence, character, and industry, which was well opened, planted with good plants and in proper time, vacancies well supplied and weeding carefully attended to ; in fact, everything done in a business-like manner and the coffee cultivated to a high degree of perfection ; and, accordingly, it was not surprising to find that the best crop in the neighbourhood was gathered there two years ago, amounting to an average of 4½ cwts. per acre. Such returns would pay well. Some other estates yield two or three cwts. per acre, which will pay sufficiently well if expenditure be kept at a minimum.

The expense of up-keep varies from Rs. 50 to Rs. 80 per acre per annum ; 70 rupees may be regarded as a fair average. A crop of two cwts. per acre would, therefore, give some profit ; but if expenses are kept at the very lowest possible point, even one cwt. per acre might be made to pay.

So much, however, depends on care and skill in the original selection of land, on shelter from wind, which cannot always be assured beforehand, on good soil, and on personal superintendence, that it does not seem worth while for young men to come out from England at present. Any one of experience on the spot, purchasing cautiously and judiciously just now, while things are at a low ebb, might do well. Purchasers or investors are not to be found. The strain of bad seasons has been so heavy on the planters that confidence has been lost ; and many Europeans are thrown out of employment, some having lost their all. The Sirkar has heavily handicapped the enterprise, and been unwilling to remit duties in bad seasons, or even, until lately, when urged by the united action of the planters, to provide sufficient roads for the carriage of the produce to the coast—needed especially, as the estates are much detached. The stoppage of sales of land some seven years ago, effectually checked the opening of fresh lands, thereby, perhaps, incidentally saving other intending investors from ruin. It is feared that the felling of the forests may diminish the rainfall ; certainly it would, in such case, run off more rapidly, producing torrents or inundations. And it is a curious fact that the returns for Trevandrum Observatory, recently made up to date, do show a diminution of the annual rainfall at that station from an average of 68 inches to 62 inches. But the proportion of forest that has been cut for coffee to the whole mountain area is extremely small ; and the decrease of rainfall has occurred not only during the last twenty years, while this cultivation has been spreading, but also in the previous twenty years, during all which time enormous additions have been made to the number of fruit and timber trees in the low country, which has everywhere been more or less reclaimed and planted.

Earnest and minute investigations have been made, and experiments conducted with a view to the prevention or cure of leaf disease, but no definite conclusion has yet been arrived at; none of the remedies proposed have yet proved certain, or sufficiently economical for application to extended areas. Sulphur and burnt lime were applied with some advantage; and Mr. Schrottky, in Ceylon, has tried inoculation and vapourisation with carbolic acid, with apparent success; but whether this can be practically carried out remains to be seen. Leaf disease seems somewhat diminishing in violence in Ceylon, and hopes are entertained that this pest, like some other diseases of widely cultivated plants, may go off by degrees, and the coffee recover itself. But in Travancore, in 1881, after a period of some diminution, the disease was worse than ever; it was widely spread, and crops almost everywhere poor. The past year has been the worst ever known among native planters, and great losses have been sustained. Indeed, the out-turn has been a serious failure to all concerned, without exception. The yearly recurrence of leaf disease during the last decade has nearly ruined this once promising adventure. The misfortune of past seasons culminated last year in the almost total destruction of crops by the excessive rainfall. The coffee market, however, has gone up of late, and hopes are entertained of improvement in the coming year. Leaf disease seems now to be an accepted difficulty to be contended against, with little or no hope of getting rid of it by any "cures." A still more serious evil is "root disease," by which some estates seem to be slowly dying out. Probably the true and only effectual remedy for all present evils would be more generous cultivation, sufficient manure, and careful management of smaller estates than hitherto: the trees should, at the same time, be kept from over-bearing year by year, rather than forced to their utmost capacity and prematurely exhausted.

It is strongly felt that planters have erred in relying so much on one special product, as did the Irish agriculturists on the potato before the terrible famine of 1848; and that, instead of restricting their efforts to coffee alone, they ought to have tried a variety sooner, so that they are now casting about for other reliable cultivation. Their researches for gold are not likely to lead to much permanent or solid benefit, but more feasible inquiries are being made after valuable fibres, farinaceous roots, and other vegetable products.

Liberian coffee has been introduced, and grows fairly; though, as yet, it has not been planted to any large extent, and will always best suit a low elevation. In Ceylon, the new species is making rapid way. Numerous plantations, amounting in all to about 5,000 acres, have been formed at a moderate height; the trees are flourishing luxuriantly, and coming well into bearing. Some time ago 93*s*. per cwt. was obtained in the New York market, that is, 12*s*. above the quotation at the time for middling plantation coffee in London.

Tea, also, has been planted to a considerable extent at Peermade and elsewhere; some "supply" tea where the coffee dies off, as the former is hardier, and requires somewhat less richness of soil for its growth. Cocoa is being tried, in some cases planted among the existing coffee, and in others in separate plots; but seeds are somewhat difficult to procure in quantity, and the young plants very tender of transportation. A large quantity of cinchona seeds from the Neilgherries has been sown in nurseries, from which, it is hoped, some hundreds of acres will soon be planted. Some of those previously planted are doing well, especially *C. succirubra.* It is a question, however, how far the cinchona will stand the wind which has destroyed so much coffee. Nutmegs and cloves, and, perhaps, as in Ceylon, cardamoms, if the Sirkar should make the necessary concessions for its cultivation, as it is now a government monopoly; and possibly, in time, the Indiarubber trees, now being introduced, would form a welcome and remunerative addition to the products of the estates.

The influence of this branch of agriculture in Travancore, and the social and economic changes which have taken place in consequence of its introduction, have not been small. Two or three years before this enterprise was commenced, public works began to receive attention, and to provide employment for labour. Public buildings were erected, new roads opened, and the old policy of isolation by jungles and the absence of roads (still adhered to by the Government of Madagascar), became impracticable and was relinquished. Wages began to increase with the demand for labour, and the price of provisions and other necessaries also naturally rose. In 1859, cooly labour in retired parts of the country was attainable for an anna per day. The canal works in the South raised this to a little over two annas. The planters, however, were obliged, in entering on their work, to give at least four annas to induce ordinary coolies to brave the dangers of the hills; and eight annas or more were paid to woodcutters. Carpenters' wages rose from four to six annas, up to eight annas, or even a rupee a day. The labour of the previously enslaved castes, which had hitherto been almost valueless, being remunerated only by a few measures of rice daily, became of as great money value as that of others; caste was nothing in the eyes of the European planter. Accordingly, Pulayars, Pariahs, Védars, and other low-castes began to obtain employment and good pay; even their children earned wages for weeding, picking, and other light work, to which they were better suited than adults; and Ilavars and Shánárs working with them in the mountains, far from the critical observation of caste neighbours, saw little need to maintain the troublesome restrictions of caste by which they were bound in the plains. The Sudra masters complained of the planters taking away their labourers. But this competition and demand for labour largely ameliorated the condition of the poor. The native Christians educated by the Mission proved themselves of great service to the new industry, became overseers, confidential clerks, and managers, to European planters; and in time were able to acquire little plantations of their own. Prosperity and social advancement followed. Comfort was introduced into the homes of the people. Good houses were built; more convenient clothing worn; and the social influence and consideration of native Christians largely increased.

Numbers of the poorest classes of the population were thus removed from the degradation under which they had suffered, and relieved from oppression; while everywhere the landed proprietors were reminded of the necessity of fair and kind treatment to retain the services of their dependants. Some exercise of choice was now open to field labourers. Few, if any, Sudras or Brahmans, nor indeed Syrian Christians, availed themselves of the opening which the coffee enterprise afforded; and their circumstances consequently remained stationary as far as this went. As in the somewhat similar case of the introduction of railways—"The demand for workmen completely changed the relation of labour to capital. To a person on the spot it seems that the railway's chief mission in India has not been so much to aggrandize our own race, as to restore the balance between labour and capital among the native population, and to root out slavery from the land.

The higher classes of Hindu Society, by their inbred dislike and contempt for manual industry, disabled themselves from becoming a wealthy or powerful people, and are, at this moment being ousted from many posts of emolument by the despised mixed multitude, who had for ages done the work of the country, and who now, for the first time, are secured by an impartial government in the fruits of their labour. Even in education, the immemorial monopoly of the Brahmans, the competition of the non-Aryan element is beginning to be felt." ("Annals of Rural Bengal," pp. 137-255.)

One result of this enterprise not unworthy of mention, is the retirement and *limitation of the wild beasts* by which so many lives are annually lost in India. Dangerous forests, once filled with elephants, tigers, and wild boars, which sallied forth from time to time for raids upon the population and the cultivation at the foot of the hills, are now cleared and brought under cultivation. "The first ardent adventurers," says Sir T. Emerson Tennent, "pioneered the way through pathless woods, and lived for months in log huts, while felling the forest and making their preliminary nurseries preparatory to planting; but within a few years the tracks by which they came were converted into highways, and their cabins replaced by bungalows, which, though rough, were picturesque, and replete with European comforts. The new life in the jungle was full of excitement and romance; the wild elephants and leopards retreated before the axe of the forester; the elk supplied his table with venison, and jungle fowl and game were at hand and abundant."

Facilities were thus made for the increase and quiet settlement of the population, and their overflow into regions farther and yet farther inland. Waste lands in the interior, and especially on either side of the roads leading to the hills, are being rapidly reclaimed, and planted with native garden cultivation of roots, fruits, and vegetables, and with rice. As clearing and cultivation progress, the malarious fever, which is so deadly at the foot of the hills, is restrained in its destructive influences.

The large and steady circulation of money from the capital invested in this enterprise and its annual returns, could not but produce a powerful effect on the industrial and commercial status of the country, in the increase of remunerative employment and the dissemination of wealth. The planters calculate that they have expended altogether nearly 90 lacs of rupees on the land, in its clearing, planting, upkeep, and taxes. European push and activity have moved and guided the inert natives. Shops and markets have been opened to supply the workers, contractors, and artificers on the estates, with the rice, tobacco, cloth, arrack, and salt, which they consume. These are transported to the foot of the hills, in numerous bullock carts, which return laden with coffee. European goods are also in due proportion imported. Products are thus exchanged, and commerce promoted. The export of coffee has revived trade at some of the ancient ports; and gives employment to numerous work-people in its curing, sizing, and packing, at

Colachel, Quilon, and Alleppey, and to British ships and seamen for its transport over the seas. The Native Government has enjoyed an increase of revenue, not only directly, but also indirectly from the increased ability of the labouring and agricultural classes to pay their dues. These facts were briefly represented in the petition of the planters addressed in October 1872, to the Sirkar, pleading for remission of the export duty imposed, in the following terms:—

"This expenditure has gone to pay for labour and supplies; and every rupee of it is now circulating among the people of the country, enabling them to purchase a larger amount of taxable articles, enabling them to pay their land assessment more easily, and thus increasing their contribution to the revenue; preserving also numbers of people from starvation where other resources fail, as has been felt and avowed during the late time of scarcity. We may also notice the benefit to the State bv recalling profitable labour which had been diverted to other countries. The British capital which has been introduced into this country by British planters, has indisputably helped to make the country richer, and indirectly to fill the Sirkar Treasury."

A more intelligent and powerful public opinion is being created by the planters, who are able to plead their own cause, and not afraid to speak out in cases of public neglect or wrong. Hospitals, missions, and schools, commerce, and industry, have all had a share in beneficially affecting the native population. And, notwithstanding various evils usually inseparable from the spread of civilization and the increase of wealth, Christianity and the use of the English language are seen to follow from these and other benignant agencies at work upon the native population of India.

CHAPTER XXII.

COTTON MANUFACTURE.

COTTON not being grown in Travancore, and the people having hitherto been accustomed, even till recently, many of them by law obliged, to go half naked, and to wear only coarse qualities of cloth, the manufacture of this material is carried on to a very limited extent. Most of the calico used for clothing purposes is imported from other parts, and a Tinnevelly man may often be recognized in Travancore by his fuller clothing. The climate does not appear to suit the growth of the cotton plant, though attempts were made, some twenty years ago, by the distribution of seeds, to introduce the better kinds of Peruvian, Persian, Bourbon, and other varieties. The raw material required for hand-spinning, and other purposes, is imported from British India. The statistics of forty years ago give the imports of raw cotton as 305 candies, or about 200,000 lbs. yielding duty 3,020 rupees; and those of last year state the tariff value as 26,675 rupees, admitted free of duty.

Hand-spinning of cotton was formerly practised to a greater degree than is now profitable, and by several castes—Chetties, Ilavars, Shánárs, and Cháliyars. It was also tried in some of the Mission Boarding Schools, but dropped for more promising industries. To some extent spinning is still continued at Quilon and elsewhere; and in Trevandrum the Pánars spin and twist gold thread.

But most of the thread used in the country for indigenous looms is English cotton twist of the coarser grades. This is now readily procurable of native dealers, and is not only cheaper, but liked as being evenly and easier woven. Number 20 is most used, but 30's and 40's are not uncommon; and even finer threads for some work. The warp and weft are usually alike.

The imports of white cotton twist in *M.E. 1018*, about forty years ago, amounted to only 30 candies, or 20,000 lbs. weight, paying duty 713 rupees. It is now wisely admitted free, mostly coming by land or backwater, to the value of between one and two lacs of rupees annually. Last year the tariff value was 152,370 rupees, say £15,237.

Weaving is carried on only in private looms or very small works, in the houses of the people. Many cultivators do a little during the intervals of agricultural labour. It is most practised in the South and at Shenkotta, where the people are Tamil and the climate drier. The largest number of looms is here, next in Quilon, and Shertala, and next in Pundalum; there are very few in the inland mountainous districts.

The old statistical tables of over sixty years ago state the total number of looms then as 4,170. The recent census does not give this item, as there is now no special tax on looms; but it supplies information as to the number of workers in dress and textile fabrics, mostly, except tailors, engaged in weaving operations. These workers are 8,687 in number, of whom the greater part are Hindus; some are Muhammadans, others Christians.

The ordinary weaving class are called CHÁLIYARS. The Ilavars and Chetties, some of the barber caste, and others engage in this work. At Kottár there are Muhammadan weavers who make a useful cotton check cloth, the coloured yarn of which is of fast blue dye.

Besides these, mention may be made of the Silk-weavers, or PATTUNÚLKÁR of Kottár, a remarkable colony from the Bombay side, some of whom speak, besides the vernacular Tamil, a language called in the census "Nagaram." They weave silk cloths for the use of the wealthier class.

The CHALIPPARS of Trevandrum, about 1,300 in number, are also colonists, from the Telugu country, retaining their own language, who fabricate a coarse kind of sacking for gunny bags from the strong fibre of *Crotalaria juncea*, which might be much more extensively cultivated.

Much of the cloth produced is of a very coarse quality, consumed in the vicinity of the towns where it is made, and adapted only to native use as waist and head cloths, &c. The looms are very rude and simple in structure, and the common cloths are woven by boys. In such a loom we have seen a cheap cloth woven from No. 20 cotton yarn, in pieces each about four feet long and twenty-six inches wide, selling for five chuckrams. The material cost about 4½ chuckrams for each piece, leaving only half a chuckram profit. Of these cloths three a day were woven.

At Válrampuram there is a village of Cháliyar weavers brought from farther south by Dewan Oominy Tamby, who founded it in 1808, and intended it for an important commercial town. There are two neat streets with about a hundred houses of one story each, thatched, with small verandahs at the front, in which women and girls may be seen busy winding the thread. In the centre of the street stands a row of cocoanut palms, and devil temples of Ammen and Agastier occupy prominent sites. The people are pleasant looking, and seem fairly comfortable; but few, either of the children or adults, can read, and only one female out of the whole number of this caste in Travancore. Inside each house are from two to four looms for plain cotton cloth, mostly rather coarse. Some cloth, however, is made of 50's yarn dyed dark blue, but not fast colours; and even some of 60's, which is sold at 16 fanams (about 2¼ rupees) for a piece nearly six yards in length and of good width.

The shuttles are made of horn, or of the large reed (*Melocanna Rheedii*) the work of carpenters or Muhammadans, and thrown across from one hand to the other, without the English box and "pluckstick," by which twice as much work might be done in a day. It would be highly desirable for the Sirkar to introduce a few light and simple looms of the English pattern, as they are now introducing English ploughs. Some help towards improvement might be had from the admirable Industrial Establishment of the Basle Mission at Calicut.

Several warping wheels are in use in this village—a great saving of labour and a convenience in rainy weather. Still some prepare the warp for the cloth in the old-fashioned way on posts, stuck upright in ranges in the street like a rope walk, boys running back and forth with the thread. Rice-water is used for dressing. A yarn merchant has settled here and built a good two-storey warehouse, where he supplies English yarn from number 20's to 40's. The profits of weaving are less than formerly; all, young and old, having now to aid diligently in the work to obtain a living. Some fine head-cloths for females are made near Anjengo.

Though there is no export of cloth from Travancore, as was formerly the case to a small extent, it is difficult to assert that the weaving of cotton by hand has declined, as in most parts of India; probably it has not, for the population has increased in numbers and in comfort, and the custom of wearing civilized clothing has at the same time spread. In some places it is admitted that hand-loom weaving has decidedly increased.

In addition to the local manufacture, long-cloth, chiefly grey, coloured handkerchiefs, and other piece goods, have always been imported as needed to meet the demands of the population, from the neighbouring provinces and from Ceylon. These goods are now admitted duty free, except those brought direct

R

from England or Ceylon. The tariff value of imports of piece goods in *M.E. 1054* was 1,117,498 rupees, and in *M.E. 1055*, Rs. 846,632. Take a large average of 10 lacs for piece goods and 2 lacs for yarn imported, and double it for retail cost, say 24 lacs of rupees would be the total sum spent by the 24 lacs of inhabitants in the country, or only one rupee per head per annum for clothing, not very much beyond what is spent upon tobacco! Here is vast room for improvement.

English long-cloth is little used by the poor native population, and the low quality sometimes imported is complained of as giving less wear than country-made cotton. They say that four or five common English steam-loom cloths will wear out for one native hand-made cloth; and that the former, when worn out, are useless even for wicks, so much required for oil lamps, burning away too rapidly.

Cotton cloth purchased by retail in a market in Travancore seems, as far as we can judge, to cost fully a fourth more than the retail price in England.

CHAPTER XXIII.

COCOANUT FIBRE AND MANUFACTURES.

WITHIN the last twenty years a vast extension has taken place of the economic uses to which this valuable fibre is put. The term "coir," usually applied to this material, is the anglicised form of the South Indian *kayaru*, cord or twine, and is not applied in India to the raw fibre, which is called in the Tamil language *savuri*. The fibrous husk or rind of the cocoanut is, though uneatable, a very valuable part of the tree. It is readily stripped from the nut, while yet green, by striking it on the point of a stake or iron spike fastened upright in the ground; and it is then at once steeped in salt and brackish water, large bundles of the husk being secured together by means of netting, or bambu stakes in the water. It lies for several months, until the softer portions of the husk rot away, and the strong fibre alone remains. This is taken out, beaten with a stick to separate and clean the fibre, and twisted with a simple rope-making machine into the coir yarn, and this again is twisted with the required number of strands into rope of various thicknesses. It is also woven into webs of matting, or single mats, and the stiffer fibres made into brushes and other articles of domestic utility. The attempt has been made to prepare the fibre from the dried husk in England, but without success.

Much of the coir fibre used in England is brought from Ceylon, but a large and increasing quantity is now exported from Bombay and the Western Coast of India, especially Travancore and Cochin. The fibre is pressed like cotton for shipping into bales weighing 200 lbs. each. Where formerly the natives allowed it to go to waste, or used it as fuel, European merchants and native agents are prepared to give a price for this fibre, and the price is steadily advancing. Of course, the supply is not inexhaustible, but as prices rice, it encourages the cultivation generally, and makes it better worth while for the cultivators to bring the fibre to market even from some distance; fortunately for this traffic, all the growth of this palm is along the sea coast, where alone the tree flourishes and where generally there is water carriage.

Factories for the weaving of Coir matting have been opened by English and American firms at Alleppey, Quilon, Colachel, Cochin, &c., and turn out a considerable quantity of goods. The buildings are in quadrangles or long ranges, with iron roofing. Spinning is not attempted in these, as it is cheaper done by hand at the place where the fibre is produced. Along the coasts of the backwaters and canals, many people may now be seen busily engaged in scraping and cleaning the fibre, and twisting it into yarn. In the factories the yarn is first sorted to its various shades and qualities. The warp is made by boys running backwards and forwards, then it is flattened and smoothed for weaving by being run through heavy rollers. The weaving is laborious work, performed by men, who earn two or three rupees a week at it. The web is again rolled to give it some finish, wound securely in a roll and marked. Single mats are also fabricated.

Large profits have been made in this manufacture in India. But it can now be carried on so much better in England with the machinery and appliances available there, that a great quantity of the plain fibre and the yarn is exported from Travancore. These are worked up, by large firms in London and elsewhere, into matting and other articles of various patterns, colours, and degrees of fineness. One firm in Lancaster have introduced steam-loom weaving of this fabric. The various shades of fibre—cream-coloured, reddish brown, and blackish—which vary greatly according to care and skill in preparation—are first carefully separated: most of the fibre, however, is used of the natural colour. Cocoanut matting is now made of fine quality, with pretty shades of colour, and in pleasing geometrical and card-loom patterns, so as to be available for higher uses than the very coarse makes; and the material is most durable. The yarn is also plaited by machinery into cinnet or belting.

Cables made from coir bear exposure to salt water better than anything else, the tannin which it contains preventing the fibre from rotting; they are exceedingly light and buoyant as well as elastic. Coir cordage in Dr. Wight's experiments broke at 224 lbs. weight. Even the refuse and broken fibre can be turned to account for stuffing mattresses, draining flower-pots, &c., as no insect will touch it.

The exports from Travancore of this material made from the apparently worthless husk of the cocoanut, in addition to the leaves, wood, shells, dried kernel (*copra*), and oil, amount to considerable items in the list, and form more than half of the whole. In the last year, under report, *M.E. 1056*, (1880-81) exports of coir yarn amounted to 137,000 cwts. valued at 12½ lacs of rupees (say £126,000), and paying to the Sirkar a duty of Rs. 62,755. Of fibre 681 cwts. were exported, valued at Rs. 4,900; and of the cocoanuts themselves nearly nine millions, valued at Rs. 243,100, and paying customs duty Rs. 12,154. Other products of this palm exported—as oil and copra or dried kernel—were valued, the former at Rs. 272,600, and the latter at no less than 28 lacs of rupees, making a total value of the export of products of the cocoanut palm from Travancore alone of 46 lacs of rupees (approaching half a million sterling), besides all that is used in the country itself. Some thousands of tons are also exported from Cochin. A valuable palm this!

Statistics of the quantity and value of the matting manufactured are not given in the annual Government reports.

The market price, of late, in Travancore and Cochin for fibre is from Rs. 11½ to Rs. 12 per bale of 200 English lbs. In London this is sold by auction, at rates varying from £22 to £31 per ton. Coir yarn is sold in India at very varying rates, from Rs. 25 per candy of 654 lbs. for the very lowest quality, to Rs. 67 for the very best. In the European market the price for the same qualities respectively now ranges from £20 to £45 per ton. The demand in England is active, and steadily increasing. Scarcely enough of the raw material can be procured to keep the present machinery going. Good prices are given for fair qualities, but complaints of bad colour, harsh fibre, and unsatisfactory preparation, are frequent.

Cocoanut fibre is so durable, useful and economical a material that a great future is assuredly before the industry; and as prices rise, the natives will pay increasing attention to the collection of the whole amount produced, and to its careful preparation. Perhaps when, through increased demand, the fibre becomes still more expensive, it may be found possible to prepare it of greatly improved quality and appearance by steaming or boiling, so as to avoid the pollution of ponds and backwaters by the decomposing pulp of the husk, and the consequent blackening of the fibre so often observed. The textile ingenuity of the present age of invention may perhaps devise some additional uses for this fibre; hats and bonnets made of this material, it is said, attracted much attention at the Great Exhibition in London.

CHAPTER XXIV.

BOATS AND FISHING.

WATER communication in Travancore being so generally available, and in some localities the only means, various classes of boats are in constant use. On the smaller rivers, tiny canoes a few feet in length, and lightly paddled by a single person, must be always at hand, to enable those who live on the banks to cross over or to get about; on the line of traffic north and south, by backwaters and junction canals, long narrow canoes for ordinary passengers, or cabin boats for those of better means, and slower baggage boats for heavy merchandise, are continually travelling hither and thither, while on the sea-coast immense numbers of fishing canoes and rafts are employed, besides a few native craft of clumsy make and small burden, which work as coasters for the carriage of cocoanuts, salt, and other bulky produce.

The ordinary canoe or *vallam*, sometimes called a "dug-out," is fashioned from a single large log hollowed out and trimmed by carpenters, generally in the forests where the tree grew. The best and most durable timber is the *anjelly* (Artocarpus hirsutus), but jack and other woods are also used. They are made from the smallest size of a few feet in length, scarcely bearing the weight of a man, and rising but a few inches above the surface of the water, to the largest, measuring perhaps 43 feet long by 3¾ in width. The commonest size for a passenger canoe (such as is represented in the illustration) is from 20 to 30 feet long and 2½ to 3 feet broad. These are propelled by a bambu pole along the shallow waters, at the rate of about two and a half miles an hour; sometimes a second man rows with a paddle at the bow, or a sail made of soft matting, hence called *pāy*, is set up on a bambu mast in the fore part of the boat, in which case it may progress at the rate of six miles an hour, where there is plenty of "sea-room," and the wind is favourable.

Being round-bottomed, however, and without any keel, these canoes rock and list heavily with waves or wind; there is much labour in propelling them under adverse circumstances and on a dark night, so that the men are often afraid to proceed. Losses do occur by the capsizing of canoes every year through mismanagement, sudden squalls, or overpowering currents.

Scores of these boats start every night with the passengers for Trevandrum, Quilon, and other towns. They are crowded and uncomfortable, usually as many as thirteen passengers in a canoe, sometimes more, in which case there is no room to lie down; but the rates are exceedingly low, say about three chuckrams for 24 miles. Passengers try to fall into the company of others of somewhat similar caste, and may spend part of the night pleasantly chatting together before falling asleep. A European can travel pretty comfortably, though slowly, in one of these canoes by engaging one for himself, at the rate of a little over a rupee for 24 miles near Trevandrum; and two and

CANOE OR VALLAM.

a-quarter rupees for 40 miles farther north. The latter distance can be done in eighteen hours. Two men take turns in poling; or one rows and the other poles. A mattress is spread in the centre of the boat, the mat covers are drawn over the whole space, and there is abundance of room for luggage, provision box, and a servant or two. Sometimes all fall asleep in the night, and the boatman slily stops work to take a snooze or go ashore to refresh himself. The men are usually Ilavars, Roman Catholics, or Muhammadans; the last I have found the most troublesome and unaccommodating to deal with. The introduction of steam navigation, long talked of, and now proposed by a Scottish company at Quilon, will doubtless be a great public convenience, as it has already proved at Cochin and Emakulam.

Names are sometimes given to these boats, such as *Colatoor-polay ódi*, from the place where the timber was felled; or

Rómakku ódi, "fly to Rome." The owners hire them out to poorer men, who work them. Some possess three or four boats, or as many as ten or twelve; and a good canoe will last, with proper treatment, fully forty years. The best and largest cost up to Rs. 200 each, the monthly hire of which class will amount to four rupees.

Baggage boats called *Kettuvallam*, or "sewed boats," also ply in great numbers on the inland navigable waters. They are built of planks sewn together with coir cordage through holes drilled in the edges, the seams also being caulked, as it were, to make them water-tight, with coir fibre and yarn, round and over which the stitching goes. The general outline is the same as that of the canoe, but of course they can be made of much larger size. A second-class one, the largest in which passengers would care to travel, as they are so very slow, though roomy and comparatively cool, is about five and a quarter feet wide, and twenty-five to thirty feet in length. Being protected with a semi-circular waggon-like cover of matting which rises to the

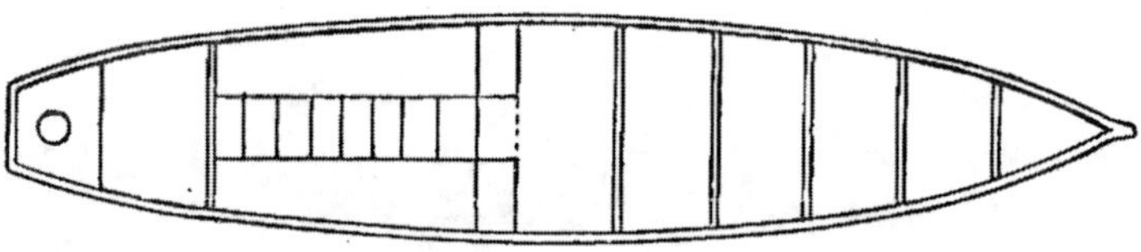

PLAN OF CABIN BOAT.

height of six feet above the bottom of the boat, one can almost stand upright or lie crosswise in it; a table and chair can even be used, much less fatiguing than being compelled to lie for a whole day, or longer, in a narrow canoe with low cover. But the time occupied in a journey is much longer.

The burden of this boat would be sixteen candies; say over four and a half tons, and the hire for sixty miles with two men about Rs. 2¾. Large baggage boats cost from Rs. 300 to Rs. 350. They are owned by various classes, and are hired out at the rate of Rs. 50 or Rs. 60 per annum to men who work them from place to place.

Graceful and swift **cabin boats**, invaluable to travellers, ply on the smooth backwaters and up the rivers. They are built at Cochin or Quilon of anjelly, teak, and jackwood; usually about thirty feet long and six feet in beam. In the front half of the boat are seats for ten to fourteen rowers; the stern part is covered in as a little cabin with wooden roof, windows, doors, and seats, which latter are more frequently fitted with planks,

CABIN BOAT.

so as to make a level floor on which the mattresses are spread for reclining or sleeping, while boxes and other luggage are neatly ranged underneath the seats. A second little box cabin and other accommodations are frequently attached for females and children, or servants. The plan is given above.

The *Marakán*, or steersman, occupies a little seat outside the cabin door, and a native servant may occupy the other. The steersman is sometimes owner of the boat; generally a clever and sharp fellow; he leads the chant, and indulges as he may see necessary in reproof, encouragement, or small wit to cause a smile amongst his men. The paddles are of bambu, with a flat saucer-shaped piece of wood secured at the end of each. An awning can be spread over the rowers in the heat of the day.

The men pull lustily, accompanying their labour with a song, or rather a responsive chant, the words of which it is very difficult to make out. I have often asked my native companions whether they could distinguish the words, and they always professed to be unable to do so. On one journey, by making special inquiries on the subject, one or two of their songs were obtained. Some are improvised and simply amusing, incoherent, or nonsensical—others are Roman Catholic religious compositions—others from the Rámáyana, and other poems appropriate to Sudras rowing their long snake-boats. There are said to be ballads on the Great Fire at Alleppey, the Inundation at Trevandrum, and such like, but no patriotic or national songs.

One of the common chants used by boatmen has been very accurately reduced to notation by Rev. R. Collins as follows:—

Some of these boatmen are very athletic, well-made, fine looking men. Their usual time from Quilon to Cochin (ninety miles) is twenty hours, resting a short time half way to eat their rice; and I have even known them after such a journey offer to go on, after taking six hours' rest, to Trichoor, forty-five miles farther, and then was amazed to learn that they were arranging to start on their return with the empty boat almost immediately again.

The fare for the above ninety miles for the whole boat, whatever travellers or luggage go in it, and a dozen rowers, inclusive of half hire for taking back the empty boat, is about Rs. 30—for sixty-four miles it is about Rs. 17.

A first-class boat will carry a great deal of luggage stowed in different parts—say up to a couple of tons—and there is quite room for several travellers, or a family. It is much more convenient, expeditious, and for a large party more economical than locomotion by bullock carts, where there is so much packing and unpacking and exposure to the weather. But the jerking of the cabin boat by the paddles is a sad hindrance to writing on the way.

These boats cost Rs. 500 to Rs. 900 each, and will last for twenty years or more. They earn, if well managed, Rs. 150 to 200 a year. Many are owned by Roman Catholic Christians. The rowers often complain of suffering from impressment for travellers, the Beach Superintendent, one of their own class appointed by the Sirkar, taking bribes from those who are better off and strong in body, and often seizing the poor, the aged, or boys, beating those who attempt to flee to avoid the inconvenience. Some better arrangement should be made, or the rates raised, to secure voluntary labour.

Boatracing is a favourite pastime, for which considerable facilities exist on the numerous rivers and lagoons. Long "snakeboats," low in the water, with ornamental bow and stern curving upwards, are the principal boats used. These are paddled by men, who keep good time in singing, and become greatly excited, yelling and shouting when warmed up with the race. At temple festivals in some parts, these boats form a striking feature of the scene. At Chembakulam, for instance, annually in June, boat races are run in honour of the Ambalapuley god, Bhagaván, by various classes of people. Certain lands are held on condition of this service, the holders of which circumambulate the temple, carrying flags of the god.

So at Aramula: "18th August, at 5 A.M.," writes Rev. W. J. Richards, "finds us opposite the great temple steps, on which an immense and excited crowd stands, some holding long lighted cressets which are reflected in the water, making a weird appearance in the grey light of morning. The river is alive with canoes, big and little, which are objects of great interest to those on the bank. There goes a stately racing-boat with its prow nine feet out of the water, and manned by a hundred rowers, besides a large number of singers standing up, and keeping time with hands and feet to the plash of the oars. These boats are reported when full to contain 200 persons each. How proudly they stand, how exultingly they sing, how gracefully they sway to and fro! Mark the feathering of the oars, and the musical motion of the paddles stretched far from the boats, and brought to the water at the end of a circular sweep. How fine the boat looks, ornamented at head and stern by plates of burnished brass and large silver-headed nails, which they call 'bubbles'? This is Onam, the great festal season of Travancore, and these are all high-caste people performing their national boat game. These five great boats abreast make the air ring with their songs as they glide in state down the river. If we could but wait till next Monday, the 23rd, we should see twenty-five together."

For fishing purposes the simplest possible invention is the raft or catamaran (*kettu-maram*, "tied-tree"), consisting of four or five logs of very light buoyant wood, such as the *Erythrina Indica*, fastened together with cross bars and ropes near the ends. It is surprising how often writers carelessly speak of the rafts and boats as made of the cocoanut tree—a wood which sinks at once in water.

Mounted on these strange floats, and of course almost nude, for the water freely washes over and through the logs, and paddling with a piece of bambu, the men go out to fish for hours, even hoisting a diminutive sail when the wind favours.

The fishing boat is like the ordinary canoe, but narrower and deeper, and not so long; provided also with a plank on either side as a kind of gunwale. These boats cost Rs. 50 to Rs. 100 each; but with outfit of nets, say Rs. 140. They are owned by Roman Catholic or Muhammadan fishermen, partners often uniting, so that thirty or forty persons may be interested in one boat. Hooks are used, or small cast nets, out at sea; and a quantity of young sharks will be brought in—some good large fish like carp, and many others. On some days nothing is taken; at other times four or eight chuckrams' worth. The least takes are in the hot season, from February to April; the largest in the S.W. monsoon, June to August, when the weather admits of their going out at all. Occasionally large quantities of seer fish, or Indian salmon, are caught,

Sharks are taken with a large hook and chain: from the liver the oil is extracted, and the flesh eaten by Muhammadans, Ilavars, and Roman Catholics. Multitudes of the young are daily caught, and it must be a great advantage that the numbers of these ferocious creatures are kept down in this way. As it is, they are sufficiently dangerous, carrying off Pulayars gathering shells for the manufacture of lime, or Védars diving in the sea outside the rocks for shell-fish, or fishermen who may fall into the water. "If a shark once seizes a man it never lets go." But in rare cases agile men may escape with the loss of one or both hands, or a leg.

A large proportion of the fish are caught with the long drag-net, consisting of a cotton bag with fine meshes in the centre, and wide meshes of knotted coir rope at either end to lead the fish into the central bag. The upper ropes are supported by wooden floats, and the under ones kept down by stone sinkers, so as to make a kind of wall of rope. An immense quantity of cordage is used for this net, which almost fills a small boat, being nearly half a mile in total length.

One end is left on shore in the hands of a few helpers, and the other end carried to sea by boat, and then payed out in a semicircle: after an hour or two it is dragged in to shore by ten or twenty men and boys. Idlers assisting in the haul are rewarded with a few of the fish. The two ends of the net are equally pulled, boys shouting and beating the water in the middle to drive the fish into the bag as it nears the shore.

Large quantities of fish are taken in these nets, chiefly ribbon fish, mullet, pomfret, mackerel, rayfish, with bushels of sardines and small-fry. Thousands of cuttle-fish are also caught and eaten. Perhaps about one and a half rupees worth is the average produce of a single haul. The fisherwomen wait with their baskets ready to run with the fish to the nearest market, and the small fishes are spread out on the sand to dry in the sun.

The supply of fish in the Indian Ocean is abundant, and practically inexhaustible, and with larger boats and better appliances a vast addition might be made to the food store of the people. "But more scientific means than the catamaran and the hook are required to gather in from the sea the harvest which nature provides. Steam trawlers pay on the English Coast, and should do so on the coast of the Madras Presidency, if worked with economy." A more liberal policy as to the salt tax should, however, be inaugurated. The *net* revenue or profit to the Government from salt in Travancore amounts to twelve and a half lacs of rupees, which averages a fraction over half a rupee per head for man, woman, and child, rich and poor, for taxation alone, besides the actual price and retailers' profits of the salt consumed. The general testimony is that numbers of the poor "have to put up with two-thirds of the proper quantity—are not able to afford sufficient—do not get enough—suffer much from this cause." But the Native States are in this matter obliged perforce to follow suit with the British Government, and to keep up with their scale of taxation of this article.

Salt might, at least, be supplied in Travancore, as in Tinnevelly, at lower rates to fishermen for curing fish. This trade is at present a nuisance and a danger to the public health, from the bad quality of the provisions cured rather by the sun than by the antiseptic. Vast numbers of good fish are found in the seas; and the people are prepared to use them largely as food, and do use them; but heavy taxes on salt, and heavy duties on exports are highly repressive of this valuable industry, which might expand and become an additional help in periods of general famine.

"If capitalists should embark on the business of fish-curing," says the British Commissioner of Salt Revenue, "the Government will be willing to aid them by the duty-free issue of salt at the lowest possible price consistent with the realization by the Department of a fair manufacturing profit; and on some such conditions as that suitable and secure premises be provided for the custody of the salt, and for the conduct of the operations of fish-curing; and that the adventurers pay for the deputation of a Government officer to supervise the work, and to prevent the removal of the salt otherwise than in corporation with the salted fish; and give such other security as may be thought necessary that the privilege granted them will not be abused." Unfortunately, however, on the West Coast the best months for fishing are the most dangerous and unsafe for boats.

At the same time greater freedom, protection, and consideration should be given to the fisher-classes. These have somehow always been helpless, uneducated, and the prey of their rulers, and ought certainly to be freed from the depressing extortions of which they still complain in Travancore.

CHAPTER XXV.

INDIAN MUSIC.

THE Hindus have an ancient system of music, which is described in some of their musical treatises; and even a rude notation, which, however, is not in common use at the present day, the national melodies sung or played by musicians in the temples or in social life, being handed down from generation to generation by ear. It is impossible to tell how far these tunes have become changed in course of time, but no doubt many of them might claim a very high antiquity. Some of the Sanskrit works explain the law of musical sounds, their divisions and succession, variations of scales by temperament and the enunciation of modes, besides a minute description of the different instruments, and the rules for playing them. Within the present century the Indian music has been investigated by several European scholars, and explained in various essays in the "Asiatic Researches" and other literary journals, and in separate dissertations upon the subject. And within the last twenty years natives of great learning and ability have devoted much time and effort to the revival of the indigenous music, writing down ancient standard tunes, composing new ones in similar style, and discussing at large the principles of Indian music. Such are Rajah Sourindro Mohun Tagore, who has published much on this subject, and has done more for the revival of Indian music than any other man, not only by his books but by his orchestra, organized to illustrate the art in the Hindu School of Music, and his Bengal Philharmonic Academy; Rajah Debendranath Tagore; L. N. Ghose; and Krishna Dhana Banerjea, of Calcutta, and others. Christian missionaries and evangelists also have within the same period introduced these tunes into public worship, and employed them for attracting audiences to the preaching of the Gospel.

The Hindus are acquainted with our **scale of seven tones**, or graduated series of sounds used in music; and denote them by letters which are the initial names of those notes, viz.: Sharja,

Rishava, Gándhára, Madhyama, Panchama, Dhaivata, and Nishada. The gamut therefore is as follows:—

sa	ri	ga	ma	pa	dha	ni
do	re	mi	fa	so	la	si *or* te.
C	D	E	F	G	A	B

This is called the *Pracrita Shurogram*, or Natural Scale. It is also called *Surgum*, from the four first notes of the scale.

Various and complicated Scales, however, are used in Hindu music. "The English Diatonic Scale," says Mr. L. N. Ghose,* "is like our Pracrita Shurogram, having five *Sooras, i.e.*, tones, viz.: sa, ri, ma, pa, and dha (C, D, F, G, and A), and two *urdhasooras, i.e.*, semi-tones, viz., ga and ni (E and B)."

"When these notes are divided into twelve semi-tones, they form our *Bicrita Shurogram* (artificial scale), like the English Chromatic Scale, having *kamala, i.e.*, flat, and sharp (*tibra*) sooras. We use also the smaller intervals than semi-tones, called *Srooties*, which are almost like those of the Enharmonic Scale. They are twenty-two in number in the compass of our Pracrita Shurogram, as specified in the following table:—

Sa	to	Ri	4	Srooties.
Ri	,,	Ga	3	,,
Ga	,,	Ma	2	,,
Ma	,,	Pa	4	,,
Pa	,,	Dha	4	,,
Dha	,,	Ni	3	,,
Ni	,,	Sa of the next Heptachord	2	,,
		Total number of Srooties ...	22	

Or, as the case is put by J. D. Paterson,† "The Hindus divide the octave into twenty-two intervals, which are called *Sruti*, by allotting four Srutis to represent the interval which we call a major tone (between the first and second, fourth and fifth, and fifth and sixth, notes of the octave); three to describe a minor tone (between the second and third, and sixth and seventh), and two the semi-tone (between the third and fourth, and seventh and eighth); not as being mathematically just, but as means of representing to the eye and to the understanding the supposed relations which these intervals bear to each other; merely to show that a semi-tone is half a major tone, and that the minor tone is a medium between the major and semi-tone, being less

* "Hindu Music." Calcutta, 1874.

† "Essay on the Gramas or Musical Scales of the Hindus." Asiatic Researches, Vol. IX.

than the former and greater than the latter. Mathematical calculation is out of the question."

A *Sruti*, or sub-tone, is therefore sometimes a quarter-tone, and at others the third of a tone, according to its position in the scale. "From the simple calculation of the number of Srooties," continues Mr. Ghose, "we can form different kinds of scales according to our present system of notation. We can write twenty-one notes in our *Stabaca*, consisting of three lines intended for the three natural *Saptacas* or Heptachords, viz.:—Udara, Moodara, and Tara. In each line we can note down seven notes belonging to each of the Saptacas, with the exception of our two additional (ledger) lines. Example of the Bengali Stabaca or Staff, containing twenty-one notes of the three natural Saptacas without ledger lines."

C D E F G A B

C D E F G A B

C D E F G A B

By varying the length of the vowels, the means of indicating notes of two different lengths are found in the gamut; other marks are used to indicate greater length. Then, for the purpose of expressing the octave as above or below, the connection and succession of notes, the process of execution or of fingering the Vina, little circles, ellipses, crescents, chains, curves, lines straight, horizontal, or perpendicular, are employed, and the close of a strain is distinguished by a lotus flower.

All singing and playing are in unison: **harmony and part-singing** seem to be almost unknown in India, which causes their music to be generally uninteresting, if not repellent, to European ears. Indian harmony, where it exists, is mostly confined to a monotonous repetition of the keynote during the flights of their instrumental or vocal melody, as in the case of the Scotch bagpipes. In this instrument the drone consists of two pipes sounding the keynote or tonic, and the fifth or dominant, one or other of which will suit all the notes of the melody.

The word *Sangíta*, symphony, or sounds in combination, as applied to music, conveys the idea of the union of voices, instruments, and action. Rev. R. Collins remarks respecting the temple music, "The hautboy is accompanied by a number of horns, some of great length, all of which sound the *tonic*, sometimes in concert with the *dominant*, the only attempt at harmony I have ever heard in Hindu music."

It has been much discussed of late years whether the Indian melodies can, with any fair degree of approximate accuracy, be

written in the European notations, even with the addition of a few special signs; and native scholars in Bengal have written strongly upon both sides of the question. Sir W. Ouseley, in his "Oriental Collections," says:—"A considerable difficulty is found in setting to music the Hindu *rágas*, as our system does not supply notes or signs sufficiently expressive of the almost imperceptible elevations and depressions of the voice in these melodies, of which the time is broken and irregular, and the modulations frequent and very wild. Many of the Hindu melodies possess the plaintive simplicity of the Scotch and Irish, and others a wild originality pleasing beyond description." It is indeed questioned whether these numerous Srutis, or quarter-tones, which are mentioned in old Sanskrit works on music, and which of course have no symbols in the European notation to represent them, are actually found in the tunes now used. But perhaps the opinion expressed by native musicians that their tunes cannot be played with perfect accuracy on such instruments as the organ or piano, and that the violin and other stringed instruments alone are suitable, may indicate that the Indian music does use intervals which are not symbolized in the European notation, and that other accidentals are used as well as the European flats and sharps.

"It is true that in rendering European music, keyed instruments (being tuned in equal temperament so as to answer, as well as possible, for all the keys) do not perfectly accord with the human voice in any except the key of C.* The reason for this is that the so-called whole tones are not equal in value. The interval between Do and Re is greater than that between Re and Mi; and that between Re and Mi is greater than that between La and Si. Organs are made to fit the scale when Do falls on C; and when the pitch is changed and Do falls on another letter, the regular succession of whole and half tones is secured by the use of flats and sharps; but the interval between C and D is too large for the interval in the scale that falls on it, and one of the shorter intervals of the staff has to do service for the long interval between Do and Re. For example, in the key of F, which has one flat in the signature, Do falls on F, and Re falls on G. But the interval between F and G is not long enough; and when a good singer sounds Do in accordance with the F of the organ, he will find G of the organ a little flatter than the Re of his voice. So when he sounds Sol in accord with C of the organ, he will find D of the organ a little sharper than the true La of his vocal scale. One playing on a viol can

*Note by Mr. J. S. Curwen:—The old organ-tuning had C in perfect tune, and other keys more or less out of tune; but modern equal temperament was specially designed as a compromise, and makes *all* keys a *little* out of tune.

produce sounds in any key that exactly harmonize with the human voice. If it be found that intervals of a quarter-tone are used in some Hindu tunes, the necessary symbols for indicating them should be invented and added to those now used to indicate flatting or sharping by half tones. It is, however, probable that the real difficulty lies in the differences between the intervals of the natural and diatonic scales that are hinted at above.

The Bengali tunes that have been printed suggest three principal points in which Hindu and European music differ. One of these is that Hindu music has *no proper harmony*. True, there is a drone in the common native bands, and the various bass and treble drums are carefully tuned to be in harmony with the drone. In singing troupes, also, children and women take part, and so the harmony of the octave is secured. But the harmony formed by the bass, tenor, soprano, and second treble sounded together, so that three other melodies are subservient to the air and harmonize with it, has no place in Hindu music. The European delights in symphonies, in which the high, low, and middle notes of the different parts, and those produced by many kinds of instruments, blend into a succession of harmonious sounds. He delights to have an air repeated, with variations in its harmonious accompaniments. He delights in a melody alone when rendered by a good voice or a favourite instrument; but still more to trace that melody amid a flood of harmonious sounds that sweeten and perfect it. But this is all unintelligible to the average Hindu.

Another point of difference regards the *time and movement* of music. In this the Hindu excels. The European is content with the simpler modes of time. He has double, triple, and quadruple movements, with their varieties of quick or slow; and he rarely indulges in a sextuple movement, or an occasional triplet. The supple Hindu uses other and more complicated modes of time. One author reckons quintuple as one of the kinds of time, and gives exercises in it. He also gives tunes in which the measures are alternately in quadruple and in triple time. Doubtless quintuple and sextuple movements would be found well nigh impracticable to Europeans.

The third point of difference is that the Hindu is trammelled by *none of the European rules with regard to key-notes*, changes of key, and closes. He indulges in an unlimited use of accidentals, and trills, and shakes, and slides. He mingles major and minor modes. He often gives to a syllable a note that includes the last part of one measure and the first part of the next. He begins and ends his tunes on any notes of the scale that please him. The first of the Bengali songs in Krishna Dhana Banerjea's 'Self-Instructor for the Sitara' begins on the fifth and ends on the seventh. Another of the songs, with a signature of four flats, begins and ends on B flat —that is on Re, the second of the scale. These will doubtless be considered defects by those used to the European rules of musical composition; but to learn to like these liberties one has need only to become used to them." All these, in fact, are *Modes.*

"It should, however, be borne in mind that the term Hindu Music is very indefinite. Each nationality of India has its own peculiar style of music. There is little similarity between the tunes of Bengal and Madras, and those sung by the Marathas are still different."*

Through the predominance of certain tones, or essential sounds, tunes are said to be in the "Mode" of that tone. The Doh mode, according to the Tonic Sol-fa nomenclature (which calls all scales starting from any one of the twelve semi-tones by the same name as it gives to the notes of the scale of C, namely, Doh, Ray, Me, Fah, Soh, Lah, Te, Doh), the Fah mode and the Soh mode are called Major modes, because they have a major third above their predominant tone. "The simple minor modes were used by the ancient Greeks, by the ecclesiastics of early ages, and are more or less used at the present day by all the great nations of the East, as well as among the hills of Scotland and Wales, and in the country places of England and Ireland."

"The old *modes* took almost any note of the major scale as a key-note, *e.g.*, 'Scots wha hae' takes the fifth: the old form of several psalm tunes now written as ordinary minors took the second. The mode taking the first as the key-note seems to be 'the survival of the fittest.'" (Curwen.)

The Chinese use the Pentatonic or ancient musical scale, easiest described as that formed by the black keys of the pianoforte. It consists of the first, second, third, fifth, and sixth degrees of a modern diatonic scale. This scale is also associated, as mentioned above, with Scotch, Irish, and other Celtic melodies. The Javanese instruments are all in the same kind of scale, and more than half the melodies of the Negro Jubilee Singers also omit the fourth and seventh tones. The Hindus, however, are by no means confined to the use of one, or a very limited number of scales.

The Rágas, or musical modes of the Hindus, are stated amongst the Tamils and Malayális as thirty-two in number, and each is supposed to have a peculiar expression capable of moving some particular sentiment or affection. They are

* *Indian Evangelical Review*, vol. i. p. 526.

regarded as appropriate to various seasons of the year or periods of the day, after which some of them are named.

It is doubtful whether the term *Rága* (in the feminine *rágini*), used in Indian music, answers precisely to our "Mode." It does not mean tune, because various pieces may be sung to the same Rága, while the tunes are obviously different. Nor does Rága in all respects correspond to Mode. Various writers assert that *Thata* (mould), in which the notes are arranged in different but peculiar orders of succession, ascending or descending, which may be formed into a variety of Rágas, comes nearest to what is implied by a mode. To each thata two or more rágas or ráginis are appropriated.

"The three predominant notes in each rága are called *graha*, *nyása*, and *ansa*. The note with which a rága begins is called *graha;* that in which it ends, *nyása;* and that which is most frequently used and predominates over all the other notes, *ansa*. The latter is the same as *bádi*, and is the origin of the graha and nyása. According to the Sanskrit authorities, the same note should be the graha and nyása; but in modern practice this rule is not strictly observed."*

There are three kinds of characteristic melody for the structure of rágas—either by the use of all, or the exclusion of one or of two, particular notes.

Tála simply means time or speed: its only object is to calculate the measure of beating time. Tálas derive different names from the variety of *mátras* (the measure of time in pronouncing a short vowel), four, six, eight, &c., that form them.

Besides the ancient rágas, various names are given to various styles of composition.

"*Kheál*, or *Kiyál*, is generally a love tale, supposed to be uttered by a female. The style is extremely graceful, and replete with studied elegance and embellishments."

"*Tuppa* or *Dappá*.—These songs were formerly sung in very rude style by the camel-drivers of the Punjab, but since brought to perfection and elegance by the famous Shoree."

Kummi is a poem in which the verses are of the same metre as that sung by women, with dancing and clapping of hands.

Unjal páttu, a swing song; and *táráttu*, a cradle or lullaby song. *Tulla páttu* is a lively or quick melody, songs with dance or mimics.

Native poems are rarely read simply, but usually chanted in a kind of recitative, which seems, however, well nigh incapable of being reduced to English notation. *Kuratti páttu*, or "Ku-

* "Six Principal Rágas," by S. M. Tagore, Mus. Doc., Introd. p. 38.

ravar woman's song," is used for Malayálam and Tamil poems; and we have a brief "Life of Christ" in the small compass of eighty-eight lines, which is committed to memory, and sung with much interest by children, and is frequently used in open-air preaching to familiarize the hearers with the grand facts on which Christian truth is based, singing a few distichs, then explaining the meaning, and so on.

The Kuratti Chant is as follows:—

MAL. LYRIC, No. 38.

In the South of India, music appears to have been maintained and cultivated as a science long after it had ceased as such in the North. Nearly a century ago a distinguished native Christian poet and songster, called Védanáyagam Sástri, of Tanjore, was raised up, in the providence of God, in the Tamil country for the benefit of the Christian Church there. He was a pupil of Father Schwartz, and died in 1864, at the ripe old age of 92. He learnt, at considerable cost, the best temple and classical tunes, to which he composed Christian lyrics and poems. His original works in poetry are said to amount to a hundred and twenty in number. Other authors have since appeared; but in the last edition of the "Tamil Christian Lyrics," Védanáyagam Sástri's hymns still form a very large proportion of the whole. His sons and talented daughter, and now his grandchildren, followed in the same line, but rather as musicians than writers of original poetry. They occasionally travel through the Christian churches in South Travancore, and had the honour of performing even before the Maharajah. Their entertainments of singing of hymns, with explanations, comments, and exhortations interspersed, and with musical accompaniments, are extremely popular amongst both Christians and Hindus, who will gladly sit up all night to hear them; and the native Christians make up handsome sums for the remuneration and travelling expenses of these minstrels. Unfortunately, however, they attempt to combine Hindu caste with Christian teaching, and most pertinaciously and bigotedly refuse to partake of *any* food, at any time, along with, or prepared by, other Christians, or Europeans, for which reason some missionaries feel unable to avail themselves of their professional services as freely as they otherwise might. I have frequently heard them, and learnt some tunes from them. At Neyoor, for instance, some ten years ago, the son of the celebrated poet came to the Mission House to sing, accompanied by his three sons and a little boy and girl with fiddles, tambourine, and small hand-cymbals. The old gentleman, the leader, was rather coarse in features and harsh-voiced. He wore a great gold-laced turban. The younger men were pleasant-looking, with long *kudumis* and nice dress. They keep fine time and sing with expression. One *suram*, or composition, was very odd, delivered with tremendous vigour and rattle at certain parts—a marvellous specimen of execution. The native poets sometimes go to hear a European military band play, and then, without knowing, or, indeed, caring (why should *they?*), what were the words associated, in English, with the tune, go at once and write a religious hymn to the pretty tune; so they had the tune of "The Ten Little Nigger Boys" for a lyric played really well and powerfully. Lastly, the leader expounded a Tamil lyric on the Incarnation (No. 47) "*Vánam búmiyó,*" &c. "Is heaven become earth? Two wonders are here," said he; "heaven become like earth, and earth like heaven. Why? How? Heaven filled with human souls saved through Christ. Earth become the residence of the Son of God." Occasionally he introduced some Eastern and fanciful illustrations and witty remarks. The tune of this lyric has been published in a small collection of Indian music by the C.V.E. Society, Madras, 1875, from which we reprint it here:—

RAGAM. SENCHURUTTI.

In conversation with the singers afterwards, they asserted that these tunes could not be written down, especially the finer tones, grace notes, &c., which could only be learnt by hearing them for ten years; in fact, by becoming Tamil songsters.

These lyrical compositions and native tunes were formerly disliked and objected to by some European missionaries, as stilted in style, full of vain repetitions, unmusical and undevotional. As far as there may be truth in these criticisms, the remedy is within reach—to write better ones; but I have not found them undevotional or in any way unsuitable to the use of the native Christian Church. Spite of all objections, they have made way, and are now adopted, to a greater or less degree, all over India, and used by the Brahmo Somaj as well. Our European music is no doubt more refined and scientific; at a few mission stations part-singing is admirably performed; and we shall always wish and endeavour to instruct select pupils in English sacred music. But the attempts of new or untrained converts at hymn-singing are generally either ludicrous or distressing; and it is not within our power to bestow an extended musical training in the English system upon the large and rapidly increasing body of native Christians. Nor do these yet appreciate the beauties and excellencies of our music; while they can readily, even at the beginning of their Christian life, with a little aid and encouragement, pick up the indigenous tunes; and these do please their taste and arouse their enthusiasm, as we have often witnessed. They still prefer their own national music to ours, and sing it with much greater accuracy and feeling.

The Hindu melodies are usually short, lengthened by repetition and variations, somewhat like the Rondo. The Chorus, or refrain, comprising sometimes one, sometimes two lines, is printed at the commencement of the hymn, and is sung first, and usually repeated after each verse. The first line of each verse is generally repeated; and native singers, in singing the chorus, often repeat lines, or parts of lines, to suit their own taste.

One distinction from English hymns is important. In Indian metres the lines are measured, not so much by the number as by the quantity, of the syllables. If, for instance, a bar in 2-4 time contains the music for two long syllables set to two crotchets, you may in the next verse find four short syllables. In that case the two crotchets must in practice be resolved into four quavers, and sung to the four short syllables. "This is at first perplexing, but the difficulty soon wears off by practice. The best plan to surmount it is, probably, to sing the chorus and first verse repeatedly till they become quite familiar; and then it will be easier to adapt the music to the rest of the hymn. Native singers find no difficulty in this." (Parsons.)

We have in Malayálam a volume of lyrical hymns and psalms, in the fourth edition, carefully revised, improved, and enlarged each time of reprinting, now containing 216 lyrics, and sold for half a rupee; besides a "Life of Christ," in standard native metres, and other compositions. Such hymns, with their appropriate melodies, were a powerful bond of union, and even a means of excitement during the recent agitation of the "Six Years People;" and they are urgently needed, and already successful, so far as tried, for attracting the heathen to the preaching of the Gospel. Any number of people can be gathered to listen, and interested, by singing these Lyrics in or near a street. The meaning of the verses may at the same time be explained. We have known Hindus accept fly-sheets containing copies of these Christian hymns interspersed with expositions or enforcement of truth, learn the tune from the preacher, and take the papers home to sing in their houses. Many of our leaflets and tracts are now issued in poetical form, as are all the Hindu religious works, and even some on medicine and other sciences. They always ask for "a song" when they see tracts in our hands for distribution. No people, in fact, are more susceptible of the charms of music than the Hindus: it is most encouraging and cheering to hear the Christian converts singing at family worship in their houses or at their work in the fields, or the dear little children in the schools, with bright eyes and glowing countenances, singing their sweet hymns of praise.

It is highly desirable, therefore, that the popular tunes of India should be reduced to notation, and made generally available, critically comparing the various renderings prevailing in different places, selecting, revising, editing, and printing the best version in a permanent form, either in the Tonic Sol-Fa or the Staff notation, or in both, in order to secure a *common standard* of song. Some beautiful tunes current in one district are not known in the neighbouring districts or languages ; and as the singing has hitherto been always by ear alone, widely differing versions are in existence, of which one will probably be found, on examination, decidedly preferable to the others.

During the last twenty years several attempts have been made to reduce these Lyric tunes to some fixed notation. A small volume called the "Hindustani Choral Book," compiled by the Rev. J. Parsons, and containing ninety tunes in Staff notation, was published at Benares in 1861. And in Madras the Christian Vernacular Education Society published in 1875, under the title of "Indian Music," twenty-four of the Lyric tunes in use among Tamil Christians, collected by Mr. De Riemer, of Jaffna, from various sources. Some were learned of the daughter of the old Tanjore poet, some from the best native singers in Madura and Jaffna. They were written out according to the English method of notation, with the aid of a musical instrument.

"One of the most needed missionary agents in India," says the *Indian Evangelical Review*,* "is a travelling missionary musician, one who can sing well, and is thoroughly acquainted with the science of music, and with both the old and the Sol-Fa notations, and the various Hindu notations, so as to be able to write down in the old or Sol-Fa notation any tune—Hindu, Mussulman, Santáli, Bengali, Tamil, or Telugu—he may hear throughout the country. Few Europeans can learn them, because they are not written in any notation known to Europeans; and being not written down, they are not fixed, and variations of them are common and confusing. If the zenana missionaries had such a book containing the music of India, with or without the words, they could carry a small harmonium or concertina with them into the zenanas and sing, with instrumental accompaniment, a Christian hymn to Hindu music, to the edification as well as delight of their pupils."

Dr. W. W. Hunter remarks: "The musical art of India still awaits investigation by some eminent Western professor; and the contempt with which Europeans in India regard it merely proves their ignorance of the system on which Hindu music is built up."

The missionaries of neighbouring provinces in South India might without much difficulty arrange to confer together, in order to fix the notation of the more popular native tunes, and to obtain uniformity as far as possible.

* July, 1881, p. 129.

Harmony, in its modern import, is, as we have seen, scarcely recognized or used in Indian music, its predominant character being melody. But to introduce and commend such music to Europeans, it seems necessary to add some simple harmony, as has mostly been done in the case of those previously published. The melody of any piece is certainly improved and set forth by the use of a judicious harmony which does not overpower, or overload, but adorn it. Harmony should be applied solely to the support of the Indian melody, which alone speaks the language of passion and sentiment. Especially is it requisite, if we wish to adapt Indian music to the public services of Christian worship, to add enough accompaniment to admit of a piece being sung by a soprano voice to the organ, harmonium, or piano. Two-part harmony may suffice: at the very least a couple of notes must be added as a primitive accompaniment somewhat in the native style—as, for instance,  to the following melody, which we have heard sung with great excitement by the Revivalists :—

MAL. LYRIC, No. 108.

Allegro agitato.

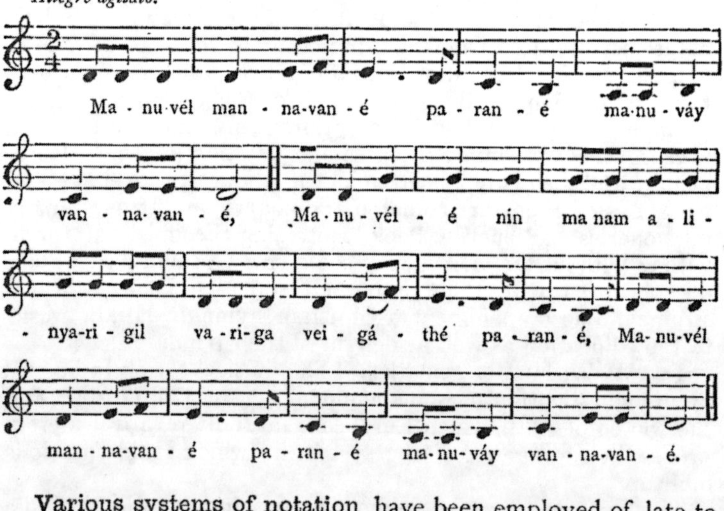

Various systems of notation have been employed of late to represent the Indian tunes. Some have thought it advisable to revive the ancient Sanskrit notation, with such modifications and improvements as are necessary for adapting it to modern requirements. This is used in S. Mohun Tagore's "Six

Rágas," but it seems more cumbrous than the English Staff notation, which he also gives.

A somewhat similar native system is advocated for writing the Tamil Lyric tunes by the Rev. J. P. Ashton, M.A., of Calcutta, who has given considerable attention to this interesting subject for many years past, in the following remarks with which he has favoured me:—

"Though for short notes sa, ri, ga, &c., are written, and sá, rí, gá for long notes, it is the custom to pronounce them all as if long, making the distinction only in the time of dwelling on each.

The Tamil way of writing the tunes is simple. A glance shows whether it is in common time or triple time. It is not used for very complicated music any more than the English Sol-Fa. Both are admirable for beginners, and for ordinary hymns and songs; but both are discarded as too clumsy for instrumental music.* Still, of course, both could be used. Again, Curwen introduces arbitrary symbols of his own to indicate changes of key. These are never used in Tamil, because at the beginning of each tune the name of the Rágam to which it belongs is written, which tells the learner at once either what notes will be entirely omitted, or what notes are to be sharpened or flattened. Again, the matter is simplified in another way, viz., that it is not the custom to change the key in the course of a piece of music, as it often is with us. To give an example—as my music teacher in Madras taught me long ago—the hymn "*Tarunam eeth*," &c., is in the Bheiravi Rága, and its characteristic is that ga or mi is flattened; or to express it otherwise, it may be sung in the key of G, but B must be B♭ in each case. This is the correct way of writing it, but native Christians ordinarily sing it as if it were in the key of F, and make the F♯ into F. But my teacher told me this was wrong, so I give it now as he gave it. The scale is as follows for Bheiravi Rága:—

F♯	G	A	B♭	C	D	E	F♯	G
ni	sa	ri	ga	ma	pa	dha	ni	sa

which may be thus expressed—key of G, with B flattened.

The tune (as sung in Madras) is as follows, in Tamil Sol-Fa:—

ni ni sa ri rì	rí ga rí sa	rì ma ga ri sa	rí — ni ni
ta - ru - nam - eeth - un	kát - chi sá - la	ar - ul a - ná - thi-	yé — div - ya

* Mr. Curwen dissents from this opinion; he has not yet found any music which is too complex to express in his notation, and finds that his pupils play very readily from it.

sa ri má gá ri	sá — pa pa	pa pa pá dha pa	ma pa pa ma ga
sa - ru - va nee - thi	yé div - ya	sa - ru - va nee - thi	yé ————

ri sa	ni ni sa ri má	ga ri sá
——	div - ya sa - ru - va	nee - thi - yé

Or, to put it in the old notation :—

RAGA, BHEIRAVI.* TAMIL LYRIC, No. 206.

"I think that the Tamil sa, ri, ga, ma, is simpler than our Sol-Fa, especially for Tamilians. A few simple additions may be made to make it more accurate and complete—as, for instance, to distinguish between the three octaves, write thus—ṣa sa ṡa, the dot above or below signifying the highest and lowest octave, and that without a dot the ordinary intermediate sa.

Again, in the triple time above, if seven short syllables occur instead of six in a bar, it is evident that two must be semiquavers: this may be indicated by a line underneath, as (ma pa pa ma ga ri sa.) Such difficulties seldom occur, except in those cadences by which they pass down from a high note at the end of one line to the low note at the beginning of the Da Capo, &c. These are, after all, left much *ad libitum*. The Tamil plan may be recommended for its greater simplicity and national character."

The European Staff notation has been generally used, and seems, with quarter-notes in small characters where required, to be quite effective; though it is perhaps not so economical in printing as the use of letters for the notes. It is supported by

* Mr. Curwen would write this tune in G minor, signature two flats. The E flat in bar seven is peculiar, but to write it in G major seems very far-fetched.

natives as well as Europeans as entirely sufficient for writing Hindu music in all its branches.

In our Travancore Mission, the Tonic Sol-Fa system has been adopted, and recommended after trial for several years, being approved as simple and convenient for teaching or writing these tunes. The Sol-Fa uses a fixed nomenclature for the proportions of the scale, but the notes in any key are called by the names they bear in the key of Do or C. For purposes of comparison, we give below the preceding Lyric tune written in this notation by Dr. T. S. Thomson, of Neyoor, as sung in South Travancore. And if the Madras and Neyoor versions be compared with the Trevandrum rendering given in "Land of Charity," p. 150, the character of the variations which commonly occur will be at once perceived.

TAMIL LYRIC, No. 206.

KEY F. CHORUS.

| d :—:r | m :m :m | m :—:m | f :—:m | r :m :f | m :—:r | m :—:— | —
Ta-ru

:d :d | r :m :f | m :—:r | r :—:— | —:—:— | s :—:s | l :—:s | m :—:—

D.C. for verse.

| —:d :d | r :m :f | m :—:r | r :—:— | —:m :r ||

A few other Lyric tunes written in the same notation by Dr. Thomson, or others, will be found in the Appendix. The following specimens, in the Staff notation, of a few of the simplest and easiest written of these melodies may afford material for study and criticism. Longer and more intricate pieces we have been unable as yet to get written.

RAGA, BHEIRAVI. MAL. LYRIC, No. 71.

CHORUS.

The above tune, having been written from a base voice, should be in a higher key.

RAGA, DAPPÁ. TAMIL LYRIC, No. 23.

Harmonized by Mr. B. Mansell Ramsey.

TAMIL LYRIC, No. 18.

CHAPTER XXVI.

MUSICAL INSTRUMENTS.

THE native instruments used in Travancore are of all three classes, pulsatile, or drums and such like to mark the rhythm—wind instruments, as pipes and horns—and stringed instruments, like the guitar. The conch shell, which is blown in temple worship, and the *kokra*, used in demon worship (p. 49), can scarcely be classed as musical instruments. The gong also, a flat plate made of a composition of copper, zinc and tin, is beaten in temple worship, or as calls to ceremony, and gives a deep rich tone. Strings of small ankle-bells are used by devil-dancers, tied round the leg as symbols of their profession. They produce a faint clashing sound. Larger ones are tied round the necks of bullocks like sleigh-bells on horses. And small hand-bells are rung in all idol-worship. "No ceremony of sacrifice or oblation is ever performed without preliminary tinkling of the bell, which is repeated at certain intervals according to the ritual. No set of sacrificial utensils is complete without them."

Drums are of various classes, some played with a stick, others with the hand. One kind, called the *tambattam*, or tom-tom, is so closely associated with devil-dancing that it is disused by Christians, as are also the kokra, chunk, &c. A performance is sometimes given on drums alone.

Small basin-shaped cymbals of bell-metal are constantly used with vocal music to beat the time. Generally the edges only are struck together, producing a sweet tinkling tone, but sometimes the faces, which make a hollow, unmusical sound.

Various wind instruments are used, resembling respectively our fife, clarionet, horns, trumpets, and bagpipe drones. Reed pipes are in universal use, like flageolets in appearance, but with a sound precisely similar to that of the bagpipes, only rather more melodious.

Stringed instruments are the most popular for private use, and are generally of the guitar or lute family, in varied forms and sizes. This will be evident from the accompanying engrav-

MUSICIANS.

ing of a party of native musicians in Trevandrum, in which five of the instruments are of this class, and one is a small drum. A rude instrument is made of the cocoanut shell as a body, covered over with parchment or bladder, a long reed or bambu for string-board, and two or four wires (in the latter case one being of brass). It is played with a small bow, or with the fingers, as a simple accompaniment to singing, and help to the voice. These are usually called *Tambúras.* "The four-stringed lutes are tuned to one chord, in whatever key is required—generally of C—and the finger passed rapidly across the strings; or the notes are played separately but quickly, so as to form the chord in vibration." The wire-strung guitar is much used by mendicants and religious devotees in recitation of hymns, and other sacred singing.

The Vina (Been) or lute is an Indian guitar of peculiar construction, the best and standard musical instrument of India, and one of the most ancient. The make somewhat varies in different parts. It is a fretted instrument, usually having seven wires or strings, and a large gourd at each end of the finger-board. Its usual extent is two octaves or two and a half. "It is the instrument," says Willard,* "of the greatest capacity and power; and a really superior Veen in the hands of an expert performer is perhaps little inferior to a fine-toned piano—and, indeed, for Hindoostanee music, the best devised, and calculated to be adapted to all practical modifications.

The Veen is strung with seven metal wires—three steel, and four brass; but, as is the case with the Sitar and the Rubab, the melody is generally played on one of the steel wires, and the rest are chiefly for accompaniment. Several fingers of the right hand striking simultaneously on several of the wires, each of the fingers to be thus employed is armed with a plectrum, usually made with the large scales of fishes, and fastened on with springs, or tied down with thread."

The finger-board of the Vina with nineteen frets is two and a half octaves; and the frets themselves represent the following notes in English music:—

D D♯ E F F♯ G G♯ A B♯ C C♯ D D♯ C F F♯ G♯ A D

The following details are given by Fowke ("Asiatic Researches," vol. i.):—"The finger-board is $21\frac{6}{8}$ inches long, and about two inches wide. The whole length of the instrument is three feet seven inches. The wires are seven in number, and consist of two steel ones, very close together, in

* "On the Music of Hindustan."

T

the right side; four brass ones on the finger-board, and one brass one on the left side.

They are tuned in the following manner:—

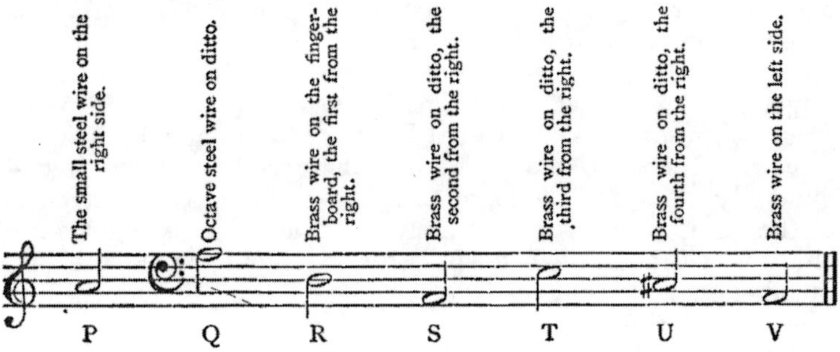

The notes given by the frets will appear on the following scale. I have added below the Indian names of the Surgum, which the performer himself gives to the notes. It is very observable that the semi-tones change their names on the same semi-tone as in the European scale:—

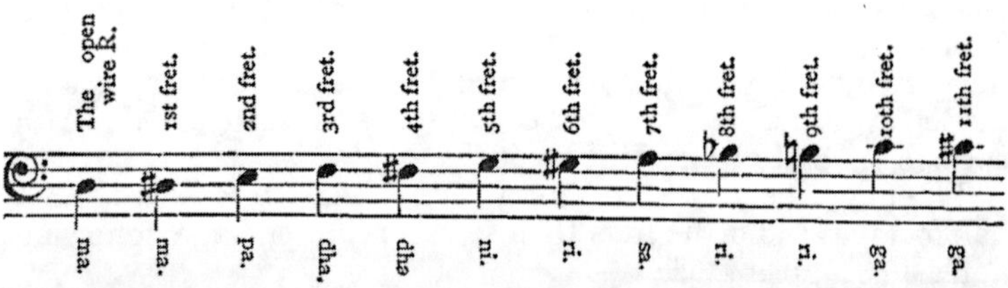

On the wires R and S, which are those principally used, there is an extent of two octaves—a whole note with all the half notes complete in the first octave, but the G♯ and B♭ wanting in the second. The performer's apology for this was that he could easily get those notes by pressing the string a little hard upon the frets F♯ and a ♮, which is very true, from the height of the frets; but he asserted that this was no defect in his particular instrument, but that all Beens were made so. The wires T U are seldom used except open. The frets are stopped with the left hand; the first and second fingers are principally used. The little finger of the hand is sometimes used to strike the note V."

"From the nature of the instrument," says Rajah S. M. Tagore,* "the Vina is tuned in fourths. Although the three Saptakas, in which the whole scope of Hindu music is confined, are considered as natural, yet the human organism of voice is not so powerful as to produce more than two and a half octaves. In imitation of vocal music, the finger-boards of our instruments also are adjusted so as to exhibit the same extent of notes. Such being the case, ma or F, which occupies the middle position in the octave, *i.e.*, between the two perfectly similar tetrachords, must be adopted as the key-note; otherwise the compass of notes would either fall short of, or exceed two and a half Saptakas, allowable in practice. Should the Vina, instead of being tuned in fourths, be successively tuned in thirds, seconds, &c., the extent of notes would fall short of two and a half octaves; and, again, should it be tuned in fifths, sixths, &c., the extent would by degrees exceed the limit."

In Travancore and South India, the Vina is the instrument which is learnt by ladies of high caste in the seclusion of their zenanas, and some of them play very prettily on it, accompanying their voices in songs. None of the music is written. The airs are very pleasing, wild, or rather plaintive, and some require great execution. The Vina, as used here, has six strings made of metal, and at the side are three very fine strings, which are played with a backward movement of the little finger before each bar or phrase of the music. The best instruments are procured from Mysore.

Vinas are made chiefly of blackwood or jackwood, which are said to give the best tone. They are generally much carved and ornamented, the long neck of the instrument ending in a carved dragon. One made of blackwood, and ornamented with silver, costs Rs. 60; but they are procurable down to ten rupees, only there is much trouble and waiting to get them. The gourd at one end is rested upon a cushion in playing.

"The musicians of Hindustan appear not to have any determined pitch by which their instruments are regulated, each person tuning his own to a certain height adapted by guess to the power of the instrument and quality of the strings, the capacity of the voice intended to be accompanied, and other adventitious circumstances." (Willard.)

The want has long been experienced of suitable musical instruments for social enjoyment at Christian marriages and other festival occasions. The people are very fond of music,

* "Six Principal Rágas."

and at times sit up to hear it night after night. But some of their amusements are simply a nuisance to neighbours not interested in them, if indulged in at hours when people require rest; and the tom-tom and other instruments produce only barbarous noises, besides being objectionable on other grounds. Rev. F. D. Ward says of the common music: "What renders the music of India so unwelcome to a cultivated ear is the limited number of their tunes, and, therefore, constant reiteration of the same notes, and the small variety of their instruments, together with the imperfect manner in which they are played. The most common article, and one that is dinging in your ear wherever you go is the tom-tom, which is nothing more than a half-tanned sheepskin drawn, when damp, over a wide-mouthed earthen or iron vessel from six to twenty or more inches across, and when dry beaten with a stick or leathern throng. This is often accompanied by a pair of sharp-sounding cymbals. A funeral procession is preceded by two persons blowing each a long horn, which emits a doleful and prolonged note of a distinctive, and, at times, very plaintive and sorrowful character. Every pagoda of any note has a band of musicians, who are obliged to attend at the temple twice every day to make it ring with their discordant sounds and inharmonious airs."

The caste difficulty also crops up here, as everywhere. Shánár Christians consider it degrading to play these instruments, and hire a lower caste to do it for them: these are mostly officiators in devil-worship, who cannot sympathize with Christian sentiments or principles, and who should not be called in at such times. A barrel organ has been thought of, but this could only meet the want to a very limited degree, being too expensive for general use, uninteresting with European tunes, and lacking sufficient variety or adaptation. Missionaries are, however, working gradually to this end by the training of Christian musicians and singers; and it is principally with this view that I have entered into the subject so fully in the present chapter, and attempted to offer practical suggestions. The violin is highly popular with the men, and readily procurable: hand-cymbals and tambourine are also in use. But some inexpensive and simple instrument is wanted for Christian females educated in the mission schools, and for the senior girls' classes under instruction. Many have acquired a simple and solid elementary education, and sing pleasantly by ear; but they have no instrument for their amusement when at leisure in the house, or on social occasions. To encourage such singing, and help the people to procure instruments, would at the same time tend to bring into notice and training any superior voices, or musical talent that exists, enable our converts to interest and benefit their Hindu neighbours, and ultimately aid in the general improvement of the service of song in the house of God. "Let the people praise Thee, O God; let all the people praise Thee."

The Vina is too costly, and is not procurable without much trouble and delay; the concertina, and some others, do not appear to meet the national taste; and if injured, would not be so easily repaired. The banjo seems the most promising instrument for this special purpose, as an accompaniment to solo or domestic singing. It is simple—of the stringed class most appreciated in India—can be had much cheaper than the guitar, say for five or six rupees—can be ordered without difficulty, and in any quantity, from makers in London—and is easily learnt and played. This instrument is capable of producing the sweetest harmony, and may be used either as an accompaniment to the voice, or with piano or guitar. Four-part music may be played with four banjos, each taking one part. With this instrument even such a simple accompaniment will be of service as the following to the Lyric tune of "*Tuthi tangiya,*" p. 270:—

CHAPTER XXVII.

DISTILLATION AND EXCISE.

FROM the most ancient books of the Hindus, and the hereditary profession and usages of some classes, it is evident that intoxicating liquors have always to some extent been manufactured and used in India. Distillation was practised more than three thousand years ago, the ancient Aryans making an inebriating juice of the *Soma* or "moonplant," which they thought an acceptable beverage both to gods and men, even for purposes of intoxication as well as exhilaration, and which was in common use in Vedic times. The Soma juice is spoken of as exhilarating to the gods, who are invited to drink of it freely and are represented as intoxicated by it. "Thy inebriety is most intense," says the Rishi to Indra, "nevertheless thy acts for our good are most beneficent." The Soma drink was the most important portion of the offering. "It was made from the juice of a creeper (*Sarcostemma viminalis*), diluted with water, mixed with barley meal, clarified butter, and the meal of wild rice, and fermented in a jar for nine days. The starchy substance of the meal supplied the material for the vinous fermentation, and the Soma juice the part of hops in beer. Its effects on gods and men were those of alcohol." ("The Vedic Religion," by Macdonald, p. 41.) In the Puranas also, of more modern composition, Siva is represented as drunken in his habits and his eyes inflamed with intemperance.

That the use of ardent spirits in India was very ancient may also be inferred from the Institutes of Manu, in which regulations for the classes of distillers and vendors of spirits are laid down with much particularity. Almost all nations, indeed, have at an early period discovered the way of procuring alcohol from grain, fruits, or vegetable juices. So in various parts of India the aboriginal races largely distil or ferment strong drink from the cocoanut, sago, date, and palmyra palms, from sugar or rice; or in the great forests of India, from the dried flowers of the *Bassia latifolia;* and this has been their custom from time immemorial.

The common fermented drink is called *kallu,* or toddy (Hindustani and Sanskrit, *tádí*), the vinous sap of the palm, drawn in North Travancore, from the cocoanut tree, by the Ilavars and Chogans ; in the South from the palmyra by the Shánárs. It ferments after standing for a few hours in the heat of the day ; and spoils, turning into sour vinegar, in two or three days. Of this pleasant sub-acid drink the people say that a pint, or a pint and a half, will intoxicate a man. It is generally employed for yeast in making wheaten bread and rice cakes.

Arrack is an ardent spirit, transparent and colourless like gin, abundant and cheap throughout India. It is, properly speaking, rum, being distilled from palm-sugar with a small quantity of acacia bark—or from the fermented sap of the palm.

To distil spirits the *jaggery* or unrefined sugar is broken up and put in water to ferment along with the bark for four days ; then the whole is boiled in an earthen pot, the vapour being caught at the top in a tube of bambu and carried on so as to fall into another pot, or into some condensing vessel placed in cold water. Distillation is effected in half a day. Sometimes the first product is re-distilled. When manufactured from toddy, a quantity, say eight *edungalies,* is taken on the second day after being drawn from the tree, put in a large earthen pot on an oven. On the top of this a small earthen pan, having three holes at the sides, is placed, and over this a brass pot containing cold water. The edge of the intermediate vessel is tightly secured with cloths so as to retain the vapour, and from a hole in one side a pipe is fixed to convey the spirits into a bottle. The cold water in the upper vessel, which is open to the air and used for condensing, is renewed from time to time as it becomes heated, until the whole quantity is distilled. Women generally attend to this work. Ten quarts of toddy will yield about two of proof spirits. A small quantity of the first product of the distillation must be thrown away, being sour and hurtful. The first bottle drawn will be first-rate arrack ; the second bottle, second quality ; the value respectively twelve and ten chuckrams ; total twenty-two chuckrams, of which the profit to the distiller will be about five chuckrams. Less than a chuckram's worth will intoxicate some men.

To make the very best arrack, toddy and arrack are mixed together and distilled. The people believe that it is in order to impart a strong intoxicating quality that the bark of *kárinja*

(*Acacia leucophlæa*) is added; but Brandis, in his "Forest Flora," p. 184, says that it is added on account of the tannin it contains, in order to precipitate the albuminous substances of the palm juice.

On the East Coast, spirits are more commonly distilled from a mixture of rice-flour, sugar and toddy, so that the Government dues are fixed with some reference to the market price of rice. The spirits produced are not considered equal in purity and excellence to those distilled from palm-juice or sugar alone on the Western Coast.

The first introduction of intemperance into India, it will be obvious, is not by any means to be laid to the charge of the European nations. The manufacture and use of such liquors is quite indigenous, and native stimulants are probably more injurious than European drinks. But besides the native habit amongst the lower classes of the population, the early European navigators also unfortunately brought the evil custom and example with them. Canter Visscher, writing about A.D. 1723, says that for strong drink in general the Portuguese have no taste. "The Dutch, on the contrary, drink to such an extent as to expose themselves to the reproaches of the Portuguese and the Natives: the English are liable to the same imputation."

Drinking of spirits, according to the modern system of Brahmanical Hinduism, is a great sin; yet this view of matters is not supported by caste discipline, except in rare cases. Bartolomeo speaks of a well-meant attempt of the King of Travancore in 1787 to prohibit the use of cocoanut brandy under pain of the confiscation of property; the smoking of ganja hemp and use of opium were at the same time forbidden. This measure could not, however, have been long maintained or effective, when so large a proportion of the people used these drugs, or were dependent on the profits of their manufacture and sale.

Revenue from tax on the sale of intoxicating liquors appears to have been very ancient, and to have existed under Mussulman and Hindu governments. In Travancore the *Abkari* or Excise Department was originally under the Amani system, the Dewán having the chief management of its affairs and the revenue being collected by a staff for the purpose. After M.E. 1010 (1834) it was leased out to the highest bidder, and a fixed number of shops were allowed to each contractor, who collected the monthly instalment of rent from sub-renters or the retailers. Each shop vendor of spirits paid annually two pagodas.

The farmer of the duty at that time was bound to purchase

toddy and *Akkáni* (the sweet sap of the palm newly drawn) from the ryots at the rate of two chuckrams per pot, containing ten edungalies, and to sell this at from four to five chuckrams a pot ; and arrack at eight and six chuckrams respectively for the first and second qualities. He was to erect shops for the retail trade, and to see that liquor was sold only within the prescribed limits.

The present system in force for the collection of Abkari revenue is prescribed in Regulation I. of M.E. 1054. The whole is under the direct management of the Dewán, who has power to assign by license the exclusive privilege of manufacture or sale of all spirituous and fermented liquors to suitable renters or others, under proper restrictions, and to determine the places at which stills and shops shall be erected, the number of such in each locality, the prices at which liquor shall be sold and the measures to be used ; also the transfer or closing of shops. No shops or stills to be opened or built within the limits of any principal town or other populous place. Excepting foreign liquors for private consumption, more than one imperial quart is not to be in the possession of any unlicensed person at one time. Drunkenness and riot are forbidden ; also adulteration and illicit distillation.

The Abkari and Opium contracts are determined by competition, and are usually taken, the former by Ilavars and the latter by Syrians. The revenue from this source has steadily and largely augmented. The amount collected in M.E. 1010 was 42,584 rupees, which rose in M.E. 1014 to 47,372 rupees. In M.E. 1037 it had risen to 78,000 rupees, and the next year to 87,000 rupees, not varying much from this sum until M.E. 1045, 91,000 rupees, and the next year 100,000 rupees ; then it has rapidly mounted up since, as follows :—

M.E. 1047	(including 10,000 rupees for opium)	108,658	rupees.
„ 1048	„ „ „ „	122,447	„
„ 1050	Abkari alone	146,781	„
„ 1052	„	159,250	„
„ 1054	„	171,648	„
„ 1056	„	190,041	„

This makes an average of 1 anna 3 pice per head of the total population for *revenue alone*, and the expenditure on intoxicating liquors must, of course, be many times greater, but no particulars are given in the published reports. To this must be added foreign wines and spirits imported, a considerable proportion of which would be for consumption by Europeans and

Eurasians; and which amounted in M.E. 1056 to 2,462 gallons. To this add licenses for the sale of foreign liquors, realizing during the year the sum of 1,206 rupees.

It may still be averred with truth that there is not a great amount of intemperance among the population of Travancore, and there is not much *visible* drunkenness, as in some European towns. Still there is more than formerly, and sufficient cause appears for anxiety and regret lest this debasing vice should increase both amongst Native Christians, to whom this may be a considerable temptation, and Hindus of the lower, and even of the higher orders. All over India the lower classes drink. The excise revenue is steadily advancing in its returns to Government, partly through better plans for its collection, and partly in consequence of the increased use of intoxicants. In 1879-80 the aggregate excise collections from all the provinces of British India for licenses and distillery fees and duties levied only on the manufacture and sale of intoxicating spirituous liquors and drugs, including opium, amounted to £2,838,021, an average of 2 annas 2½ pice per head of the total population of British India, taking it at 200 millions. To this must be added malt liquors, spirits and wines, probably a large part of which is for European consumption, value £1,306,113, the customs duty on which is not separately given. The excise income of the Madras Presidency is about 62 lacs of rupees for 31 millions of population, say 3 annas 2 pice per head.

It is to be feared that drinking habits and the use of European wines and spirits are spreading amongst the educated and wealthy classes of natives. I have heard a thoughtful Brahman gentleman complain of this evil as existing amongst students at Combaconum through the too free and inconsiderate recommendation of alcohol as a medicinal agent by European physicians. Probably the use of wines and spirits for luxury or medicine must inevitably spring from the increase of wealth and intellectual labour, whether this increase came from external contact with European nations or from internal sources. But such habits need to be counteracted and controlled by moral principle and a constant sense of their great danger, and they cannot but prove on the whole a vast evil to the Hindus in even greater degree than they have proved to the more muscular, active, and high-fed European nations. Already cases are known of disease and death brought on by intemperance. "European brandy is the curse of most of the rich idle men, and the evil seems increasing rather than diminishing. They are forbidden by their Shastras to indulge in strong drink of any kind; consequently all they take is in private after dark. They sometimes shut themselves up for days with the enemy close at hand, and feign sickness, so that their drunken state should not be found out."

As to other classes we have the testimony of Connor's "Memoir of the Survey," written about sixty years ago. "Most classes (nor have the Brahmans quite escaped the imputation) indulge in the use of spirits; the temptation is great, as it is so easily indulged, the quantity purchased by a few copper coins being sufficient to intoxicate. Like all other natives, their potations are unsocial, the harsh spirit sufficient for the purposes of their coarse intemperance being more calculated to produce oblivion rather than conviviality: the better ranks, too, are addicted to the use of soporifics (particularly opium), a vice by no means uncommon even amongst the Christians (Syrians), whose pastors are not proof against its allurements; but the placid intoxication it produces is not followed by ferocity, nor do their orgies, however intemperate, ever end in riot."

The Hill tribes are constantly in distress through the prevalence of drunkenness, and instances have occurred in which European planters or sportsmen have thoughtlessly given them brandy, forgetting that the use of strong drink is almost death to such races, who have little self-restraint or knowledge of moral duty in this matter. Coolies employed on coffee estates are also often exposed to great temptation from liquor shops. The Hill people suffer much injury from Muhammadan dealers, who set them to drink, let them finish the whole, and can then take what they like out of their houses. Pariahs and Chucklers also drink and quarrel much. Pulayars drink excessively at their harvest festivals, and on other special occasions.

Shánárs have often been remarked as abstaining as a caste from intoxicating liquors, and we trust they will retain their reputation for sobriety, especially with the advantages of Christian instruction and discipline, which so many of them are now blessed with. Yet instances of intemperance again and again occur amongst them, such as that mentioned by the Rev. W. Lee in his report for 1867.

"In the village of Santhayadi a rich heathen Shánár was a confirmed drunkard. On one occasion when I went to the village, as a little child of his was being educated in our school I called to see him. I found him locked up in one of the rooms of his house, with his feet in fetters, to restrain him from gratifying his frightful propensity for drink. I induced his sons to knock off the fetters and come with him to the sanctuary. His case was made a subject for special prayer by the congregation, and he was induced to make a solemn promise that he would henceforth abstain from drinking. During the year which has elapsed he has not even once yielded to temptation, and has continued regularly to attend Divine service."

Amongst the ancient Syrian Christians who are thus referred to by Lieutenant Connor, less intemperance appears to exist now than in the beginning of the century. Still the evil is present and serious. At Kandenád I was grieved to witness much drinking on their Easter Sunday in 1878, those who had partaken of the holy communion on the previous Thursday, according to their rule, now screaming, yelling, and fighting after the long Lenten fast of fifty days, during which many keep from drunkenness, bursting out again when the time has expired. Having thus kept right for some weeks, they are allowed to partake, then indulge in excesses and riot. I have seen wine, too, offered as a beverage at a native marriage feast, a most dangerous custom to introduce in India, while it is being got rid of by thoughtful people in England for the sake of the public good.

Amongst the Roman Catholic fishermen there appears to be a good deal of intemperance. Towards Anjengo, drunkenness is said to be very prevalent, chiefly amongst Ilavars and Roman Catholic Christians. Several may be seen intoxicated in a single day. Even children learn early to drink, going with their parents and getting a little from them.

Complaints are also made by our Mission Catechists of trouble in the management of some congregations from the drinking customs of neighbouring people, or even of attendants on their ministry. Of these, and of the earnest efforts put forth by the mission teachers to rescue the unfortunate victims of intemperance, and the good result of their labours, the following quotations may be made in conclusion of this chapter:—

"At the beginning of the year," writes an Evangelist, "one difficulty seemed to my sight insurmountable; it was the constant quarrelling of the people living near the chapel. Their nearness to the chapel would lead everybody to suppose they were Christians, and I was under that impression at first; but with the exception of one, all are heathens.

They were addicted to drinking; and every baneful effect which intoxicating drink produces manifested itself amongst them. Often I was tempted to despondency, supposing that all my efforts would be in vain; but I am glad to record that, although they may not be wholly converted to God, they have undergone a great moral change, and the village is now calm and peaceful. They are ashamed of their previous misconduct. There was one family, however, which long withstood all my efforts. The chief man of the family and his wife were both drunkards, and foremost in impiety and quarrelling with others.

One day there was a great contention in the family. Every one was in the highest fit of angry passion. Immediately I ran to them, lest any mischief should happen, and addressed the father emphatically, as he was the leader and cause of all the disturbances. 'My friend, you are marching to a shameful and ignominious death. You are on the road to ruin, the road which leads to shame and misery. Drink, the curse of millions, leads you on the way as it has led others. Drink, first blinding you, takes you by the hand and leads you step by step on the way, which assuredly ends in everlasting destruction.' This solemn truth, timely spoken, was impressed deeply upon the hearts of the old man and his wife. The quarrels and brawls have entirely ceased, and they are now improving in worldly circumstances. Some of them now attend the services at the house of God."

Again, a native missionary writes:—"At Puliady, the last time I visited the congregation, observing a better attendance of the people at Divine Service, I inquired into the reason. 'It is owing to the co-operation of Caleb with the catechist,' replied the people. 'This man,' said the catechist, 'goes among his friends, crying out, "Dear friends, you know what a drunkard I have been—what a terror to the village. Few escaped my abusive language day and night. I paid no regard to the earnest remonstrances and advices of my catechist and other friends, and was more than once handed over to the police, to my great shame; but still I would not give up the arrack. Many a time the catechist knelt down in prayer with me for Divine mercy: but I went on as naughtily as ever in my self-murdering career; when one night I got so drunk that while staggering homewards I tumbled into a dung-pit, and lay there insensible all night. In the morning as soon as I came to my senses I ran hastily to the distiller's house, resolved to drink more than ever. There I was met by my uncle, who, having heard of what befell me the previous night, shed tears over me, and very earnestly addressed me: 'O son, the only offspring and hope of our family—how is it that you have turned out such a sot? I am deeply solicitous about you, and beseech you not to kill yourself in this way and plunge me and our family into grief and misery.' These words entered deeply into my heart. I felt I could not stay longer in the arrack shop; and went home at once strongly convinced of the evil effects of drinking. Increasing terror and thoughtfulness seized me during the restless night, a great part of which I passed in earnest prayer to God for mercy. The prayer-hearing God listened to my poor entreaties and graciously worked the change which you now witness in me."

A Temperance Society was formed at Nagercoil by Mr. Duthie and his native friends, as an additional means of combined effort in this direction.

CHAPTER XXVIII.

POLITICAL AND SOCIAL CONDITION IN FORMER TIMES.

THE political condition and government of the country in past, but still modern, times, is of importance as bearing upon practical reforms in the present day. Take, for instance, the period from the middle of the eighteenth century, when Vanji Mártánda Vurmah Rajah began his reign, to the end of the century, when the British political power became established, and introduced a new element urging and enforcing enlightened and righteous rule. The various reforms which have taken place clearly indicate the former condition of things, and the corresponding urgency of need for them which existed. Information may also be gathered from the detailed testimony of writers since the beginning of the present century and from the evils still prevailing, which cry for further and sustained effort towards amelioration.

At the period referred to, the **territory under the rule of** the Rajah of Travancore was but small, extending only from about Cape Comorin to Quilon, and comprising but a small portion of the present kingdom. A system of small States obtained, as in other parts of India, and as once in England. The neighbouring States of Káyenkulam, Tekkankúr, Vadakkankúr, Changanácherry, Ambalapulay, Alangádu, and Paravúr, afterwards subdued by intrigue and fraud, and incorporated with Travancore, were still intact and ruled by their respective Rajahs, while even within a short distance of the capital the "Eight Barons" seem to have not yet fully acknowledged the sway of Travancore, and the southern district of Nánjinád appears to have had still some remnants of popular and constitutional right. From the persistent claims of other chieftains it appears somewhat doubtful whether the authority of the Rajah was really sovereign. Was it not then rather an aristocracy of military leaders than a consolidated monarchy, the most powerful chief afterwards reaching the stage of territorial sovereignty?

"Till the beginning of the eighteenth century," says Sir Madava Row, "the territory which now constitutes this State was mostly cut up into little principalities, each with a chief of its own, who had a favourite pagoda at his capital—a shrine with the splendour of which he regarded his fortunes as indissolubly bound up. When conquest welded the numerous little chiefships into one State, the pagoda at Trevandrum naturally acquired a predominant ascendancy, and other institutions of the kind had to take a more subordinate position."*

With this view agrees Buchanan in his "Journey":—"The Rajahs (of Malabar) were formerly head of a feudal aristocracy with limited authority; afterwards they became despotic princes, with a military force to chastise any chieftains who might be disobedient." And an able exposition of the Malabar land tenures in "Standing Information" of the Madras Government says:—"The characteristic of the whole of the Kerala country was the presence of a strongly developed personal and individual land property, the absence of a government tax on land, the absence of a concentrated village system such as obtained in the Carnatic, and the existence of a military tenure similar to the feudal system of Europe. The country was originally subdivided between a race of Brahman priests called Namboories, and a military tribe called Nairs: these two holding in subjection the agriculturists of the country, consisting of persons called Teers, and others. The Nairs paid no land tax, but attended the kings to the field with their retainers. The Namboories also paid no land tax, but furnished the expenses for the support of the temples. In the absence of land tax, the kings of the country had considerable domains assigned to them, which were cultivated by slaves, and yielded a sufficient revenue for household expenses. The subordinate chiefs maintained their own internal police arrangements, and, except in time of war, the personal expenses of the rajahs were not large. But they were not without other branches of revenue. A succession duty equal to twenty-five per cent. was levied on Mahomedan subjects being landholders. There were also import and export duties, mint duties, fines, escheats, confiscations, protection money received from persons of other states who claimed asylum, benevolences in the shape of offerings made to the Crown at great festivals or on an occasion, and fees on marriages of important persons. There were also license taxes, and royalties on gold ore, elephants, ivory, teak trees, bamboos, and vessels wrecked on the coast. For fiscal arrangements, there were authorities in charge of defined tracts of country."

* "Administration Report," *M.E. 1045.*

Of this period we have some notices by Canter Visscher, a Dutch chaplain at Cochin, about A.D. 1723. The country was almost isolated from foreign intercourse, the roads and communications by land being kept as obscure and difficult as possible, by the jealousy of the governments and their disinclination to admit strangers. They were but semi-civilized; scarcely any indigenous literature existed; and the customs handed down from that age, remnants of which are still visible, testify to the low social condition of the inhabitants.

Except in so far as it was checked by the counteracting power of a number of refractory chieftains the form of government was altogether despotic, the chieftain being regarded by the common people with almost superstitious dread, as in the South Sea Islands, Africa, and elsewhere. The restraint of law was faintly acknowledged by the sovereign, and but slightly felt by those who conducted the administration, even at the best; while, at the worst, it was ignored altogether. All authority was centred in the rajah and distributed by him amongst various officials at his pleasure, and these were rewarded not by regular salaries, but by grants and the profits of oppression. There were no independent judicial tribunals, but the executive officers were invested with judicial powers, and determined causes according to caprice or interest. The Rajah was the final court of appeal, if any dared to prefer appeals against the decision of powerful officials. One advantage, certainly, was that justice (or injustice!) was swift and decisive.

"Their legal suits are tried, according to old customs, *vivâ voce.* No lengthy proceedings are required to obtain the decision of the causes, which are always concluded within a few days by the fiat of the Rajah, who, in obscure cases, consults with his Brahmans" (Canter Visscher). But, of course, the low castes were not taken into account in these matters; they had no rights, and could make no claims.

The subordinate governors and officials, as in all Oriental despotisms, ground down all beneath them. Paying for their appointments and giving also annual "presents," they were obliged to squeeze the necessary amounts from the unfortunate people. The heads of the respective castes also paid an annual sum for their dignity. Bribes and pecuniary gratifications were everywhere expected, and nowhere forbidden. The ruling power and subordinate officials were ever ready to snatch from the people as much as possible. When a cruel ruler was on the throne, the country suffered much; when a benevolent one, it gained little.

Religion was used as an engine for government, yet the

rajahs themselves were enslaved to the Brahman priests. No Brahman could be sentenced to death, however heinous his crime.

Warfare with neighbouring rulers was frequent, as throughout India; not that there was generally great bloodshed in these parts, but the country was devastated and laid waste, cattle were driven away, and the miserable subjects sorely oppressed: the time and treasure of rulers and people were wasted in war and on forts and arms, while the lower castes were made to serve in menial attendance, only occasionally Tiers, or Shánárs, weavers, and others, being entrusted with arms. Petty princes attacked each other's territories, and carried away the people as captives.

The grossest cruelties were practised, and oppressions of the labouring classes and the predial slaves. Most severe punishments were inflicted on the disobedient and criminal. Simple imprisonment was not much resorted to, but cruel torture to force confession, mutilation, cutting in pieces, impalement, and other inhuman punishments, even for theft, unchastity, killing of cows, and other minor offences. Ordeals were common.

"The prisons of Malabar are mere quadrangular cages, the size of a man in length, breadth and height, made of wooden gratings nailed together. Such prisons as these would in Europe be more fit to keep fowls in than human beings." To the present day Pulayars and others are thrust into cages not much better. One which I measured was fifteen feet long by eight feet wide, and five and three-quarters in height, in which twenty-five persons have at times been incarcerated, supplied with stocks all round, and no separation of the sexes. Another was eighteen by eight feet, in which thirty persons have been confined at once; and another was a "black hole" about eight feet square and five and a quarter high, with no opening whatever for ventilation, not now used "except," said the peon, "there were a woman, who would be put in there for her comfort!" The Sirkar has long been urged to remedy this serious evil, and has promised amendment, and done something in the larger towns; but much yet remains to be effected throughout the country. In somewhat recent times Shánárs also, if they neglected to supply jaggery for public work, were put into cages armed with spikes, and made to eat a quantity of salt with a little rice, or chained to trees like monkeys to their cage-posts.

"I once saw," says Fra Bartolomeo, about A.D. 1780, "five natives suspended from a tree in a forest near Ambalapusha, on account of the supposed crime of killing a cow." Again he says: "At Quilon, I saw a native of the caste of the Shánárs hanging on a gallows for having stolen three cocoanuts in the house of a Nayr. The *corpus delicti* was suspended from his neck, in order that it might serve as a warning to all passengers."

"For the restoration of peace at that time" (A.D. 1802), says the native historian, Páchu Mútthathu, "punishments were too severe, beyond the law. Krishna Pillai sepoy, and others who rebelled, were tied to the feet of elephants and torn asunder. Blowing from the mouth of a cannon, impaling and hanging, gouging out the eyes, cutting off hands, nose and ears, were inflicted for trifling offences." Devasagáyam Pillai, a convert to Christianity in 1752, was "taken from village to village riding on a buffalo, daily beaten with eighty stripes, pepper rubbed in his wounds and nostrils, exposed to the sun, and had only stagnant water to drink."

Severe fines, pecuniary mulcts, and confiscation were also resorted to. "The rajahs understand how to make the most of the opportunity of making criminals bleed well in their purses; and there is hardly any crime which may not be expiated by money."

Slavery in the most unmitigated form, that is, united with caste restrictions, prevailed. A large proportion of the population were actual slaves of the soil, while others of the proscribed classes were in a condition but little removed from this. "The rajah might sell into slavery persons of various castes who had committed any crime by which they lost caste, or were liable to capital punishment." They also laid hold of vagabonds and sold them. Slaves were sometimes exported to other parts of India.

Crimes of murder, assault, and robbery were prevalent in those days; and outrages were freely committed upon the weak and defenceless.

Narrow and short-sighted laws, exclusive legislation, and oppressive monopolies, effectually hindered the extension of trade, the growth of commerce, and the spread of agriculture, while barbarous caste restrictions produced disunion and national weakness. The use of the public highways was forbidden to outcasts, and any one daring to pass on within polluting distance of a Náyar would be cut down at once. To secure immediate recognition of such classes they were required to be uncovered above the waist; shoes, umbrellas, fine cloth, and costly ornaments were interdicted to them. The holding of umbrellas was prohibited to all castes, except Brahmans, on public occasions, though the rain were pouring upon them. The proper salutation from a female to persons of rank was to uncover the bosom.

The erection of lofty or large houses was forbidden to all but kings and nobles. Even the King of Cochin, it appears from Barbosa, was prohibited tiling his palace without special permission of the Zamorin. Licenses were given in consideration of large payments, granting various social privileges and distinctions, as the use of certain lamps, particular kinds of music, ornaments, or conveyances, with other honours, immunities, and titles.

Burdensome taxes were also imposed, a poll-tax being a favourite mode of levying rates. In 1754, for instance, a head tax was imposed on the Shánárs to meet the military expenditure. In 1787, a poll tax was imposed on the Syrian Christians. Fees were levied on low-caste marriages. The Administration Report for *M.E. 1040* gives a surprising list of no less than 110 distinct taxes, which were in that year happily abolished with a stroke of the pen, to the unspeakable relief of a great multitude of the industrious poor. A perusal of this curious list is very suggestive as to what must have been the previous state of the country, and the miserable interference with trade and industry, social freedom, and domestic comfort. Everything at all taxable was availed of, and every special occasion made an excuse for squeezing the laborious classes of their hard earnings. They produced small revenue at the cost of great vexation, partaking often of the character of poll taxes and taxes on implements of industry, and the proceeds were wasted on Brahmans, temples, and ceremonies. "These taxes," the Report modestly says, "used to be a source of vexation and embarrassment." Yet their total proceeds amounted to but 8,500 rupees annually. Their very titles are suggestive, though not in all instances explanatory of the actual import. *Kuppa kátcha*, "refuse offering," was so called because it was the meanest tax—really a house tax—one fanam for each hut. Pariahs, Pallars, and some Shánárs paid this. There was also a house tax on Ilavars. "Grass cutting" was paid by Pariahs only in Nánjinád. The widow of a weaver continued to pay the tax on the loom (about a rupee per annum) long after the death of her husband and the cessation of the work. The catalogue goes on enumerating various forms of house tax, taxes on oil-mills, bows, iron and forges, exchangers, palankeens, boats and nets, hunting, keeping civet-cats, on the industries of goldsmiths, fishermen, musicians and drummers, bearers, dyers, schoolmasters, Kuravar dancers, &c.; dues at the festivals of Onam, Dípávali, harvest, the end of the year, and various anniversaries, and or occasion of royal marriages, birthdays, &c., besides more defensible fees on royal grants, on agreements, on timber cutting, &c. A little oil was taken from each oilmonger; and service in village watching was demanded.

Though these cesses were professedly relinquished under a Royal Proclamation, many of them are still retained and partially collected, the people being ignorant of their rights, and the inferior officials grasping and oppressive.

Sirkar Ooliam, or personal gratuitous services and forced labour for government and temples, is an institution common in countries that are backward in civilization; but in Travancore imposed on the poorest classes, and to an unwarrantable degree. This led to very serious evils and complaints, and to great suffering and loss, up to quite recent times, and, indeed, is partly continued in *Vritty* service, and forced labour of several kinds. "These demands," wrote Sir Madava Row, "were of the most uncertain character, involved a good deal of oppression and vexation, and interfered with the freedom which industry of all kinds is entitled to." The small nominal sums that were in some cases allowed for work did not reach the labourer's hands, the underlings keeping what they could for themselves, or to bribe their superiors to continue them in employment, while the people dared not complain, lest counter-charges be brought against the complainant, and himself condemned as a malefactor, imprisoned, or perhaps, tortured to death.

When looking with admiration at the noble examples of Indian architecture and engineering—temples, forts, public buildings—the first thought that sometimes occurs to us is of the vast amount of misery and expenditure of human life imposed on the multitudes, as in Egypt, who did the unskilled labour. In the case of irrigation-works, perhaps, this was excusable, though even in these the higher classes should have taken full share; but the attendance upon the military forces, cutting of grass for the horses, supplying of fodder for state elephants, palm leaves for writing, oil for lights, and firewood and provisions for temples, formed a heavy and oppressive burden on the poor. Of a single one of these, the report for M.E. 1040 says:—

"The cocoanut plantations of the country were for a long time subject to a demand for feeding the Sirkar elephants. The demand was of an uncertain and oppressive character; the rich contrived to evade it, and it fell with great severity upon the poor. The required leaves could be cut from any garden on payment of a nominal price, and even this scarcely reached the owner. This year a notification was issued declaring that elephant fodder should thereafter be purchased in the open market at the ruling prices of the day. The extent of the relief may to some extent be measured by the fact that under the new arrangement the fodder of a first-class elephant cost Rs. 540 a year, while under the old it cost only Rs. 144; but the relief is really more valuable than represented by the difference of cost. Many oppressions and exactions for which the old system gave scope have been swept away."

In another paper from the same able pen, in 1869, numerous disabilities and established abuses to which the lower castes were subject, but which had been happily, to a greater or less extent, removed of late years, are recounted as follows:—

"Gratuitous services of various kinds used to be exacted from them. They had to guard Sirkar properties in several places. They were compelled to work in the Sirkar forests in cutting down or transporting timber. They had to carry Sirkar things from place to place. They were largely impressed to convey Sirkar salt from the pans to the place of export. They had to supply firewood to certain charitable institutions—and so on. Families of these low castes were even allotted to certain private individuals, who were at liberty to obtain gratuitous services from such families.

Then, again, there were many restrictions placed upon their personal liberty. A proportion of the low-castes were, indeed, subjected to avowed slavery. As such they were attached to lands, like chattels, and were bought and sold. Their masters were authorized themselves to punish them for refractory conduct—a power which it may be imagined was frequently abused in no small degree. Even those that were not avowed slaves used to be treated almost as such. They were not at liberty to keep milch cows. They could not use oil-mills. They were interdicted from carrying on trade as bazaar-men. They were debarred the use of any but coarse cloths. It was improper in them to wear any but the most ordinary personal ornaments, whether for males or females. It was not open to them to decorate the sheds they erected on marriage occasions. They were restricted to particular music. They were denied permission to move in conveyances. They could not even wear shoes or use umbrellas. It was considered improper to allow them to use metallic utensils. They could not build substantial or tiled houses. Nor could they acquire landed property with impunity."

Such was the sad condition of millions of human beings throughout Malabar for hundreds, if not thousands, of years.

Superstition, with its attendant cruelties, multiplied the sorrows arising from ignorance and pitiless oppression, and still further darkened the gloomy picture. It sank the slave still lower by the caste notion of his essential pollution, so that he could not approach his master, enter the dwelling of any superior, or offer worship in any temple of the higher castes. The Pulayan was, therefore, in an infinitely worse condition than ever the American slave was. Caste also prevented the access of the lower castes, in their various degrees, to public officials and courts : it even deprived the higher classes of many comforts and conveniences in travel, food, labour, and trade. On a long journey amongst people of strange caste, with whom they cannot eat, or drink water, their sufferings must be great.

Human sacrifices also appear to have been offered occasionally, as in other parts of India. "It is not fifty years since an instance occurred of this inhuman and diabolical practice in the immediate neighbourhood of Cottayam. A Zemindar was endeavouring to build up a bund, which the waters carried away as often as he made the attempt. Some Brahmans told him he would never succeed till he had offered up on the bund three young girls. Three, of the age of fourteen or fifteen were selected ; the dreadful sacrifice was made, and the ground was stained by the blood of these innocent victims. Mr. Chapman showed me a place where some very large earthen vases have been recently discovered buried in a hollow in the laterite. All the natives without hesitation declare that they must have been the receptacles of human victims when this awful practice prevailed. Near each was another and minor vase, in which, it is said, the knife used in the sacrifice was buried."*

Slaves were so little valued by the higher classes, that in cases of repeated and destructive breaches in banks of rivers and tanks they ascribed the catastrophe to the displeasure of some deity or devil ; and propitiated his anger by throwing a slave into the breach and quickly heaping earth on him. It was this horrid custom that gave rise to the common remark with reference to a lazy and worthless man, "What would this man do for ? Only for being thrown into a breach." They were sometimes cast into the holes dug for foundations, and buried there for good luck, also that their ghosts might protect secret haunts of treasure. Rajah Vurmah Kulasékhara barbarously buried alive fifteen infants to ensure success in his wars with his neighbours.

Enormous expenses also were incurred in idolatrous worship. In M.E. 919 the whole kingdom was solemnly dedicated, by the will of one man, the reigning Rajah, to the deity worshipped at Trevandrum, Patmanábhan, who became the tutelary deity of the whole State. Thenceforward new expenses were under-

* *Madras C. M. Record*, April, 1849.

taken for special festivals, such as the Bhadradipam in M.E. 919; the Murajapam, which was first observed in M.E. 924, and thenceforward every six years; and a large number of Ootoopuras, or Feeding Houses for Brahmans, established in M.E. 948, which cost the country three lacs of rupees per annum, a very small proportion of which can be regarded as useful, or even harmless, expenditure.

The Syrian and Roman Churches were, at the same time, in a condition of utter spiritual deadness, doing little or nothing, either by preaching or circulating the Scriptures, to enlighten the people as to the way of salvation. They themselves too often followed heathen customs, and mingled superstitious notions and practices with the truths they still retained from their forefathers.

CHAPTER XXIX.

SLAVERY.

SLAVERY in Malabar doubtless took its rise historically from the conquest of the aboriginal inhabitants by invaders and settlers from the north. Several strata of population are easily discoverable—the earliest composed of the lowest castes, and, perhaps, also the hill tribes—next the Dravidians, who now form the mass of the respectable Hindu population—and over all, the Aryan Brahmans, few in number, but clever, intelligent, and possessed of great religious and social authority. For thousands of years these lowest castes have continued in a state of hereditary servitude and abject poverty, exposed to the caprice or brutality of the owner, and disposable according to his pleasure; too abhorrent, at the same time, on account of caste pollution, to be touched or closely approached by their superiors, or to be admitted to any of the privileges or amenities of religion. Every wealthy man, and even individuals of inferior castes, had a number of bondsmen born in slavery. Syrian Christians also possessed slaves.

The number of persons originally reduced to a state of slavery was increased by the sale of children in times of famine and distress, which has occurred even in our own day. Other additions have been made from time to time by petty princes carrying away captives in their wars, by the fraud or violence of kidnappers, as a judgment on criminals, as a punishment on females of the higher classes who have fallen, and are cast out to associate with the lowest of the population. Muhammadans and Roman Catholics of property, also purchased slaves in order to proselytise them to their own religion.

On account of the law of caste pollution, these slaves have all been engaged solely in predial or field work, not domestic service, as they could not enter the houses of their masters, nor be used for personal attendance: even in the fields their work must be superintended from a certain distance. The unhappy influence of Hindu caste was thus added to the usual evils of slavery. With reference to this double infliction a writer in the *Asiatic Review* says: "The condition of the predial or rustic slaves of Malabar cannot bear a favourable comparison with that of household or domestic slaves among the Mahommedans. The latter are received with them into a fraternity; and are no longer kept at a suspicious distance. In Arabia their treatment is said to be like that of children, and they go by the appellation of sons with their masters. They often rise to the most confidential station in the family; and the external appearance of the master and slave is hardly distinguishable, they are so much upon a par."

The **proportion of the population** formerly held in slavery may easily be gathered from the Census Report for 1875, which gives the Pallars, Pariahs, and Pulayars, "soil-slaves" now freed, at 258,401 out of 2,311,379, being 11·2 per cent. of the total population. But other classes should be added, who were in a very similar condition, as the Kuravars, some 56,000 in number, and the Védars and Ulládans, who are designated in the Memoir of Travancore, as "the least domesticated of the predial slaves;" so that we may fairly state that *one-eighth* of the entire population were sunk in outright and acknowledged slavery of the worst kind; while about *a fourth* of the population, *besides*, were regarded as decidedly polluting in caste, and were to nearly as great an extent as the soil slaves deprived of the rights and enjoyments of freemen and citizens. These servile classes may, therefore, be put down as constituting *over one-third of the entire population.*

We have already seen that the rajahs sold into slavery felons and criminals liable to capital punishment, in which case the penalty, if justly imposed, might be compared to ours of transportation beyond the seas. This ostracism was also reserved for female criminals, on whom the punishment of death is never inflicted.

Another source of the supply of slaves consisted of **high-caste females** exposed to this punishment when detected in immorality or breach of caste rules. As there are many unmarried women amongst the Nambúri Brahmans some amount of temptation and evil necessarily springs up, notwithstanding severe restrictions and the care exercised. Now-a-days there is a better resort open to such—to join the Syrian or Roman Catholic Church, or the Muhammadans—which is sometimes done in the northern districts. Recently, the illegitimate child of a Brahman woman was given away to a Nair woman. According to Day, a Brahman woman erring with a low-caste man became the Rajah's slave: a low-caste woman allowing improper intimacy with a Brahman was sold to the Muhammadans. Pácha

Múttathu says that the women of the "Eight Knights" who were extirpated in *M.E. 908*, were handed over to fishermen, a hard enough fate for ladies of rank and authority. Barbosa describes Náyar females as sold in this way when not put to death by relatives for their fault. "If any woman of Nayr family should offend against the law of her sect, and the King know of it before her relations and brothers, he commands her to be taken and sold out of the kingdom to Moors or Christians. And if her male relations or sons know of it first, they shut her up and kill her with dagger or spear wounds, saying that if they did not do so they would remain greatly dishonoured."

A curious custom also existed, which is said to have added to the number of the enslaved. The various castes met at fighting grounds at Pallam, Ochira, &c.; and at this season it was supposed that low-caste men were at liberty to seize high-caste women if they could manage it, and to retain them. Perhaps this practice took its origin in some kind of faction fights. A certain woman at Mundakáyam, with fair Syrian features, is said to have been carried off thus. Hence arose a popular error that during the months of Kumbha and Meena (February and March), if a Pulayan meets a Sudra woman alone he may seize her, unless she is accompanied by a Shánár boy. This time of year was called *Pula pidi kálam.* Gundert says that this time of terror was in "the month Karkadam (15th July to 15th August), during which high caste women may lose caste if a slave happen to throw a stone at them after sunset." So the slave owners had their own troubles to bear from this institution.

The Pariahs in North Travancore formerly kidnapped females of high caste, whom they were said to treat afterwards in a brutal manner. Their custom was to turn robbers in the month of February, just after the ingathering of the harvest, when they were free from field work, and at the same time excited by demon worship, dancing, and drink. They broke into the houses of Brahmans and Náyars, carrying away their children and property, in excuse for which they pretended motives of revenge rather than interest, urging a tradition that they were once a division of the Brahmans, but entrapped into a breach of caste rules by their enemies making them eat beef. These crimes were once committed almost with impunity in some parts, but have now disappeared. Once having lost caste, even by no fault of their own, restoration to home and friends is impossible to Hindus.

Barbosa, writing about A.D. 1516, refers to this strange custom as practised by the *poleas* (Pulayars). "These low people during certain months of the year try as hard as they can to touch some of the Nayr women, as best they may be able to manage it, and secretly by night, to do them harm. So they go by night amongst the houses of the Nayrs to touch women; and these take many precautions against this injury during this season. And if they touch any woman, even though no one see it, and though there should be no witnesses, she, the Nayr woman herself, publishes it immediately, crying out, and leaves her house without choosing to enter it again to damage her lineage. And what she most thinks of doing is to run to the house of some low people to hide herself, that her relations may not kill her as a remedy for what has happened, or sell her to some strangers, as they are accustomed to do." Somewhat hard this upon feeble and helpless women, who should have been protected, if necessary, from such risks by their husbands and other male relatives, who had themselves virtually invented and created the imaginary crime, yet strictly carried out the retribution for it!

In times of famine also, parents sold their children for the sake of sustenance to any one who appeared able to support them. During the famine of 1860 in South Travancore, Mr. Cox wrote:—"The people are selling their own children, and this for a mere trifle. I hesitate to mention the lowest sum I have heard, but for a quarter of a rupee, and less, they sell their children into slavery to the Muhammadans and others on the seacoast; and these have the means of disposing of them again so as to make much profit—of course they make converts of them at once. The poor starving parents, instead of seeing their children dying with hunger which they are unable to appease, know or hope that they have something to live upon. How deeply we should pity them in this extremity of misery!"

A century ago a similar practice was described by Forbes. "The number of poor people who come down to Anjengo and the other seaports, from the inland country during a famine, either to sell themselves or to dispose of their children as slaves, is astonishing. During my residence at Anjengo there was no famine, nor any unnatural scarcity of rain, but during the rainy season many were weekly brought down from the mountains to be sold on the coast. They did not appear to think it so great a hardship as we imagine. I must and do think the feelings of a Malabar peasant and those of a cottage family in England are very different: the former certainly part with their children apparently with very little compunction; the latter are united with every tender sympathetic tie."

These various circumstances would naturally lead to **trading in slaves**, in which the early Europeans themselves set an evil example by importing Kafir and Mozambique slaves. Barbosa mentions the trade:—"If it should happen any year not to rain, Chormendel falls into such a state of famine that many die of it, and some sell their own children for a few provisions, or for two or three fanams (say sixpence). And in these times the Malabars carry rice and cocoanuts to them, and return with their ships laden with slaves." Bartolomeo also speaks of the trade in "Cafre slaves from the coast of Africa." Reference to the same subject is made in the *Asiatic Review* for 1828. Mr. Baber heard of the traffic in children, even of good castes, from Travancore into Malabar, especially, strange to say, by a European planter. Pulayars and others were purchased at Alleppey; and some free children of good caste were also secured, and cruelly compelled to eat with these, so that they lost caste as well as freedom. Colonel Munro reproved this misconduct, and the Muhammadan agent in effecting the purchases, was punished by the native court in Travancore for his crime.

Colonel Munro had also discovered, in 1812, a number of half-starved and naked natives in irons as slaves at the Dutch settlement at Chunganàcherry. The proprietor was a Pondicherry man, and the inhabitants of Chunganàcherry persisted in the traffic in slaves in defiance of the proclamation of Government.

It was remarked on the above circumstances that "where the severe Mussulman Government most prevailed, the condition of the slave was the easiest; while his condition is the most abject in those countries where the ancient institutions of the Hindus have been least disturbed, where the public demand on the soil is most light, and private property in the land is universal and of the highest value."

Even in later days instances of traffic in slaves have occurred. The Muhammadans found in large towns are ever ready to prey upon orphans and enslave them. Complaints are still made of slaves being taken from Northern India to Persia; and a Mussulman has quite recently been convicted of importing girls as slaves for Bhopal, and detaining them in Bombay against their will. Some years ago, the Rev. H. Baker rescued a family of heathen Shánárs from the hands of Muhammadan merchants, who would have carried them to Zanzibar, by paying Rs. 21 as their price. They had been sold by their parents; and after their rescue were educated and employed in various capacities. One girl of whom he knew was actually taken away to Zanzibar by a Muhammadan, who secured her in Travancore ostensibly as a wife, then sold her off in Zanzibar. Her release and return to her native country were procured by Dr. Kirk.

In Trichúr a friend of mine was present in the mission-house in 1872, when some Náyar landholders came and actually carried off a woman and child who had put themselves under instruction for baptism. The missionary started off to prevent the kidnapper, and overtook him on the public road. The man was punished by the Cochin Sirkar. Shortly after, some Brahmans made a similar attempt, and the court sentenced the culprit to six months' imprisonment; but as the offender was of the "twice-born" caste, intercession was made by the authorities for his forgiveness by the missionary, which was agreed to, on condition that a proclamation should be issued to the effect that no one could hereafter have or hold, buy or sell any person, under penalties, the highest of which was seven years' imprisonment. This valuable document the missionary had printed for circulation. Only the other day, also, a bride was kidnapped on the way to Mundakayam by a strong party.

As to the **classes of soil slaves,** the lowest were the Pulayars, whose customs and condition are described in a previous chapter. Information respecting their deplorable condition in North Travancore before emancipation is given in the *Church Mission Record* for 1850:—"The condition of these unhappy beings is, I think, without a parallel in the whole range of history. They are so wretchedly provided with the necessaries of life that the most loathsome things are a treat to them. They are bought and sold like cattle, and are often worse treated. The owners had formerly power to flog them and enchain them, and in some cases to maim them, and even to deprive them of their lives. They are everywhere paid for labour at the lowest possible rate consistent with keeping life. They are valued differently in different places. The price of an able-bodied slave in the low country, where their wages are comparatively high, is not more than six rupees. In Mallapally it comes to nearly 18 rupees; and in places nearer the hills it rises considerably higher, even to double the last amount. The children of slaves do not belong to the father's master, but are the property of the mother's owner. In some places, however, the father is allowed a right to one child, which, of course, is the property of his master. This succession is by the female line, in accordance with the custom of the Náyars, the principal slaveholders of the country.

"A great landlord in a village near Mallapally has nearly 200 of them daily employed on his farm, while three times that number are let out on rent to inferior farmers. The slaves are chiefly composed of two races—the Pariahs and the Puliahs—of whom the latter form the more numerous class."

Further interesting details are supplied in the same periodical for February, 1854, in the form of questions and answers, as follows:—"Why do you not learn?" "We have no time—must attend to work by day, and watch at night,—but our children teach us some prayers and lessons." "What are your wages?" "Three-quarters of an edungaly of paddy for adults over fifteen years of age, men and women alike." "What are the wages of slaves in other districts?" "Half an edungaly, with a trifling present once a year at Onam." "In sickness, is relief given by the masters?" "At first a little medicine, but this is soon discontinued. No food is supplied." "What is your usual food?" "Besides rice when able to work, often only the leaves of a plant called *tagara* (Cassia tora) boiled; and for six months the roots of wild yams are dug from the jungle." "How do you get salt?" "We exchange one-sixth of our daily wages in paddy for a day's supply of salt." "And for tobacco?" "We give the same quantity for tobacco." "How do you do for extra expenses as weddings, &c.?" "We borrow, and re-pay at harvest time, when we get extra gleanings." "Are slaves sold and transferred to other countries, or to distant districts?" "Four days ago we saw a man and woman and two children brought for sale." "In your neighbourhood, are wives and children separated from the father by these sales?" "This sometimes occurs—the Wattacherry Syrian Christian family have four slave women, who had been married, but were compelled to separate from their husbands and to take others chosen for them by their masters." "Are slave children brought for sale?" "About six months ago two children were brought and sold to T. Narayanan: the relatives afterwards came to take them away, but the master would not suffer it." "Are slaves sometimes chained and beaten?" "Not now chained, but sometimes beaten and disabled for work for months." "In old age when disabled for work what support is given?" "No pension or support of any kind." "How are children paid?" "Not having proper food, the children are weak and unable to do hard work, therefore they are not paid any wages until they are fifteen years of age; they are not even allowed to attend the mission school, if their masters can hinder it."

Rev. J. Abbs also, in 1841, described the condition of the Pulayars in the South from personal observation, and as reported to him by "a rich Soodra, who possesses a number of slaves." He informed me that the highest price for which a slave could be sold was sixty fanams (Rs. 8½). He says that he is at liberty to let or transfer his servants as he pleases—to separate the children from the parents, and the wife from the husband—to give them as presents to his friends, or allot them as the wedding dowry of his daughters—to assign them over as a payment for his debts—and in short, as he expressed it, to him they are "as cattle." Many fell victims to fever, rheumatism, and other diseases; and very few lived to old age. They were but poorly fed, and scantily clothed, and were notorious for drunkenness, dishonesty, and evil passions.

"We cannot calculate," adds Mr. Abbs, "how many of the sons of bondage are prematurely removed from this world in childhood and youth, for want of sufficient nourishment and clothing. Those who reach maturity are doomed to work like beasts of burden, to live in wretched hovels, to eat the most offensive animals and reptiles, and to be treated as outcasts by their fellow creatures. Their evidence is not admitted against their masters; and if they meet a free person on the road they are bound to run from him lest they pollute him. They draw out a miserable existence; and are often left in old age to beg for their support, or to perish with hunger. By few are they comforted, pitied or relieved; none seek to remove their distresses; and no man cares for their souls."

The Pallars are very similar in condition to the Pulayars, and though properly a Tamil caste, their designation is so like that of the Pulayars that they regard themselves as a branch of that caste. Next come the Pariahs, respecting whom in North Travancore further quotations from the same source will be appreciated:—"The carcases of all domestic animals are claimed by the Pariahs as belonging to them by right. They frequently poison cows, and otherwise kill them, for the sake of their flesh. Lying, stealing, and drunkenness are the prevailing vices of the different tribes of slaves; but crimes of an aggravated nature are very rare among them, except the Pariahs, who are frequently chargeable with robbery, burglary, kidnapping, murder, and other heinous crimes. Nowhere is the degradation of this caste so complete as in this country." (*Church Mission Record*, 1850.)

The Kuravars, Védars, and others, were many of them attached to the fields, and in circumstances quite similar to those of the other slave castes.

Other castes also appear to have retained some of their own number in a state of serfdom or semi-slavery. Amongst Shánárs the *Kalla*, or "Pseudo" Shánárs were slaves of wealthy Shánárs, to whose descendants this fact is scarcely yet forgiven or forgotten; and the miserable prejudice against them not yet quite abandoned. Of the great tribe of Ilavars, the Válanmár are still, through forced services, virtually in the condition of slaves belonging to the State.

The attention of the British Government was first attracted to the *Cherumars*, or Pulayar slaves in Malabar; and various inquiries were instituted into their condition. In 1838, the Census gave the number of slaves in that province as 144,371; and in 1843 slavery was entirely abolished.

Early in 1847 a petition on the subject was signed by thirteen missionaries labouring in Travancore, in which they showed from the Census of 1836 that the soil slaves there numbered 164,864. Official reports were also forwarded, in which the slaves were described as "in the lowest possible state of degradation." Not only were they held by private persons, but some were the property of the Government, which derived a small revenue from letting out their services to such cultivators as required them. The British Resident pressed upon the Dewán the manumission of the children of these slaves; in addition to which, the home authorities suggested the emancipation of the parents also; and the subject of predial slavery generally, with a view to its entire abolition at an early period, was recommended to special attention. In consequence of this pressure a proclamation was issued in 1853 (*30th Cunny* M.E. *1029*), declaring free the *children* of slaves of the State who may be *subsequently born;* forbidding the seizure of private slaves in satisfaction of debts; recognising the right of slaves to possess property and to enjoy the protection of the law; directing the emancipation of slaves connected with property escheating to the State; prohibiting, without consent, the sale and separation to a greater distance than fifteen miles of slave parents and children; and prescribing regulations intended to preserve that unhappy class from oppression. "How far," remarks Thornton, "these rules will be effective against the opposition of both prince and people remains to be seen; but it is something to have obtained a recognition of the right of slaves to be dealt with as human beings." ("Gazetteer," Art. Travancore.)

This measure having been found, as was anticipated in such a state of society, utterly inoperative to any practical result, another Proclamation was, by the influence of the Madras Government, issued in June, 1855 (12th *Mithunam* M.E. *1030*), as follows:—

"Whereas we are anxious to better the condition of our slave population; and it is but just that they should have conceded to them those advantages which are enjoyed by the same class of subjects in the extensive territories of the Hon. E. I. Company; and whereas it appears that our Proclamation of the *6th Coombhum 1029* has not fully accomplished that object, we therefore deem it right to rescind the same, and to proclaim:—

"1st. That from and after the date of this Proclamation, all those who are included in the denomination of Sirkar slaves shall be considered free, as well as their posterity, the tax hitherto leviable on them being hereby abolished.

"2nd. That no Public Officer shall, in execution of any decree or order of Court, or for the enforcement of any demand of

Rent or Revenue, sell or cause to be sold any person, or the right to the compulsory labour or services of any person, on the ground that such person is in a state of slavery.

"3rd. That no rights arising out of an alleged property in the person or services of any individual as a slave, shall be enforced by any Civil or Criminal Court, or Magistrate, within this territory.

"4th. That no person who may have acquired property by his own industry, or by the exercise of any art, calling, or profession, or by inheritance, assignment, gift, or bequest, shall be dispossessed of such property, or prevented from taking possession thereof on the ground that such person, or that the person from whom the property may have been derived, was a slave.

"5th. That any act which would be a penal offence, if done to a free man, shall be equally an offence if done to any person on the pretext of his being in a condition of slavery."

This was followed by another royal Proclamation in August 1858, as follows:—"To all Police Officers. Whereas in some Districts the low-caste people are put to great inconvenience because they cannot approach the places where the Tahsildars sit, to represent their grievances, the Tahsildars shall therefore hear their complaints every day in such places as the low-castes also can approach to prefer their petitions, and shall decide such petitions without delay."

This again was followed by a Circular Order in the next month:—"To all Police Officers. Whereas it is reported that since slavery has been abolished by Royal Proclamation, some persons do not allow those who were formerly slaves to work for whom they chose; and also that these persons, with the view of bringing back those who have gone to work under others, use intimidation and prefer false accusations of theft, &c. against them, and thereby trouble and oppress them; and whereas, it is also reported that such persons are helped by Sirkar officials, the Samprathies are hereby ordered to inform the Police Gumasthas, Tanah Naicks, Provertykars, and others, that the Royal Proclamation must be strictly carried out, and that those who in opposition to it persecute these people with false charges shall be duly punished; and all Sirkar officers who are abettors to such complainants shall be at once dismissed the service. The Tahsildars also shall give the matter special attention; and for the future, inquiries shall be made without unnecessary delay into the truth of charges brought against the low-castes, such as Pulayans, Pariahs, and Coravans, &c.; inquiries shall also be made to ascertain in whose employ they are; and should it be found that the charge is true and should be accepted, or on the other hand that it is false, they shall file, investigate, and decide according to law and in obedience to this Circular Order."

These measures were variously carried out by officials, but by most with little zest. As remarked in Admin. Report for M.E. *1038*, "Cruel treatment of predial slaves by their masters has been attempted to be repressed by committing the latter to the Courts, whenever the charges against them were brought to notice, and sufficiently established. Those servants, who belong to a very low and ignorant class, are gradually awakening to a sense of their liberty to take employment under any master they like, as is evident by certain complaints of the landlords. It must, however, be feared that a proportion of cases of ill-treatment are never brought to the notice of authority; and also that they are not, in some places, sought out by the local officials with the requisite degree of zeal. But it should not be overlooked that time is required to counteract the prejudices and traditions of centuries." A few, like Sir Madava Row, nobly and honourably supported the cause of right; but cases of complaint rarely succeeded in those days, as the subordinate magistracy were so deeply prejudiced and naturally partial to their own intimates and caste connections.

The former slave-owners grudged, as they still do, the emancipation of the serfs, fearing the ruin of their agricultural interests; and sought to hinder freedom and keep the Pulayars down in every possible way. They laboured to prevent the slaves getting lands, reclaimed by themselves, registered in their own names as private property, and appropriated adjacent gardens actually cleared by them. They terrified their serfs by absurd and wicked reports, especially from coming under Christian influence and enlightenment. And they resisted their access to Courts of Justice, Government schools, public markets, and high roads. Slaveholders have ever kept their slaves as much as possible from schools and education.

The liberated slaves also have been, as a body, slow to avail themselves of their freedom, and in many instances remain in their former condition. This is not without its advantages. A sudden revolution in the social condition of such multitudes is not desirable—especially as other Hindus are unwilling to educate them—or a complete upturning of the arrangements of society, but fair, steady progress and gradual development as the times improve, and as diligence, moral character, and natural ability develop themselves. With the spread of civilization and education, and an increased demand for labour, these classes are able to procure somewhat better terms from their employers, or are falling in with other employments and other masters, and society is slowly coming somewhat nearer to a healthy state.

The Pulayars and Pariahs who have been Christianized are being educated by the Missionary Societies, towards the secular instruction supplied by whom grants-in-aid are made by the Sirkar, rather than admit these low-castes into their schools. They begin, especially in South Travancore, to dress decently, to use the public roads, enter the markets, and acquire private property.

Their present condition varies in different parts of the country. In the South, where Protestant Christian congregations are numerous, their condition is improving. In the far North, distant from the capital, from civilization, and from the observation of Europeans, their circumstances have been but slightly ameliorated. Dewán Sashiah Sástri gave it as his opinion that "Though slavery has been abolished, it is doubtful whether it has tended to improve the condition of the serf classes very materially; freed from oppression on the one hand, they have lost to some extent the *paternal* care and protection they used to receive from their masters." No satisfaction is expressed here with the emancipation of the slaves, nor is expression given to any hope as to their improvement in the future. But the testimony of influential and able officials who exhibit a practical interest in the social advancement of the people is to the effect that the slave-castes are rising by degrees, "acquiring in some cases by their own labour independent property in land, an advantage long denied them, first by open opposition and subsequently by intrigues on the part of the high castes." Still, no doubt, the present condition of the great mass, especially in North Travancore, is fairly represented by a well-informed writer in the *Travancore Diocesan Gazette* (Apl. 1882) as follows:—

"These proclamations and advancing civilization doubtless have made a marked improvement in their favour; and yet one has only to make a slight inquiry to find that, even in the present day, their condition is most wretched and pitiable, and that in some important points these edicts are a dead letter. We are assured that in many parts in the eastern districts of Travancore *slavery practically exists*, and that *many are unaware of their emancipation.* However this may be, and we are not disposed to doubt the testimony on this point, the condition of those in the large western villages or towns in North Travancore is bad enough.

In some places they are not allowed on the public roads; in others, they are driven from them to seek shelter in the jungle on the approach of a high-caste man; hence it is most difficult for them to travel from place to place. Should they be engaged in work in or near the roads, they are compelled to place leaves, as a mark to warn the high-caste of their presence, who, on seeing it, shout for them to retire while they pass. They may not approach within 64 feet of a high-caste man.

They are still not allowed to enter any public markets, and hence stand at great disadvantage in selling any little produce they may happen to possess; and consequently are kept in a state of poverty. They are not permitted to build their houses near the public roads; nor are they, as a rule, allowed to avail themselves of the Sirkar ferry-boats to cross swollen rivers.

They are not allowed to enter a shop, but should they wish to purchase articles, they must lay down their money at some distance from the shop, shout out their wants, and retire while the owner comes forth, takes up the money, and places instead the articles required. As a rule, though nominally allowed to possess property, they possess none. Should they clear a little waste land, their rich masters generally get the land registered in their own names, and thus they are deprived of the fruit of their industry.

We have used the phrase "not allowed" throughout, for we can find no written laws by which such privileges are forbidden them. But this state of things arises from the fact, not that the Government makes decrees for their oppression, but that it does not adequately protect them; or, as is stated in the last proclamation, that its officers and servants in very many cases do not interfere to protect them, but even connive at their oppression. Can any one suppose, for instance, that if Government officials set their faces against Pulayars being driven from the public roads, or protected them in their endeavours to enter the public markets, or allowed them to approach close to the Law Courts, that this state of things would continue? Would it not soon cease under British rule?

Such a state of things is revolting to the instincts of humanity, repugnant to the feelings of all civilized men, and that it should be winked at under a civilized Government is surprising. May we not hope that under a new and enlightened Rajah such a state of things may soon be abolished, and all men feel that they have a right to the paternal protection of government while they faithfully observe its laws—nay, that the more helpless they are themselves, the more right they have to it."

The continued existence up to a few years ago of the practice of buying and selling slaves in some of the northern districts, where there are almost no schools, and where the slaves are still scarcely informed of the fact of their legal emancipation, as it has never officially been made known to them, was admitted in the Administration Report for M.E.

1045. "It is here that the practice of buying and selling the right of servitude still prevails. But it is clandestinely carried on; and the buyer and seller are well aware that the right parted with, or acquired, cannot be enforced by law. Legally the transaction is quite invalid. . . . . The fetters have been broken, but the emancipated labourer, from attachment, habit, or helplessness, chooses to continue where he was. . . . . European Missionaries have been instrumental in gradually awakening the liberated bondman to a sense of freedom and self-reliance."

The causes which operate to **hinder the rise** of these classes are clearly and ably set forth in the following remarks of Rev. C. Yesudian, a native missionary of lengthened experience. He says: "The following considerations, humanly speaking, may be given as reasons for the failure of these classes to avail themselves more largely of the blessed opportunity offered to them by Christianity for the promotion of their temporal and eternal interests:—

1st. The length of servitude under which they have groaned from time immemorial has so much crippled them that they are too weak to stand on their own feet without a crutch. Hence they look for support and protection to their old masters, on whose premises or farms they can pick up, honestly or dishonestly, what they want for a livelihood.

2nd. Christianity advises its minister to urge upon his hearers the necessity of giving for the support of the ministry.

3rd. The poor slaves were to the Sudra landholders what the damsel of Philippi was to her masters. Finding the hope of their gains is gone, they are highly incensed at the emancipation from slavery as the result of the introduction of the Gospel among them, and try their utmost by enticements or by persecution to retain them in their former condition.

By way of enticement, they hold out promises of increased wages. They pretend to sympathize with them in straits by loans and small presents, or let them hold bits of paddy land, occasionally supplying them with seed, plough, and bullocks. They secretly persuade their friends to raise up lawsuits against the slaves, and soon after stand as mediators to effect a compromise.

When the slaves see through these stratagems, and this pretended kindness, they are persecuted in various ways, such as—

1st. Their rented lands are taken from them.

2nd. They are deprived of their hire, in part or wholly, whenever they have to do Sirkar work. On the occasion of any high official passing through the country, these poor people are forced to give, without payment, such things as fowls, eggs, milk, straw, &c., which they can hardly spare without great inconvenience and distress. Should they refuse to part with their property, they are beaten, taken to the local officers as disloyal, and shut up in the Tanna (prison).

3rd. The hamlets of these people lying in the midst of paddy fields without village roads, they have to drive their cattle or carry their dead along the narrow ridges of rice fields, and are falsely complained against for damage to cultivation or crop, and heavily fined.

4th. Bond deeds are also forged against them, and got proved as genuine before courts, where decisions are sometimes passed, requiring them to pay what they never owed, though the persecutors at length offer to forgive the debt on condition of their returning to their former servitude. They are thus intimidated. Some may be surprised to know that this state of things prevails in Travancore, which at present enjoys the privilege of being under a mild government; but it must be borne in mind that as these people are the most obscure portion of the community, simple and mouthless, they are unable to defend themselves and their rights against the violence of their masters, who, forming the ruling class in the district, and occupying one of the remotest recesses of the country, can, to a great extent, commit acts of injustice with impunity."

A particular instance of fraud, which occurred a few years ago, may be mentioned. "A Pariah got a piece of jungle as mortgage from a Sudra, cleared and planted the land, so that it became worth about a hundred rupees Then the Sudra called the man and told him to bring his document, along with sixty fanams, for which, he assured him, he should get the land registered in the man's name. The Sudra afterwards produced a new document, assuring the Pariah (who could not read) that it was the proper deed, and he received it with pleasure. But soon afterwards, the land he had cleared was registered in another person's name, and taken from the poor man, who was unable to obtain any redress. The Sudras in these parts, being connected with the police clerks, can get anything they like done against these poor people, who are easily cheated and oppressed."

Again, an agricultural labourer borrows a sum of money from a landowner, and gives his service and the service of his children to pay the interest. He lives all his lifetime with his wife and children giving service under these conditions; and so generations pass, and the principal can never be repaid. The landowner of course feeds them, as it is to his interest to keep them in health. This system extends, more or less, all over the country, but it specially holds in the more distant and hilly districts.

CHAPTER XXX.

CHRISTIAN WORK AMONG THE SLAVE CASTES.

IN spite of opposition and persecution, open or concealed, in spite of natural defects of character and evil habits long cherished, **Christianity has done much** for those who have embraced it in Travancore. They have risen, not slowly, but with marvellous rapidity, as soon as the unnatural incubus of their superstitions was removed, and the light of intelligence and religion shed upon their hearts and upon their path in life. Through their improvement in industry, sobriety, and domestic order, and through the Divine blessing upon those who seek Him, their temporal circumstances speedily begin to improve. The children of Christian Pulayars, Kuravars, Védars, and other castes learn in the Mission schools; some have even been able to render service to illiterate masters by reading for them documents and letters. A Sudra conversing with an Evangelist, said:—"Kuravars cannot learn anything—that is quite impossible." The teacher called several of his congregation to him and bade them repeat their Scripture lessons. When the man heard this, he was astonished and confounded: an illustration this of the inspired words, "Out of the mouths of babes and sucklings hast thou ordained strength because of thine enemies, *that thou mightest still* the enemy and the avenger." Some who have had much to do with these outcaste races testify that the converts are, as a rule, persons of excellent natural abilities, as I myself have frequently found them. They are quite capable of rapid improvement.

"At Venkódu," says a native missionary, "I saw a wonderful instance showing the rapid progress of these once most degraded slaves, both in temporal and spiritual circumstances, which has been made solely by the gracious and mighty arm of our Lord. I saw the newly built house of a Christian, who was fifteen years ago a slave, and the whole of his property then did not exceed three rupees. Now his house itself is worth Rs. 1,000, and he has besides landed property and cattle worth more than Rs. 500.

Reading and singing, which I have heard from a house while passing the jungle in the dark of the night, was a proof of what Christianity is spiritually doing among them."

Another report contains some remarkable illustrations of the good influence of Christianity upon this class of people. Writing in 1873 of his own congregation, numbering nearly four hundred, the native missionary says:—

"Twelve years ago, most of these Christians were zealous heathens and oppressed slaves. They lived in huts some ten feet long by ten broad, worth about seven rupees each; huddled together in filthy villages rendered disgusting by the remains of dead animals on which the people fed, and other foul refuse. Carpenters and masons dared not work for them, even if some one possessed the means to employ such. Eleven years ago one of these men, who had become a Christian, undertook to employ carpenters in building a decent abode. The Brahmans interfered, prevented the carpenters from working, and put the man in prison for making the effort to better himself, where he stayed until one of the missionaries interposed and procured his release. At another time the Government caused several houses of the native Christians to be pulled down because they were too good for such people to live in. But now the times are changing. Last year a native Christian, who was formerly of the class described, erected a house of two stories, worth a thousand rupees. This same man, who a few years ago was prohibited from owning any other property than a wretched mud house, now owns besides his house other property, valued at over a thousand rupees, and pays rent and taxes to the amount of 250 rupees a year. Another case is mentioned of a man once a slave to a cruel Brahman, who now owns a house worth Rs. 350, and other property worth about a thousand. These are *exceptional cases;* yet the social status of all those Christians has improved wonderfully as well as their style of living, and they are now building neat houses, in clean and orderly villages."

"Most of these Christians," he adds, "are now advanced in spiritual knowledge and in worldly circumstances. They had not formerly any foot of ground to call their own, but have now bought lands from their masters by money earned after the abolition of slavery. They have now cattle of their own, and lease lands from the Sudras for cultivation. Some Sudras even work on the lands of those who were once their slaves. One is now bullock driver for his former slave."

In their former condition it was their custom to deceive their Brahman and Sudra masters, and to steal their property. If one wanted to take a girl in marriage for his son, he would not inquire into her beauty, property, or education, but her cleverness to steal. Children were taught by their parents to steal—it was about all the education they had. So lying, quarrelling, and the use of foul language were fixed and constant habits. These have all been renounced, and creditable instances are given of self control under severe provocation. Drunkenness was common, but is being abandoned.

The improvement in moral character of the freed slaves under Christian instruction and discipline, renders them more acceptable to sensible and well-disposed employers and landowners. Some of these have been observed to walk past a Christian prayer-house where converts were assembled for worship, just to hear and see what was going on inside. An intelligent Sudra woman, residing near such a congregation, bore clear testimony not long since to the effect of Christian teaching upon these people. "We acknowledge," said she, "that Christianity is a good religion, because formerly the Pulayars and Pariahs were afraid of demons : they used to spend all their earnings in time of harvest for offerings to their terrible demons—but now a great change is seen. They also used to steal our property, but do not do so now; and we must acknowledge that it is your religion that has produced such good results."

Interested and struck by this marked reformation of their former slaves, the master will sometimes make inquiries of his servant as to this Way; or ask him to repeat some of his Scripture texts, or sing a hymn to him, as they are very fond of singing. These poor Christians are becoming able to converse with and exhort their masters and superiors in caste; and are sometimes listened to with pleasure and interest. One we have known purchase tracts to present to the children of his employer. The other day a respectable Sudran came to one of our catechists, and said, "I want all my Pulayars taught Christianity, and I will help you to build a prayer-house for them."

They are also remarked as exemplary in giving, according to their small ability, for the support and spread of the gospel; they help in building chapels with unpaid labour, or for mere food in cases where they are so poor that if they do not earn something for a day they must want. Some of them go about when they can to pray with their fellow Christians, and exhort heathens of the same class to embrace the truth.

A native missionary from a distance recently paid a visit to some of these congregations, and was struck with the wonderful changes which Christianity and education are working. "My tour in the hilly districts, he writes, was very trying, but how pleasing it was to behold here and there among these jungles, chapels for the worship of Jehovah rising up like towers of refuge, and to see those poor ignorant wild people—Puliars, Pariahs, and Vedars—who live in little huts scattered in different parts of the jungle, and who earn their maintenance by hard daily labour in the fields, coming on Sundays with neat dress and cheerful countenance into the sanctuary of the Lord to worship and sing His praise, having cast off their former superstitions. It was also delightful to witness the devotedness of the catechists to the noble work of the Lord, leaving their own homes and properties to live and labour, with their dear wives and children, in places infested with wild beasts and malarious fevers."

A sketch of these converts was given in 1874 by the Rev. J. Emlyn, who has several thousands of them under his spiritual care in the Pareychaley District. He writes:—

"The people that have, as a body, made the greatest progress during the last few years are the converts from the Pariahs and Puliars. While in slavery, and for some time after the proclamation of their freedom by the Sirkar, fearing their masters, they rarely ventured to speak with Christians, and when spoken to by mission agents generally ran away. But after a while they became less timid, and venturing, in jungle paths and other sheltered places, to listen to the words addressed to them, they gradually obtained more enlightened views, both of the Gospel and of their own degraded condition; and understanding the aims and motives of their instructors, they eventually placed full confidence in them, as well as in their teaching. A few in this district made an open profession of Christianity in 1862 and 1863, but it was not till 1867 that large numbers did so: that year the increase reported in the adherents in this district was 2,649 persons, the majority of whom were from these castes. Since then they have every year become more numerous.

Some notion of their former ignorance may be formed from the fact that once when I visited a congregation of learners for the first or second time, nearly all the hearers had absented themselves, having been told by their masters that I intended catching them, and sending them to Great Britain to serve as food for gold-producing rats!

Their character corresponded with their knowledge. Marriage, properly speaking, they had none, men and women living together only as long as they pleased; and so addicted were they to stealing, lying and drinking, and so low was public opinion among them, hardly any considerable evil being considered disgraceful, that the attempts to elevate them used to be ridiculed by many of the higher heathen.

The majority are now acquainted with the leading truths

of the Scriptures; scores of adults as well as children have learnt to read; five have become mission schoolmasters; many have been baptized; a few have been admitted into the church; a good proportion are married; civilization advances, and godliness increases. The Hindus who used to ridicule the efforts of the Mission now acknowledge their wonder at the results.

These converts do their own part well, and are worthy of continued help from us. They strive to learn; they give up their evil habits, and many of them certainly endeavour to walk in the ways of the Lord. They, moreover, contribute very liberally according to their means. In one respect these have an advantage over many of their fellow Christians of the Shánár caste—they have no special work to occupy them on Sundays, and are, therefore, able to spend several hours at the services. And in general they have much greater ability and love for singing than the converts from the Shánárs; assembling for divine service, therefore, has perhaps more attractions for them."

A few years later, in 1878, Rev. W. Lee, in charge of the same district, thus writes:—"In the north of the district the people who have joined us were altogether without education, and grossly ignorant and superstitious. Lying, theft, polygamy, were common amongst them. A wife was kept as long as the husband pleased, and then sent away. In like manner, also, the wife forsook her husband whenever she liked; and if illness or any other calamity overtook either, he or she was invariably forsaken. In morality they might be described as the lowest in the kingdom.

But within fifteen years the power of the Gospel to elevate men has been shown in remarkable instances and in many respects."

In the **Church Mission** in North Travancore the work among the Pulayars began about 1851, three years before the emancipation. It was not suffered to proceed without great opposition on the part of the owners, not only Hindus, but Syrians: the slaves who came to learn were oppressed and cruelly maltreated, and those who ventured to teach them were treated as utterly polluted, and expelled from society. Twice the Mallapalli school was burnt down.

There are now in this Mission eight or nine thousand converts from these castes, of whom nearly a thousand have been taught to read. Fifty-one schools are conducted amongst them. Many more are willing to come under instruction were sufficient means and teachers available. The missionaries and pastors report that many have exhibited striking examples of a holy and humble life. There have been cases to mourn over, of lying, pride, and the grosser sins; but taken as a body, and considering what they have been and their present social condition, they are regarded as most satisfactory converts, who would put many more highly-privileged Christians to shame. They may now be heard singing hymns, instead of howling to drive off wild animals while watching the fields at night.

The following **translation of a pathetic Lyric,** which they delight to sing at their work, will illustrate their sentiments and character:—

CHORUS.

Our slave work is done, our slave bonds are gone,
For this we shall never henceforth forsake Thee, O Jesus!

1. To purchase cattle, fields, houses, and many luxuries (we were sold);
(Now) Messiah himself has settled in the land a people who once fled in terror.
Our, &c.

2. The father was sold to one place, the mother to another; the children also separated. But now
Our, &c.

3. The owners who enslaved us often caused us much suffering:
But will it comfort us to relate all the oppressions in full?
Our, &c.

4. After exhaustion with labour in burning heat, in rain and cold and dew,
They beat us cruelly, with thousands of strokes.
Our, &c.

5. Dogs might enter streets, markets, courts, and lands; (but) if *we* went near they beat and chased us to a distance.
Our, &c.

6. As unclean lepers must run and hide in the jungles, so we outcastes must leave the road after warning those who approach. But now
Our, &c.

7. As the Lord freed from slavery the much-suffering Israelites in Egypt,
So He has freed us from our distresses.
Our, &c.

8 The Scripture teachers came, sent by the Triune God:
Through this, slavery ended and liberty was gained.
Our, &c.

9. They diligently taught letters, arithmetic and hymns; made us clearly see the path to heaven, and set us therein.

Our, &c.

10. Come in crowds, brethren, let none hang back,
Heartily to trust and worship Jesus, the great and wise God.

Our, &c.

11. Come, ye elders! gather the people unitedly into the church:
To-day and evermore remember the love of Jesus and the Judgment Cry.

Our, &c.

12. Observe Baptism and Communion. Advance,
And walk wisely in the path of a renewed nature.

Our, &c.

CHAPTER XXXI.

SERPENT WORSHIP.

SNAKES abound everywhere throughout India; and it will be difficult, or impossible, in such a wide territory and with such large areas of forest, hill, and jungle, ever wholly to eradicate them; though they have numerous enemies, birds, mangooses, monkeys, wild pigs, as well as mankind. Though generally small creatures, these reptiles compel the notice of man, for a very little one may by its bite cause death within an hour or two. The monstrous pythons in the hills, some thirteen or more feet in length, are not venemous, while the deadly cobra rarely exceeds three or four feet in length. The great abundance of snakes may be gathered from the fact that in Burdwan district a dozen years ago above Rs. 30,000 were paid in a short time for the destruction of poisonous snakes, though only two annas were paid for each head; and in 1880 in the Bombay Presidency 177,078 snakes were destroyed, as many municipalities there have begun to offer rewards for their destruction.

It is difficult to realize the melancholy fact that 20,000 human lives and over 50,000 head of cattle are yearly lost in India through the ravages of wild beasts and snakes; by far the greater proportion of the loss of *human* life being caused by serpents, while *cattle* are more frequently carried off by wild beasts. These odious reptiles kill about 17,000 persons annually throughout India; while, on the other side of the account, about 200,000 snakes are killed. The number of deaths reported is, doubtless, far short of the actual truth, as many parts of the country are beyond the minute observation of Europeans and officials. The Governor-General in Council has recently urged increased attention to the subject to diminish this grievous and augmenting, but preventible mortality.

Although no statistics of deaths by snake bite have ever been published in the Travancore Government reports, there is no reason to suppose that deaths are fewer in proportion than in other parts of India; and I know from painful experience that such deaths frequently occur. The whole country is full of cobras, and I have known many deaths, and still more narrow escapes—snakes falling on the shoulders or hands when doors or windows are opened; snakes winding round the leg of the chair on which one is sitting; snakes found under the bed or the floor mat, in bedrooms and verandahs, or darting out when houses long closed are opened; not to speak of laying the hand unwittingly on one coiled up on the bough of a tree, another gliding over me while resting on the floor of a chapel, and a lady gathering flowers for a bouquet actually seizing and clipping off the head of a snake along with an opening rosebud, besides all kinds of risks in travelling, bathing, gardening, or botanizing in the jungles. The good providence of God and his constant guardian care over our lives is ever needed.

It is no wonder, then, that the serpent should be regarded with dread, and that this dread should assume a religious aspect. The endeavour is ignorantly made to pacify the serpent by worshipping it as a deity, instead of using the appropriate means, and following the example of the Jews, who said in their time of need, "Pray unto the Lord that He take away the serpents from us." Most nations of antiquity appear to have rendered divine homage to serpents.

The serpent is mixed up with all the superstitions, mythology, and traditions of India. Various places are named after it, as Nágore, Negapatam, Nágercoil, Nágpore. The last-named place is said by Sir W. Elliott to be called after the Nags, a race of Scythian lineage, who invaded India about 600 B.C., and had the figure of a snake as their national emblem and standard.

Certain demigods are fabled to exist, called Nágas, having a human face with the tail of a serpent, and the expanded neck of a cobra. The king of the serpent race, Ananta, is described as superior in wisdom and intelligence, having one thousand heads, on one of which he supports the world. He is reputed as forming both the couch and canopy of Vishnu, and is venerated in various parts of India. Snake worshippers expect after death to go to a heaven called *Nágalóka*, where many snakes live, and are happy.

Siva wears a snake as an ornament in the hair of his head; and the same creature is worn as a ring by his wife. Legends are told of the gods churning the sea to recover the elixir of immortality, with a great mountain for a churning stick, and the five-headed serpent Ananta for a rope, the poison issuing from whose mouth was drunk up by Siva, and made his neck blue. He is hence called *Nílakandan*, a favourite name in Travancore.

Natives are careful not to speak disrespectfully of such powerful creatures: as the Malayalies of the Shervaroy Hills while hunting the tiger only speak of it as a dog—so the cobra is called *nalla tambirán*, "the good lord," or *nalla pámbu*, "the good snake."

Serpent worship is closely connected with demon worship, and the figure is frequently carved on their shrines. Images of the serpent god are very common. In the Fort at Trevandrum about fifty of these images stand together under the shade of a noble banyan-tree. Idol gods are often surrounded by numerous figures of serpents and elephants.

The origin of this cultus in Malabar is stated as follows in the Kéralólpatti :—

The first Brahman colonists brought by Parasu Ráma did not long remain, because they were unable to bear the incessant attacks of serpents which infested the country. After they left Kérala, it was for some time under the undisturbed control of

THE COBRA.

the serpents. Other Brahmans were then brought by Parasu Ráma; their *kudumi* was removed from the back to the front of the head to prevent their returning to their former home and people. Dividing them into sixty-four villages, he granted to them freehold lands in various parts of the country; and a portion of the Brahmans' estates he allotted to the serpents who had injured them before, ordering the Brahmans to regard these as their demigods, and to present offerings to them. The serpents were thus pacified. Parasu Ráma established the goddess Dúrga on the sea-coast, Sástávu on the hills, and serpents and *Bhúthas* (demons) in the interior, and dedicated temples to all. Hearing of the pleasant and peaceful settlement of things in Kérala, the Brahmans who had fled from the serpents returned, and became the Tulu Brahmans, distinct from the "Sixty-four Villagers."

The snake is to this day an object of worship to the Nambúri Brahmans. It is also prominent in the image of Patmanábhan, or Vishnu, and in the legend of his fane in Trevandrum, which is properly *Tiru-ananta-puram*, "the city of the serpent Ananta." One form of the legend is given in "Land of Charity," p. 161: another version states that Ráma and his brother appeared at Ananta Kádu to a priest, who prepared food for them. After eating, Ráma fell asleep, and Latchmana, finding no mat or pillow for his brother's comfort, kindly changed himself into a large five-headed snake, and made Ráma sleep on this.

It is singular, however, that the killing of the black serpent Káliya was one of the most momentous of Krishna's exploits, frequently represented in sculpture, a fine example of which may be seen in the temple at Tenkási in Tinnevelly. The story is given by Maurice* thus:—

"The monster's infectious breath had poisoned the whole current of the Jumna. The great envenomed serpent *Kali nága* thus determined to try his strength with Krishna. Cattle and men died as soon as they drank. Krishna restored them to life, combated with the serpent, which aimed at once a thousand bites with his thousand heads, and twisted his folds round Krishna's body. He at length took hold of the serpent's heads, one after another, and tearing them from his body, set his foot on them, and began to dance in triumph on each of them." Some figures are said also to show the reptile biting his foot.

Snake worship is especially common in the west and south of India. Throughout the whole of Travancore this strange and degrading superstition prevails. Silver representations of Vishnu trampling under foot a snake are kept by Brahmans in their houses and worshipped in private.† But the worship is practised chiefly by Sudras, Brahmans of an inferior order officiating as their priests. When Sudras find a snake, they catch it by a cord with a noose tied to the end of a long rod, place it carefully in an earthen pot, and bring it to the place of worship, or let it loose in the jungles. Should they find others killing these precious reptiles, they earnestly beg for their protection, or lavish abuse on the persons who have committed the sacrilegious act. Offerings of fruits, cakes, flour, milk, or rice are made to the snake god, and once a year a lamp is kept burning before it.

Live snakes are kept in small temples dedicated to them,

* "Indian Antiquities."

† The accompanying small engraving is taken from a copper idol of this kind in my possession. The larger one is kindly lent by the Religious Tract Society.

and fed and worshipped by the people. Sometimes wealthy Náyars spend much money in this worship, even in cases where members of their own families have been bitten and died.

Snakes were formerly used in the **trial by ordeal.** "When a man will not confess a crime, they take a mantle and wrap up in it one of these reptiles: after calling on the gods, the accused must thrust his hand into the mantle and lift up the snake. If he be bitten, he is considered guilty. . . . . To such an extent do the Canarese carry the superstition, that whenever they find a dead cobra they consider themselves bound to

KRISHNA DESTROYING THE SERPENT.

burn its body with a small piece of sandalwood, a grain of gold dust, corals, &c., using the same ceremonies as at the burning of the body of one of the high castes." (Canter Visscher.)

Some of the priests and temples profess to be able to grant special immunity from snakebite, or miraculous cures; and the ignorant credulity of the people, as well as the uncertainty, after a snake has escaped, whether it was venomous or innocuous, aids in maintaining the imposition. Incantations are sometimes performed by the charmers to the loss of the life of the unfortunate patient. Sacred ashes are kept in the pagoda of *Perunturi Koilappan*, or Siva, at Vaikkam, a dose of which is administered in case of snakebite.

Nagercoil (snake-temple) is one of the centres of this worship, near Cape Comorin. The principal image of *Nága Amman*, or "the Snake Mother," of copper-gilt, and in the form of a serpent, is carried in procession in a car, like other idols, once a year. Inside the temple and without, are numerous stone images of snakes. People assemble on Sundays and other special days from many quarters, bringing milk, sugar, and cocoanuts to worship the serpent goddess. The priests keep up the report that within a circuit of a mile from the temple no snakebite will be mortal; and daily some sand from the seashore is distributed from the temple as a charm or protection. Live snakes also are said to be kept there for purposes of worship.

Perhaps the principal seat of this superstition in Travancore is at **Manárchála** in Kartigapalli district, which I visited in 1880. All that country is devoted to serpent worship. At a distance we heard extraordinary tales of this place, even from intelligent natives—that there was a vast grove, in which was a kind of cave where snakes were kept in large numbers—the priestess, a Nambúri virgin devoted to this service, who cannot leave the grove, and is fed by her mother carrying food to her—no one else dare approach the reptiles—she becomes very beautiful and shining in appearance, and lives to a great age—milk is put in a tub and offered to the serpents at evening, and has all been drunk up by the morning!

A very different state of things was found on a personal visit. Situated in a fine rich country, dotted with comfortable houses of Náyars and Syrians, and many domestic groves, so that it is a common saying that each Hindu house has one, the temple is readily approached by boat, as waterways abound. The place steadily shrunk in importance as we approached it. Instead of a grove miles in extent, there was a fine clump certainly, containing noble specimens of Hopea, Vateria, Hydnocarpus, and Calophyllum trees, but only, say a hundred and fifty yards in diameter, besides another grove much smaller. Instead of a sacred virgin of resplendent beauty, we found Nambiár or Ilayathu priests, a low class of Brahmans living with Sudra concubines. The priests have a good tiled dwelling-house, adorned with excellent wood carvings and brass decorations, provided with a vegetable and fruit garden, and a neat courtyard, in the centre of which stands a small group of trees—Tamarind, Palmyra, and Poinciana—having a circular platform built round the stems, as is common in the vicinity of temples. On the other side of the road stood a neat little cottage, where their wives resided. Several small buildings, consisting of a house for purificatory ablutions, the principal temple, and lesser fanes dedicated respectively to the snake king and the snake goddess, in which the large images are kept, stood in the centre of the grove. These are surrounded by a long wall, and on two sides of the temple projects a square platform of stone, raised about a yard above the ground, as a stand for the display of the stone images of the snake, which are ranged along the outer edge of the platform, and number nearly a thousand in all. The images are of several kinds, most of them about a foot in height, but some very small, many of them copies of the usual representation of the serpent; others having three or five heads, others Krishna, or Siva, or the Siva lingam, engraved within the hood. These figures have been presented from time to time by devotees or persons exposed to danger from snakes. In such cases offerings are made at this shrine. While we were there, some one brought an offering of raw rice, and laid it on the platform. We could see no live snakes, and, of course, could not be allowed to enter either the grove or the temple.

The annual festival is held in September, on Ayilliam day, auspicious for serpent worship, and is attended by all castes. Wealthy people usually offer two or three rupees; the poorer classes a quarter or half a rupee. Some Hindus in time of sickness present golden jewels and five-headed serpents to this temple and grove. Pulayars also come to make presents, but are kept standing at a great distance, whence they must send their gifts. They are told that if they do not propitiate the serpents, they shall suffer from them, and that they must not attempt to kill snakes, else they will be afflicted with leprosy as a punishment. Thus the priests, the more intelligent and influential order, for their own purposes, actually terrify and hinder the poor and uninstructed from protecting themselves.

This worship is a source of much profit to the priests, who pretend that no one bitten within the distance of a mile from the place dies. They showed a Sudra who had been bitten, but he admitted that the accident occurred at night, and that he could not, therefore, be certain that it was caused by a cobra. In conversation the priest justified this cultus from the Keralólpatti, according to the legend given above. A Nambúri in the neighbourhood is applied to by any who have suffered from snakes, and he gives them *a stone*, repeating mantrams over it, and promising that if it be kept in their houses they shall not be molested in future.

Superstitious natives are unwilling to kill snakes, believing that revenge will be taken upon them for the offence. In the Tamil country the curse of the cobra is supposed to be inflicted on a person for killing it, and this is supposed to prevent offspring. A five-headed cobra is made and worshipped to expiate the sin of killing it by a person or his ancestors. In North Travancore, Syrian Christians kill snakes when they come in their way, but other classes do not. In Trevandrum, while a colporteur was reading to some people, a serpent passed by him into the courtyard. He wished to kill it, but was forbidden. "It is our god," they said.

Dr. Doran, of Cottayam, mentions that he met with a family in the Cochin country who made a household god of a cobra. It dwelt on the premises where they resided, and was served with daily offerings of food by each member of the family; while, at the same time, its power as a divinity was regarded with uncommon awe. It happened that one day a native girl, one of the children of the family, about ten years of age, was bitten by it, and Dr. Doran, in the course of his visits to the people, approached the dwelling just as she had breathed her last. On hearing the cause of the poor child's death, he asked them if they had killed the snake, and he relates that never will he forget the expression of countenance of the child's mother when she replied: "Sir, if we were to kill the cobra, which is still about the house, all the other members of the family would die likewise."

When the serpent gods are supposed to be offended in any way, domestic or local festivals may be held to propitiate them. At Vakkam, near Anjengo, such a festival was conducted in a private garden, of which the following account was given:—

"In former days there was a grove in this place, where the Serpent King resided. An inhabitant cut down the grove, and built houses instead, for which he was cursed by the offended god. Most of his family died, and those who survived were reduced to poverty. To remove the curse, an astrologer, who was consulted, advised the celebration of a festival in honour of the god, and at an expenditure of no less than a thousand fanams."

Not long since, at Warkkala, several members of a family of Ilavars having been attacked, one after another, with leprosy, they had recourse to witchcraft to find out the cause of the calamity. The sorcerer advised them that they had failed to pay due homage to *Nága Raja*, the serpent king, and should erect a domicile for him to reside in, and make special offerings to pacify his wrath. A large quantity of rice, cocoanuts, and other provisions was offered; and a number of Kuravars were invited to feast upon these, after going through some ceremonies.

In a lecture on Travancore by Sir Madava Row, the subject is treated in a rather humorous manner. He says:—

"Though people die from their venomous bites, serpents are worshipped as a living deity. Respectable natives deem it a duty to set apart a cool patch in their gardens for the comfortable residence of snakes. Occasionally they creep out, and get out into the house itself, just by way of a little change. He had seen many title-deeds in which the snakes of the estate are conveyed along with other rights to the purchaser. It is reserved to the rising generation of Travancore lawyers to determine whether the snakes constitute movable or immovable property. Cobras wander about freely, and in broad daylight, in certain of the famous Pagodas. There is a temple dedicated to Krishna, which is peculiarly sacred to cobras. Every time he visited the temple he was greeted by one or more of these reptiles. Once he saw a huge cobra quietly passing a few yards off, followed by a band of devotees with clasped hands. Suddenly it turned, and began to wriggle on towards the speaker, who instantly recollected that he had some urgent business elsewhere, and hurriedly left the sacred precincts!"

In parts of the country where these dangerous reptiles are regarded with most veneration, it is possible that the danger to human life arising from the great abundance of snakes is slightly diminished by the comparative tameness of the creatures, though of course this would not lessen the risk from inadvertently treading on them in the dark, or turning over them in sleep, and thus forcing them to bite. Serpents, happily, do not chase men, or seek to attack them, but rather try to escape; they only bite when trodden upon or driven to bay. No doubt they are more familiar, and even audacious, where the poor superstitious people fear to drive them away or annoy them, but only throw a piece of stick or clap their hands, crying "*Po, adá,*" "Go, you fellow"; and it usually goes off. But it is quite an error to say that they never do injury, for a recent instance occurred of a Nambúri Brahman dying at Ambalapuley of snakebite.

A serious practical difficulty, involving many human lives and the interests of many families, arises out of this miserable superstition in the reluctance of most Hindus to kill snakes, and of the Sirkar to offer rewards for their destruction. It is very remarkable that no reference is made in any State Administration Report to the number of deaths by snakebite, except to the few cases who survive long enough, and reside sufficiently near, to be brought to the hospitals, and thus included in the reports of the European physician. There might be some difficulty in collecting full and reliable statistics of all deaths from this cause in the more distant and hilly parts of the country, but no attempt at a separate enumeration of this class of accidents is made, and one cannot but fear that it is the superstition alone which leads the authorities to dread looking the facts in the face.

The contrast between British India and Travancore as regards the offer of rewards for the destruction of venomous serpents is very marked, and is often referred to by those who take an interest in the subject. In a little corner of the territory, Tangacherry, which belongs to the British, two annas are paid per head; and in the Cantonment of Quilon, considerate British officers frequently offer rewards and take a great interest in the protection of the lives of their people; while in Travancore nothing of this kind is ever done. The missionaries endeavour to help in a good cause by offering small rewards, but, from the scanty means at their disposal, their efforts are scarcely worth mentioning in view of the importance of the whole subject.

It is most distressing to think of such trifling with the lives of men under the cover of religious prejudice. "*Ahimsa paramo dharmmah,*" "Not killing"—the first law of Buddhism—"is the highest charity," has been adopted as the official motto of the Cochin State; but *charity to the snake* is *death to the poor man* and his children. It is often said that there is something good in every religion; but it is extremely difficult to see any good whatever in the serpent cultus. A cruel selfishness and apathy must probably bear a part of the blame. Each one thinks that himself will escape, and cares little for others, so that men will often not take the trouble to remove a dangerous stone out of the road, much less to destroy a dangerous reptile. To Europeans the risk is practically almost *nil;* I have never known a death amongst them from snakebite. The few wealthy natives, also, who have conveyances, servants, lamps, and other conveniences, and are able to exercise caution, are proportionately less exposed to danger. The peril increases in proportion to the poverty and rough work, the thoughtlessness and exposure of the people. Yet the lives of the poor and labouring classes are not without their value to the State by their money earnings and production, not to speak of the value of their lives to themselves and those dependent upon them. And even the highest are not quite exempt from this danger; it threatens every household; nowhere is there absolute security. Serpents most infest the fields, woods, and waste places, to procure their prey of small animals; but they also get into houses and towns, haunting holes in the gardens, or the roofs and purlieus of dwellings, whence they dart out and kill people.

Cases of snakebite usually, in fact, occur near habitations; for while twenty times as many more cattle than persons are killed by tigers and other wild beasts, snakes kill many more human beings than cattle. The greater proportion of casualties occur in the night time, and more than half of these during sleep. The reptile creeps near the sleeper for warmth, or in its quest for prey—he turns in his sleep, or throws out a hand or foot, and is bitten. Death takes place after great suffering in from two to twelve hours. It is rare that cases of mortal bite reach the hospitals; and there seems to be no specific yet discovered for the poison of the cobra.

We look to the spread of enlightenment and true religion to abolish the superstitious veneration of the serpent, and the havoc and miseries thence arising. The Sirkar might, however, very well adopt immediate measures to encourage Christians, Muhammadans, and others, to join together in exterminating these hateful and noxious reptiles, and so reduce the present melancholy loss of life.

CHAPTER XXXII.

HINDU CASTE AND POLLUTION.

According to the census of 1875, the number of distinct castes found in Travancore is no less than 420; but many of these are merely subdivisions of other castes, or large families separated from the parent stock through various causes. Some may eat together, but individuals belonging to distinct castes never intermarry. People of any caste coming from a neighbouring country are usually treated as distinct by their fellows here, their customs and social consideration often being, in some respects, different. Thus there are Ilavars in Tinnevelly, and Ilavars in Canara, who are in a much more degraded condition than with us. Caste is not a mere form of "division of labour." This theory is but an excuse offered by some for Hindu Caste. The institution is based and defended on definite religious grounds, and is strictly maintained in practice, being woven into the very texture of Hindu society. "Caste," says Barth in his 'Religions of India,' "is the express badge of Hinduism. Caste is not merely the symbol of Hinduism; but, according to the testimony of all who have studied it on the spot, it is its stronghold. It is, therefore, a religious fact of the first order." The gulf which separates one caste from another is often very great, as great, almost, as between distinct species of animals; or as that which exists between mankind and their cattle or dogs. The cordon of division is strangely effective and complete in its operation. There are little hamlets of low-caste people situated in secluded valleys and corners of the rice fields, near which one might pass for years without observing them; and there are Brahman *agrárams* or closes, intentionally retired from public view, where the entrance of a stranger would be regarded with hostility, horror, and alarm, and would lead at once to personal attack upon him.

Pretences are sometimes made by individuals to higher than their real caste. During a festival at Trevandrum, several goldsmiths putting on the dress and ornaments of a superior caste, walked boldly into the temple. We have known one or two apostates from Christianity, well educated in English, who assumed Sudra names, and passed in distant parts of the country as such. But impostors are detected by very simple means. A Shánár youth who took the high-caste seat at a public cook-shop was discovered by his mode of eating rice, picking it up with the fingers, while a Brahman scoops it up gently with the side of the hand lest he should tear with his nails the leaves which they are accustomed to use as plates. Strangers at feasts are therefore closely scrutinized and watched. Still, changes in caste do, in odd instances, succeed. A Tamilian, for instance, readily alters his *kudumi* from the back to the front of the head; and becomes a Malayáli.

Eating together is one of the grand tests of identity of caste, and earnest discussions are often held as to what constitutes pollution in eating. A typical case occurred in Calicut. A Brahman had been confined in the jail there, and bathed in the common well; but after his release asserted that he had eaten no cooked food, only fruits, which do not convey pollution, and drank only the water of the cocoanut. The Ranee of Calicut charged him with polluting the temple, of which she is manager, by entering it, he being now impure and out-caste, and his daily prayers without efficacy. Tamil Brahmans, it is said, might do all this without losing caste, but in Malabar opinions differ. The suit, as such, was dismissed by the British Courts, but it was very properly held that the Ranee's permission was needed to enter her temple. Brahman prisoners in the jail at Trevandrum are taken outside for their meals, so that their caste standing may not be affected.

In the Pújapura jail, where there are no Brahmans, but a few caste men, it is somewhat amusing to see small clay walls of about a foot in height built to separate between the cooking places of the different castes—a feeble but harmless attempt to preserve their caste purity.

In 1873, when the Nagercoil temple was declared to have been polluted by the entrance of the children of Sesha Iyengar, a Brahman who had given his young virgin daughter again in marriage after the death of her betrothed husband, expensive ceremonies were performed for the purification of the sacred edifice. The priests, though professedly celibate, were known to live in intercourse with the temple women; wicked men and cheats of various kinds might enter, but not a remarried widow, or any who had "aided and abetted" in her crime. A minor purification was first performed, but a greater and more thorough cleansing being required, Nambúri Brahmans skilled in the Tantras were called. The ceremonies cost the Sirkar over

Rs. 320. A sacrificial fire was kindled and fed with choice material, sprigs of *Ficus religiosa*, milk, butter, and ghee. Around this fire were one large and twenty-one small pots representative of demons, each girt with cotton cloth, painted with mystic diagrams, and adorned with flowers and mango leaves. Propitiatory offerings were made and incantations uttered; then the contents of the smaller vessels were poured into the large one, and all emptied over the head of the serpent god who had been insulted. The ceremony closed with the gift of a cow to Brahmans.

In the Satapatha Brahmana of the White Yajur Veda, ceremonial impurity proceeding during the celebration of sacrificial rites from the touch of a carpenter, or any other sacrificially impure person, is represented as removed by the sprinkling of sacrificial water. This passage Dr. John Wilson thinks "forms a key to the caste institution of *sparsha*, or defilement by contact. What occurred at sacrifices was afterwards extended to what may occur in any circumstance in social life, to the debasement of large classes of the community."

This absurd notion is carried to a preposterous extreme in Travancore, and is certainly one of the greatest evils that afflict the country—the *fons et origo* of much distress and suffering to nearly all classes. Ordinary cleanliness is doubtless a virtue, and the pretty tanks close by the temples are, when supplied with *clean* water, both ornamental and useful. But the idea of ceremonial caste pollution sadly hinders the people from social intercourse with one another and from improving intimacy with other nations. Europeans, because they eat flesh and mingle with all castes, are excluded from access to the interior of a native house, or entering beyond the common reception hall of a Hindu palace. After shaking hands with a European, the caste Hindu must bathe to remove the pollution; and there are special occasions when it is highly inconvenient to them to meet foreigners even in the most casual manner.

A native gentleman once conversing with an English visitor at such a time, was obliged to ask him to excuse the omission of the usual shaking of hands, and to lay his letter on the table, whence it could be lifted without pollution. A distinguished Brahman priest and Rajah once granted an interview on the express condition that I should not expect to shake hands, as the old gentleman could not conveniently bathe just then! Some intelligent natives, however, are beginning to feel weary of these absurd and tiresome regulations, and express the wish that they were rid of them.

A British military officer of rank offering his hand to a

young Hindu noble one day, the latter drew back exclaiming, "I cannot touch you to-day. I am holy just now. We are a very religious people, you know." The gallant officer only remarked, "Well, you will shake hands with me the next time that I ask you." "Oh, certainly," replied the innocent youth. This is precisely the spirit so severely condemned in Holy Scripture—"Stand by thyself, come not near to me; for I am holier than thou."

Some naughty boys, however, after playing with others of inferior caste, only go round the corner, wait a while there, and then return and tell their mother they have bathed.

Should a Pulayan touch a Brahman, the latter must make expiation by immediately bathing, and reading much of the sacred books, and changing his Brahmanical thread. If the same man touch a Náyar, he has only to bathe afterwards.

Temples must not be approached within a certain distance by the low castes. The stone lingam in front of the temple at Cottayam is said to be a slave, turned into stone for too near approach! A European unwittingly passed along the Brahmans' pathway with his palankeen bearers, between the temple and the tank. Complaint was at once made that the temple was polluted; and the Sirkar had to pay the expense of reconsecration. During the continuance of the Murajapam festival, Europeans are excluded from nearly the whole of the fort in Trevandrum. In former times the Mission catechists had difficulty even in passing through the streets outside the fort to attend for report at the Mission House.

Brahman temples, therefore, are not for the use of all classes. The low castes have their own temples and deities of an inferior kind, and dare not touch even the outer walls of a Hindu temple. They may, indeed, make offerings to noted shrines from a distance; their *money*, fortunately, is not polluted, nor raw *rice* and other provisions which it is their work to cultivate and gather, else the Brahmans would starve outright. At several temples there are special festival days on which the lower castes have permission to approach a little nearer for worship and amusement.

Because of this theory of pollution, our mission churches, to which persons of all castes are freely welcomed, could only be built, in former times, in retired localities, or at some distance from the public road. Scarcely could a desirable site be sought for purchase, or reclaimed from waste, but the objection was raised that it was near some road used by a religious procession, or some sacred stone, or well. The official reply to a formal request for permission to purchase the land on which one mission church now stands was that it was too near the road by which some procession went, therefore permission could not be granted. The result has proved this all nonsense. In asking the Sirkar for permission to take up another piece of waste land, the Gumastha measured our land, omitting thirty feet all along the side of the road on the ground that the native Christians *would pollute the public* passing by it. The matter had to be brought before the Dewán and pressed; and a second registration was made for this narrow strip of land in order to give us frontage to the road.

All dread the raising of the lower classes and their admission to the common rights of humanity. "The very essence of caste lies in the degradation of others." Hence, as Rev. H. Baker wrote, "Every slight objection to any site that is chosen for the building of churches is attended to, false statements are made by the district officers, and five or six years pass away before a decision is come to; and that is mostly unfavourable."

All this superstitious punctiliousness is fraught with serious inconvenience to the unenlightened high castes themselves. They are unable to travel by sea unless they could land daily to cook and eat their food, that prepared with the water on board ship being ceremonially unclean. When travelling by rail along with other classes, they dare not even take a draught of water to refresh themselves; and often there is great suffering from hunger where habitations belonging to their own caste are not at hand. A friend of ours calling a native doctor to the Hills for a serious emergency, the poor man could eat nothing but plaintain fruits during the two days he was in patient and kindly attendance. Barbosa, however, says that, in his day, "during the time the Náyrs are at war, they may touch any peasant, and eat and drink with them in their houses, without any penalty." But such a sensible arrangement is not recognized now.

It will be easy to see how the idea of caste pollution affects **the use of the public road** by people of low caste. Each caste is familiar with the prescribed distances within which they may approach, or be approached by every other caste in the whole scale. A Nair, for example, may approach but must not touch a Nambúri Brahman—a Pulayan must remain at a distance of ninety-six steps. Until lately Pulayans were not allowed even to approach the roads.

When they had palm-leaf umbrellas and other small articles to sell, they laid them down near the highway, and standing at the appointed distance shouted to their customers. Landowners could not approach their labourers in the rice fields, but must call to them from the boundary. Hence the habit of shouting aloud in conversation, which many respectable men have acquired. Cottayam Pulayars put a few green twigs on the road side, near where they are working, to warn off high-castes.

Pulayars walking on the high road are required to run off into the jungles or fields when high-caste people pass along. Where there is plenty of room, a kind of side-walk is sometimes formed in this way. It is most painful to see a poor and inoffensive woman, with a load on her back, or burdened with an infant, compelled to scramble up the steep sides of the road and retire into the jungle, to allow a high-caste man to pass ; or seeking for a favourable chance to cross the highway, or go along it. She waits till one party has gone on—then makes a dash—but perhaps is balked by meeting another party in the opposite direction. What discomfort, misery, and waste of time all over the country, and that for no rational purpose or appreciable advantage to any one! If the Pulayar did not speedily move out of the way, instant death was the penalty : the low-caste man in former times would be at once cut down by the sword of the Nair. Now-a-days respectable passengers, when polluted by accident or by the obstinacy of inferiors, sometimes, on the principle that they "may as well be hanged for a sheep as a lamb," join in giving a good thrashing to the disrespectful low-caste passengers. On one occasion a party of Brahman travellers meeting a set of coolies carrying a heavy log of timber, ordered them to put it down and run off the road. This they positively declined, under the circumstances, to do, and the Brahmans began to beat them ; but the coolies did, at last, lay down their load, and gave them as much as they got. There are, again, cases in which high-caste people are glad, for the moment, quietly to ignore these rules, and a Chogan or Ilavan gets a good thrashing for his over-anxiety to keep a Brahman pure by informing the latter that he was defiled by too near approach, when he would have passed on unconsciously and without further disturbance.

At one period I was quite surprised to see all Pulayars get far out of my way when driving along the roads, as most of them should know that a missionary cared nothing for their approach. After being puzzled for some time as to the cause of this, I detected my horsekeeper, an Ilavan, behind me making threatening signs and gestures to Pulayars approaching, that they might run off, in order to save his caste dignity! Yet Ilavars and Chogans were, and still are in most parts, similarly driven out of the way by Brahmans. Missionaries have pleaded the cause of all classes alike, and to a large extent succeeded in procuring the emancipation of Shánárs and Ilavars from such bonds, but as soon as one caste has somewhat risen from their degradation they inflict similar indignities upon their inferiors, unless restrained by the fear of God, or a sense of justice to their fellow-men. A most cruel and selfish thing is Hindu caste!

Where the road is too narrow, or closed in with walls, it may suffice for the inferior to keep to the far side; but sometimes no quarter is shown to the unfortunate low-caste passenger. On one occasion I found three native Christians, who had kindly accompanied me to help the cart across a river, tied, on attempting to return to their homes, to the wheels of the carts belonging to certain bandymen, because they did not leave the road, which in fact was impossible at that place, there being strong hedges on either side. Happily, as I myself was able to bear testimony on behalf of my poor friends, there was no great difficulty or delay in procuring the punishment of the brutal bandymen by a fine of three rupees each.

In 1878, a Sudra, a drunken and violent character, happening to pass by the road from the market, saw a Pariah Christian woman, fatigued and footsore, sitting down by the roadside to rest a while. The man assaulted and struck her with his stick on account of her not moving to a distance to avoid polluting him. Her son, who was present, defended his mother, giving the assailant two strokes in return, with a stick he had in his hand. This was supposed by the judge, who afterwards dealt with the case, to be "natural enough, though it may be a grievous offence for a low-caste man, especially a Pariah, to strike one of the higher caste, according to the Dharma Sástram. But it must be remembered that the prisoner was a catechumen of the Mission, and that the necessary results of education and civilization are a feeling of self-worthiness, and a yearning after independent thought and action. With these, one's rights as recognized, or not recognized, by Society and by political Government are felt and dwelt upon."

About a month afterwards the Sudra died of intermittent fever, and a noble opportunity was presented to the police officials, who came to bury the poor man, to magnify a petty case into a great crime, and win fame by displaying their zeal and ability in detecting murder; at the same time to inflict a blow on the spread of religion and freedom amongst the obnoxious Pariahs. Accordingly seven Christian men were seized, mostly heads of families, and charged with the murder of the Sudra, and they were kept in prison for more than a month before they were acquitted and released, while their persecutors went scot free. In the judgment, the Court remarked, "This is a petty case: the circumstances lie in narrow compass though, evidently, from caste prejudice, of which the committing officer may be supposed not to be free, it has been made to assume the formidable proportions of murder. One witness says, 'I deposed none of those things—what further they might have written at the Police Cutcherry I am not able to say, since my statement was not read over to me. I simply affix my mark in the paper presented to me, as I was desired to do.'—There was sufficient in the affair to excite the strong caste prejudice of the scribe who took down the evidence; and the opportunity for spicing it with extravagant statements, in order, perhaps, to supply at least some grounds that might seem *primâ facie* to justify the prisoner's commitment, was not to be lost when *impunity was secure,* and *they could be subjected to imprisonment, pending their trial and acquittal,* if not found guilty." Such is Travancore justice as administered by the inferior officials, with whom the people have firstly and mostly to do!

In former times, Europeans were not allowed to travel in the interior of the country, but were obliged to keep to the sea-shore. The first British Residents also lived near the coast, the present Residency in the town having been built only in 1820. Early missionaries, travelling, as they did, much about the country, occasionally came across processions, and were driven out of the way: in some cases their palankeens also were broken.

Great improvement is manifest, however, in this respect. A few years ago, a friend and myself were returning in two bullock carts from a meeting in the South, along the main road, when we met the gods being carried back from their annual visit to the capital. An escort of sepoys accompanied them, their officer walking in front with sword drawn. We pulled up our carts as close to one side as possible, but as high walls stood on either side, we could not go quite out of the way; nor, indeed, was I desirous to do so, as it seems a plain duty to claim all the rights of citizens and taxpayers for the sake of the humbler classes of the community, who are afraid to insist upon any right, scarcely knowing what their legal rights are, and are unable to plead their own cause. The officer bade us get out of the way for the gods. I showed him that this was impossible, neither was it required in these days of freedom, when all Christians enjoyed the right to use the public highways. "But there is a proclamation that you must get out of the way." "No," we replied, "there is not. You may remove us, or our carts, as you please; but we have gone quite close to the side, and you have plenty of room to pass." "I will report you," said he. "Very well, do so," and they quietly passed on. We heard nothing further on the subject.

"A Védan, it is said, pollutes the road while he is upon it, but a Pulayan pollutes all the road by which he has gone."

Englishmen can scarcely realise the horror which superstitious natives feel when there is any chance of being approached by a Pulayan, and the disgust with which these unfortunate people are viewed. It is a great struggle for a caste Hindu to pay us a visit, or to enter a Church, even to ask medicine or other aid, when there is risk of coming near such. Yet it is certain that no true civilization or progress, no national prosperity, no true religion is possible till this wicked hatred and aversion are removed by the improvement in cleanliness, education, and moral character of the low castes on the one hand, and by the enlightenment, philanthropy and spiritual conversion of the high castes on the other. "A house divided against itself cannot stand."

In proportion as civilization is introduced, popular education spreads, and new life is inspired into the activities of the people, these barbarous restrictions become intolerable and are continually broken through, sometimes leading to the commission of breaches of the peace by those offended at the impudence, as it is deemed, of the lower castes.

After the commencement of evangelistic work amongst the Pulayars by the Church Missionary Society, in 1851, at Mallapalli, great opposition was shown by the slaveholders; the slaves who came to learn were oppressed, and those who ventured to teach them were treated as utterly polluted, and expelled from society. Soon there arose the question whether Christian converts from such classes should be allowed to walk along the public roads, as Syrians and Muhammadans are permitted to do, or should be kept in the same degraded state as before.

The Dewán decided that this liberty should not be granted, and an order was issued on the occasion of a recent convert, an Ilavan, passing near a temple in the neighbourhood of the Mission House, asserting that "though an Illowan becomes a Christian, he still remained an Illowan," and directing that converts to the Christian religion *should not pass through the public highway*, but must pass through the field road, that is the road the jackals go!

It was urged by the Society that this placed Protestant Christian converts at an unfair disadvantage as compared with converts to the Syrian Church, or to Muhammadanism, who are permitted to enjoy the status accorded to these bodies. And after much delay the adverse decision, happily, was overruled by the Madras Government.

In 1870, again, the Madras Government, urged by a case which had occurred some time previously, in which an Englishman was assaulted for passing through a Brahman village, and his assailants were only punished by a trifling fine, passed a censure on the Sirkar for permitting numerous caste disabilities, urged their removal, and expressed surprise that any class of the public should be excluded from public thoroughfares. They recommended the adoption of the principle that "the public high streets of all towns are the property, not of any particular caste, but of the whole community; and that every man, be his caste or religion what it may, has a right to the full use of them, provided that he does not obstruct or molest others in the use of them; and must be supported in the exercise of that right."

About the same time the matter was made the subject of lengthened public discussion in consequence of a proclamation which was made with beat of drum through the streets, by the officers of the district, excluding Pulayars from the main road near Trevandrum. This having been noticed and taken up by the Acting Resident, an announcement appeared in the "Travancore Government Gazette" that the notification was unauthorized and improper, for which the Tahsildar was punished, and the Provertikar dismissed from the service; and that the road in question is open to all classes of the people at all times. But in the very next issue appeared a special proclamation that the Maharajah himself directed that the Provertikar should not be dismissed, but only fined a month's salary, that being a sufficient punishment for his fault.

Search has been made, and inquiries instituted of high officials, but no copy of any *general* Proclamation has been found, conceding the right of all subjects to the use of the highways, so that there is nothing in black and white and readily accessible, for those outside the capital, where this right is disputed or practically denied, to appeal to. It would appear that no such proclamation has ever been issued, so no one is assured of his rights. Why should this not be done now? Is the Sirkar still unwilling, or is it afraid, to grant liberty? It is, indeed, said that a notification was to be issued, coming into force from the beginning of *M.E. 1058*—15th August, 1882, allowing these castes henceforward full liberty to walk through public roads, and to appear before public courts without inconvenience; but I have been unable to learn whether this report is correct or not, or to procure a copy. Has it been widely published—or published at all?

Throughout the whole of North Travancore, the low castes enjoy practically no right of way; and caste divisions and evils are rampant. Even Christian converts of low-caste origin have gained no right of way on the public roads yet; and it is said that they are advised by the missionaries not to claim this, but to give way under all circumstances, else they will get beaten and persecuted, and false charges will be raised against them. Even Syrians are accustomed to bathe after touching a Pulayan, and will not admit converts from this class. Respectable Hindus with whom I conversed in the Cottayam District denied strongly, and with apparent sincerity of conviction, that there is any law making the public roads free to all classes. The native Christians had not heard of it either; and a missionary of whom I made inquiries had not been able to procure any copy of such law or proclamation, being informed by the Dewan that he could not find anything of the kind. Accordingly, Válan boatmen must keep 50 or 60 paces off Nambúris. A Chogan must walk on the far side of the road, if a Nair passes; but must go out of the road altogether for a Brahman. Pulayars meeting me, cried *po, po* ("go"), and stood still, till I assured them they need not fear me. At Cottayam, low-caste people are not allowed to appear in the common market to dispose of the small articles they bring for sale on market days. In taking the sick to the Hospital at Cottayam, the gauntlet had to be run. A separate hospital has now been built for low castes, but it is rather difficult of access, and a long détour is to be taken through the rice fields, the distance by road being about a quarter of a mile. A poor slave has been known to let his child die—and they love their offspring—rather than undergo the delay and chance of a beating in a visit to the hospital. Caste takes no account of necessities, charities, or infirmities. Yet Pulayar criminals are taken through the Chetty Street. In the Cochin state it is said that the condition of the low castes is not so bad, Pulayars being allowed to go through the streets and even into houses.

Another serious evil arising out of the idea of caste pollution is that the **covering of the bosom with clothing** is forbidden, in order to the easy recognition and avoidance of the lower castes by their masters. This rule of going uncovered above the waist as a mark of respect to superiors is carried through all grades of society, except the Brahmans. The highest subject uncovers in the presence of the Sovereign, and His Highness also before his god Patmanábhan. This was also the form of salutation even from females to any respectable person. Hence deadly offence was given by persons who had resided for some time in Tinnevelly and Ceylon, or by Christians who were taught in the churches to cover themselves in accordance with the claims of modesty and health.

Such marks of degradation have sometimes been imposed on slaves by other nations. In Batavia, at the beginning of this century, all slaves were strictly prohibited from walking on the flagged causeway in front of the houses, as also from wearing stockings and shoes, in order that their naked feet might be the means of making their condition notorious. While, on the other hand, the Roman people would not agree to a proposition which was made in the Senate, to distinguish the slaves by a particular dress from citizens, lest the number of the former being thus easily ascertainable might become dangerous to the state.

The upper-cloth covering the bosom is taken off before a superior, and tied either round the waist or the head. Ornaments and jewels were similarly dealt with, being forbidden to persons of inferior caste, except by special grant. Each caste and class had its own ornaments and style of dress, differing in pattern, value, and material. The higher castes wear gold on the upper part of the body only, and silver, as being less honourable, on the lower members. Pulayars could only wear brass, and Hill people, Védars, Kuravars, &c., a large number of strings of glass beads around the neck and hanging on the breast. Even to wear the ornaments *customary to each caste* it was supposed that special permission was required from the Sirkar, showing how the officers kept back the humblest rights of the people; and a notification was published by the Ranee when General Munro was Dewan, and again republished in *M.E. 1040* (1864) by Sir Madava Row, that ornaments such as they *have been in the habit* of wearing *according to the custom* of each caste might be worn without asking special permission of the Sirkar, or paying a fee for the privilege.

It will now be seen that the **free access of the lower classes** of the population to **Courts of Justice**, Government officials, and fairs and markets, however essential to the public peace, security, and prosperity, is still more difficult of attainment. In consequence of the mingling and interference of superstition with every event and business of life, and the consecration of the country to idols, most of the public buildings were in the vicinity of the temples, and to them the lower castes could not be allowed access. Nor could the officials, being all of high caste, afford to be continually polluted by the near approach of low-caste witnesses, complainants, or petitioners. As the witness could not come to the court, the court must go to the witness. But it must not go too near him, and the frequent result is that the witness's evidence is taken by the court, or a clerk deputed for the purpose, calling the questions to an intermediate peon, and the peon shouting them to the witness and repeating his replies to the presiding officer, the distance at which the witness is obliged to keep from that functionary being too great to allow of the questions and replies being distinctly audible, or intelligible.

A painful picture has been drawn in one of the public papers of the sufferings of students at these places in the Cochin territory, but equally true of Travancore, and by no means overdrawn. The writer says, "Notwithstanding the civilization that education ought to inculcate in the minds of the rulers of a State, we are sorry to say that neither time nor education seems to have worked any change in the old usages of the Tahsildars' Cutcherries. Parties to a suit, if they be of low caste, are not privileged to approach such places, but have to keep away at a distance of fifty or sixty paces from them, the examination of witnesses and every other proceeding of a suit being conducted at that respectable distance. It is very amusing to watch a case of this description going on, for the Gumashta (clerk) of the cutcherry has to cry out at the top of his voice every question, and the witnesses or defendants, as the case may be, have in turn to respond to them by as loud yells, so that all the proceedings are not only audible to those in court, but to those out of and far from it, presenting a scene more like a serious quarrel than a court of law.

The low-caste people who wish to present petitions are thus kept away from the court, and are made to stand day after day in the hot sun, their heads not being permitted to be covered, or they are exposed to merciless rain until by some chance they come to be discovered, or the Tahsildar is pleased to call for the petition. This procedure is diametrically opposite to the distinct orders of the British Resident conveyed upon the subject several years ago, abolishing the barbarous practice in the local courts, and we hope, therefore, that the Dewán will take the necessary steps to put a stop to the invidious distinction of caste prejudice and pollution so rampant in public places of business."*

Rev. J. H. Hawksworth, writing in 1855 of the shameful attempts made by the slaves' owners to deter the Pulayars from attending Christian instruction, tells how a schoolhouse was maliciously burnt down a second time, and a slave cruelly beaten and left lying senseless for attending it. His own master sent him a day or two afterwards to prefer a complaint at the police office, and he called to ask the gentleman how he could get within shouting distance of the officials. A slave acquainted with the neighbourhood was sent to accompany the complainant. They had to pass through rice fields, jungles and gardens, keeping out of reach of the owners. In this they failed; a man caught them and gave one of them a thrashing, while the other escaped. The attempt to reach the police office was abandoned for the day. A second attempt was subsequently made, and

* *Western Star*, 1879.

resulted in a second thrashing. However, the complaint was ultimately lodged, the slave's deposition was taken at the top of his voice, and all attempts to get the case beyond that stage proved abortive.

So also a distinguished native clergyman, the Rev. George Matthan, in 1856, relating a case of cruel beating of a slave by his master for keeping the Sabbath day, says, "I thought it would be of no use to complain to the authorities; for I despair of justice being obtained, from the general corruption of the courts of law in this country, and from the jealous eye with which any attempt to raise the slaves would be viewed by the officials."

Such arrangements are tantamount to a positive denial of justice in many cases. Taxes also are paid by go-betweens; and rents to Brahman or Chetry nobles, some of whose agents are almost inaccessible to their humbler tenants; who can only induce some high-caste friend to take their letters, or applications, into the sacred street in which the officials reside.

The position of many of the public buildings has long been the subject of serious complaint by various classes of the inhabitants. The ordinary and only road to the cutcherry at Suchindram is through the Brahman street, and only open to high castes, so that even the native missionaries—men equal in character, attainments, and influence for good, to any Brahman in the country—dare not, on account of caste defilement, approach by it, but must go by a circuitous and filthy path through the rice swamps: the site for new offices has therefore been selected at Kottár. Several cutcherries have been rebuilt in more accessible situations, but even this has not wholly remedied the state of things. In some of the new buildings business was not regularly conducted for a considerable time. The officials occupied them only occasionally, when they could not help it, and especially when superior inspection was anticipated. They naturally prefer working in the vicinity of the temples, sharing in their privileges and pleasures, and being themselves thereby to a great extent protected from personal pollution by low-caste suitors. The more hindrances that are presented to such, the better and the easier for officials of this temperament. In ordinary cases the low classes are not allowed nearer to the cutcherry than from 40 to 100 yards.

At Mávelikara a new cutcherry was professedly erected, but being only a temporary building with mud walls, it was not in use more than ten days; afterwards it tumbled to pieces, and has only recently been re-erected. At Chenganúr a new building was put up, afterwards it disappeared, and it is again rebuilt, but very close to the temple. At Ambalapuley the officials resort to the new office when low castes apply; but as there are almost always some such in attendance, the officials should remain permanently in the new building. At Karunágapally there is a new cutcherry; but the officials are mostly Brahmans, so that low castes, and even Chogan Christians, must stand at a distance. The Cottayam cutcherry is an old building and very inconvenient, Chogans being unable to enter, or Pulayans to approach very near. The distance required is about sixty yards. Changanácherry standing close to a temple, is worst of all, as Pulayars are not allowed to approach within about 200 yards, and cannot give their evidence with convenience.

At Neduvengaud, though the new public offices are in an accessible spot, yet the caste prejudices of the Government servants are so strong that access is not yet allowed to low caste people—they are all kept, even Christians, at a distance of at least twenty feet; and were they to complain or intrude, the officials, being all of one mind and having a common interest on this question, and being the wealthy employers, masters and neighbours of the poor people, could readily take revenge when opportunity presented itself.

At Kotárakara, even in the new Munsiff's Court, no one thinks of admitting any low caste men *into* the court house as component parts of "the public," and such a thing dare not be proposed. One kindly official whom I saw there took great credit to himself for having ventured to propose that witnesses or suitors of low caste should be allowed to come up quite close to the window *on the outside*, and that a verandah should even be erected for their protection from sun and rain.

Such reforms, though continually pressed on the Sirkar by the British Government and by enlightened public opinion, and from time to time promised and even begun, are carried on slowly and grudgingly, and are still very incomplete. As to means, the amount expended for the admiration of European visitors on the costly Museum at Trevandrum, or for the Brahmans on a single Sexennial Festival, would have sufficed to rebuild all the district cutcherries in Travancore, and thus benefit thousands of households amongst the humbler population; or would have sufficed to establish a hunded village schools open to all classes. A thorough and universal reform in this one matter would confer unspeakable benefit upon the masses of the population, of whom nearly one half are subject to these serious disabilities, born to toil and to contempt. Some of the very same classes in Malabar now creditably fill most important appointments. It is not right that large classes who contribute their quota to the revenue should be excluded from the courts, schools, and other institutions maintained by

FALLS AT COURTALLUM

the public funds. It is now *caste*, not *slavery*, that stands in the way of further progress. Public servants in their public capacity should be expected, as some of the ablest and best of the higher officers already do to a large extent, to lay aside all consideration of the pollution by low-castes; and, as in British India, permit the approach of all for business in business hours, or when the exigencies of the public service demand it.

The Metropolitan of India lately expressed his great disappointment and astonishment to find, during his late tour in South India, that in Travancore, the position of women should be so degraded, even compared to other parts of India, and that the most oppressive and degrading of caste rules should still be in force, the lower orders being compelled to leave the public roads and retire to the jungle to allow high-caste men to pass unmolested. Degraded by the oppression of centuries, loaded with such disabilities that it is impossible for them to rise or take any social standing in the country, their condition even yet is indeed pitiable. The present able and enlightened Maharajah could do nothing to render his reign more illustrious than by adopting effectual measures to ameliorate the condition of these poor people. (*Diocesan Gazette*, March, 1882.)

The same pernicious notion of caste pollution hinders the **obtaining of public employment** by persons who have belonged to the lower castes, however they may rise in character, ability or reputation. The union with civil duties of religious functions which have no necessary connection with them, such as the administration and management of the Temples and Government Free Inns for Brahmans, not only occupies the time of the revenue officers, but makes it impossible for Christians or persons of humble birth ever to occupy such posts in the public service. They would pollute their more sacred fellow-officials and the temple buildings. At one time when a small proportion of respectable Syrian Christians were admitted into the service of the Sirkar through the influence of Colonel Munro, it was quite ridiculous to see them standing at the appointed distance professedly superintending the measurement of grain and the writing of accounts, outside the gate of the sacred enclosure. Native Christians are thus excluded from the Revenue and Magisterial Departments of the public service, which are the best paid and most honourable. Those native Christians who make up the total of 6 in Government employment are mostly in inferior positions as messengers, &c., chiefly under the European officials. So long as the present plan of administering the temple funds and superintending the feeding of Brahmans obtains, only Brahmans and Sudras can be appointed in the principal departments. Recently, however, a separate Sheristadar has been appointed for the superintendence of these religious duties; and there is no good reason why separate Devassam and Ootooperah establishments should not be organized in each District, thus removing the main substantial difficulty in the way of admitting a fair and equal proportion of all classes to the responsibilities, honours, and emoluments of the public service now so largely monopolised by a few.

Over and above the religious aspect of this question there is of course, a strong conservative feeling among high castes, that if a man of low-caste birth were admitted to positions of authority, high-caste men would, on occcasions, have to stand before him, a situation very repugnant to caste prejudice. But this does not present any practical difficulty in British India.

The same obstacle stands in the way of **primary education,** caste prejudice being allowed to hinder the admission of low-caste children into most of the Government schools in Travancore. To the lower castes, both Christian and heathen, is still denied the very essential right to a full share in the education supplied by the State at the public cost. Of the English and Vernacular District Schools only about a third are open to low-castes, while from the 199 Village Schools established all over the country, except in the far north they are absolutely and universally excluded. A grant-in-aid is indeed made to Mission Schools; but it is highly undesirable that these should be regarded or forced into the position of being schools for low-caste children only. To remove this stigma and unite the people into one nation, the whole of the Sirkar schools should be opened, as in British India, to all classes of the population.

Personal experience certainly corroborates the remark of a recent writer on India. "So fiercely are the higher castes opposed, not only to associating with low-caste pupils, but to their being educated at all, that it is with the greatest difficulty we can obtain sites for Christian schools in the villages, if the high-caste people can throw impediments in our way." ("Every Day Life in India," by Rowe, p. 80.) In certain Government village schools to the north of Cottayam, even Syrian Christian boys (who are admitted as of good caste), are seated apart, at a distance from the other children, lest the Hindu boys should be polluted by accidentally touching them; when this does happen, complaint is made to the teacher. The Chogans form the principal part of the population in those parts, but dare not approach the school, and are deprived of the privileges of education and civilization on account of the supposed inferiority of their caste.

The objection urged against granting to the lower castes

admission into the public schools is the trite and futile one that, if they were admitted, the higher castes would at once leave the school. Even so able an administrator and scholar as Sir Madava Row was led astray by this notion. "The religion," said he in his Report for *M.E. 1042*, "of the high-caste pupil forbids his associating with the low-caste pupil; and if the State in present circumstances throw the schools open indiscriminately to all castes, the practical alternatives offered to the high-castes are either that they should forego the advantage of State education, or secure that advantage under serious violence to religious feelings."

But what becomes of the religious and conscientious objections of the high-caste pupils in the High School and College at Trevandrum, which are open to all who can manage to obtain the primary education and the means to continue it, and are actually attended by lads of low-castes and Christian converts of all sorts, except Pulayars? Do the Brahman and Sudra scholars of those institutions feel that they are losing their souls by sitting on the same benches with low-caste scholars, for the poor reward of an English education and the temporal benefits anticipated therefrom? So of the few District Schools open to all. And if it were a part of the religion of a moiety of the people to deprive the other moiety of their civil rights, such religious prejudices must give way, if common justice and the public good are to prevail.

Just think of the amazing selfishness and effrontery of the demand made on the part of the wealthier and more respectable inhabitants. They have any amount of pecuniary means at command to establish schools for themselves as exclusive in principle as they please. To save their own pockets, however, they claim admission to the public schools, which may be regarded as a kind of charity. And they not only accept this charity, but they even venture to assert a claim to its exclusive enjoyment. The wealthier classes are to benefit by the public expenditure for benevolent purposes: they will also drive off the poorer classes who shall dare to apply for the same, and who yet have contributed their proportionate share towards the general expenditure!

But the experiment has been made over and over again in the railways, government service, army, and schools of British India. So long, indeed, as but a few schools are open to all, we may expect the high-castes to hold aloof from them as inferior and stigmatized by the presence of the despised children, and to hold out the threat in other schools, that if the low-castes are admitted they will leave. Mission schools in various parts of India have met with the same objection, and by manfully holding out against caste assumption they have gained the day, and their scholars have yielded within, at most, a few weeks. Let the experiment be but fairly and heartily tried in Travancore, and it will be seen how soon pretended "religious" objections will drop in all, as they have in the schools already open, and in British India. A broad and whole-hearted policy will command respect and secure the desired end, where timid and partial efforts might fail in presence of popular ignorance and ingrained prejudice.

It was once proposed to open separate schools for the instruction of Christian converts and others of low-caste. We trust that such a suggestion will never be carried into effect. For what would it be but to "aggravate as well as perpetuate unnecessary and hurtful distinctions of caste" which have already brought such mischief. Such a movement could not be other that retrogressive, tending to prop up the decaying system of caste, and lending fresh life to the evils still in existence, but now declining in strength through the spread of knowledge. Nor would it be fair to the Christian community rapidly increasing in numbers, growing in intelligence, and rising in social position, to deny them opportunities for beneficial educational intercourse with respectable Hindus, and the advantages of emulation in the race for instruction and progress. Separate schools cannot properly be called *public* schools.

As to the indefeasible right of native Christians to a share in the public institutions of the country, few in these days will entertain any doubt. In a petition presented to the Maharajah in 1873, the point was dealt with as follows:—

"The native Protestant Christian community realize very strongly the disabilities to which they are still subjected, notwithstanding the remarkable manner and extent to which they have, as a body, risen in the social scale, despite of many obstacles. They deeply feel their anomalous and undeserved exclusion from the benefits of the Sirkar schools, while they are strenuously endeavouring to fulfil their part as your Highness's loyal and obedient subjects; and as upright, peaceable, and industrious citizens. They have been already educated to a greater or less extent in the Vernaculars or in English, some of them for several generations past. They willingly contribute their full quota to the funds of the State, the amount of which is annually increasing. Several of them are actually paying annually much larger sums than neighbours of other castes, who are allowed access to the Sirkar schools. We therefore beg your Highness to issue orders for the admission of *all* cleanly, decently-dressed, and well-behaved children into *all* the schools supported at the public expense."

It would be highly to the interest of the Travancore Government itself to elevate its subjects from the unfortunate condition of servitude and disability in which one third of the entire population are found at the present day, and to prevent their rising from which every effort is put forth by certain classes. Greater intelligence amongst the labourers would result in an enormous increase of production, and accession of wealth. The waste lands in the interior of the country would soon be fully brought under cultivation, producing a most gratifying addition to the revenue. New manufactures and employments, as well as improvements in processes, might then with ease be introduced and augmented: comfort, enlightenment, and prosperity would assuredly follow the amelioration of the social condition of the people.

In these days it can scarcely be disputed that it is highly to the interest and advantage of a government to seek the welfare of all its subjects alike, not only to enlighten the upper classes and create in them a thirst for knowledge and refinement suited to their station, but also to raise the masses of the people to some incipient degree of intelligence and civilization. This indeed is the professed principle of the Sirkar. The administration Report for *M.E. 1043* (1867) says—"The vernacular schools are growing extremely popular and will receive far greater development in a few years more, so that *no subject* of His Highness, *however humble*, will have any excuse for being ignorant of reading and writing, and of arithmetic, geography, history, and the principles of morality." Even the lowest in caste, it would appear from these words, are intended to be considered in their educational schemes, and this is undoubtedly right and desirable. But at present the excuse is available to them that they are not yet admitted into the Sirkar schools. Were the low-caste population permitted fully to share in the advantages of government education, the utter helplessness, arising from ignorance, which places them at the mercy of the high-caste employers, inferior officials, and writers of legal documents, would be removed; they would be emboldened to claim the enjoyment of rights to which they are now entitled by law; and would be enabled by their ability to read and write, to judge whether they are being imposed upon or not, and to represent their grievances to the proper quarter for redress. (Unfortunately, this is precisely what the majority of the higher castes do not wish.) Absurd and groundless alarms, which produce endless suffering among these poor people, would then of necessity cease. On one occasion, the Muhammadans of a certain locality near the capital, took advantage of the census to work upon the ignorance and fears of the surrounding Pulayar population, asserting that all their fowls and sheep were to be confiscated on the final day of enumeration, and that therefore they had better sell them off at any price; which was accordingly done, much to the profit of the wily rogues; and the unfortunate low-castes were thus deprived of their domestic animals. This could not have occurred had some little instruction, however elementary, been enjoyed by the Pulayars.

The education of the lower castes would also tend largely to develop the industrial and agricultural resources of the State. Considerable quantities of waste land are from time to time cleared by these people on private account; but they know not how to secure and register their rights over the property thus formed; and indeed receive but scant attention when they venture to apply to Sirkar officials for formal registration, so that lands cleared by them are, perhaps, enjoyed during the lifetime of the enterprising labourer, but fall, after his death, into the hands of the nearest high-caste employer or capitalist. There is thus a lack of encouragement to these hardy people to clear and cultivate the jungle lands abounding at the foot of the Ghauts. Some little education would enable them to help themselves and to defend their own interests against unscrupulous oppressors; and the result would soon appear in their augmented ability to contribute to the public income.

Nearly all the expense incurred and effort put forth at present by the Sirkar is on behalf of the higher castes, and for higher and secondary education; with some exceptions, the *mass* of the labouring population has not yet been materially benefited or allowed to benefit. The expenditure, according to last published Report (*M.E. 1056*) on "Education, Science, and Art," amounted to Rs. 183,696, but of this only Rs. 60,131 were for *vernacular* education, and this sum included the large District Schools, mostly for Brahman and Sudra boys.

About Rs. 19,000 is the expenditure for grants-in-aid to Mission Schools and a few others, to which alone all castes are admitted—say one tenth of the whole expenditure for one-third of the entire population. Ilavars, Shánárs, Pariahs, Pulayars, and such like, constituting over a third of the population, are refused admission into the village or primary schools. These castes are not yet regarded as of the masses that are to be educated; they are *too* humble in rank to be as yet admitted into the circle of "subjects of His Highness who are to be left without any excuse for being ignorant of reading and writing." It was natural and proper that the Sirkar should begin with the higher classes. The higher educational institutions are now in full and very successful operation, and yearly increasing in efficiency, but the educated natives are doing little or nothing to raise the slave castes, and the great want of the country now is primary elementary education for the mass of the people, down to the very humblest. Once let them get a start in education and they can go on.

The words of Lord Mayo in his noble despatch of 1869, on the subject of education in British India, reaffirming the policy prescribed in 1854, very appropriately describe the present state of the case in Travancore. "In 1854, the Court of Directors declared that up to that date the efforts of the Government had been too exclusively directed towards providing the means of acquiring a very high degree of education for a small number of natives of India, drawn for the most part from what we should call here the higher classes. Our attention should now be directed to a consideration, if possible, still more important, and one which has been hitherto, we are bound to admit, too much neglected, namely, how useful and practical knowledge suited to every station in life, may be best conveyed to the mass of the people who are utterly incapable of obtaining any education worthy of the name by their own unaided efforts. The higher classes will now be gradually called upon to depend more upon themselves."

Certainly the Annual Reports of the Administration of Travancore for the last twenty years show a highly admirable increase of attention to higher education, and of expenditure upon it which reflects great credit on the Government, yet we cannot forget that nearly all the effort and most of the expenditure have been on behalf of the higher castes, who really have it in their power to help themselves did they desire to do so, while the lower castes are left almost untouched by the present system of education. The last Census Report states that out of 32 *tàluks*, or counties, there are six in which less than 4 per cent of the population can read and write; and one with less than 3 per cent. Out of 97,730 Shánárs, only 1,924 males and 8 females can read and write; and out of 383,017 Ilavars only 5,928 males and 93 females. Of 56,274 Coravens only 58 males and no females; of 63,688 Pariahs only 192 males and no females; and *of* 188,916 *Pulayars only* 183 *males and no females.*

This is all that has been effected, notwithstanding abundance of funds and loud professions of high aims, for the most necessitous portions of the population, by the English education of the nobles and high-caste people of Travancore; and even of this small amount of education, much must be attributable to the labours of the Missionary Societies, strangers and foreigners, who have so long laboured and pleaded for the outcasts. Is it not high time to do something for these unfortunates? Let the educated natives of Travancore show the practical effect of the higher education enjoyed by themselves, by allowing it to filter downwards a little. Let them take a decided stand against the social evils of caste. Let them make an attempt in real earnest to raise the masses by primary education and by a few firm and resolute measures against the cruel oppression of the poor and helpless; and a solid and general advance in national prosperity, power, and happiness will speedily be evident to the world.

CHAPTER XXXIII.

RECENT MEASURES OF REFORM.

THE system of Government in Travancore practically consists of two benevolent despotisms, the Native and the British, the one acting as a counteraction to the other. The desirability of some kind of constitution has been spoken of, but the practical difficulties are great, the people being not yet fitted by education, training, or solidarity for a share of sovereign power. At present, therefore, the public are unrepresented and unable to explain their requirements. Indeed, it would be no great exaggeration to say that there is no public, no community. The Travancoreans are not a nation, but a congeries of artificially and widely-separated, for the most part mutually opposing, sections of population. Yet a capacity for the conduct of representative government can never be developed except by the practice of it. The Supreme Government are leading the way by legislative councils; by the publicity given to legislative proceedings, and opportunities afforded to the public of examining them and expressing an opinion on them, and by raising trustworthy natives to high office and position. In proportion as we thus show the example native rulers will follow it; and so will the higher castes among the Hindus, who are as much separated from the low-castes as Europeans are from Indians, or more; as much afraid of their rise, and as unwilling to concede liberty and social rights to them as the *most* intolerant and selfish individuals that can be found amongst Europeans.

Some action, however, in the direction of **popular deliberation and representation** has recently been taken by the Sirkar, in imitation of the Mysore Government, who hold meetings of representative landholders and others, to listen to an exposition of the annual budget and of the aims and plans of the Government. The survey and re-assessment of garden and rice lands just entered upon in Travancore is essential to an equitable and proportionate adjustment of the land tax, as many properties brought under cultivation, and trees into bearing, within the half-century which has elapsed since the last general survey, have not been entered in the Government records. The result will be a large increase to the public revenue if the present rates of assessment are maintained, and for such increase of revenue there is no immediate or urgent need. Much, however, depends upon the use that is to be made of the expected increment to the income of the State—whether the rates of taxation on trees and land are to be lowered, or customs and other imports repressive of industry and interfering with the operations of trade abolished, so as to keep the income at the present figure—or whether the overplus is to be spent on the increased support of temples and priests, on great religious ceremonies, or military display; or to be devoted wholly to elementary education, so loudly called for by the degraded condition of the low-caste population; and to roads, railways, post offices, hospitals, vaccination, and other civilizing agencies and remunerative works; and to the adequate remuneration of subordinates in the judicial, revenue, and medical departments.

Some uneasiness has been felt throughout the country with regard to the re-assessment, as the people are beginning to look into such subjects; and also those landowners who now escape taxation for portions of their property, desire to continue to profit by their exemption. A representative assembly of landholders from all the táluks was, therefore, invited to meet the Dewan at the capital, on 24th March, 1883, to receive information respecting the proposed new survey and settlement. On this occasion an able and statesmanlike speech, exposing present evils and inequalities, and explaining proposed reforms and the benevolent intentions of the Sirkar, was delivered by the Dewan to the gratification of those assembled.

It is to be hoped that this will prove but a beginning in this direction, and that the public, Christians as well as Hindus, will be taken into confidence in questions affecting legislation, taxation, and expenditure of public funds; and that instead of passing empirical measures hatched in private consultation alone, without sufficient criticism from without, as has sometimes been done, the evils of which are only discovered by their practical working after the lapse of years, various sections of intelligent people will be consulted, and the influence of any given measure upon the humbler, as well as upon the higher classes, taken into consideration.

Again, a very serious form of **oppression**, from which some of the poorer classes have just been released, was the **compulsory supply of firewood** for temples and ootooperahs.

Large quantities of firewood are daily consumed, while the sum allotted for the purchase was a third, or a sixth, or even a much smaller ratio of the fair market value. Ilavars especially were the sufferers. At Ambalapuley and Quilon this long-standing grievance was remedied in 1864, though not without much difficulty; and the increased expense was actually met by funds realized from the same institutions by the suppression of abuses.

At Vaikkam, Ilavars and others not enjoying a single acre of Devassam or Government lands, and under no contract or special obligation to this service, were forced by the Provertikars to supply the entire quantity of fuel demanded by the temple authorities, at almost nominal prices, while there were ample funds available from the temple revenues to meet the just expenditure; and much of the fuel went, not for direct temple service, but to meet the demand of private individuals connected with the temple. There was also a great deal of oppression and vexation in the measurement of the wood, loss of time in waiting, and personal annoyances pressing most heavily upon the poorest and most helpless. The people in some parts have now been released from the obligation, and arrangements made for purchasing the firewood in the open market.

Re-arrangements of the judicial machinery have also recently been made, promising much advantage to the public. Defective laws had been administered, in many instances, by judges devoid of judicial training and experience, with a community much given to litigation, the number of civil suits filed in *M.E. 1056* being 31,361. The Zillah Courts were clogged, not only with pending suits, but with judges so numerous that responsibility was hopelessly divided; the reduction of their number was, therefore, long contemplated. The pecuniary jurisdiction of the lowest grade of judicial officers, the Munsiffs, was restricted to suits not exceeding in value 200 Rupees. The salaries of the Zillah judges and Munsiffs were altogether inadequate, considering their position and responsibility, while yet there was a superabundance of funds, and a large profit made on the administration of justice, the judicial revenue being nearly double the entire cost of the establishment. The number of Zillah judges was therefore reduced, and their pay somewhat increased. The *personnel* of the Munsiffs was improved by the removal of some of the old school and the substitution in their places of better qualified men: their jurisdiction has been increased to suits valued at 500 Rupees, and their pay considerably augmented—a most necessary condition of successful reform. Appeals from the decisions of Munsiffs lie to the Zillah Courts ; and appeals from the latter to the Sadr, now termed the **High Court.**

The last Court has again been re-organized, in order that in all civil and criminal appeals the parties might have the advantage of the presence of two Judges on the bench, and to find a mode of disposing of appeals to the Maharajah. Scarcely any one, indeed, knew that such appeals lay, but the theory is still tenaciously clung to that the power of appeal rests with the Maharajah, though happily it is rarely exercised. The High Court has now five judges, two of whom sit in turn to hear and dispose of Criminal and Civil appeals coming from the Zillah Courts. If these two judges differ in their opinion the case is referred to a full Bench of five judges : the opinion of the majority prevails, and is final. If the two judges agree, a further appeal lies in special cases from the Division Bench to the remaining three judges, who are called the *Judicial Committee.* The decision of this Committee must in all cases be submitted to the Maharajah for approval. It is said, however, that the only appeal heard by the new tribunal was finished in February, 1882, and judgment had not yet been pronounced up to the end of the year.

The want of systematic substantive Law for the guidance of Courts in Criminal business having long been felt, and several attempts been made unsuccessfully to form a new Penal Code adapted to the backward civilization and peculiar usages of Travancore, a Regulation has been passed, enacting that the Indian Penal Code (omitting chapter VII.), and also the Whipping Act, should come into force, excepting any customary Law exempting any classes from any particular kinds of punishment, *e.g.*, Brahmans and females are exempted from capital punishment for murder ; and only one person of a gang who unite to commit murder can be executed. Another Regulation introduces the Indian Criminal Procedure Code, excepting that no trial is to be by the aid of jurors or assessors.

Regulations are still required, or clearer precedents, to meet various needs, as with respect to Divorce in the one sole case allowed in Holy Scripture, Wills of Christians, Female Inheritance, Widow Re-marriage, and freedom from loss of property in case of conversion to another religion. But the measures recently passed may be regarded as placing the judicial affairs of Travancore on the fair road to uniformity, order, and efficiency, if the reform of prevailing corruption and incompetence could be so far effected as to ensure their due administration. May order and loyalty long continue, and keep pace with the progress of liberty and independence.

The **Irrigation Works** in the South, on which so much depends, have also been placed under special supervision, which is said to be giving satisfaction to the people generally.

By far the most important and fertile reform recently effected is the withdrawal from the Magistracy and Revenue Officials of their police functions, and the organization of a **regular Police force** after the British Indian Pattern, and in accordance with more enlightened and modern views of political economy than had previously prevailed. The duties of Tahsildars were manifold, some of them mutually incompatible, and they were overwhelmed with work, or at least in a position to make this an excuse for inattention to the business of the humbler classes. The Tahsildar was superintendent of Police, of minor Public Works, especially repairs of Temples, of Revenue Collections, of Escheat, Inam, and Survey departments, of Ootooperah and Pagoda administration; and various Magisterial duties devolve upon him, providing supplies, conveyances, and coolies for travellers; and all arrangements for the comfort, progress and public reception of members of the royal family when they travel, and for great religious ceremonies. Occasionally, a royal visit, a special ceremony, and two or three temple car-festivals occurring close together, sorely pressed these officials.

The heaping of so many onerous and multifarious burdens on one shoulder leads to the unsatisfactory performance of public business; and the time of the people is wasted in attending day after day at the Cutcherries. While one set of duties is receiving attention, another set lies in abeyance, and neither is performed satisfactorily. The authority conferred for one purpose is sure to be misused in the administration of other functions. The separation of police duties has now brought the first instalment of relief to these officials.

The Police force lately organized are as yet quite new to their duties, and can scarcely be expected to work satisfactorily till better trained and brought under thorough discipline. Indeed, it will require a firm hand, strict supervision, careful inquiry into complaints, and complete and equitable *representation* in the force of *all classes* of the population to see that they do not establish a system of general vexation and oppression, and become a terror to the poor people in out of-the-way places. The power of the Indian police has too often been used to gratify petty spite, and for motives of revenge and cupidity. An oppressive police, which has hitherto been the rule in Travancore, is a thousand times more baneful than an inefficient one; and the new body will be tempted to incessant interference with the liberty of the subject through ignorance of the public rights, and to display their diligence and authority. Some little antipathy between the magistracy and the police is already discoverable, but mutual jealousy will work less harm than united conspiracy in wrong-doing. We hear of petty officious interference with missionary preachers, driving off people quietly assembled to listen or to obtain medical treatment, threatening with dismissal those who wish to receive tracts, driving Pulayars off the road, and so forth. One head constable arrested and locked up a Mission Catechist of the highest character and standing, and kept him beyond the legal time, on a charge (proved false) of obtaining bambus from the jungles for mission work without permission. The officers concerned were, however, duly punished, which is likely to prove a warning for the future.

Great complaints are made in various quarters. The police are certainly not as yet effective; and there is reason to fear that they still collect evidence by the old methods, with which we are too familiar.

Some degree of relief has been afforded to a number of **Vrittikár** or feudal service tenants of the Sirkar, who were bound, in consideration of lands, free of all assessment, except a succession duty (*Adukkuvathu*) on every change of incumbency, or held at a light assessment, to supply at low rates vegetables and provisions for Pagodas, Ootooperahs, and for the royal birthday, to erect sheds, to thatch public buildings, to watch them in some places, and to do peon's duty occasionally.

This service tenure dates from a period long back, many of the lands having been granted by former chieftains, but only as remuneration for personal service, while much more was afterwards demanded from most of the holders; and when prices rose in the market no increase was granted to the Vrittikars. The original military pledge was converted into a permanent contract with Government to supply provisions for State needs, and especially for the temples; miscellaneous menial kinds of work were added by degrees. The grievance was felt especially in North Travancore, yet the holders are generally unwilling to surrender the lands and the position which they have so long enjoyed, preferring quietly to bear the loss.

It appears from recent inquiries that "about 5,000 families, consisting of 25,000 souls, are directly subject to the operation of this system—that the full assessment of the lands held by them on favourable rent amounts in round numbers to Rs. 200,000, and that the amount of the loans of money to them or their ancestors in satisfaction of the interest on which service is rendered amounts to a further sum of Rs. 200,000. In process of time the obligation has become extremely onerous and oppressive, and the source of much abuse and demoralization. Prices of provisions and wages of labour have risen at least three or four times since M.E. 948, when the contract was entered into. Still, the Vrittikars are bound to supply provisions at the rates fixed in that year."*

Various attempts at amendment have been made, and the evil sometimes limited, or again increased. Now the prices of the supplies furnished to the large feeding-house at Trevandrum by Vrittikars of that and the two adjoining Táluks, who "had almost sunk under the weight of their obligations and been reduced to poverty, have been raised to nearly the market rates;" which must be a great relief to those resident near the capital. It would, however, assuredly be a better and sounder policy if the Vritti system were entirely abolished all over the country, and money payments in all cases substituted for the service, relieving a large extent of valuable property from such restraints, and bringing in its train many advantages to the interests of agriculture. Most of the holders would be disposed to pay a reasonable rate of additional assessment, which would to a large extent re-imburse the Sirkar for increased expenditure on the purchase of provisions for temples and Brahman feeding-houses in the open market. The annoyances and evils of the Vritti system, which is but one of the complications produced by the temple claims, would thus be judiciously done away with altogether.

In addition to these recent measures, a comprehensive scheme of **Revenue reform** is said to be in contemplation, to include "a separation of the duties connected with the management of the extensive religious and charitable establishments from purely revenue and magisterial duties,"—a most essential and urgent item of needed reform.

It is not easy to give in a few sentences an accurate and comprehensive view of the **present state of public affairs** in Travancore, as very divergent opinions are expressed by the Press and by individuals: no doubt the state of various departments and of various districts also differs to a corresponding degree, as it always did, so as to admit of a variety of criticism, improvement being shown in some respects and not in others. In such a slow moving country progress is not speedily achieved, especially as to the raising of the moral character of the subordinate officials; which is after all the main point, and which, we believe, can never be completely accomplished while idolatry and superstition prevail. Some seriously doubt whether any recent "reforms" have as yet touched the seat of the

* "Dewan's Address," March 24, 1883.

disease, the magistracy and revenue officials being, with certain praiseworthy exceptions, incapable, uneducated, and lazy; the police untrained; the subordinate judicial officers conducting business loosely and negligently, and requiring incessant super-

HIS HIGHNESS THE MAHARAJAH OF TRAVANCORE, G.C.S.I.*

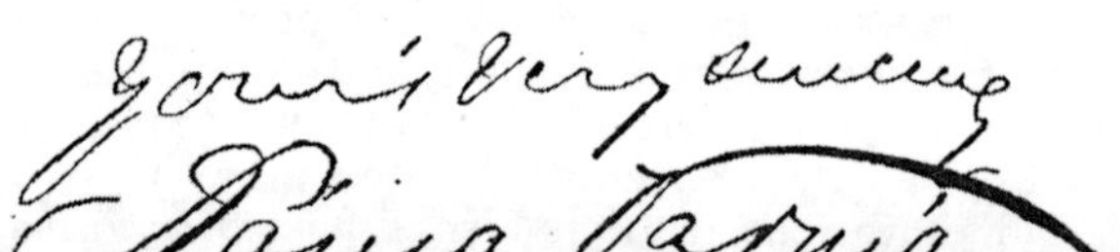

vision and frequent warning from the Sadr Court, as seen by their "Select Decisions and Reports"; and the Bar still to a great extent incompetent and promotive of unnecessary or unjust litigation.

* From a Photograph by Messrs. Bourne and Shepherd, by permission of the Publishers, Messrs. Marion & Co.

Besides, the religious and caste difficulty still remains, and must operate prejudicially (except where the spirit of the age, and pressure from without, will not possibly allow of it), demanding large expenditure on the support of temples and Brahmans, and on special ceremonies, the maintenance of injurious caste distinctions and rules, and of ancient privileges, vested interests, and institutions inimical to true progress. Much unfavourable comment, for instance, has been excited by the passing over of the second judge of the High Court, an English barrister and university graduate, of tried integrity, firmness and legal knowledge, for a young Brahman lawyer from Madras, introduced as Chief Justice, because no Christian, it is said, can be promoted to this high office. The religion of the Christian judge, it appears, disqualified him for further promotion, though it was freely admitted that he had every other qualification for the post.*

Still, there is no doubt that progress is being made, and that in the right direction. **The present Maharajah**, before coming to the *musnud* at a mature age, enjoyed and fully availed himself of ample opportunity for study and travel in India, intercourse with the people, and familiarity with current affairs, and with the corruption which previously prevailed, and is certainly the most enlightened of all the princes of India. His knowledge of history enables him to appreciate the necessity of the British supremacy and its power for good; his sympathies are with what is good and right; and he evidently wishes to rule for the benefit of the people, hastening on the correction of abuses and the improvement of the administration during his reign. The Maharajah is prompt and decisive in business, and while naturally of a somewhat severe disposition, very gracious in private intercourse with those whom he esteems.

The present Minister also, Hon. V. Ramiengar, is generally admitted to be an honest man, firm, prudent, and of great ability, noted for absence of caste prejudices, doing his best to benefit the country, spite of opposition from parties who intrigue against every British-trained administrator. His aim appears to be the public weal, the removal of oppression, and the attainment of efficiency amongst the members of the public service. Officials are sharply looked after; and, of course, those who are set aside through re-arrangement, or dismissed for incompetence, or otherwise disappointed, bitterly complain.

A great work of improvement, reconstruction and reform,

* *Madras Mail*, December, 1881, and *Madras Standard*.

and of rendering of justice and freedom to the poor and oppressed, lies before the rulers and administrators of Travancore, to aid in which, if possible, in some small measure, I venture to offer sundry suggestions in the following chapter, not indeed of an original character, though always tallying with personal experience, but carefully compiled from intercourse with all classes, and from the writings of those who are competent judges of such matters.

CHAPTER XXXIV.

FURTHER REFORMS NEEDED.

BESIDES what has been incidentally pointed out in previous chapters with regard to the re-building of Cutcherries, and the free access of the public to them, the re-building and re-arrangement of the smaller prisons, the grievances of various orders of the people, rewards for snake-killing, the right of way on the public roads of low-castes, and other points, much still remains to be done in the public administration of Travancore, for the true end and aim of all government—the greatest happiness of the greatest number.

One of the first steps to general improvement seems to be to widen the area of political activity by a more equal **distribution of public office** amongst the various respectable and educated classes of the inhabitants. The Syrian, Roman Catholic, and Protestant Christians jointly form as large a proportion of the population as the Malayálam Sudras, yet being admitted to no department where they have political influence, able men are driven for employment to British India. The Malayálam Sudras, although they number rather less (440,932) than the native Christians in Travancore (466,874), yet, according to the census report, absorb no fewer than 8,647 Government posts in all grades of the service, out of 14,703, while but 651 native Christians were in Government employ, mostly in inferior posts, as messengers and such like. And this, too, in spite of the fact that of the Malayálam Sudras, who, according to the same authority, stand beneath twelve other castes as to the percentage of education among males, only 21·27 per cent. of the males (counting from *twelve* years of age) were able to read and write, while we could show that of the Christians connected with the London Mission, 29·4 per cent. of the males (counting only those from *fifteen* years of age) were, to a similar extent, educated.

Although the Travancore Government is Hindu, Christians have a just claim to share in the administration, as urged by the Madras Government in 1870, and as in Malabar; in reply to which, the only feasible excuse made is that the magistracy have committed to them the superintendence of temples, which would be polluted by the contact of Christians, or persons of inferior caste. Let these duties, then, be separated, as is now promised, from those civil functions which rightly devolve upon the magistracy, and which are already sufficiently onerous; and let the ecclesiastical and quasi-charitable establishments be placed under the supervision of special officers, who would soon, if diligent and efficient, save to the extent of their own salaries, and thus really cost nothing to the institutions themselves.

The separation of the work of furnishing supplies to temples on the part of the revenue servants would facilitate the transaction of public business, admit of a considerable reduction of the number of subordinate petty officials, and greatly simplify the accounts, besides permitting the employment of Christians and others in the Revenue Department. It would, at the same time, admit of the **conversion** on equitable principles, of the whole of the **grain assessment into money tax**, a highly desirable measure, which has been partly carried out in Nánjinád; as it has lately been in Cashmere also. The evils and inequalities, vexations and oppressions which accompany the collection of tax in grain, its measurement and estimate of value and its storage by the Sirkar, are great, and universally felt. The proposed change has been effected in the Cochin State; and the supply of rice for the temples and free inns is purchased in the open market, which could also be done in Travancore.

On this subject Hon. V. Ramiengar remarks: "The varying proportions in which the Government demand is collected at present in grain and money, and the differing rates of commutation at which the grain is converted into cash, are a source of oppression and exaction on the one hand, and of fraud and evasion on the other."

The further **extension of popular education** would also tend to improvement in every direction. The exclusive caste schools, supported at the public expense, should be opened to all, and a larger proportion spent on primary education for the classes who need it most. In fact, the most serious real difficulty in the way of practical reform consists in the *abject condition of the lower castes*, who have been kept under and oppressed by the powerful official and landed classes so long, that they are now often content with their degradation, and rarely lay claim to the commonest rights of humanity. As Mr. Porter of Cumbaconam remarked, "A strong official class side by side with a timid and ignorant cultivating class—here is a combination full of temptation to an unscrupulous man, and requiring to be watched with peculiar care."

The intellectual development of the people would relieve them from much suffering, and prepare them for increased usefulness to the State. False and mysterious reports would no longer be bruited abroad. The humbler classes would become able to defend themselves from the injustice and cruelties of the more powerful. I have seen, for instance, tax receipts given for half the sum actually paid, the unfortunate taxpayers, who could not read, being told that the receipts specified the whole amount. A badly written petition is sometimes rejected by an official on the pretence that "he cannot read it." Documents are collected by the landlord professedly for renewal, and never returned; or are altered *ad libitum*. By receiving a little education the people will become able to understand the precise nature and extent of their rights, and to claim them. Popular liberty could no longer be denied when "the schoolmaster is abroad." Education, which quickens the sense of hardship, also happily tends to emancipate the subject of it. The extension of education and intelligence would rapidly tend to the introduction and growth of arts and manufactures, and an improved system of agriculture.

The necessity which exists for some reform **in weight and grain measures**, especially the latter; to introduce uniformity, aid commerce, and save the poor and ignorant from fraud and imposition, is by no means unworthy of mention in this connection.

The great variety of rice measures used in South Travancore has long been a subject of complaint, a source of much evil and serious inconvenience to the population generally. For instance, people usually suppose that the Kottár stamped *puddy* is exactly half an *edungaly;* but those which I have tested contained 52½ cubic inches: this point should be decided correctly. Authorised measures are difficult to obtain. even in Trevandrum months have been spent in the endeavour to obtain a stamped edungaly. Could not the Sirkar prepare a number of these, and have them ready for sale at the Book Depot, or elsewhere?

The extraordinary confusion in grain measures which prevails would make it so much the easier for the Government to remedy the evil: it might be done with a stroke of the pen, providing the reform were but followed up by the officials throughout the country. The people would hail with gladness an improvement which would enable them to purchase the staff of life with so much more facility, and to compare the prices of grain &c., prevalent in different parts of the country. As the Nánjinád measure is not even the standard Tamil *paddy* of 100 cubic inches, and affords no facilities for trade with Tinnevelly, there is no sufficient reason for retaining the local measurement. The Malayálam edungaly might be introduced everywhere, and that with a slight alteration, making it 92·425 cubic inches, so as to be exactly one third of a gallon, and so as to make 24 edungalies equal to a bushel, instead of $24\frac{1}{9}$ as at present. Reform in weights is of less pressing urgency, and perhaps not so easily effected.

In legislation and administration the **popular liberties and public rights** should, in accordance with the liberal tendencies of the age, be steadily kept in view, and the lower classes enfranchised from their hereditary servitude and rigid adherence to old restrictions and pernicious usages. Knowledge and patriotism will thus by degrees make the nation prosperous and happy. The State, and caste customs having the force of Common Law, exercise at present too much control over civil and social life, and intrude upon the sphere of civilization and modern progress. For example, the Government Astrologer in his study in Trevandrum calculates what he thinks ought to be an auspicious day for the first ploughing and sowing of rice, early in the year, which is announced by beat of drum in every village in Nánjinád ; and none dare sow his seed before. Bitter complaints are made of the evil of postponing the preliminary operation of rice culture till the beginning of April, in which month this Nallérpúttu ceremony usually falls, thus losing the benefit of the earlier rains.

The privilege of *using palankeens* in travelling, or at marriages, has long been claimed by some castes regarded as inferior ; and a curious case occurred some years ago, in which a wealthy Shánár from Tinnevelly was severely fined for this by some officious subordinates, though the fine was afterwards remitted by the Dewan. In all British India the palankeen is freely used ; and in Travancore by tailors, workers in gold, silver, and iron, and by masons and others. A proclamation was issued in *M.E. 1041* announcing the removal of such disabilities generally; but the use of the palankeen is still sometimes denied to members of the caste of Oilmongers, and to all beneath them. The oilmongers of Trevandrum were the first to confront the prohibition by conducting, about the year 1874, a marriage palankeen procession along a public road in the capital. The narrow-minded Sudras of the town preferred a complaint before the local magistrate, who imposed a heavy fine upon the oilmongers as having violated a caste usage. On appeal, the fine was cancelled by the superior Courts, to the great astonishment and confusion of the Sudras, on the just ground that the quiet use of a vehicle on the public road cannot be considered and punished as a criminal offence. Some time afterwards the oilmongers of Kottár imitated the example of their fellows in Trevandrum, but were fined, on complaint by the Vellálars, by the local magistrate, who, strange to say, was supported by the Peishcar. This decision also, happily, was reversed by the superior Courts. Encouraged by these liberal decisions, the Potters of Kottár used a palankeen, and were in turn fined by the magistrate, a Brahman too bigoted to see the equity of their claims; and this was again supported by the Peischar, on the ground that there were some Vellálar houses on the road by which the procession was conducted, though it was a part of the great trunk road from Trevandrum to the Cape. The Ilavániers or Vegetable Venders of Kottár next followed suit, but the Vellálars threatened a breach of the peace unless their permission was first obtained by presents, and a sum of Rs. 200 paid in token of subordination and homage.

Popular liberty is thus being achieved by slow degrees. The struggle on this apparently trifling question curiously illustrates the battle for liberty which has often been waged in England.

In the census of 1875, it was conceded by the late Maharajah that the *former caste designation of Christians* should be omitted; which was a great step in advance of the ruling in 1851, that if a man of low caste became a Christian he must ever be considered and treated as of low caste, and that converts to the Christian religion should not pass through the public highway, but only by the field paths. The omission of the invidious caste designation carried with it pregnant consequences as to the rights of citizenship, and implied that the former caste must be absolutely sunk, as it is in Madras and Bombay. But in many cases this is not carried out. In the census taken in the early part of 1881 some Christians, unable to write, were recorded under their heathen caste designations, and many were enumerated, to my own knowledge, in a rather original and ingenious manner. The enumerators being unwilling to defile their purity by approaching the houses of the lower castes to affix a house number on the door, or elsewhere, as required by law, called to the householders to bring out into the open some piece of matting, or board, or old cap, on which the house number was stencilled, while the owner stood at a non-polluting distance, and afterwards picked up his property with the number upon it.

Quite recently, too, it is said, a practice has sprung up in a Court at Nagercoil of insisting upon Christians declaring their former caste, and threatening any who may hesitate to do so with committal for contempt of court.

The subject of forced labour also requires the attention of the Government and demands a thorough remedy. The oppressions arising from this cause have already been much alleviated, but they are still considerable. The extent to which the poor are impressed is shameful for a country calling itself civilized. Many boats beyond what are required for public necessities are seized, and kept waiting for days. Numbers of coolies are impressed, and sometimes kept, as on the occasion of the visit of the last Governor of Madras, locked up till required to carry His Grace's luggage, so that they may not run away in the meantime. Bandies are seized and detained, often without the least necessity, simply to extort a bribe for letting them off. On my own journey homewards the bandies engaged by me. were seized, and only released on personal application to the Dewan. On the journeys of members of the royal family public business is dropped by the Tahsildars and their subordinates, in order to attend to the supply of provisions and arrangements for travel and sojourn. Boatmen and bandymen flee for fear of impressment; and the roads and canals are cleared, to the hindrance of industry and delay of ordinary passengers.

Forced labour is made an excuse for all kinds of impositions and exactions, many people paying the peons to be relieved of it. The Roman Catholic Vicar of Poonthory, within two miles of Trevandrum, revealed from personal knowledge a melancholy state of things, in a letter which he addressed to the Dewán early in 1881. From this letter the following extracts will tell their own tale. The facts are known to many, and are simply illustrative of the usual practice :—

" The subordinate officials take advantage of any exigencies to enlist forced labour for State purposes, with an indifference to the hardships they entail on the poor, approaching to utter recklessness. The press-gang system is employed by the Granary Superintendent of Valiatory and the Némum Police, to secure boats, and men to man them whenever required for Sirkar purposes. Every boat and every man in this parish is seized, and black mail levied from such as wish to escape this oppression. On the last occasion that boats were required for His Highness and suite to proceed to Attingal, 35 fanams were contributed by the people of Poonthoray as blackmail, while the people at Vilenjam, being required to furnish 14 boats, had to purchase immunity to themselves with another bribe, when the demand at once fell down to *two* boats. The boatmen prefer infinitely to engage in any service, rather than to hire out their labour to the Sirkar, simply to escape hunger by their being called away for several days from their ordinary pursuits, to be, in the end, fleeced of payment It not unfrequently happens that the boatmen decamp ; and the head villager buys off the myrmidons of the press-gang by a bribe assessed on the whole village, to escape the grudge that would otherwise inevitably follow in the shape of fines and imprisonments.

"The most flagitious oppression and extortion are practised in the name of the Travancore Government under the pretence of supplying fresh fish every day for the Resident's table, by which the poor Christian fishermen, already ground down by the iron hand of poverty, are deprived even of the means of daily subsistence. A daily contribution is levied, sometimes in fish and sometimes in money, when there may happen to be no fish."

Boats are also seized for shipping salt, with much loss to the fishermen. The compulsory carriage of salt, and the compulsory supply of writing leaves to Government have long been a formidable engine of oppression and injustice in South Travancore.

I have been unable to learn whether the *impressment of Ilavars in the North* for watching jails and salt storehouses at night, without any remuneration, has yet been stopped or not. This forced service prevented those liable to it from pursuing their employments, and subjected them to privation and distress ; as did also the forest department formerly, by seizing poor miserable wretches for sawing timber in the mountains many miles distant from their homes.

Whatever may be said in favour of the expenditure on Temples as being principally provided for by ancient endowments assumed and managed by the State, it seems evident that the **Ootooperahs for feeding Brahmans** should by degrees be **abolished** ; and the funds, over three lacs of rupees per annum, put to better and more general use, or expended on Education, Science and Art, on which not much more than half this sum is spent throughout the kingdom. Those institutions are of comparatively modern origin, having been established only between M.E. *930* and *950*, a little over a century ago.

Nowhere is there a parallel in civilized countries to the waste on Brahmans, the undue preference of this class of subjects, and the abuses hitherto prevalent in the administration of this so-called charity. The proportion which goes towards real charity is insignificant, a large part being for mere strangers and vagrants. The whole system tends to foster mendicancy and pauperism, and to increase the number of unproductive and useless members of the community. Brahmans (and other classes in times of famine) are allured from British territory and demoralised by this mistaken hospitality, so unfair and injurious to the mass of the indigenous population; while the resident Brahmans are kept in a state of real degradation and dependency, and self-respect destroyed, instead of being impelled by the ordinary motives which actuate mankind into useful and profitable channels of activity.

It is only in times of famine that the Travancore Ootooperahs are of any real service to British India; and it would be much better that the people should be provided for considerately in their own country than drawn to a distance by the promise of indiscriminate charity.

The expenditure on Brahmans in Travancore is altogether disproportionate to their numbers, and unfair to other elements of the population. This false charity is confined, with the most trifling exceptions, to those who least need it. A very moderate sum would suffice to meet the demands of real charity for the poor of 40,000 Brahmans; or there need be no great difficulty in their supporting their own poor, as other classes do. The Christians strongly object to this expenditure of the public funds against their convictions of right; and complain that this institution is the principal cause preventing their obtaining office in the revenue service. The low castes have been sorely oppressed by the temple services; and the Náyars, who have had some little pleasure and benefit from this expenditure, are more and more indulging in complaints of sacerdotal pretensions, and beginning to rebel against their inequitable exclusion on various occasions. Intelligent Sudras are far from being content with the present state of things. "The question of feeding the Brahmans at the expense of the State is, from the Malayáli point of view, an undue advantage given to one portion of the subject population. The Brahmans uphold that the custom is ancient. So also was suttee—put down by law; trial by ordeal also, resorted to occasionally before the god at Suchindram, and put down in Sir Madava Row's time. These are unjust and foolish customs. There are no State Ootooperahs in British India. The system of feeding the Brahmans is detrimental alike to the Malayáli and to the Brahman. To the Malayáli, because the funds that go to defray the expenses of feeding come from the general income of the country. The poor taxpayer supplies food to a non-taxpaying and even ungrateful class of people. It is also detrimental to the Brahmans, for it encourages idleness."*

If this grievance be not remedied now that popular rights are beginning to be understood, the mutual bitterness and jealousies of various and rival classes will be sure to increase until it is removed.

* *Western Star*, June, 1881.

Perhaps, after all that has been said on sundry topics, the principal desideratum essential for the onward progress of Travancore is the **improvement of the character and conduct** of the lower **officials** and ministerial servants of the Sirkar. Their tyrannical and unjust conduct has always produced the greatest portion of the suffering experienced by the common people; it has been worse and more complained of than even the backward and uncivilized state of the laws. Though some improvement, doubtless, has taken place, this arises rather from the action of the higher officials and Courts, the publicity now given to grievances, and the increased ability of the people to protect themselves and to speak in their own defence, than from any radical improvement in the character of the dominant classes. It is hard work even for the superior officers with the most strenuous endeavours to stem the flood of official corruption; as they are sometimes so overburdened with routine and a variety of duties that they have scarcely time to attend to complaints, and it is difficult to watch over so many officials scattered over the country, banded together to help and to make excuses for one another, and cunning in deception through long practice and established custom. This is the standing difficulty of rulers and administrators. Notwithstanding admirable reforms recently initiated, Travancore in the present seems to be much the same as Travancore in the past; while the character of the inferior officials remains the same as it was, different systems of administration or reforms pressed from above fail to make so much difference in actual beneficial result to the community as might be hoped for if men of higher principle were employed, or could be had. Much injustice still prevails in the third class magistrates' cutcherries. Some are unfamiliar with the new rules. Others, who quite expect dismissal through further reform, are grasping at the utmost gain before that comes, seeking to "make hay while the sun shines."

Still, the efforts made by enlightened rulers are always, in greater or less degree, successful, and it has been noticed that bribery and corruption rise and fall in prevalence with the purity, assiduity, and strictness of administration of each sovereign or dewan. Bribery almost disappeared under Sir Madava Row's administration, he himself always setting a notable example of incorruptibility.

Hitherto the lowest employés of the State have been regarded by those in the country best acquainted with their character as, in many cases, but a gang of plunderers, rather than protectors of the people and guardians of law and justice. Unequal laws might be modified in their ill effects (as they often have been in England) by kindly and judicious administration; but the public benefit is the farthest thing from the thoughts of the peons, gumasthas, and other assistants, and even some of the Tahsildars. General corruption, incapacity, and dense ignorance of their duty, cruelty and bribery, as far as they dare to indulge in these, still prevail. Only personal interests and private profit are considered by many. A remarkable testimony was borne in October 1881, to the State of the judicial department in Travancore before 1864, when Mr. M. Sadasiva Pilley was appointed to the head of the Sadr Court, in an address presented to that gentleman by a large number of influential and well-informed natives, under the presidency of the Senior Coil Tamburán. They say :—"When the judicial branch of the service appeared most hopelessly tainted with unblushing corruption, and when its administration was characterized by laxity of discipline and want of system, you were called upon to take the helm as the Presiding Judge of the highest Court in the land.—At a time when intrigue and counter intrigue were rampant, and the ranks of the service under you were leavened with corruption and venality, you had oftentimes to face conflicting interests and inveterate prejudices."

Next to the general corruption of morals in a heathen land, these public servants of the subordinate grades are driven to such misconduct by the miserable pay which they receive. They are notoriously ill-paid, and common justice to them, as well as to those who are at their mercy, demands a great and speedy reform in the scale of salaries. Until they are fairly paid it is impossible to expect fair service of them ; though, of course, proper pay will not of itself make men honest or attentive. Nothing, however, would help the country so much as some expenditure in this direction. In 1879, the Government of Madras suggested that a portion of the large surplus revenues of the State might be utilised in giving a general increase to all departments. In old times, servants of the State were probably expected to live partly on private means, or, as so often in Oriental countries, to make up their salaries by private charges and bribes. A *Tandakáran* (a kind of peon collecting taxes), whom I knew in a large town, had Rs. 3 per month of Sirkar pay, and constant work. " People give him something besides," he said—that is, he must make a living by bribery and extortion. Posts with a small salary are gladly accepted because the holders are sure of bettering themselves by bribes ; how otherwise could these men live ?

Yet on some of these subordinate servants of the Sirkar, especially on the **Proverticars** or Village sub-magistracy, the people must greatly depend for the conduct of business in smaller matters which make up the sum of their daily life, and prosperity or loss in agriculture or trade; and these officials have hitherto been the worst oppressors. As has been well said, "An ill-disposed Provertikaran is the very personification of oppression, injustice, bribery, and illegality; and no official in the ranks of the public service combines in a single person so many evils as are daily found in the doings of such a man."

In a decision of the Sadr Court on a dispute regarding landed property, the remark is made: "The case in question appears to us to illustrate very well the way in which Proverticars fabricate evidence and foment litigation. The Pillai who furnished these conflicting accounts must, we think, be dismissed from the service.".

These remarks may be illustrated from events which have occurred within the last few years, for reports of some of which I am indebted to the public papers, and for others to personal observation, and information derived from Administration Reports and other immediate sources.

Oppression and unkindness are exercised *towards the poor* and low-castes, who can rarely prefer complaints, as they are in other respects dependent on the masters; and could rarely succeed in doing so for lack of means. None of the low-castes, even if they become wealthy or educated, can attain to magisterial honours, just as converts to Christianity were for three centuries excluded from Roman political life. By this arrangement class is set against class and deep-rooted prejudices fostered.

Courtesy to the poor is almost unknown among the lower officials. In nothing will they oblige, except duly feed for it. The Cutcherries cannot yet be freely approached. Peons receive petitions or papers from Pulayars with unconcealed abhorrence, ordering them to lay them on the ground. One worthy Peischar took the trouble to make his peons receive these into their hands to carry to the magistrate.

A few of the officials are scarcely accessible, being usually about the Temples or Palaces. Poor suppliants or tenants must induce some high-caste friend to take their letters in. The Peons also endeavour to hinder the low-castes from near approach to bazaars or markets. even where this is allowed by law.

Some Tahsildars we have known abuse all of the poorer classes who apply to them, and keep them at a distance. These men hate to see a decent dress on any man of humble origin, or the chest covered with a cloth; and such are openly reviled, their letters declined on various pretexts, and their business left undone.

Peons have come with summonses (or without any) when the

Christians were at worship, or just going to prayer, to seize or forcibly take them away. They are afterwards ill-used, kept waiting about for a few days and then sent off. We have even known them to enter a Christian Church, or stand ready at the door to seize the worshippers on Sunday. They terrify ignorant complainants by a loud and threatening manner, catching at every verbal error, and threatening them with punishment as false witnesses. Witnesses are forced to sign whatever has been written by the clerks, notwithstanding protests against its accuracy, or ignorance of what has been written, on threats of worse punishment if they do not consent.

Unconscionable delays occur in attending to business, so that suitors are tired out and it becomes not worth their while to continue. One great resort of some officials is to leave letters unanswered, so that people get tired out on smaller matters. In attendance on the public offices and courts, witnesses have been compelled frequently to trudge over roads and kept waiting for days, sometimes hungry, faint and sick, while their private affairs go to ruin. This has been sharply reproved by the Sadr Court.

At the end of the year, when reports have to be made up and forwarded, it is an object to appear to have few arrears on their files, so as to seem very diligent and attentive; work is then hurried up and cleared off in any hasty way, and admission of any new complaints deferred till after the new year has commenced.

Tax receipts are written in a most indefinite manner, without specifying the particular property for which the tax is paid: the people believe this is done to keep the payer in the power of the Sirkar clerks. Such documents are of little use in the Courts, where tax receipts are often relied on as proving possession and rights to property. Great difficulty is in consequence experienced by those who own several compounds, in making out which receipt belongs to each; and worse still, the tax collectors often deny that the tax belongs to the land for which it was actually paid. In various parts of the country this is a source of much evil, especially to small holders and uneducated people.

Common sense would surely require some definition, name, or number of the particular property referred to in such receipts. A tax receipt for a plot of land on which a mission school was situated was forwarded to the Dewán for his inspection, in 1880, pointing out this omission, as well as that of even the name of the Proverty (village) in which the land lay. The reply, however, was to the effect that the specification of such particulars in the receipt is highly desirable, but it is never done—evidently to economize the time and labour of Proverty accountants; but that perhaps the desired modification might be made at a future time.

Receipts are also given to persons who cannot read, for sums less than those actually paid. A poor man is told he has to pay, say *five* fanams, "and here is a receipt for that sum." He brings the receipt to some one who can read, and finds it is for *three* only. I have known one pay ten fanams and get a receipt for only two.

A certain Pulayan whose annual tax was two chuckrams was charged more than fifty for a receipt for the same. He refused to pay it. Meantime a transfer was made; the first official left and was succeeded by another, who now demanded money and tobacco equal to a hundred chuckrams. Complaint being made to the Peishkar, he had the unjust official arrested and sent before the judges at Alleppey, and he was dismissed the service and otherwise punished.

An utter want of humanity in the *treatment of low-caste prisoners* is not uncommon amongst the peons and local officers, embezzling the allowance for the prisoners' food, by which some have been actually starved to death. An increased allowance is now made, though still, in the smaller and more distant prisons, scarcely sufficient for sustenance; while in the jails at Trevandrum due attention is paid to the diet and medical care. Various other evils prevailed, in the use of long and heavy iron fetters and chains, wooden stocks and instruments of torture, the confinement of debtors and other defaulters or persons on trial, along with convicted criminals, and of men with women, and the detention of accused persons in other than the legal and suitable places of confinement. I have known coarse wooden stocks made impromptu, and a poor man confined for several days in the courtyard of his own cottage; while his cattle were dying for want of care, and his little property exposed to robbery and going to ruin in every way.

Not long since, a Pulayan escaped from a cage prison in South Travancore. When again caught, he confessed that he had run off because he had been starved for four days, the peons pocketing the allowance for food. The Sadr Court reduced his punishment for escaping, from sixty days' imprisonment, to which he had been sentenced by the lower Court, to fifteen days, which had, in fact, nearly expired; and they expressed the wish that they had the two peons before them to answer for their misconduct.

Tax is sometimes demanded of persons for lands which they neither possess nor owed for in any way. In a case which I knew, there was some uncertainty as to whether a particular village was in a certain district or in the next, so some poor men who had paid the demand in the one district, for which they had proper receipts, were seized for not again paying in the next district, and only released on application by a friend to the higher authorities.

A low-caste man bought a piece of land from a Sudran, but for three years was unable to obtain the certificate of transfer from the Pillai, or clerk. The magistrate found that the fee due for this was half a fanam, yet the purchaser had already paid five fanams, and was asked for thirty-five fanams more. Many such cases occur.

In *assessing and collecting the taxes on jungle cultivation* especially, (*Sanjayam*) which is variable and lies in distant hills and jungles, many opportunities for oppression and fraud occur. The Kuravars, Védars, and others reclaim plots of waste land in the hills, cutting down small trees, and clearing away the grass. These they cultivate for a year, then leave fallow again for several years. For this there is a fixed *méladi* or *Malavâram* tax. But the Provertikaran, tax collector, and clerks ask four or six times the proper rate, or profess to measure the land, and say it is much greater in extent than it really is. The Pillai will say, "give me a rupee, and I will make the tax light for you." The cultivators pay on the seed sown, not on the produce; which is sometimes insufficient to repay expenses, or is destroyed by wild boars, deer, &c.: then they must borrow to pay all demands, else suffer imprisonment. The village Provertikaran and others come and take nearly all the produce, and thus dishearten these poor people from rice cultivation. They say they would give a tenth or two tenths willingly; but at present they cannot tell what the rules are, or how to calculate the government dues, and whether what they pay goes to the government or to the servants. "The Government," said an official who understands the matter, "do not get an eighth of what is collected by the tax-gatherers for Malavâram."

To procure registry of waste lands reclaimed, the poor always have to give from a rupee and a half to three rupees as a present to the Samprithies and other clerks; but still they make excuses, and the business is often not attended to for years. Without a substantial gratuity it would be idle to expect these men to do their duty. Yet nothing would be more profitable for the government and the country than the reclamation and permanent cultivation of waste lands by these hardy labourers, who would also themselves be raised and benefited by it. One or two of the higher officers deserve great credit for the interest which they take in this subject.

Insatiable greed and extraordinary cunning are displayed in the taking of bribes by the underlings; and indeed there have been times when it was said that there was scarcely an official of any grade free from this vice. Bribes are even extorted by threats of implicating the parties in charges of murder and other serious crimes, if not paid. To allow criminal complaint to be withdrawn, cloths and money are presented to the official. In criminal cases the police naick, similarly influenced, reports the charge a factitious one. An official invites people to a feast and some domestic ceremony, and gets large presents of money, ornaments, &c. Gratuitous service is demanded of work people and bandymen; if refused, charges are got up against them; or they are over punished on some real charge. Sometimes a judicial servant quietly takes bribes from both sides, but honestly returns that which he received from the losing party!

The village guards extort money and property on the slightest pretexts. Their demand for cloths, money and other goods have sometimes differed but little from highway robbery. In collecting provisions for travellers and officers on circuit, they often robbed the people of fowls, sheep, eggs, fruit, &c., or gave the merest nominal payment for the provisions.

Bribes are taken in the evening to the house of the tax assessor, begging him kindly to charge only what is right and fair and really due to the Government. The Pilleymar (writers and clerks) thus reap a harvest of bribes. Some *gumasthas* and others regularly earn three or four times their fixed pay.

To complain of all this unfairness, bribery, and corruption, only exposes poor and illiterate men to the getting up of false charges of the most serious character. As the Tahsildars have been until now police as well as revenue officers, they could touch the people on many points, and affect their peace and comfort in many ways.

It is exceedingly unpleasant and painful to have been obliged to say so much on such a topic; but faithfulness to the cause of truth and righteousness, and of the helpless and oppressed, demands it; very few of those acquainted with the subject are at liberty to speak plainly and freely upon it; and much more might have been said with perfect truth.

CHAPTER XXXV.

HISTORY OF TRAVANCORE.

It is refreshing to find the natives of India, who are, of course, best acquainted with the details of their own manners and customs, undertaking the task of publishing them for the information of English readers. Hindu writers may not, as yet, be generally capable of reasoning or commenting accurately upon facts, or displaying them with impartiality and independence of judgment, for history never has been their forte. But whatever errors they may fall into in the philosophical view of historical questions, there is no doubt that the rough materials are, to a large extent, in their hands: their views of their own history and usages, even if illogical or warped by party spirit, are of high interest to observers; and it is only by calm and frank discussion between Europeans and natives that the whole of the facts connected with any particular topic can be brought to light. Truth must gain in the end, and that not a little, on Indian subjects, by almost any mode of treatment that a Hindu writer may bestow on them. At the least, the peculiar characteristics of the Indian mind are more fully revealed by the indigenous literature.

A handsome volume on the history of Travancore, published a few years ago, furnishes a good illustration of these remarks.* It is written in very respectable English by the late Mr. Shungoonny Menon, a talented official in high office of the native Government. He appears to have had access to direct sources of information, and to have been encouraged in his literary task by individuals high in rank in the country. Many of these sources of information have long been accessible to scholars acquainted with the vernacular languages and literature; as for example, Sir Madava Row's and Páchu Moothathu's histories, the Keralolpatti and other Malayálam classics, Bartolomeo's, Welsh's, and Day's volumes, pamphlets by "A Travancorean,"

* "History of Travancore from the Earliest Times." By P. Shungoonny Menon; Madras: 1878.

the Madras Journal of Literature and Science, and other publications. Sundry political records and letters, however, are for the first time published, and many remarks by the author himself on the native manners and customs are new—some of them worthy of further investigation. But it must be admitted —and it has been known from the period of the publication of the "History"—that the statements and views of the author are by no means reliable in point of impartiality; and require a great amount of sifting and balancing, limitation, and discussion as to their actual historical value. This done, considerable light may be obtained from the work. Many of Mr. Shungoonny Menon's allegations and opinions might, if left on record without some protest and exposure of their inaccuracy, come, in course of time and by dint of constant reiteration, to be regarded as correct; especially as the book seems to be highly thought of by natives as a defence of their peculiar usages and institutions. This would seriously damage our prospects of ever recovering the true history of this most interesting and now renascent kingdom.

It was with some curiosity that one applied to this goodly volume in order to discover what information would be communicated as to the real facts of the history of Travancore and their true causes—the secret history of legislative and political measures—the precise origin and results of incidents which have been placed before the public in an official and diplomatic light in state annals, proclamations, and polite communications. As events transpire, their true history and antecedents are more or less known to contemporaries; but sometimes they dare not be revealed for want of legal proof, or for other reasons; sometimes they are forgotten and lost for ever. Little or nothing unfavourable to his own side is, however, divulged by this writer; and damaging facts that are well known to many are either courageously denied, or quietly glossed over. It seems evident that we shall never, in all probability, in such a country, obtain complete information as to the history of court intrigues, immoralities, and follies, as well as of reforms and political progress—the sale of offices, bribery, and interference with the course of justice—factions and cabals in favour of the sovereign, or of the heir, or of rival ministers—secret executions and assassinations, and other events that would reveal the actual state of things in the past or at present, and prove a warning beacon for the future. What a history all this would make! But, indeed, this author seems neither desirous to furnish full and impartial information concerning Travancore, nor scarcely endowed with the capacity for doing so. The historical faculty appears absolutely wanting, and the gift of weighing facts and evidence, and of estimating the relative importance of events. He begins long before the earliest ages—assigns "the origin of the present dynasty" to "the beginning of the world"—gives "many hundred thousands of years without interruption" as the period of rule of a single dynasty, for which circumstance he has "valuable evidence"—refers to "a peculiar adventure by which Ilen, a male, became a female"—and supplies a portrait, in modern Malabar dress and accoutrements, of the Emperor Yayathi, who reigned we know not how many ages ago! The last chapters, again, read somewhat like a court journal, giving particulars of the furniture, down to the lining of the sofas, and the list of game for dinner at the reception of a distinguished visitor to the country; and even ludicrous details of the sea-sickness of sepoys, and the cleaning of the decks. The author proves native historical works to be almost entirely worthless, yet appeals to them.

Every one who differs from him, even with the fullest available opportunities for information, is one-sided, inconsiderate, or misled. He endeavours to cast the blame of local official waste or indifference on the British Resident—falls foul of Páchu Moothathu, who has not sufficiently exalted his country, for undue exercise of imagination, and for want of literary diligence—and attacks Sashiah Sastri, Dewan, for admitting into the Almanac some historical memoranda compiled on the basis of the hitherto recognised histories, even though accompanied by a note declining responsibility for their historical accuracy. He argues largely on assumption and by guess; and throughout the whole work freely indulges in exaggeration, suppression of the truth, and special pleading. In a word, the whole production appears to be an eulogium on Travancore and its rulers and customs. The degrading adulation of an oriental courtier appears everywhere. His kings are almost divine—were formerly Emperors of a wide extent of territory—were ever the wisest, most valiant, and best of men; except, indeed, one of them, who is admitted to have erred through the evil advice of his counsellors in attacking the British power. Each ruler, we are told, introduced such great and comprehensive improvements in the government that it is difficult to see where any room was left for the radical reforms which every one knows have been carried out during the last twenty years. Men are still alive who remember what Travancore was some thirty years ago—who found it then in the lowest depths of misrule, oppression, and corruption prevalent amongst all grades of society. Officials occupying the very position of our author received bribes with both hands, and administered the country with shameless and unblushing corruption, as every native knows; and yet, except in so far as Mr. Shungoonny Menon incidentally, or by implication, reveals the true state of things, these facts are concealed, misrepresented, or extenuated. Notwithstanding that so much improvement has been effected, for which due credit ought gladly to be accorded, the country is still but semi-civilised; wide reforms and radical changes are still required; for some of which the public are looking with hope to the present Maharajah, whose intelligence, ability, and desire to rule well are undoubted, as his opportunities for the enlightened study of the principles of political and social science have, of necessity, been far beyond those of his predecessors.

In the work before us, the **connection of Travancore with the paramount British power,** and the subsidy paid in consideration of the essential aid rendered by the latter, are not placed before the reader with sufficient clearness, and in an accurate light. It is evident on the surface that the raj of Travancore would have been easily and completely extinguished by Tippu Sáib; and the Rajah knew that, and was glad to be rescued from utter destruction at any price. He had only "a dastardly crew not deserving the name of soldiers" to defend the country; and was obliged "to trust for all that was valuable to him, his territory, his honour, and even his personal safety," to the East India Company, who carried on the war undertaken on his account, with all their forces, and at an enormous expense, "appropriating to this great undertaking not only the revenues of Madras Presidency, but those of Bengal, and the greatest part of the resources of the Carnatic and Tanjore." Owing all this to the British power, whatever independence remained was also owing to them, and was, at the time, gratefully accepted and acknowledged. It was not merely the power of a particular dynasty that was at stake, but the national liberties and religion, domestic security, and even the existence of the kingdom. What, indeed, if the British had *not* then aided Travancore?

The treaty of 1795 virtually surrendered all real independence. The Rajah also bound himself to pay the utmost attention to such advice as the English Government should judge it necessary to offer him, with a view to the good government of the State; and this has been the foundation and origin of all the reforms that have been effected since. He admitted himself to be "an ally and dependent of the British Government." The tone of the letters shows the subjugation of Travancore; and the forfeiture of the Company's protection, in case of obstinate resistance to good advice, is threatened. After the rebellion of 1808, Travancore was virtually conquered by the British arms, and surrendered at discretion; but was again spared, and the administration of the country was undertaken by Col. Munro, who nursed it into financial vigour, re-established order, and set it on the fair road to prosperity. Of this period the 'Standing Information' of the Madras Government states:—"The Rajah tendered his submission, and disclaimed any sympathy with the insurgents. The debts, however, into which the country was thrown by these events, prevented the punctual payment of the subsidy, and the administration of the territory would have been assumed under the terms of the treaty of 1805, had not the death of the Rajah and the succession of a female led to the union, in the person of Col. Munro, of the combined functions of Resident and Dewan." The term *sovereign*, therefore, applied of late to the Maharajah, is evidently used in the modified sense referred to by Wheaton. "Tributary states, and states having a feudal relation to each other, are still considered as sovereign so far as their sovereignty is not affected by this relation."*

It was but natural and customary under the circumstances, to expect the Native State to contribute its quota of the imperial expenditure incurred on its account; and as the expenditure for the external protection of the Indian Empire still continues, and peace is henceforth absolutely assured to Travancore and other Native States so long as the British supremacy abides, the subsidy, amounting to some £80,000 per annum, is still paid. The military expenses, indeed, were, as is perhaps always the case in war, much greater than had been anticipated. A good deal of grumbling is indulged in; but there seems no doubt that Travancore has received, and is receiving, good value for its contribution, in the form of efficient and complete protection from external outrage, and a share in the general advancement of the Empire. The subsidy is but a small payment for immense advantages permanently secured; and is fixed at a rate which is now far below the average proportion of military expenditure for the whole of India.

The moral obliquity displayed in the book now under review is at times quite startling, and is remarkable even for a Hindu. Illustrations of this frequently occur. We find, for instance, that the only burden that bore heavy on the conscience of a distinguished statesman on his death-bed, was that he had never had a chance to seize upon the neighbouring kingdom of Cochin, as several other states had been reduced by him to subjection. A curious specimen of the domestic morals of this minister is given. Too conscientious and devoted to public duty to marry properly, he simply kept a concubine;

* International Law, p. 45.

but, though she tended him with the greatest devotion, he left no provision for her support, merely commending her to the charity of the Rajah after his death. So also Vurmah Kulasekhara Rajah, who ruthlessly attacked all his neighbours and seized on their territories, slew the sons of the last King for aspiring to inherit the throne, barbarously buried alive fifteen infants to ensure good luck in his undertakings, and tortured and put to death Devasagayam Pilley, a Nair convert to Christianity, is pointed out as specially pious and favoured with Divine protection. And we read that for the correction and warning of a selfish and illiberal subject who refused alms, he summarily confiscated the whole property of the unlucky miser, and dedicated it to the support of a charitable foundation!

A point here brought under discussion and of considerable scientific interest to the ethnological student is the position in the scale of Hindu caste of the royal family of Travancore, as well as of the other Rajahs and chieftains of Malabar. It is unfortunate that this curious historical question is not only somewhat obscure from the absence of reliable records, and from the existence of puzzling anomalies in their domestic usages; but it is also unavoidably encumbered with various personal and political considerations which tend to take it out of the region of abstract discussion. The Rajahs of Malabar are undoubtedly kings of very ancient lineage, and were formerly, of course, to a greater or less degree, warriors; but the question discussed by Mr. Shungoonny Menon is, whether they are descended by birth from the ancient Aryan Kshatriyas, who are reckoned as the royal or military caste of India. Much delicacy must naturally be felt in discussing the genealogy of distinguished families; but certainly an official, dependent, as was Mr. S. Menon, solely on personal favour for promotion and honours, could not approach the subject with an unbiassed mind, nor feel at liberty, if unbiassed, to express his views without reserve. I have heard a distinguished Brahman acknowledge that he felt restrained by delicacy and prudence from carrying out his own convictions as to individuals really lower in the scale of caste than himself, but higher in authority and social influence. Happily the Rajahs of Travancore have, in a most dignified manner, refrained from interposing in the discussion of this question; but while, up till somewhat recently, it was almost universally admitted that the dynasty was of Náyar lineage, attempts have of late been made by partisans to claim for them Kshatriya rank and birth as respects Hindu caste, and to becloud the right apprehension of various considerations on which the decision of this purely historical question depends. Our historian, for instance, says "We wonder how, and upon what authority, the authors of 'The Land of the Perumals,' and 'The Land of Charity,' and other learned writers, state that the Rajah of Travancore is a Sudra. If these authors will but search the Sanscrit works they will be obliged to acknowledge that they are in the wrong, as no mention is made therein as regards the caste of the Travancore sovereigns, except that they are Soma Vamsa Kshatrias."

As bearing upon this subject, it is very curious to notice with what tenacity the Hindus cling to caste, and what sticklers they are for its minutest distinctions and privileges. It is difficult for Europeans to form any adequate conception of the sway of caste and the power of its traditions over the minds of each class of native society—the amount of research bestowed by each to discover local traditions, verbal derivations, analogies in ceremonies or usages, or anything whatever that might enable them to outvie rival castes—the contempt felt for the boasting of others—and the age-long memories of reported or imagined honours once enjoyed by them. The ancient Puranas are ransacked to find something that can be twisted by ingenious special pleading into allusions to the ancestors of each modern caste; aged sires hand down traditions to their descendants; and incessant controversy is waged, even to blows, on the recurrence of public festivals or processions. Titles are altered, new customs adopted, lawsuits conducted to checkmate opposing castes or clans. And each caste reproaches the other with any peculiarities or absurdities which they themselves do not practise. Not that they are at all unlike other men in this respect; for everywhere social prestige and titles are valued, and not unreasonably so. But caste, the form which the claim for precedence and respectability takes amongst the Hindus, is really a most injurious and hurtful distinction, prohibitory of all progress and improvement.

In this way "right hand" and "left hand" castes carry on interminable disputes, often leading to breaches of the peace. The Pánars, or tailors of Travancore, pretend to be Sudras, but are repudiated by the latter. Between the Pariahs and the Pallars of Tinnevelley there is an unsettled dispute respecting precedence; as also between the Shánárs and the Ilavars of Travancore, a moot question which, we fancy, must be decided differently in the north and in the south. Some Shánárs, who ought to have regarded themselves as simply "Christians," without claiming any merit on the ground of heathen caste, published a pamphlet in 1871, seeking to prove by a variety of far-fetched and ridiculous arguments that they once belonged to the Chetry or kingly caste; and in the census of that year some thousands of them in Tinnevelly described themselves as Kshatriyas, in so far falsifying and invalidating the enumeration. And now English writers, unacquainted with this circumstance, are quoting the supposed fact that the converts to Christianity in Tinnevelly comprise some thousands of Kshatriyas. The Kuravars have a tradition that they were once kings of the hill country in the south. The Pariahs also claim, on the most trifling and unhistoric grounds, to have been once a royal caste; and we have even known the degraded Pulayars, than whom none can be conceived lower both in ceremonial caste and in social circumstances, pride themselves on their superiority to Pariahs on the ground that they do not eat beef like the latter. The enslaved Pulayar also keeps, in his turn, the Parayan twelve feet from his sacred person. Indeed, this very competition, along with the spread of education and the acquisition of wealth and office through the knowledge of English, is breaking down the artificial system of caste, in individual instances, at the present day.

The struggle for caste superiority is incessant throughout the whole of India, and Christian Missionaries at times find it difficult to restrain even their converts from taking part in it. Various Mahratta castes and some of the Gond Hill Rajas are pretenders to the honour of Kshatriya descent. "It is a fact," says Dalton, in his "Descriptive Ethnology of Bengal," "that many Rajahs and chiefs who are invested by Brahmans in due form, at the proper age, with the sacred string, and who may show you a pedigree proclaiming their descent through fifty generations from a Rishi, or a cow, or a snake, or some other animal or thing, are Kols, or Bhuiyas, or Gonds." The Brahmans, who located themselves in Nepaul a few centuries ago, accorded to their earliest Turanian converts, and also to their own offspring by mountaineer concubines, the lofty rank and honours of the Kshatriya tribe. A curious instance of a kind of fiction, which probably was in more common use in the earlier ages of Hinduism, is seen in the conversion of the border tribes of Manipuri, about a century ago, by a wandering Sanyási, who prescribed a suitable expiation for their neglect of orthodox faith and practice; and then declared that the whole people were received back into the Kshatriya caste, to which they had formerly belonged. ("Indian Caste," Vol. II. p. 221.)

Even the humble Bhil tribes claim descent from the Rajputs, who themselves are simply the least degenerate descendants of the Aryan Kshatryas. The Pandian Kings are traditionally supposed to have been Kshatriyas, but there is no proof whatever of this, and little reason to make such a supposition. The

Vadiyar dynasty of Mysore, though commencing about the beginning of the 16th century, had no difficulty of getting certification of the most ancient descent even from the Yadava line. "After the establishment of the chiefs of Marawa or Ramnad as independent princes," says Prof. H. H. Wilson, "adulatory ingenuity was employed to devise for them an honourable origin. The founder of the family was accordingly made contemporary with Rama: who was said to have consigned the hereditary charge of the deity and temple at Rameswaram to the Adi Setupati or 'first lord of the causeway.'"

Manifold instances occur in which the position in the scale of Hindu caste does not precisely connote that in the scale of actual rank and dignity. Some of the reigning dynasties of India have been really of humble origin. The Gaikwar (or "cowherd," as the name denotes) was a Sudra official of the Peishwa, having charge of flocks. He became independent of his former master, and, by entering into treaty with the English, saved a part of Guzerat and Kattiawar, which is now held by his successors. Holkar is of the shepherd caste; the Rajah of Soondee a Védar; Pattiala and others descended from peasants of the Jat tribe; and the Tondiman of Puthucotta a Marava chieftain, as were also the Polygars of Tinnevelly. All such are Kshatriyas only by courtesy. Mr. S. Menon himself correctly states that "each of the various rulers of India, *irrespective of caste,* became supreme in his own kingdom." Sudras occasionally rose to power and eminence even during the political ascendency of the Brahmans. Sudra dynasties are sometimes mentioned as dominant in certain parts of Hindustan. The Brahma Vaibarta makes mention of Dramila, king of Kanyakubja, a Chandála by caste. Chandragupta also was a Sudra. Such instances of Indian rulers, who are Sudras by caste, but by office kings and warriors, tend to introduce uncertainty into the historical question; and courtiers by their flatteries soon cause still greater confusion.

A considerable portion of the work before us is occupied with the subject of the descent and caste of the royal family of Travancore, who, it is repeatedly urged, are not Sudras but Kshatriyas—a somewhat unnecessary anxiety for their reputation; for in the South of India, Sudras, and especially the Náyars of the Western Coast, though not regarded as "twice born," are yet not socially a low caste, but constitute the mass of the respectable population—the landowners and employers of labour, the agricultural and military classes. Some are nobles and even kings. "This caste," says Monier Williams, "was probably formed from the more respectable of the aboriginal inhabitants, who joined themselves to the conquering Hindus, and preferred serving them to leaving their homes."

On this subject various arguments are brought forward, some of which may be noticed.

"The Keralolpathi does not say that the King of Travancore is a Sudra, nor is this stated in Sanscrit works." But Mr. Shungoonny Menon has already given his opinion, and that a correct one, of the compositions which he calls Sanscrit, that they are "embellished with ideas and statements supplied by imagination, a practice common among Sanscrit authors." Again, he says: "On such a work as the Kerala Ulpathy little reliance can be placed." As to the Keralolpathi, though said by some to be translated from the Sanscrit, such an original is nowhere to be found, and it is comparatively a recent composition, dating only from the 16th or 17th century, than which there is no earlier Malayálam literature.

It is asserted that the investiture with the Brahmanical thread, and the use of Sanscrit names and titles, prove the Kshatriya origin of the princes of Malabar. But this is no proof whatever, for we know that aboriginal tribes have often picked up, and are still adopting, high-sounding and Brahmanical names, rites, and institutions. Many Roman Catholic natives have assumed the patronymics of distinguished Portuguese families, a precisely similar case. The Kallar or robber caste of Tinnevelly add *deva*, "god," to their names as a caste title, as also did the Pandian kings; and this has been regarded by some as an objection to the Christian use of *dévan* to denote the Supreme Being. Some Shánárs have asserted that the true form of their caste name is *sándor*, "the learned," in order to apply to themselves the frequent allusions in Tamil literature to "the learned" and their superior excellence in comparison with the illiterate.

So of the Brahmanical thread. Being worn by various castes in imitation of the Brahmans, who are naturally everywhere taken as models, it is no proof of Aryan descent. Besides some castes in Bengal and Bombay who are of dubious purity or of acknowledged inferiority, all the artisans of the South—goldsmiths, blacksmiths, carpenters, stonemasons, and braziers—none of whom are supposed to be higher than Sudras—wear it. Even Pariahs don the thread occasionally—a few of their Vallavar priests constantly—and at marriages the bride and groom for sixteen days, after which they leave it off; and this they are accustomed to appeal to as a remnant and token of their Chetry descent.

Next, the Rajahs of Cochin, Calicut and Colastri are respectively referred to, and their relation to Travancore. Cochin is said to be of the same caste and original stock as Travancore; the Zamorin inferior, "not being permitted to wear the Brahmanical thread, or touch a Brahman or Kshatriya without contamination;" and Colastri or Cherical is given as the stock from which children were usually adopted into the Travancore house when heirs failed.

Now the Zamorin is admitted by all to be simply a Náyar chieftain and decidedly inferior to Cochin. The males consort only with Náyar women: the princes are called *Eráttu* or cowherd, and they have no ceremony to raise them to caste rank. But Travancore also is admitted by almost every native to be beneath Cochin in caste; and this has, at times, caused some little difficulties as to the forms of courtesy to be observed on public occasions. Kolastri, again, is usually asserted to be the origin of the Travancore dynasty. But all these royal houses are inter-related—their traditions point in the same direction and to a similarity of origin; as their names and customs are also in some respects identical, the descent of the throne by nepotistic law, and their children falling into the ranks of the ordinary Náyars of Malabar. The Zamŏrin's family and that of Neeleswaram, a branch of Kolastri, partake in each other's funeral ceremonies. Travancore, also, is said to be connected with Neeleswaram. All, until recently, claimed descent and grant of authority from Cheraman Perumal, who is supposed to have been a Kshatriya, yet there is a tradition that the last of the Perumals *was a Sudra.* This appears to have hit upon the truth, that all alike are of Náyar or Sudra lineage. Travancore, by extreme subservience to the Brahmans, to the extent of devoting the whole country to religious service, and by extravagant donations and costly ceremonies, has been rewarded with various Brahmanical privileges and distinctions; and Cochin, mainly by paying Nambúri Brahmans to consort with their females, has won an admitted superiority of caste.

"Two of our oldest and most faithful allies in the Madras Presidency," says Dr. Hunter,* "the enlightened dynasty of Travancore and the ancient princes of Púdukotta, are survivals of the time when non-Aryan sovereigns ruled over Southern India."

It is asserted, again, that the aim of the **Hiranya Garbha** (golden womb) ceremony is not to advance the celebrator in caste rank, but a mere donation, or religious coronation ceremony. This ceremony has to be performed by the Maharajah of Travancore. His Highness is weighed in a scale against his weight of gold. This is made into a hollow vessel or tub (*see*

* "Indian Empire," p. 176.

frontispiece), which is half filled with holy water and *panchagavya* —"the five products of the cow"—into which the Maharajah enters, is covered in with the lid, bathes, and comes out again. In "The Land of Charity," I have given my authority for the assertion that the intention of the ceremony is the regeneration of the Sudra King—a detailed description, written by a Brahman who had access to the ceremonies, published on the spot and at the time, and never repudiated nor rebutted. Mr. S. Menon makes no allusion to this document. It says:—

"The performance of this ceremony was thought indispensably necessary in order that the Maharajah might assume the crown which, according to the Vedas and the custom of the country, he could not wear till he should be re-born from a cow, or a lotus flower.—The prince about to be crowned enters and sits for a short time within the belly of a cow, or the corolla of a lotus flower, made of the purest gold procurable, and issues thence as if born again. Such ceremony is termed Hiranya Garbham, or Padma Garbham, according as the vessel employed is made in the shape of a cow or of a lotus flower."

Amongst Hindus *garbha dhána* is the ceremony on conception of a child. The phrase constantly applied by every Sudra in the country to those who have performed this ceremony is *pasuvin vayittil piranna tamburán*, "the prince born of the womb of the cow." Mr. S. Menon himself refers to the construction of "a golden cow" for some such occasion. The *panchagavya*, or five products of the cow—milk, butter, curd, dung, and urine—half filling the vessel, are the very things always used for restoration to caste, and the only substance sacred enough to effect this important purpose. The Bombay prescription to this end is to swallow a pill of this mixture. It is said that Ragonath Row the Mahratta Peishwa, when expelled from his capital and defeated by his enemies, passed through a golden cow, in hopes of better fortune: and two Brahmans whom he* sent as ambassadors to England, were on their return to Hindustan, compelled to pass through the sacred *yoni*, made of the finest gold. After performing this ordeal, and making valuable presents to the Brahmans, they were restored to the privileges of their caste, which they had lost by the impurities contracted in travelling through so many polluted countries." (Forbes, *Or. Mem.* vol. i. p. 240.) Men are not rarely raised in caste, or restored to its privileges, by penances for expiation, or by largesses to Brahmans; just as some sink by marrying their inferiors, or in other ways. Cheaper and easier methods than bestowing one's weight in gold have been invented by the Brahmans.

* Not sent from Travancore, as stated by Day.

While it is conceded that the *Tulabhâram* or scale-weighing is primarily a religious donation as atonement for sin, or as a deed of merit not uncommonly practised in Bengal, where not only gold, but silver, rice and other articles are weighed against the donor and presented to the Brahmans; the Hiranya Garbha, (which is very briefly referred to by our author, while the other is quoted *in extenso*), is altogether distinct. The two ceremonies are lumped together under the head of "coronation ceremonies;" and it is worthy of notice that no descriptive accounts have been published of the last celebration of the latter ceremony, and it is passed over with but the barest mention in the Administration Report for M.E. 1047 as being "to complete the coronation." This very ceremony has been used by others, and for similar purposes. Some time ago "the illegitimate son of a Collector by a Moor-woman was privately raised to the Brahmanical order, the child's weight in gold poured over its head being the preliminary ceremony." (Taylor's First Century, p. 363.) The quiet change in modern times from the shape of a cow to that of a flower shows the influence of the enlightenment of the present age in making the Hindus ashamed of the absurdities of superstition. The Tanjore Rajah also performed this ceremony.*

The social effect of the second ceremony also is patent and most significant. The Maharajah ceases to partake of food, as formerly, along with the members of his family, but is yet not allowed to eat with Brahmans, only admitted to be present at their meals.

The opinion which I have formed respecting this interesting question after lengthened consideration of all that has hitherto been advanced upon it, and after considerable inquiry amongst various classes of natives, is that the European writers referred to in the volume before us, who have no personal interest in the discussion, and who are usually best able to reason upon the interesting facts supplied by native witnesses, and to form a broad and unbiassed opinion *ab extra*, and have also paid more attention to Hindu literature and ethnology than most of the natives themselves, are, in the main, right as to those Malabar princes being virtually Sudras, which is admitted also by many of the natives. The facts that they can only marry Sudra ladies—that their children are simply Náyars according to the ordinary Malabar law, without any caste pre-eminence on account of their father's rank—that the laws of nepotism prevail in the descent of the throne and inheritance—that all the chieftains of Malabar agree to a large extent in traditions and

* "Manual of Madura," pp. 111, 188.

usages—and that the mass of the population of Malabar, over whom they exercise rule and with whom they are so intimately connected, are Sudras—all indubitably point to the orignal Náyar origin of those families. Even if the father be of higher caste, this makes no difference to a Náyar—the male parent being of little or no account in the Malabar domestic system, and many respectable families regarding themselves as honoured by the visits of Brahmans in this way. Indeed, there seems little ground for supposing that the so-called Kshatriya families who intermarry with the royal ladies, are really such, for their social and domestic usages also point to a Náyar origin. Even the Malayáli Brahmans have been supposed to have no higher original, as some of their own traditions assert. The whole case is put in a nutshell by the learned Bishop Caldwell—"The Aryan immigrants to the South appear to have been generally Brahmanical priests and instructors, rather than Kshatriya soldiers, and the Kings of the Pandyas, Cholas, Kalingas, and other Dravidians, appear to have been simply Dravidian chieftains, whom their Brahmanical preceptors and spiritual directors dignified with Aryan titles, and taught to imitate and emulate the grandeur and cultivated tastes of the Solar, Lunar, and Agni-Kula races of Kings. In later times we may see the progress of a similar process in Gondwana, where we find that Gond chieftains have learned from their Brahman preceptors, not only to style themselves Rajahs, but even to assume the sacred thread of the 'twice-born' Kshatriyas. The gradual transformation of these semi-barbarous chieftains into Kshatriya princes shows how the Pandya and Chola chieftains of the South may originally have been Polygars like those of Ramnad and Puducottah in later times; and may, in process of time, have risen in rank as in power, assuming, as they did so, the Kshatriya titles of Deva, Vurma, &c. and finally, in some instances at least, succeeding in getting themselves recognized as Kshatriyas by the orignal Kshatriyas of the North."

When natives are asked how otherwise can they account for these royal families being unable to intermarry with Chetry ladies, or any higher than Sudras, they sometimes answer that the warriors from the north might have brought no females with them; or, as G. V. Tirumulpad suggests, that these families all belong to one *gotra* or clan, so closely related as to be unable to intermarry; and when asked how, if the principal Rajahs be descended from Cheraman Perumal, tney are supposed to be of diverse castes, the reply is that Cheraman Perumal married four wives from four separate castes, whose posterity consequently vary in this respect. These explanations are simply absurd and *ex post facto* inventions of persons hard driven to find some basis for their theories.

The last point which I would here particularly notice is the spirit of shallowness, unfairness, and scarcely concealed antagonism which Mr. Shungoonny Menon displays towards Christian truth and Christian missions. In one brought up with such surroundings, and under the power of such prejudices, this is not altogether to be wondered at. Still, he had considerable opportunities for learning what Christians really are, opportunities quite equal to those of some of his compatriots who have borne very different testimony concerning the missionaries and their work ; and he might, for the sake even of his own reputation, have shown some leanings in favour of popular liberties and the progress of reform. Would that this talented man had better known, and had sought, the blessings bestowed by Jesus Christ, the Saviour of the world.

The course often adopted by educated Hindus hard pressed by the enlightenment of the age, is to apply Christian phraseology to the heathen deities as if they were but synonymous with the One and Living God ; or, at times, to brazen out their degrading superstitions by audacious assertions of the truth and excellence of Hinduism, and the evils of the Christian religion, just as in the flattery of individuals they apply it most vigorously, precisely where it is not deserved, and could not for a moment be justified. Here we find the Hindu Puranas, with their monstrous tales and immoral superstitions, placed on a level with the Bible—the idolatrous worship of Padmanábha Swamy (who is enumerated in the Census Report simply as one of a long list of deities) is made synonymous with "the praises of God" and "supplicating the Creator ;" and "the will of Sri Padmanábha Swamy" equivalent to "the divine will." "Padmanábha Swamy alone protects"—What then about the multitude of other deities and demons worshipped in the country, and how comes it that this god is clothed with rich garments, anointed, and bathed, if he is the Almighty Creator of the universe ?

As to the *origin of modern missions* in Travancore we find the marvellous assertion that Rani Gouri Parwathi Bhye "was the founder and supporter of the English missions in Travancore." It is, on the contrary, well-known, and even apparent from some portions of the History, that it was due, if to any local patrons, to the English officers, who procured for the missionaries permission to reside and to labour in the country. Such were Col. Macaulay, who obtained a passport for Ringeltaube, and gave personal contributions to his work ; and the distinguished Col. Munro, who was at the same time a zealous friend of missions, and a lover of beautiful Travancore. To reduce the administration to order, and save the country from the effects of misrule, he assumed almost autocratic power by uniting in himself the functions of Resident and Dewan. He was the real author of the grants referred to, which were intended for, and are still devoted to, the education of the native Christian youth, rather than the direct work of the Missions—it was he who appointed Mr. Mead a judge, as he found so few trustworthy persons available, which office, however, the Missionary Society requested Mr. Mead to resign, as unsuitable to his position—and it was he who applied to the Church Missionary Society for missionaries, and helped them in manifold ways. It is often difficult in the history of Travancore to distinguish between the spontaneous movements of the Sirkar towards reform, and those which really originated with the British Government, and which simply could not well have been declined by the Native State. It could easily be proved that most of the early reforms were imposed by moral pressure on the Sirkar, though credit is now claimed for these, as it is of course officially due, and willingly accorded by us.

The boasted *tolerance of Christianity* in Travancore took its rise from a long series of circumstances, rather than from any deliberate policy on the part of the Hindu rulers; and it could not have been successfully refused, though attempts were made from time to time to do so, and even to repress the rising cause. It was not by the "strong protection" of the Sirkar, but of the British officials, and in spite of native intolerance, that the full liberty was won, by which Christian missions have so greatly prospered. The early Syrian settlers were valuable traders, colonists, and allies to the Hindu chieftains; but even the Syrians with their descendants and converts have, especially since the conquest of the region they inhabit by Travancore, by degrees fallen under various disabilities, and are allowed but little share in the administration or public employment. In an address to the Madras Government dated from Quilon in 1818, the Resident, Col. Munro, says "The Syrians were exposed to still greater calamities in the conquest of their country by the Rajah of Travancore. The blighting influence of that despotic and merciless government was felt by them in the most aggravated degree, and they were reduced to the lowest state of poverty and depression."

The Portuguese power aided the admission to the country of Xavier and other early Roman Catholic missionaries. The Portuguese were accustomed to demand toleration and freedom for converts; and the native rulers were quite unable to resist. The Dutch Government also were, unfortuately, always ready to take up arms in defence of religion. But even in the time of Bartolomeo, little over a century ago, though extravagant privileges were sometimes fitfully granted to the Roman Catholic missionaries in response to personal appeals from the Pope, their native converts were required to be present at idolatrous festivals, and their females were dragged by force to heathen dances. Proselytism being a transgression of the laws of the country, converts could only be baptized in the night, or at Verapoly under the protection of the Dutch Protestant Government. "The king of Travancore," says Bartolomeo, "threatens with imprisonment and death every nobleman who shall quit his court to become a Christian, and who shall afterwards fall into his hands; and indeed Nilam Pilla, an officer of a noble family, was shot at Aramballi* because he refused to renounce the religion of Jesus Christ. In the year 1787, I saw four Nairs thrown into prison at Tiruvanda-puram because they would not apostatise from the Catholic Church. The Sampradi did everything in his power to make these four Sudras abjure Christianity—even paid them a visit himself, and to gain his point employed every art of persuasion. As these were not attended with success, his substitute proceeded to coercive means; and not only tortured the prisoners with hunger and thirst, but even caused them to be scourged twice a day. They were, at last, transported beyond the boundaries of Tovala." Such cruelties operated as an effectual warning, so that conversions from the Sudra caste have since been very few.

So when the Protestant Mission was commenced by Ringeltaube in 1806, great difficulty was experienced in obtaining the requisite permission. The Dewan told him frankly the thing was not to be done; evasive answers were given; and it was only through the pertinacious intercession of Col. Macaulay that liberty was at last granted. Afterwards, at various times, the jealousy and rage of the higher caste Hindus, excited by the marked progress of the Gospel and its accompanying civilization, raged against the Christian converts. From 1827 for nearly three years, a storm of persecution raged in South Travancore; and again in 1858 persecution broke out, ostensibly on the question of Christian women covering the bosom contrary to ancient usage, which was only settled by the powerful interposition of the Madras Government. Even yet, the letter of the law only allows the use of *coarse* cloth to cover the bosom; but this is not enforced, and the Protestant Christian community are achieving their

* In 1752.

just liberties and equal rights of citizenship; and gaining social influence by good conduct and steady advance in moral and material progress.

The London Mission had determined upon the capital being the site of a mission almost from the day of their coming into the country; but permission could not be obtained on account of the strong prejudices of the native government and of the Brahmans, and their dread of pollution by Europeans and Native Christians. For this reason they were obliged to commence their Malayálam Mission in 1821 at Quilon. In 1827, Mr. Miller applied to the Sirkar for permission to establish a mission station at Trevandrum, but was refused. Mr. Addis was also decidedly forbidden to reside even at Valiatory; and in 1838, it was only through the patronage of General Fraser, that a plot of waste ground at Cannamoola was allowed for the erection of mission premises.

The Church Missionary Society experienced less difficulty in opening and conducting their mission in Northern Travancore, partly perhaps, because it was begun after the London Mission had been ten years at work in the South; but chiefly arising from the fact that their first proselytes were from Syrianism, not converts from heathenism, to which therefore the Hindu Government was perfect indifferent. Complaints, however, of opposition and oppression after the conversion of Hindus, frequently occur in the official chronicles of the Mission, and in the reports of Messrs. Peet, Baker, and others.

CHAPTER XXXVI.

EDUCATED NATIVES.

THROUGH the introduction of Western civilization, science, and religion, and the influence of the British paramount power, the English language has been introduced, more or less, everywhere throughout our Indian Empire; and in Travancore the number of educated men and students in the Public offices, the College and District Schools is large, and continually increasing. An English education is eagerly sought by all who can afford it for their children, as the only avenue to new and higher spheres of activity, preferment, and profit. Without it, now-a-days, there is no hope of high Government employment, or of signal success in the battle of life.

Such an exotic training bestowed on the young from an early period of childhood cannot but profoundly affect the moral sentiments and habits, and the religious views of the people, as well as raise their general intelligence. We are giving to the Indians the scientific method, and a critical spirit which destroys their faith in the old and degrading superstitions of Hinduism. Amongst the educated men of Travancore, the number of those who appear heartily to believe in the old-fashioned heathenism might be counted on one's fingers. Such a thing as a man educated in English, and at the same time a devout idolater, is quite a rarity; though, of course, all are obliged outwardly to conform to the national religion; some strongly cling to caste prejudices and aversions, chiefly through the pride of race; and many retain a measure of faith in the minor superstitions in which they have been nurtured from earliest infancy.

It is true, indeed, that, notwithstanding all their opportunities of knowing better, some are utterly godless and indifferent to the vital subject of religious truth, sceptical with regard to all forms of religion, entirely devoid of moral stamina, absorbed in worldliness, hardened and unimpressible; or even scoffing and sneering at the indefeasible claims of Jesus Christ on the allegiance of mankind. Some are atheists, pretending to a lofty intellectual superiority to, and contempt for, all revealed religions—all, according to them, being equally false. Others more or less completely reject all social and moral restraints, and fall into intemperance, sensuality, and slavish vices. Great diversities of thought, opinion, and character prevail amongst this class. Several schoolboys, with whom conversation was once held, probably but re-echoed the respective views of their parents and seniors, when one replied, "Your Christ and our Krishna are the same person under different names." Another said, "If the mother of Christ was Mary, how can you regard him as God?" A third, "I am an Atheist: Mr. Bain, the philosopher, teaches that there is no God in the universe." Again said one, "If you require a proof of the power of our *mantrams*, I can strike you dumb by them." Another sneeringly asked "How many people have you converted?" And yet another, "It is because our Government are so generous to you that people are permitted to become Christians, and to proclaim their religion in our streets."

A few superficially clever and educated young Hindus, conscious of the difficulty of defending idolatry in these days of light and knowledge, endeavour to put a good face on their position, and brave it out, by bold and brazen assertions of the excellence and truth of Hinduism (if they only understood it thoroughly, as Christians do their religion) and the divine origin of the licentious Nepotistic Law; and by boasting of the *true* God whom, it seems, they and their ancestors have ever worshipped, and of the innumerable ages during which their caste, customs, and religion have subsisted.

We deplore the error and infatuation of such deliberate rejectors of the Gospel, and the loss they incur by not seeking the blessings which flow from faith in God; and we trust that they and their children may speedily be brought to know and to rejoice in His salvation.

Generally, however, one of the first results of intellectual enlightenment is the weakening of the power of superstition and idolatry over the mind. These evils are but rarely defended by the most intelligent men, indeed, they feel rather sore on the subject of their gross idolatry when witnessed by others—like the backsliding Israelites of old, "ashamed, they, their kings, their princes, and their priests, and their prophets, saying to a stock 'Thou art my father'; and to a stone 'Thou hast brought me forth.'"

Already we observe some tokens of decay and disintegration in the idolatries of India, in districts where evangelical missions have had reasonable time to operate effectually. Vast and fundamental changes are observable. The Tanjore bull-god which, they tell us, was originally carved of small size, but grew by degrees to its present colossal proportions, has *ceased to grow* since the white men came—an emblem of the inertness of Hinduism. Learned Pandits now-a-days attempt to explain away and spiritualise the worst features of idolatry and the grossest tales of the Puránas. During the present century the shape of the golden vessel through which the Maharajah of Travancore passes in order to become 'twice-born,' has quietly been altered from the form of a cow to that of a lily. The priesthood is less feared, the religious orders and astrologers less venerated, the annual festivals have lost something of their enthusiasm; and offerings, car-drawing, and other services are rendered grudgingly. Caste observances are somewhat loosening their hold even in Travancore, their chief stronghold, where the fostering protection of the Government is profusely bestowed upon the temples and priests.

In an English lecture on "Our Superstitions," delivered by a Brahman judge not long since to a large native audience, with a high Brahman magistrate occupying the chair, the lecturer, in closing his address, touchingly and impressively referred to a striking incident which had occurred, a fisherman having had both arms amputated in the Mission Hospital after a hard struggle in the sea for life with a ferocious shark. "Our case," said the lecturer, "is exactly similar to this fisherman's case. While we were sunk in the ocean of ignorance, the shark of superstition seized us strongly, and we had to fight against it 'for our life.' The wave of English education has brought us to a place of safety with a little life. It is absolutely necessary that we should save our souls from being condemned to Hell. To do this we, like Michael, must undergo the amputation of the crippled and diseased mind, however painful the operation may be. Let us then kneel down and pray to the Great Doctor of doctors to do the operation, and make our souls healthy, so that they may become fit to enter His kingdom."

"The Christian preachers," say some, "have taken away from the hearts of the people the fear of their native gods. People now rob the gods of their gold and silver jewellery; and the gods are afraid that even themselves will be stolen." Others, in excuse for the practice of idolatry, which they admit is only for ignorant people, say that they attend the pagodas only for amusement; or to show their respect for the religion of the Government; or very often because their women beg them to go. "Since I read your tract on the 'Errors of the Rámáyana,'" says another, "I have ceased worshipping Rama." Thus there is an incipient turning away from gross idolatry and a religion of the senses, so that we may readily believe that "the old gods of Hinduism will die in these new elements of intellectual light and air, as quickly as a net-full of fishes lifted up out of the water."

Good moral principles and opinions are also instilled into their minds by an English education. In 1861, for instance, an excellent little manual in English of the "Principles of Morality," was reprinted by the Sirkar at the instance of Sir Madava Row, the distinguished Dewán, and also translated into the vernacular. It inculcates the observance of moral duties from the fear and love of God; and the obligation of prayer for Divine aid in their fulfilment. This tract was found by the Dewán among some books received from Bombay for the use of his children; and he thought it so good that he got copies printed for his Government schools.

Similarly, in an English lecture on "Our Morals," delivered in 1874, His Highness the First Prince, now Maharajah, earnestly reprobated the low standard of morality prevailing in India, and urged the necessity of moral culture. "Marvellous," he says, "has been the effect of Christianity in the moral moulding and leavening of Europe. I am *not* a Christian. I do not accept the cardinal tenets of Christianity as they concern man in the next world. On these matters I have my own beliefs. But I accept Christian ethics in their entirety. I have the highest admiration for them. Speaking, then, of Christianity as it concerns this world, I repeat that it has effected a wonderful moral revolution in Europe. I can imagine the question which probably quivers on the lips of some of you. You will ask 'Does not vice exist among Christians?' I do not hesitate a moment to affirm that vice, crime, and immorality exist in Christendom to the same extent as they do in India. You have only to look at the great Tichborne trial, which has so recently scandalized civilized England. Under the heading of Law and Crime, in the English dailies, you will always find abundant records of crimes of the worst description. Electioneering, again, is a mine of corruption. I fully grant all this. But yet there is a difference. That difference consists in the standard of morality which an average Christian and an average Hindu respectively acknowledge. Except, perhaps, among the very scum of society, an immoral act is never applauded among Christian nations. The most truthless Christian is fired by being called a liar. But turn to an average countryman of our own who has not yet studied to adopt European externals, and see how blandly and unconcernedly the epithet 'liar' is taken by him. You must have seen people even complimenting one another with the epithet 'clever rogue.' On the other hand, nothing is more common than to ridicule men of truth and honesty as fools. Again, when two young and intimate friends meet, the staple subject of conversation is—the beauties of the locality, their paramours; their intrigues, their successes, disappointments and revenges—spiced with the needful scandal. Or, the subject is bribes, bribe-givers, bribe-brokers, and bribe-takers."

Persons not intimately acquainted with the present state of Indian society of this class, might be surprised at the *tone of the lectures, essays, and correspondence* of Hindus educated in English, and would ask, "Are the writers not Christians?" They write freely, often very accurately in the English language. I have known them to republish English lectures on science and morals. They correspond with Europeans quite in the style and tone of Englishmen, though with, perhaps, a little more attention to politeness and form. I have heard some of them lecture admirably on the electric telegraph, on astronomy, on art and science, on female education, and similar topics.

Educated Hindus frequently indulge in fine talk about moral obligations—the importance of solid worth as compared with mere gold and social rank—the value of knowledge, and the grand mission which educated men have to perform in the world. Many of them are beginning to use our religious language and phraseology, though, of course, not with the same precision and fulness of meaning that it bears with us—rather in a vague theistic than in a Christian sense. They will freely express themselves in such handsome terms as these:—"We have passed another milestone in our life's journey. May the beacon of God's light glow brighter and brighter to all of us." Another says, "In grateful memory of one long since dead, I may say that I first drew my breath of knowledge—so to say—from a missionary; and I am a witness of the much silent good work that is being done by this class of servants of God." Another, "I wish you a very happy New Year, attended with all the choicest blessings the great Author of the Universe may be pleased to vouchsafe."

I have repeatedly heard with pleasure such expressions at the inauguration of public institutions, as were used by the Hon. V. Ramiengar Dewán, recently, in opening a Mission Dispensary:—"It is not enough in passing through life to do no ill to others: we should omit no opportunity of doing good; and in this respect we should be guided by the example of those good men who dedicate their lives to the good of others; and use such powers and faculties as they are endowed with for the glory of God, and the relief of man's estate. I thank you," he added, "for your kindness in asking me to open this new Dispensary, on which I join you all in humbly invoking the blessing of God."

And, lastly, in illustration of this point:—In the reply of the present Maharajah to the address of the missionaries on the occasion of his accession to the throne, His Highness says:—"While I do as distinctly recognize the hand of God as any of you, in the great change which has so suddenly taken place, I cannot conceal from myself that the mantle has fallen on unworthy shoulders. Nevertheless, I can promise my utmost and conscientious devotion to the solemn duties which have devolved upon me. In the discharge of those duties, next to the wisdom and power which I eminently need from God, I shall prize the moral support of gentlemen like you who are the links of civilization, enlightened progress, and moral regeneration between the West and the East."

It is with men such as these that Christianity has to deal now-a-days; but having been brought by general enlightenment, intercourse with Europeans, and the indirect influence of Christian truth so far on the way to a right state as to use such admirable language, even though partly from imitation, and the desire to be thought advanced in enlightenment; and even though its full force be not felt, something, certainly, has been accomplished; and the next step we may look for is the actual carrying of such liberal views into effect by individuals under the constraining impulse of the Spirit of God, and personal conviction of the truth.

At the same time, **doubts as to all Revelation** and religion, and a general spirit of scepticism and unrest, are often produced by a merely secular education in the minds of Indian students. They experience a constant oscillation of ideas and opinions which puzzle and distress them, without seeing their way to accept the definite teaching and authoritative revelation of Divine truth which the Bible conveys. "If we believe in one revelation, or incarnation," argue some, "we might as easily believe in ten." In India, a purely secular education and an acquaintance with Western science, are taking from the people their ancestral religion, and destroying all faith. Infidelity, atheism, and universal scepticism are being introduced along with European literature and culture; and unless we hasten to give them the Gospel of Jesus Christ, they will be cast adrift, without chart or compass, on a sea of doubts and errors.

The Christian Church should, therefore, **be prepared** for the intellectual crisis which is fast approaching in India, when the temples shall be forsaken, the national superstitions and religious beliefs abandoned, and society agitated and revolutionized to its very foundation, by the spread of secular knowledge, which may lead to the most disastrous issues of atheism in creed, licentiousness in life, and lawlessness in morals, if the Gospel of Jesus

Christ be not in the meantime presented to enlighten and guide the popular mind to right principles of action and obedience to God. It is no longer a question whether the old systems of heathenism will fall, but whether the Christian Church will be able to take up the work in time to prevent the people falling into utter scepticism, atheism, and godlessness. Happily much is actually being accomplished towards this end in Travancore, Tinnevelly, and elsewhere, by the scriptural training of native churches and preachers and teachers, the establishment of Christian institutions, and the preparation of a sound Christian literature.

"The sum total of what we call civilization," says Sir A. C. Lyall, "is to such a society as that in India a dissolving force: it is the pouring of new wine into old skins—the cutting away of anchors instead of hauling them up, so that, in the next emergency, there are none to throw out. Conquest and civilization together must sweep away the old convictions and prejudices; and unless some great enthusiasm rushes in to fill the vacancy thus created, we may find ourselves called to preside over some sort of spiritual interregnum."

Superficially acquainted with the works of Herbert Spencer, and Bain, and Mill, and Tyndall, and other English materialists and pantheists, and devoting almost no time or attention to the study of the evidences of Christianity, or the devout perusal of the Holy Scriptures, which is better still, they naturally fall into a state of perplexity and vacillation, and become unsettled, without any fixed belief. "I have found," writes Rev. I. H. Hacker, "in Hindus who have been educated in the Government Colleges, much courtesy and kindly feeling, but a feeling of scepticism with respect to nearly all forms of religion. Many have read such works as those of John Stuart Mill and Herbert Spencer, but not very deeply. They have read just enough to lay hold of materialistic objections, but not enough to rise above them; and the result is much mental bewilderment. May God help them to see the wonderful attractiveness of our Lord Jesus Christ, and find how graciously He can solve their perplexities and give then true rest."

The self-same questions and mysteries puzzle inquiring Hindus, and similar difficulties retard from faith as operate amongst ourselves—the origin of evil, the sovereignty of God, the atonement and Deity of Jesus Christ. "Religion," they say, "is too strict for frail men." "It is difficult to attain to certitude." "Let each be sincere and upright in his own faith, and hope for the best as to the future world."

Moreover, through the indirect as well as the direct influence of Christianity, which is at present so largely permeating the country, there is a good deal of **inquiry and longing after certainty,** and seeking for truth. This spirit, along with the intellectual renaissance that is in operation, has led to the formation of the numerous debating societies, clubs, and literary unions, which are a striking feature of native life amongst educated young men in Trevandrum. The claim might fairly be made that the first impetus and outward direction was given to this movement by our lectures to educated natives delivered in Trevandrum for five years, from 1863 to 1867, which were attended by crowded and influential audiences. The missionaries, and other Europeans friendly to the scheme, delivered lectures on scientific, literary, social, and moral topics, while the First Prince, the Dewán, and the Chief Justice were pleased to join in the movement. Since then, lectures have been delivered at Eraneel, Nagercoil, and other places in the south, and at Cottayam in the north, in which some of the ablest and most intelligent Hindu officers, as well as Christian preachers, take part.

Trevandrum being the capital and the seat of the Court, the College, High School, Law courts, and the bulk of the educated community, is naturally the headquarters of these meetings. Societies have been formed for various classes of students, with various ends in view, and have met with varied degrees of popularity and success and varying fates. Some rose, and speedily fell again, and new ones are being instituted. There are the Infant Club, the Juvenile Circle, the Reform Club, the Malayalee Union, the Debating Society, and the Students' Literary Circle; and of a more decidedly religious cast, the Young Men's Christian Association, the Moral Class, once conducted by the First Prince, and the Moral Improvement Society (*Saunmárga Pravarthaka Sangham*).

Some of these associations have been in reality curious and interesting experiments in religion, which one could not but view with profound sympathy, and wish that the true way had been known and tried. The Prince, in his lecture on Our Morals, sketched the outline of a suggested society or order, each member to subscribe solemnly to articles of faith, to which he should unswervingly adhere; and, after due probation, to be admitted into the society, and thenceforth wear a ring as a badge of membership. The society, as a whole, to possess the full freedom of reprehending any member for misconduct, or dismissing him from the body, without being amenable to the general public. This plan of the praise and censure of a body of enlightened men, guarding one another's morals and expelling unworthy members, he thought would prove a very effective means of promoting morality. A few of the personal friends of His Highness were happy to join such an association; they met for a time quarterly in the palace, heard addresses on morals, and engaged in conversation on the subject for mutual edification. But there could be no spiritual power in such a scheme, and it soon came to nought.

The membership of the Moral Improvement Association comprised a number of young men, who appeared to be sincerely seeking after truth amongst the various systems of religion and philosophy with which they were, more or less, acquainted. Their association was never, indeed, a power to move those outside it, but, doubtless, helped on its own members, and it was hoped would develop into a means of real public good. They began to translate useful books, and read with attention Christian publications lent them by the Young Men's Christian Association. They believed in a personal Deity, opened their meetings, which were held on Sunday afternoons, with prayers out of the Brahmo book, and had a kind of lay sermon delivered to the little congregation, sometimes from a Bible text. These were but feeble imitations of our Christian meetings for worship, but showed a desire to move in the right direction, and furnished a remarkable illustration of the indirect and unacknowledged influence of Christian ideas on the minds of inquiring young Hindus.

This society is unfortunately now quite defunct. There seems at present a cloud over such societies, as some of their most prominent members have, of late, shown lamentable moral weakness.

A unique opportunity was once afforded of getting direct at the **views of some educated Hindus**, by the unexpected absence of the appointed essayist at the meeting of a Debating Society in Trevandrum, which I attended. Being asked to suggest some topic to occupy the time to advantage, I proposed the query—"What is the opinion of Educated Hindus on the subject of Christianity?" opening with a few observations on the desire of many persons in England for reliable information on this point, and requesting a frank and unreserved expression of their real sentiments.

The first speaker rose and said that he regarded God as an aggregate of moral principles—an idea like that of a mathematical point—not a person. He brought moral principles and acts to the test of his own rational faculty and conscience, and felt that this was sufficient. Christianity certainly had many excellent moral principles, but also, like other religions, made statements which were without proof; therefore he did not feel bound to embrace it. He believes in "pure Theism." I thought however that the opening remark was atheistic.

The second speaker had read the New Testament and portions of the Old Testament in the High School (several made the same reference), but did not feel quite competent to pronounce on the truth or otherwise of Christianity. It certainly inculcated excellent moral teaching, which he thought it quite right to follow, though he did not wish to be called a Christian. Jesus Christ was only a man, but certainly a saint in the true sense of the term, as an example and teacher of the highest virtue.

Yet he did not wish to depreciate his own religion. The fact must be confessed with shame that he was not fully acquainted with Hindu modern and ancient Sanskrit literature; and was informed by Hindu scholars that if competent to form a judgment on Hinduism he would at once see its excellence and superiority. He was aware that Europeans who seek to make converts, do not seek to make them Christians merely in name, but instruct them in true morality. It is little matter by what name a man is called. We must prepare ourselves as well as we can for the future world.

Another young man, who had been chanting a Hindu song in praise of Rama before the meeting opened, said—"There is not sufficient proof that Jesus Christ ever really existed, but if He did, He taught much that was good." (His incredulity with regard to the historical fact of Jesus Christ having existed was received with laughter.) "He believes there is a God, a creator, ruler, and sustainer, to whom he prays to keep him in the paths of righteousness. There are many excellent moral principles in Hinduism, as in the Kural (written by a Pariah!) which deserve to be followed. Any religion is sufficient. We might select from Hinduism and Christianity, taking the pure essence and leaving the dregs of both. A Christian may be a Hindu (by inconsistency of conduct), and a Hindu may be a Christian (in heart and in the truest sense)."

Lastly, an able Christian youth rose and said—"Education has done much for the Hindus; they are now ashamed of the idolatry which they formerly believed in. They appreciate the excellence of the Christian religion, but are unwilling to embrace it through fear of worldly loss. Brahmans regard themselves as of high birth, and will not embrace Christianity, even when partly convinced of its truth."

In conclusion I thanked them for their frank statements and for the information they had communicated, which perhaps could have been obtained nowhere else in Travancore so readily, and offered my own views of Christianity as an authoritative declaration of the Divine will and of our duty. Several had referred to their having read the Bible in the High School; we claim their present enlightenment as the indirect result of Christian effort. Even the admirable ethical precepts occasionally found in their literature were owing largely to external influence from Jewish, Muhammadan and Christian sources. Sin is a deplorable fact, to which only one speaker had even alluded; the idea of "preparing one's self as well as one can for the future world" is in direct opposition to the distinctive teaching of the Gospel as to our need of a Saviour, of mercy and pardon through Jesus Christ, and Divine grace to renew the soul, and help in the paths of righteousness.

This was a most interesting and touching occasion, and the remarks, being unpremeditated, presented no doubt a fair and accurate view of the state of mind, the doubts and errors and hopes of Young Travancore.

Throughout not the educated classes only, but amongst all classes, the **objections to Christianity** formerly raised, and the aversion shown to the gospel, are, in a very marked degree, **less bitter and violent** than in former times. There is apparent a readiness to listen to judicious and kindly expositions of the Christian revelation, and a favourable estimate is often expressed of our religion. A better feeling towards the truth everywhere prevails, and young men are eager to obtain the tracts distributed at open air services. Tracts and other publications are in general well received, and thousands, says Mr. Yesudian, "do not hesitate freely to discuss and compare the merits of Hinduism with those of Christianity, and candidly to confess that the Christian religion is destined to erect its fortifications upon the ruins of Hinduism and all other systems of worship. They are also heard to express a wish to see the downfall of idolatry in their lifetime, and to enjoy the privilege of worshipping the true God as one that looks at the love and sincerity of the heart of the worshipper, and not at external formalities, however costly or awe-inspiring they may be."

In his mission district this distinguished Native Missionary considers that "about one-fourth of the heathen population are apparently well disposed towards Christianity, as is evident from their welcoming our agents with every mark of love and respect, refreshing them with food or drink when fatigued, or exhausted by journeys or exertion, and then sitting up for hours together to receive from them, in return, the food that never perisheth. They not unfrequently deplore their spiritual condition, and mourn over the system of idolatry which the Sirkar upholds."

Educated Hindus are always delighted to converse with cultivated Europeans, and to form even intimate friendships with them, as far as the unsociable system of caste will allow.

They are seldom reluctant to enter into religious conversation, and are quite accessible to discreet and appropriate effort.

Many appreciate the efforts of the missionaries and their native helpers, continually at work to spread the gospel over the country. A general conviction prevails amongst many of the people that Christianity is destined ultimately to conquer. The unity of God is now admitted by our hearers: conscience is being aroused, and a sense of spiritual need awakened. Christian ideas are permeating many minds, and Christian influences everywhere at work. The truth has entered more deeply into the hearts and modes of thought of many than they themselves are aware of, and society is being quietly leavened by it. A new spirit is penetrating even into the homes of the Hindu.

Only last year we were privileged to hear of tokens of a feeling for which we have been long looking—the **reflex influence on heathenism** of the marvellous illustration of the **practical operation of the Christian religion** furnished by those who have embraced it in South Travancore. "The idea," writes Mr. Hacker, "of what were called low-caste people teaching divine truth, which at one time was such an abomination to the orthodox Hindu, is now becoming familiar. It is not an unfrequent sight now to see one of our Christian teachers talking about the highest truths to members of the so-called higher castes."

The caste Hindus must soon be convinced by their own common sense that they are losing much blessing in every way, by not placing themselves in the van of the movement towards Christianity, as the Malagasy rulers so wisely did. One lately remarked to a mission catechist: "To-day, when passing by your schoolroom, I heard the children sing their sweet and instructive lyrics with great delight. We Sudras, regarded as of high caste, are now becoming comparatively lower; while you, who were once so low, are being exalted through Christianity. I fear," he added, "Sudra children in the rural districts will soon be fit for nothing better than feeding cattle."

"How pleasant," said the master of a house visited by the Bible-woman, "is it to see your women and girls with their books, and to hear the singing in the very place where devil worship was practised a few years ago. This results from the efforts of the missionary ladies. You must make *our* women like the Christian women in Nagercoil. And when the *women* are willing, the whole country will embrace Christianity."

"There is in general," says Mr. Yesudian, "a movement observable in favour of Christianity among the higher classes. Many are now more than ever setting themselves to examine the nature of the truths contained in the wonderful Book of God; some study the ten commandments and the Lord's prayer; some (women and children included) have committed to memory short prayers and Christian lyrics, while others are observed to *lament their sad failure to embrace the Christian religion earlier*, to regret their folly in having *allowed the lower castes to step in before them*, and to consider the best way they should adopt for availing themselves of all the privileges offered by the Gospel."

Some of the **higher classes have seen the folly of idolatry,** look upon the name of Christ with profound respect, express a high regard for the Bible, and say that they daily peruse it for spiritual light, solace under affliction, and help in the path of rectitude. The Bible is still read once a week in the Maharajah's High School, the only Government School, perhaps, in India, in which it is taught, and we hope that it will not be allowed to drop. Respectable caste-men frequently converse with our native teachers, and even admit them into their houses, read the Holy Scriptures with them, ask to be taught to pray, and to have prayer offered with them, and make anxious inquiries on the solemn topics of the resurrection, the final judgment, and the eternal world. They even contribute to the funds of the Mission. One Sudra corresponds with a Christian catechist by post, asking explanations of Scripture and the solution of various doubts and difficulties. Many are now thankful for help in sickness, and consolation from Christian teaching in times of sorrow and bereavement. A wealthy and intelligent Brahman purchased a Bible from a native Christian doctor, and brought out the sacred volume one day to ask whether it is mentioned in the Bible that we may pray to God in time of trouble. The 15th verse of the fiftieth Psalm was shown to him, and he gladly committed the text to memory.

Chiefly, perhaps, in the South, where political freedom is greater, and active missionary operations have been always directed towards Hindus, and have had greater room and longer time to work, the number of those who may be called **secret believers** is noticeable: not uncommonly in such cases courage to confess Christ as the Saviour is only gained on the death-bed, when the world and its trifles begin to fade, and to be seen in their true light, and eternity approaches. For example:—

"We rejoiced to find a certain intelligent Sudra who was powerfully impressed by the saving truths of the Gospel giving vent to such expressions as the following:—'I feel I am a sinner, and that Jesus the Son of God is my only Saviour;' then lowering his head with pensive tears, and after some moments of solemn silence raising his head upwards, he said, 'Jesus! thou art the way to Heaven. I pray thou wilt pity me, and pardon my sins, and take me to that place of bliss, though I feel that I have not the courage to make a public confession of my spiritual adherence to Thee.' This interesting man died within two weeks or so after he had made this serious confession."

The last words which another Sudra of large property and influence, whose changed life had signally evidenced his true conversion to God, uttered to his wife and friends were these: "I see now nothing else but Jesus. He appears to me to be everything. Commit your souls to His care and protection."

There must be several hundreds of such in Travancore, who, though now weak and timid, restrained by strong social and domestic obstacles from assuming a distinctively Christian position, and halting between two opinions, sorely struggling between conviction and self-interest, between God and mammon, would at once embrace our faith, and profess Christ openly were the caste difficulties and social persecution removed out of their way, or a sufficient number of them ready to come forward, so as to encourage and stand by one another. They would be glad and thankful to be carried in safely and pleasantly on a wave of Christian movement and revival, and such a movement may begin at any time, and come with a rush upon us.

Serious impediments, indeed, lie in the way of conversion on the part of high-castes. House and home, wife and children, office and emoluments—all must be surrendered. Under present circumstances, it would be, humanly speaking, a perfect impossibility for a Christian Maharajah to remain in the palace, a Christian Dewan to retain his administration, or a Christian revenue collector to fulfil the duties required of him. Even in posts where the religion professed might not make an essential difference, government patronage and dependence on government office, which is, unfortunately, the sole aim of almost every educated native in Travancore, stifles all independence of thought and action. Professional advancement seems often to quench convictions of sin and longings after spiritual light, or to tempt men to feign a heartier zeal in the cause of idolatry than appears to be sincere. The cares of this world and the deceitfulness of riches choke the good seed. A merely intellectual is commonly substituted for a real, living, moral standard. All the temporal hopes and interests of a young Travancorean demand his continuance in Hinduism. Conversion to Christianity is, in fact, civil death, the funeral rites of a Brahman convert being performed as soon as it is ascertained that he has been baptized.

Caste customs and laws also check conversion. The opposition of relatives and hostility of caste companions it is hard to brave. A Náyar who was suspected of a leaning towards Christianity was actually threatened by his daughters' partners that they would return all their wives and children on his hands if he dared to follow out his convictions.

The obstructive power exercised by **uneducated women** is also very great. "The native, on retiring to his domicile, usually takes off his turban, his upper garment, and his ideas of Western civilization which are incompatible with his domestic life: all are equally donned and doffed for use in a world that is unknown within his household. He is alive to the theories gathered from Western books, but he fails to carry them into practice within the precincts of his own house. Why? Because, probably, the husband, in reality, no more reigns supreme in the house of a native than in that of the European. Women do not bluster or order; but they can offer irresistible passive opposition in the limits of their own domain, that is, the household. The man who, using the superior knowledge with which he is gifted, would wish to accomplish a deed contrary to caste prejudice, would not so much fear the resistance of his fellow castemen as that of his female relatives. They are the persons who would organize a *guerre à outrance* against him, for it must be remembered that caste, with all the little ceremonies it entails, is essentially an observance of domestic life. However much, then, the liberal-minded native would wish to break the bonds, he can but see that he pushes himself forward in a contest that would only result in his being isolated, and would not make the slighest impression on the vast question at stake.*

Amid all these difficulties and discouragements, it is no wonder that the general **weakness of character**, want of conscientiousness, and absence of moral courage and self-help, which the Hindus themselves admit, the effect of an enervating climate and the long reign of ignorance and error, deter many from openly declaring themselves. Some confidentially express their regret that they have not the courage to save their widowed virgin daughters from an unhappy and desolate life, by again giving them in marriage; or that they dare not refuse in the company of their rulers to "bow the knee in the house of Rimmon." Some present one side of devout idolatry to the Brahman priests, another of liberal thought and enlightenment

* *Madras Mail*, 1881.

to the European, and it is often difficult to reconcile these with entire sincerity. They acknowledge and bewail their frailty and hesitancy. I have heard one frankly and publicly acknowledge:—"In our country one cannot express one's opinions freely. We should *never get on* if we did. A beggar must not displease his patron!" This insincerity, double-dealing, and servility are terrible and damning evils. Educated Hindus will talk contemptuously of the Brahman priests and their authority, of superstition and injurious customs, of reform and true nobility, and of patriotism, while they have not the self-sacrifice or courage to put forth a finger to bear the burden of the true reformer, who is prepared to suffer for the good of others, and to live or to die for his country or his fellow men. They indulge in vague looking out of themselves for the forces that are to regenerate the society in which they move. "Education is appealed to with weariful iteration as the cure for all the social and moral evils of the country; but those who appeal to it do not, many of them, seem to dream that anything more is due from them than to suffer themselves to be educated without resistance, and to abstain from offering resistance to the education of others."

What has this class of men as yet attempted or effected for the suffering masses in Travancore? Not long since two young men of gentle birth and liberal education, being disgusted with the world, and the corrupt state of society around them, became ascetics, and wandered away from the sphere of duty, instead of setting themselves manfully and prayerfully to fight in the name of the Lord against the prevailing evils. A solemn responsibility rests upon those who are at the head of Hindu society, and whose patronage and support are given to idolatry and error.

Owing to the comminuting and **insulating action of Caste,** the conversion of large numbers of the lower classes in some of our missions, though it will ultimately, through the beneficent action of the Gospel, so raise them in character and social position (as it is already doing) that they will become the really higher classes; and will thus, in the end, give them an influence calculated to bring about the conversion of the whole country; yet does not, at present, directly or speedily affect the high castes, the nobles, priests, rulers, landholders. The common people are being brought under instruction, and this work of evangelization has only to go on in the same way as hitherto to win over the masses. But for the "upper ten thousand" distinct and special efforts are claimed, and in some places being initiated. We long to see the Rajahs of India converted, the men of rank and leaders of public opinion brought to

God. In the introduction of Christianity into Europe it was usually the conversion of the chieftains that opened up the way for the Gospel amongst the common people. So also in Madagascar, when the Queen and Prime Minister placed themselves at the head of the new civilization and religious reform, the national idols were burnt, and the whole population held themselves ready to listen to the voice of the Christian preacher. Some of the princes and nobles of various parts of India now permit the visits of the Zenana missionary to their palaces, and speak appreciatively of the Bible and the benignant operation of the Christian religion. May they be brought to accept for themselves the message of salvation, and receive Jesus Christ as their Saviour! Then those secret disciples who now hang back through fear of persecution and worldly loss, will be emboldened to come forward at once; many of the overwhelming obstacles which hinder the spread of truth in India shall be removed; and the whole population favourably disposed towards Christian teaching.

The marvellous advance which has already been made among the higher classes in India, and the moral and social revolution which has begun, through the introduction and diffusion of Western knowledge and the English language, fully repay all the labour that has, so far, been expended for the elevation of the country. The education which the Hindus are gaining fits them for the exercise of rational thought, and for wise and manly action. It is no small thing that men of liberal education are raised up and prepared (if they will but divest themselves of caste prejudice and moral vacillation) to occupy positions of influence and responsibility. Civilization and secular knowledge, though accompanied by certain evils and dangers, are, on the whole, helping on the good work of amelioration—female education is rapidly spreading, and widow re-marriage advocated—the railway, the telegraph, and the press, the "increase of knowledge" and the "running to and fro," modern industries and commerce, and a strong and righteous supreme Government influencing the life of the country, all combine to aid in "preparing the way of the Lord and making his paths straight." Vast possibilities lie before a believing and witnessing Church in the immediate future, if she will but rise to the crisis of India. A noble work indeed it is to spread the knowledge of the Lord Jesus Christ amongst the nations, and to make our brother men hear the voice of God speaking in His Word.

The masses are at the same time, to some extent, being educated, though not nearly so much as might be were the British Indian Government to direct more of its energies and expenditure towards primary education, as it is hoped it will henceforth do. Still, many are being prepared to read useful books and the Holy Scriptures. The whole country is in a state of transition, and we feel assured that the truth will at last conquer, through the might of our Divine and glorious King. Gracious and potent influences, and varied instrumentalities are already at work everywhere for the uplifting and regeneration of India, all combining towards one end which no power on earth or hell can effectually hinder.

> The fount is open'd, from whose streams
>   Celestial life and knowledge spread :
> The sun hath risen, whose radiant beams
>   Restore the sick, and raise the dead.
> And nought their glorious course shall check,
>   Till earth with moral verdure glows ;
> Till they her desert wilds shall deck
>   With blooming Eden's deathless rose.

CHAPTER XXXVII.

MISSION WORK.

ONE of the most obvious characteristics of the Travancore mission is its location in a Native State under the rule of a Maharajah and his Ministers, subject in a varying and undefined degree to the control of the British Resident and the paramount Government of India. This circumstance has had a very marked influence on the history of the mission, and has affected our work variously at different times, but has, doubtless, on the whole, in the wonderful providence of God, been made a help rather than a hindrance. About a century ago, the British were the means of preserving the king of Travancore from the devastating power of Tippu Saib, Sultan of Mysore, and they thereby gained the gratitude of the Native State, and the right, by treaty, to offer advice and exercise some supervision over it. The missionaries were supported by the English officials in asking permission of the despotic and exclusive, but now somewhat humbled, Native Government to enter upon evangelistic labours in the country. Then, while at work and resident in the midst of the native population, it was scarcely possible for them, as Englishmen, to witness the cruel oppressions practised on the poor without indignantly exposing them to public reprehension, and occasionally even interfering by petition, publication, or other legal means, for the redress of grievances and the amelioration of the condition of the people, and more especially for the protection of those who placed themselves under their instruction, and sought liberty to observe Christian rules and worship and ordinances. This necessarily gave the missionaries much influence in addition to that derived from their life and teaching; and, when the Native Government was at its worst, they were even feared by oppressors, as the only persons intimately acquainted, from their knowledge of the languages and free intercourse with all classes, with the true condition of the country, and fearless in the exposure of clamant evils.

As the native rule improved, this kind of influence naturally ceased, and there are now many other Europeans in the country capable of forming intelligent and accurate opinions on questions of public polity and administration. But still openings present themselves for the acquirement of personal influence in a small kingdom like Travancore, by extensive knowledge of the country and its requirements, by steady adherence to right, and by philanthropic labour for the public weal. Right-minded natives, even thorough Hindus, give credit to the missionaries for what they have effected and are doing for the country. Some of the nobles and officials are personally friendly, and even helpful, in benevolent undertakings, such as hospitals, female education, and popular lectures on useful topics; and, since foreign funds are expended on the primary education of over seventeen thousand children in our village schools, the Sirkar makes an annual grant in aid of the secular education afforded, which is but fair and reasonable under the circumstances. The poorer classes, at the same time, identify the missionaries, and the British influence generally, with the great amelioration in their condition which has gradually taken place. Everwhere Europeans in Travancore are regarded with the utmost confidence and respect. There have not, as yet, been numbers of indigent or illiterate Europeans in the country—those whom the people are familiar with are officials, military, and professional men, very rarely indeed of immoral or vicious life; and Travancore has been exceptionally fortunate in the decided Christian character of several of the Residents, and of many English officials in the service of the Maharajah, not least of the Masters and Professors of the College at Trevandrum, who have from the beginning been men of Christian character, as well as superior abilities, and have had in their hands, for thirty years past, the training of nearly all the educated officials in the employment of the State.

Another distinctive feature of the mission arising, in the providence of God, in large measure, from the oppressions practised on the lower castes, and from the beneficent dominance of the British, was the coming over of the people in masses, influenced no doubt at first, and to some extent still, by inferior and selfish considerations; not, of course, for temporal support, but for sympathy protection, and aid in their distresses. They were deeply impressed by the kindness of the missionaries, so unwonted an experience to them; they were aided in times of persecution by their intercession; and they witnessed Christianity elevating the first and each successive generation of converts in education, social status, and personal worth. Acting, as the Hindus prefer to do, unitedly, they came over to Christianity in large numbers; whole families and villages joined the mission; others followed the good example of their fellows, and expected like benefits. They were generally guided by a few leading minds, who saw more clearly the excellence of what was proclaimed by the missionaries. Most did not fully understand the Christian religion when they first came, but, as far as they did understand, they appreciated it, and recognized its sacred obligations.

Our congregations are still largely recruited from without, not so much by individuals becoming deeply concerned about their salvation, as by families brought over by Christian sympathy, by the prevalent opinion of the supreme excellence of the Christian religion, and by the education, civilization, and friendly aid that necessarily follow from Christianity. Such persons are not at once baptized or admitted to church fellowship; this is only done by degrees, and with especial caution and reserve in our own mission, as one or another gives evidence of personal piety and love to God; but all the adherents are organized into congregations, and carefully taught in the doctrines and trained to the practice of our holy religion. While we freely admit the worldly motives by which many were led to place themselves under Christian instruction, it is important to remember how far personal friendship and external environments have often aided the progress of the truth.

The mode of working which was demanded by these circumstances, and which naturally sprang from them, was to form the multitudes of adherents into local congregations, placing over them native Scripture-readers or catechists to instruct them. These numerous congregations are visited frequently by the missionary for inspection, instruction, and discipline; the English missionaries being thus placed in a peculiar position as the trusted and accredited messengers and representatives of the English churches, and the leaders and directors of the native churches. This whole scheme of English administration is intended to drop off by degrees, and is already yielding in proportion as the native church arrives at maturity for the purposes of self-support, self-government, and self-propagation.

The progress which has already been achieved is marked, continuous, and even surprising, leading us to exclaim with gratitude and joy, What hath God wrought! The first missionary, Ringeltaube, working quite alone, amid difficulties and discouragements of every kind, and often suffering under heavy depression of spirit in view of the unpromising character of the early converts, was not able to realise the grand proportions which the mission would ultimately assume, nor the full value of the work which he was doing in laying the foundations of a noble Christian church in Travancore. Tempted by low spirits and long-continued solitude to unbelief, bitterness of mind, and a somewhat undue depreciation of native character, he wrote to his sister:—"I have little hope, and almost no desire to see once more in this world my beloved ones. My life is almost without any joy; for the soul finds nothing new, and, therefore, nothing that gladdens it. The artificial help of books, society, &c., is lacking here entirely. However, I am not cast down. You will ask, how many have you baptized (in 1810) in Travancore? About four hundred. What do you think of them? Not much of the most; about forty of them may be children of grace. Some have died already in the Lord. They are not so cunning and insolent as the people under the English Government." Three years later he writes: "I have now about six hundred Christians, who are not worse than the other Christians in India. About three or four of them may have a longing for their salvation. The rest have come through all kinds of other motives, which we can only know of after years have passed." Yet, before he left India, in 1815, through ill-health, debility, and depression of mind, he was able to say, "I have brought a mission to good standing by the assistance of our merciful Lord, and given it over to an honest Englishman. About 1,100 have been baptized by me in Travancore."

When I arrived in the beginning of 1859, there were then in our mission nearly 17,000 adherents of all ages: now there are 41,347 worshipping in 253 congregations. Of those, there were but 980 in full communion as church members: these now number 4,124. There was not a single ordained native minister in 1865, now there are 18; and their annual meetings for mutual consultation and united prayer are an interesting feature of the time. The native converts having been regularly instructed in the duty of giving to the cause of God, their contributions have steadily advanced from Rs. 3,500 in 1858, to Rs. 12,165 in the past year. Corresponding progress has been made in the education of males and females, both children and adults. There are now 10,696 children learning in our schools of whom 2,375 are girls. Eleven native pastorates or sub-districts have been formed, with their own distinct churches, pastors, and agencies, largely self-supporting; one of them has not received any pecuniary help from any quarter for upwards of twenty years. The mission has, upon the whole, been established and worked upon sound and Evangelical principles as to the authority and dissemination of God's Holy Word, the saving doctrines of the

Cross of Christ, the entire rejection of all that is heathenish and evil, Scriptural discipline in the church, and the duty of spreading the Gospel of Jesus Christ. We have never had more than eight, often only six, missionaries at work in South Travancore.

A similar work is carried on by the **Church Missionary Society,** in North Travancore and in Cochin, to which reference has been made throughout this volume, on principles and lines similar in essentials to those of the London Mission, and with like efficiency and success. Their converts are drawn from the Syrian Church, the Chogans, and the Pulayars, the last now constituting nearly a half of the total number, which amounts to 19,505 of whom 5,418 are communicants. Ordained clergy number 15, and catechists 59, under a learned and devoted missionary Bishop. Children learning in the schools 5,173; and contributions of native Christians, according to the latest reports received Rs. 5,772.

The state of transition through which the mission is now passing, from its former almost entire dependence on foreign aid to a measure of **vigour and maturity**—from looking solely for direction to their European instructors, to the formation of independent character and opinion—from the payment by the Society of most of the native teachers, to the beginning of a union of Congregational churches, supporting their own chosen ministry and Christian ordinances—is not without its trials and dangers to the missionaries and the native converts. Our early difficulty was how to obtain access to the country, and win any converts whatever: we are now called to consider where we can find men and means to overtake the work open to us, and how to settle on a solid basis for the future the two hundred and fifty congregations committed by the Lord to our care, and to bring them on to the stature of perfect men in Christ Jesus. We have arrived at the stage when new and perplexing problems spring up, which require for their solution great wisdom, experience and grace; regulations must be made and plans entered upon, which may prove in future times a source of great spiritual power and profit—or, it might be, trammels and snares—to the Native Church. As an independent position is won, mistakes will probably be made, and severe trials and painful revelations of character may be expected. The evils of the Indian character in heathenism will crop up in cases of wicked and hypocritical men endeavouring to make a gain of godliness—others grasping at power before they are fitted to use it aright—and others yielding to supineness and sloth, or to laxity of discipline through the fear of man, when placed in positions of trust and independent action.

An additional difficulty in the way of self-support and extension springs from the changes which have taken place in the economic condition of the country, and the retrenchments which have been necessary within the last ten or twelve years. These have caused some retrogression and loss in various institutions and agencies connected with the mission, and especially some falling off of personal attention on the part of missions' agents, whose pay is now insufficient for subsistence, and who are, therefore, driven to spend a portion of their time in adding to their domestic income, in order to make both ends meet. The old class of native catechists were usually persons of

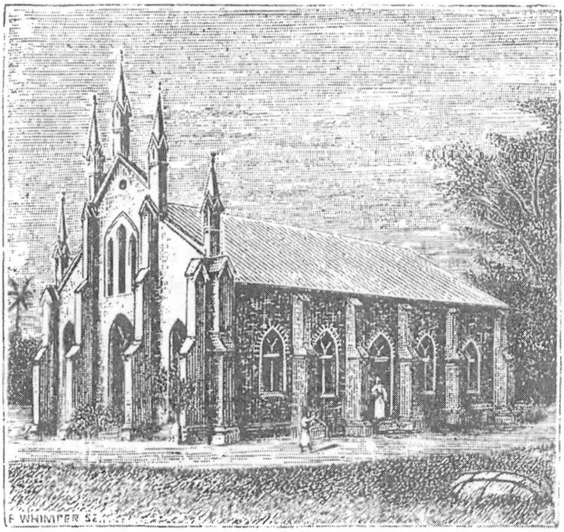

TITTUVILEI CHAPEL.

humble attainments as to education, but of general intelligence and sound piety, possessed of some little property and influence amongst their neighbours; to them any small monthly pay was acceptable, and sufficed when eked out from private resources. A better salary must be given to the present class of agents, educated in the Boarding Schools and Seminary, and devoting their whole time to the service of the mission.

Some of the agents have two, or even three, congregations to attend to in such fashion as they can; so that there is reason to fear that Scripture teaching, catechising, and individual dealing with souls have been of late years less efficiently performed through the pressure of routine work. Defections thus occur: many individuals and families were once, for a time, attendants on Christian teaching, but, having apostatized, are now harder in heart and farther from grace than ever.

Native agents specially trained in English and the vernacular under a missionary at the Nagercoil Seminary have always been employed in the mission; and the proportion of such is now greater than ever; but a still larger number of these is required, for which more reliable means of support for the Seminary, and increased facilities for training agents for the Malayálam Districts are needed to enable us to keep up with the progress of the age, particularly as the neighbouring missions of other societies are better equipped, in these respects, than ourselves.

Much prayerful effort is still demanded for the spiritual conversion and growth in grace of the mass of nominal Christians, whom we enumerate in our reports as adherents, who are still unbaptized, and, we fear, in many cases, still unsaved.

One very obvious duty resting on the mission is the increase of distinct efforts for the **evangelisation of the higher classes** in Travancore. Amongst these we have sown comparatively little and, of course, reaped but little. It happened that, in the early stage of the mission, the lower castes joined first, and in large numbers; and this circumstance of itself proved a hindrance to the higher castes coming in and mixing with them. "Where conversions are made from the lower strata of the Hindu polity in large numbers, great difficulties will arise in getting the better classes to join such rising churches: no doubt the early Christians felt the same difficulty in the congregations at Rome, consisting of slaves, Jews, and Syrians, to which the lordly Roman of the conquering race was invited in the name of Christ to join."* Our successes have thus created a caste prejudice against the native Christians. Then the pressure of work in the care of so many congregations has gradually deprived both missionaries and native teachers of time to devote to this special form of labour; and for the last few years pecuniary embarrassments also have disabled us from employing evangelists for itinerating amongst the heathen, as we were formerly accustomed to do. Not that very little has been effected in this direction. The higher classes always have had a share of attention from the mission. Lectures have been delivered to educated natives, and the Medical Mission has exercised a highly beneficial influence upon such as it reaches. For some years past all the native ministers have undertaken an itinerant tour of a month each year amongst the heathen, the

* Cust's Pictures of Indian Life.

results of which have often been of the greatest value. And, within the last year, two of the brethren have initiated a new form of labour—tent-preaching amongst the caste villages—which has excited much attention. They were surprised and gratified with one thing—the intense interest manifested by Brahman women to glean anything that might be heard.

The once despised native Christians also, and especially those of the third generation, who show the cumulative effects of continuous Christian teaching and privileges, begin to exert a

NATIVE CHRISTIAN DOCTOR.

beneficial influence on the higher classes. A new force is thus at work. The public opinion of Christians is now considered worthy of notice by public men; and they own and edit an English and Tamil paper published at Nagercoil. A considerable amount of voluntary effort for the surrounding heathen is put forth in several pastorates—earnest Christian women, for instance, first uniting in prayer on the afternoon of the Lord's day, and then going out to visit and read to Hindu women. This is a marked feature in the last report, which shows that a powerful impression is being made on heathen women by the ardour, intelligence, and sympathy of their Christian countrywomen, by means of which several converts have been made in the past year.

When the **Deputation from the Missionary Society** visited Travancore in December last, what did they find? Along their whole course, from Quilon to Trevandrum, Pareychaley, Neyoor, and Nagercoil, they found Christian congregations scattered all over the country—fruitful oases in a spiritual desert—and were received with demonstrations of the utmost

NATIVE CHRISTIAN'S HOUSE.

affection and gratitude from the native converts, who know how much they owe to the British churches who have sent them the Gospel with all its civilizing and elevating influences. Entering the Christian town of Nagercoil, they were received with triumphal arches and canopies tastefully decorated in Indian fashion with garlands of flowers, rows of lamps, texts and mottoes; and welcomed with singing and music by the Christians who went out in crowds to meet them. They addressed an eager and attentive audience of some two thousand persons in the great church at Nagercoil, where they also administered the holy communion to a thousand church members.

To the address of welcome presented to them, there was appended a cheque for a hundred rupees for the purchase of a chair for the use of the chairman of the Board of Directors in London, that they might never forget the Christians of Travancore.

The deputation visited the Seminary, now for nearly a quarter of a century under the able and indefatigable superintendence of Rev. J. Duthie, the Girls' Boarding and Day Schools, the lace workers, the Mission Press, whence Scriptures, magazines, school books, and tracts are issued in large numbers—the Hospital at Neyoor under Dr. Thomson, and dispensaries in other towns, where 25,000 patients are tenderly and skilfully treated every year, four-fifths of the expense being provided by local contributions—and the houses of several prominent Christian laymen, presenting to one of them a Bible in recognition of valuable voluntary services rendered to the church. They lectured in the Kottár Reading-room to a crowded audience, after which an address was presented by the non-Christian community, expressing their thanks for the philanthropic and educational work of the mission. At other places also, Hindus decorated the schoolrooms, and presented addresses of commendation and thanks for the labours of the Society in Travancore.

From Quilon, in the centre of the State, to Cape Comorin, at its extremity, where the waters of two oceans mingle, they met the agents of the mission, native missionaries and preachers, school teachers and zenana workers, made inquiries of each, and heard their detailed reports of work on the spot, where they could be tested, and addressed to all suitable words of counsel, encouragement, and stimulus. They laid the foundation of a new chapel to be built at native cost, opened a new reading-room and caste girls' school, and greatly cheered and animated the people by their kind words and earnest exhortations to increased faithfulness, devotion, and activity in the service of our Lord and Master. It was a more than royal progress to these representatives of English Christianity, everywhere surrounded with prayerful and loving hearts.

It is a marvellous thing that men are found who deny or sneer at these striking results of evangelical labour, which are patent to the eyes of all who care to see them, and are a splendid feature of the age. Christian missions have certainly not failed in India, where there is now (exclusive of Burmah and Ceylon, and in addition to Roman Catholic and Syrian Christians) a Protestant Christian community of 417,373 souls, which may be expected at the present rate of increase to number nearly a million in another decade. We are, at the same time, reaping the fruits of past labours, limited and inadequate as they have been, and sowing seed for a future harvest. "Every accession to the Christian ranks loosens some portion, however small, of the consolidated mass of heathenism; and every advancement in piety, culture, respectability, material prosperity, and visible strength on the part of the Christian community removes some measure of prejudice, and awakens the minds of observant heathen onlookers to a sense of the power of Christianity to elevate and bless mankind."

Could my readers but witness in person, as we who labour in India have been privileged to do, the beneficent effects of the Gospel of the grace of God in society, in the family, and in individuals—in reforming the laws and civil institutions of governments—in ameliorating the social condition of semi-civilized castes and races, and conferring upon them freedom, comfort, and decency—in moulding, sweetening and rescuing society, raising woman to her proper sphere as the intelligent companion of man, and introducing the blessings of marriage and family order into domestic life, where polyandry, concubinage, and immorality prevailed, and were recognised by caste law—in brightening and gladdening the poor homes of the peasantry with a joy and satisfaction which false religion can never supply; teaching the dear children and the outcastes, who dared not approach a school or walk through a village street, to read and write, to pray and praise and work—in reforming the lives and saving the souls of individuals; consoling them under the sorrows of life, and conquering the baseless and degrading fear of demons and unknown maleficent agencies, from which they have so terribly suffered, by a more ennobling fear of God, and supporting them in the dying hour—in raising up and directing the labours of native preachers of noble and exemplary character, of whom any society or church might be proud—and in opening the gates of heaven to multitudes now in glory—they would think no gifts too generous, no efforts or self-denial too great for such noble ends. To plant Christianity in India is a task worthy of a great nation. At but a trifling cost of life and labour, we can confer incalculable and endless benefits upon a perishing world.

Our fellow-countrymen go to Travancore and elsewhere to engage in the cultivation of coffee and other useful products of the soil. They ascend the lofty mountains in search of suitable soil and climate for their enterprise. They fell the dense primeval forests filled with jungle trees, prickly canes, and thorns which tear the hands and clothing and endanger the eyes, and with damp dense vegetation exhaling a poisonous malaria, by which the planters are often prostrated, and some die. They let the light of heaven into deep valleys and dismal dells previously haunted by ferocious tigers, leopards and bears, powerful elephants, deadly serpents, and other creatures whose strange cries and unearthly howls are taken by the ignorant and superstitious mountaineers for the voice of forest demons and satyrs. They clear and burn and level and fence; make roads, bridges, irrigation channels, and build their bungalows on charming and romantic sites. The estate is soon filled with the beautiful laurel-like coffee, the camellia-like tea, the chocolate, cinchona, nutmeg, clove, and other spice trees; while the house is surrounded by trim gardens, rich fruit trees, and lovely hedges of roses.

That is the work which we also are striving to do in the moral wastes of India, cutting down the poison tree of idolatry and superstition, clearing the dark dells of devil worship with its accompanying cruelties and vices, turning up the fruitful soil, and sowing in it the seed of life eternal. And already we are permitted to see, in some not inconsiderable measure, the fulfilment of the promise, "The desert shall rejoice and blossom as the rose—instead of the thorn shall come up the fir tree, and instead of the brier shall come up the myrtle tree; and it shall be *to the Lord* for a name, and for an everlasting sign that shall not be cut off."

Happy, thrice happy, are they who are permitted to take part in so great a work—to introduce Christianity into new castes and tribes and villages; to lay the foundations of a Christian Church in India, which shall be the admiration of the world a hundred years hence; to train the future teachers and preachers, the future fathers and mothers and citizens of India; to help the poor and needy; to rescue the perishing; to proclaim liberty to the captives of sin, and the opening of the prison to them that are bound.

> To comfort and to bless,
> To find a balm for woe,
> To tend the lone and fatherless,
> Is angels' work below.
> The captive to release,
> To God the lost to bring,
> To teach the way of life and peace,
> Is a most Christ-like thing.

CHAPTER XXXVIII.

APPENDIX.—INDIAN TUNES.

Tamil Lyric, No. 185.

RAGA, MALEIYAMI.

"*Dévá, tirukkadeikkan pár eiyá.*"

KEY G. M. 40.

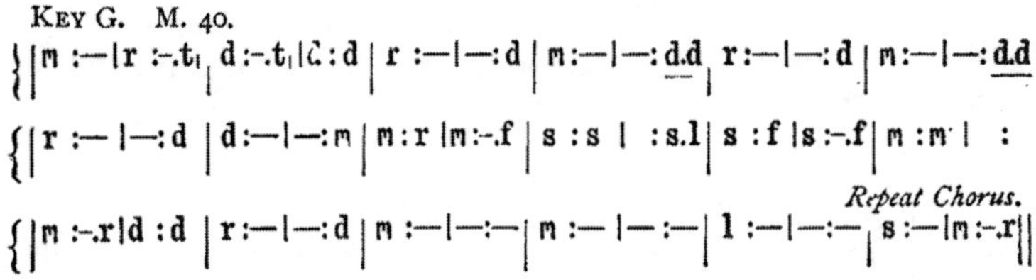

Tamil Lyric, No. 25.

RAGA, YAMUNAKALIYANI.

"*Pátham vandanamé.*"

KEY D. M. 60.

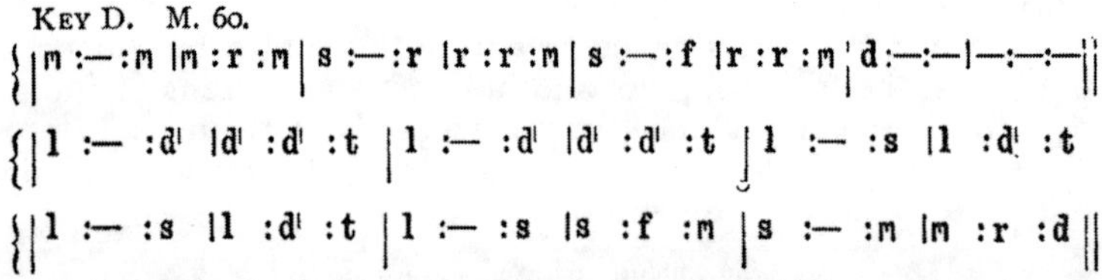

Tamil Lyric, No. 237.

RAGA, BHUPALAM.

"*Kathiravan eruginda káleiyil.*"

KEY G. M. 60.

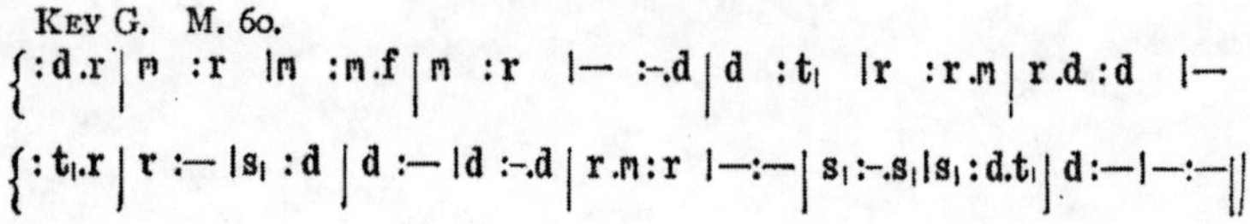

Tamil Lyric, No. 15.

RAGA, PUNNAGARAVARALI.

"Dévathé ór éga vastu."

```
 p.
{|m :—:m |f :—:m |r :—:d |d :—:r |m :—:m |f :—:m |r :—:d |d :—:r
{|m :— :m |f :— :m |m :— :r |r :— :— ||s :— :s |l :— :s
                                                      Repeat Chorus.
{|m :— :d |d :— :r |m :— :m |f :— :m |m :— :r |r :— :d.r ||
```

Tamil Lyric, No. 15.

MADURA VERSION.

By Rev. J. S. CHANDLER, M.A.

```
 KEY F.  M. 60. p
{|r :-.m |f :-.m |m :-.r |d :d |r :-.m |f :-.m |m :-.r |d :d
{|r :- .m |f :- .m |m :- .r |r :— ||l :- .l |ta :- .l
                                                      Repeat Chorus.
{|l :- .s |f .m :r .d |r :- .m |f :- .m |m :- .r |d :d .d ||
```

Tamil Lyric, No. 117.

RAGA, ANANTABHEIRAVI.

"Nittiyánandané, sittam."

```
 KEY D.  M. 40.            cres.                          D.C. FINE.
{|s :s |s :-.l |s.f :m |r :— |m :r |d :-.r |m :s |s :—
                                                      Repeat Chorus.
{|s :l.t |d' :-.t |t.l :l.s |l :— |d' :d' |s :-.l |s.f :m |r :— ||
```

Tamil Lyric, No. 264.

RAGA, SENCHURUTTI.

"Eiyané naẓar mithirangi."

```
 KEY G.  M. 40.
{|m :-.d |r :— |— :m.f |s :— |— :f |m :-.r |d :d |m :-.d |r :— |— :-.t,
{|d :— |— :— ||m :— |m :m |m :m |f .m |r :m.f |m :-.r |m :-.r |d :d
                                                      Repeat Chorus.
{|r :-.r |r :— |— :— ||m :f |m :s |— :f |m :-.r |d :d ||
```

Tamil Lyric, No. 263.

RAGA, SAYINDAVI.

"O, stri vittéseiyá."

KEY G. CHORUS.

{| s_1.d :— |d :—.d | d.m :—.l_1 | l_1 :— .r | r :r.m | r.d :—.t_1 | l_1.s_1 : l_1.t_1 | d :—.s_1

VERSE.

{| t_1 :— | s_1 :— | — : | || .r | f :—.m | r :—.m | r.d : t_1.d | r :—.r | f :—.m

Repeat Chorus.

{ | r :r.m | r.d :—.t_1 | l_1 :—.r | r :r.m | r.d :—.t_1 | l.s : l.t | d :—.s_1 | t_1 :— | s :— ||

The following three Lyric tunes are communicated by Rev. J. S. Chandler, M.A., Madura.

Tamil Lyric, No. 107.

RAGA, LAVANI.

"Tén inimeiyilum."

KEY G. M. 40.

{| d :d.d | d.d : d.r | m :m.r | m :s | r :m.r | d :t_1.d | m :r | — :r.r

{| r.m : f.f | f.f : f | m :m.m | r.r : d.t_1 | d.d : r.r | m :r | d :— | — :— ||

Tamil Lyric, No. 123.

RAGA, KIYAL.

"Yendeikku kánbénó."

KEY F. M. 40.

{ :d.r | m :m | r :— | r :m | f :— | m :—.r | d :d | r :— | d :m.f

{| s :s | s :— | r :m | f :— | m :r | m :—.r | d :d | — :— ||

Tamil Lyric, No. 134.

RAGA, MOHANA.

"Un tan áviyé, swámi."

KEY D. M. 60. *p*

{ :t .t | t :s .l | t :— .t | d :— | l_1.t_1 : s_1 | — .m : s | — ||

Repeat Chorus.

{ :l .l | l :l .l | t .s :— .m | s :— | m .m :m | d .r :m | — ||

CHAPTER XXXIX.

GLOSSARY.

A'bkary	Hind. *A'bkári.* (Strong) water manufacture.	Excise revenue, derived from duties levied on the manufacture and sale of spirituous liquors.
Adiyaray	Mal. *Adiyara.*	Fee on purchase of privileges, levied by the Sirkar in cases of adoption, inheritance by distant heirs, &c.
Adookoovathu ...	Mal. *Adukkuvathu.* Rights retained by the original proprietor from the purchaser.	Fine or fee payable to a Jenmi at the periodical renewal of a lease. Succession duty levied on every change of incumbency of Vritti tenure.
Amáni	Hind. Held in trust or deposit.	Collection of revenue direct from the cultivators or manufacturers by the officers of Government.
Ambalam	Mal....	An open building for the accommodation of travellers, &c.
Anubhógam ...	Mal. Enjoyment, usufruct.	Hereditary lands, granted to persons by sovereigns in reward of service, at a peppercorn rent, or small Rajabhogam tax.
Athigari	Mal. *Adhikári.* Ruler, officer.	Same as Provertykáran.
A'ttuvari	Mal. River-tax ..	Irrigation tax.
Anandaravan ...	Mal. From Sans (Succeeding) without an interval.	Successor, heir, younger brothers, children and grandchildren in Makkatayam system : younger brothers and nephews in Marumakkatayam.
Ayacut	Mal. *A'yakettu.* From *áyam*, income.	Register of assessed land. Original lands belonging to a village.
Bankshall	Mal. *Pándisála.* A warehouse.	Government warehouse for salt, tobacco, &c.
Bandy	Tam. & Mal. *Vandi*	Cart, carriage.
Candy	Mal. *Kandi*	Measure of weight—654 English pounds.
,, of timber...	,, ...	One kol or 28¾ English inches, cubic measure.
Cash	Tam and Tel. *Kásu*	A small copper coin, sixteenth of a chuckram.
Cawnie (of Madras).	Tam *Káni.* The eightieth part.	6,400 square yards or 1·32 acre. Acre is 4,840 square yards.
Cattanár	... ...	Syrian priest.
Codyettoo	Mal. *Kodiyéttu.* Hoisting a flag.	Temple festival.

Conjee	Tam. *Kanji*	Rice gruel.
Cooly...	Mal. *Kúli.* Hire, daily wages.	Hired labourer or porter.
Choultry	Hind. *Châwati.* Mal. *Châvadi.*	Public building, open on one side for public lodging place, post station, &c.
Chit	Mal. *Chittu*	Note, bond, or deed.
Chokkárer	Tam...	Co-heirs.
Chowkey	Hind. *Chaukí* ...	Station of police or of customs.
Chuckram	Sans. *Chakram.* Wheel, circle.	A small silver coin, worth about six-sevenths of a penny.
Chumadupanam..	Mal. Expense of carriage.	Commuted value of supplies due by Vritti holders without price.
Cutcherry	Hind. *Kachahrí.* Court, hall, office.	Public office of the Dewan or Tahsildar.
Dalavoy	Mal. *Dalavá.* From Kanarese *dala*, an army.	Commander-in-chief, minister of state.
Dendoo	Mal. *Dandham.* A stick, measure.	A lineal measure of 4 kol or 10 feet. 435·6 square Dendoos=1 English acre.
Dewan	Pers *Díván*	Chief officer of state, prime minister.
Durbar	Hind. *Darbár*... ...	Court levee.
Durkhast	Pers. *Darkhwást.* Tender for a rent or farm.	Reduced tenure on which certain Sirkar Pauttom lands are allowed to occupants at rates lower than their full or ayacut assessment.
Edungaly	Mal. *Idangári*... ...	A grain measure holding 4 nári and containing 92 cubic inches, or a third of a gallon. 24⅛ edungalies=1 Eng. bushel, which is 2,218 cubic inches.
Fanam	Mal. *Panam.* Money	A coin worth 4 chuckrams, or one-seventh of a rupee—about 3½d.
Garce of Salt ...	Tel. *Garisa*	A measured garce is 424 mercals, the official equivalent of 120 Indian maunds of 82⅘ lbs. avoir. each, say about 4·4 tons. Trav. Admin. Report makes 365 7 paras=1 garce.
Ghee	Hind. *Ghí*	Clarified butter used in cooking. Boiled and set to cool; when it remains in a semi-liquid state.
Gumastah	Pers. *Gumáshta.* Commissioned.	A native accountant in the revenue department.
Huzzoor	Ar. *Húzur.* The presence.	The place where the chief officer presides.
Iyeenzafter	Hind. *A'in* or *Ayeen*, laws, rules; and *Zabti*, sequestration.	Lands which had been held free, now subjected to a money assessment. Wet lands in Shencottah.
Jenmi...	... ...	A proprietor of Jenmam lands.
Jenmum	Sans. *Janma*, Birth, birthright.	Freehold property viewed as hardly alienable. It cannot be sold without the concurrence of the heir-at-law. In Travancore, nominally free from all tax: when alienated, a light tax called Rajabhogam is imposed.
Jummabundy ...	Hind. *Jamá*, amount; *bandí*, binding, settlement.	The annual settlement made under the ryotwari system.
Kánappauttem ...	Mal. *Kanam*, Possession, mortgage.	A redeemable tenure.
Kanderuttu ...	Mal. Record of what was seen.	Survey of actual produce. Assessment.

Kandukrishi ...	Mal.	Government agriculture. The home farms of the sovereign. Grain rent collected in kind.
Káranavan ...	Mal.	Head of the family. In Makkatayam the father,. elder brother, &c. In Marumakkatayam, the maternal uncle or eldest brother.
Kottah or Cottah	Tam. *Kóttei*	In Nánjinád 164 Kottar padies or 8 mercal. Nearly 4 bushels, or half a "quarter" of grain.
,, of land ...	,, ...	In Tinnevelly 1·62 acre.
Kudiváram ...	Mal.	Cultivator's share of the produce.
Kudumi	Tam. and Mal. ...	The Hindu tuft or lock of hair.
Kurava cry ...	Mal.	A shrill ululation produced by the vibration of the tongue between the lips and teeth. By women at marriages, devil dancing, &c.
Kurikánam ...	Mal. *Kuri.* Hole ...	Lease allowing compensation for value of trees planted or other improvements by the tenant or mortgagee on relinquishing possession. A kind of tenant-right.
Kuttikánam ...	Mal. *Kutti.* Log ...	Fee on timber trees cut down.
Lac or Lakh ...	Sans. *Laksha*	A hundred thousand.
Maicad	Kanarese. *Maikadu.* Daily hire.	Works executed without previous estimate.
Makkatáyam ...	Mal.	The right of sons to inherit as distinguished from Marumakkatáyam.
M. E.	Malabar Era	Quilon year. The date of its foundation. *M. E. 1059* begins on 16th August, 1883.
Malaváram ...	Mal. Hill, Share ...	Tax on waste land cleared. The proportion of such produce to the Sirkar.
Mantram	Sans. Production of the mind.	Prayer, text, charm, or incantation.
Marahmut	Ar. *Marámmat.* Repair.	Public works.
Marumakkatáyam.	Mal.	Succession to inheritance by sister's sons, or in the female line. Nepotism.
Maund	Hind. *Man*	At Madras 25 or 30 lbs. Indian maund of salt $82\frac{2}{7}$ pounds avoir. (100 lbs. troy), supposed to measure 3 paras.
Méladi	Mal.	Rent paid in kind.
Meleltoopillay ...	Mal. Registry clerk .	Accountant-general. Head of the Pilleymar.
Mélwárom	Mal. *Mélváram* ..	The proportion of the crop or produce claimed by Government.
Mercal	Tam. *Marakkál* ...	Grain measure, now fixed at 800 cub ins. = $2\frac{9}{10}$ imperial gallons. Of salt weighs 24 lbs. 6 oz.
Michaváram ...	Mal. Remainder, share.	The proprietor's rent of Jenmi property, after deducting the interest of the Kánam, or money advanced by the tenant.
Mofussil	Hind. *Mufassal.* Separate, distinct.	The country, as opposed to the principal station or town.
Munsif	Hind. Equitable, just.	A native judge subordinate to the zillah judge.
Mooparah	Mal. *Muppara.* Three measures (three in ten).	Assessment of three-tenths of the average of full tax on paddy lands.
Musnud	Ar. *Masnad.* The Muhammadan seat of power at Delhi.	The throne of Travancore.

Naduvukúru ...	Mal. Planting share.	Allowance for expense of planting and rearing young trees.
Nair or Náyar ...	Mal. Leader, lord ...	The Sudras of Malabar.
Nári or Nauly ...	Mal. *Nári*	A measure, chiefly of rice. Quarter of an edungaly. 23 cub. ins. or nearly 13 fluid ounces
Neet	Ar. *Niyat.* Will, allotment.	Royal decree.
Nirthal	Mal. *Niruttal.* Cessation.	Land abandoned on account of becoming unfit for cultivation. Sirkar lands left waste.
Nunjah	Tam. *Nanjei*	Soil fit for the cultivation of rice, admitting of artificial irrigation.
Ola	Mal.	Leaf of palm used for writing or thatch
Oloogoo	Mal. *Orugu.* Boundary.	Register of the measurement and extent of fields and holdings.
Oobhayempalisa.	Mal. *Ubhayam*, covenant; *palisa*, interest.	Interest paid in kind.
Ootooperah ...	Mal. *Uttu.* Giving rice to Brahmans. *Pura.* House.	Free inn, where Brahmans are fed.
Otti	Mal....	Mortgage, especially a usufructuary mortgage, in which the Janmi yields to the tenant all the produce of the field in lieu of interest for his advances; or if the receipts exceed the interest, the difference (michavára m) is paid to the proprietor.
Paddy	Malay. *Pádi*	Rice in the husk, whether growing or cut.
Pagoda	Sans. *Bhagavathi.* A deity.	Hindu temple. A gold coin worth 3½ rupees.
Pandal	Mal. Tam.	Temporary shed of leaves or wickerwork erected especially for marriage feasts, &c.
Pandára vaga ...	Mal. *Pandáram.* Treasury, government.	Government property.
Pandit	Sans. *Pandita*... .	A Brahman learned in the law and shastras. A law officer.
Para or Purrah...	Mal....	Grain measure = 10 edungalies = ·414 of a bushel. Para of seed may be taken at two-fifths of a bushel. Para of rice land is equivalent to from one-eleventh to one-eighth of an acre, according to locality. Now fixed at 8 × 9 dendoos.
Pathivu chit ...	Mal. Register document.	Document to acknowledge the ryots' right to cultivate.
Pattayam	Mal....	Deed of lease or gift.
Payittu páttam ...	Mal. Pulse rent ...	Rent or tax levied on dry lands or gardens. An edungaly of such land is 8 × 8 dendoos.
Peon	... ...	Inferior officer of police or customs or of courts of justice, usually wearing a badge.
Peishcar	Pers. *Péshkár.* A foreman, manager.	Collector, or magistrate over a province in Travancore.
Pidipádu	Mal....	Any deed or security of possession.
Pilley...	Mal. Tam. *Pillei.* A child.	Honorary title of Sudras and others. An accountant.
Plantain	Lat. *Plantago*	Same as banana. Fruit of Musa sapientum.
Pokkuvaravu ...	Mal....	Transfer of registry of lands ... ...

Provertykaran ... or Parvatyakaran	Sans. *Pravarttaka.* Presiding over. Mal. *Pravruttikáran*	A subordinate revenue officer having charge of the collections of one or more villages.
Puddy	Tam. *Padi.* A measure.	Seer Puddy of rice in Tinnevelly is nearly an English quart. It measures about 66½ cub. ins., containing 7[illegible] tolahs' weight of rice when struck, and 82 heaped pretty full. 168 of these = 1 kottah. Kottar stamped puddy said to be 42 = 1 bushel, which would be 52·8 cub. ins.
Poojah	Tam. Mal. *Púja* ...	Worship. Adoration of the gods with the proper ceremonies.
Punjah	Mal....	Land fit for dry grain cultivation, not being irrigated.
Puthuval	Mal. Newness... ...	Reclaimed or newly cultivated land.
Ranee	Hind. *Rání*	A princess. The sisters or nieces of the Rajah of Travancore.
Royassom	Mal. *Ráyasam* ...	Secretaryship.
Rupee	Hind. *Rúpáy*	An Indian silver coin, nominally worth two shillings, though at present the current value is nearly a fifth less. Throughout this book, where pounds sterling are mentioned, the pound is used to represent 10 rupees.
Ryot	Ar. *Ráyat.* Protected one, subject, commoner.	A cultivator of the soil.
Ryotwari	,, ,,	The system by which each landholder is dealt with directly, and land tax collected from each by the servants of the Government.
Sadr or Sudder...	Hind. *Sadr.* Eminence.	Supreme (Court).
Sanjáyam	Mal. Collection ...	Collection of tax on the temporary and occasional cultivation of waste lands.
Sepoy...	Pers. *Sipáhí*	A soldier of native infantry.
Séshakár	Mal....	Survivors, relatives, descendants.
Sheristadar ...	Pers. *Sirishtahdar.* Keeper of the records.	Head native officer of a cutcherry or department.
Sirkar	Pers. *Sar,* head; *kar,* business.	The native Government.
Strídhanam ...	Sans. Woman's wealth.	Dowry. The peculiar property of a woman or wife, over which she has independent control, and which descends to her daughter or next of kin.
Sumprithy or Samprathy.	Mal. *Samprathi* ...	Principal accountant in the Tahsildar's cutcherry, and immediate assistant to the Tahsildar.
Tahsildar	Hind. *Tahsíl.* Collection.	A native collector and sub-magistrate in charge of a Taluk.
Taiteeroo	Tam. *Teittir*	Sale of trees and produce without the land on which the trees stand.
Táli and Minnu..	Tam. Mal.	Marriage badge. The centre or sole ornament of a necklace which is tied on the neck of the bride by the bridegroom at the time of marriage.
Taluk...	Hind. *Tadlluk.* Dependence.	Division of a province. District under the management of a Tahsildar. (A county.)

Tarawád	Mal....	The Malabar family or united community, whose entire property is managed by its senior member for the benefit of the family—the strictest and oldest form of corporate union.
Tola	Hind. *Tol.* Weight..	A weight usually regarded as equivalent to the weight of the Sicca rupee or 179·666 troy grains. Now fixed at 180 troy grains, the weight of the current rupee. British rupees 38·9 weigh 1 lb. avoir. 350 tolas = 9 lbs. Weight of a florin is 174·54 grains.
Unjel	Mal. *Anchal.* A stage, relay.	Letter post.
Vakálatnámah ...	... ...	Power of attorney.
Vakeel	Hind. *Wakil* Delegate, agent	An authorized attorney. A pleader in a court of justice.
Vedam or Vetham	Sans. *Véda*	The four ancient scriptures of the Hindus. A religion having a sacred book.
Vellóla	Mal. Blank leaf ...	Unregistered document.
Vempáttam ...	Mal. *Verumpáttam.* Simple rent.	Rent of lands without any advance or loan. Lands paying full tax.
Virutti or Vritty.	Sans. Increase, prosperity; and Mal.	Feudal tenure. Lands granted rent and tax free for services formerly due, or still required without pay or at nominal rates.
Zillah	Hind. *Zilá.* Side, division.	Province.

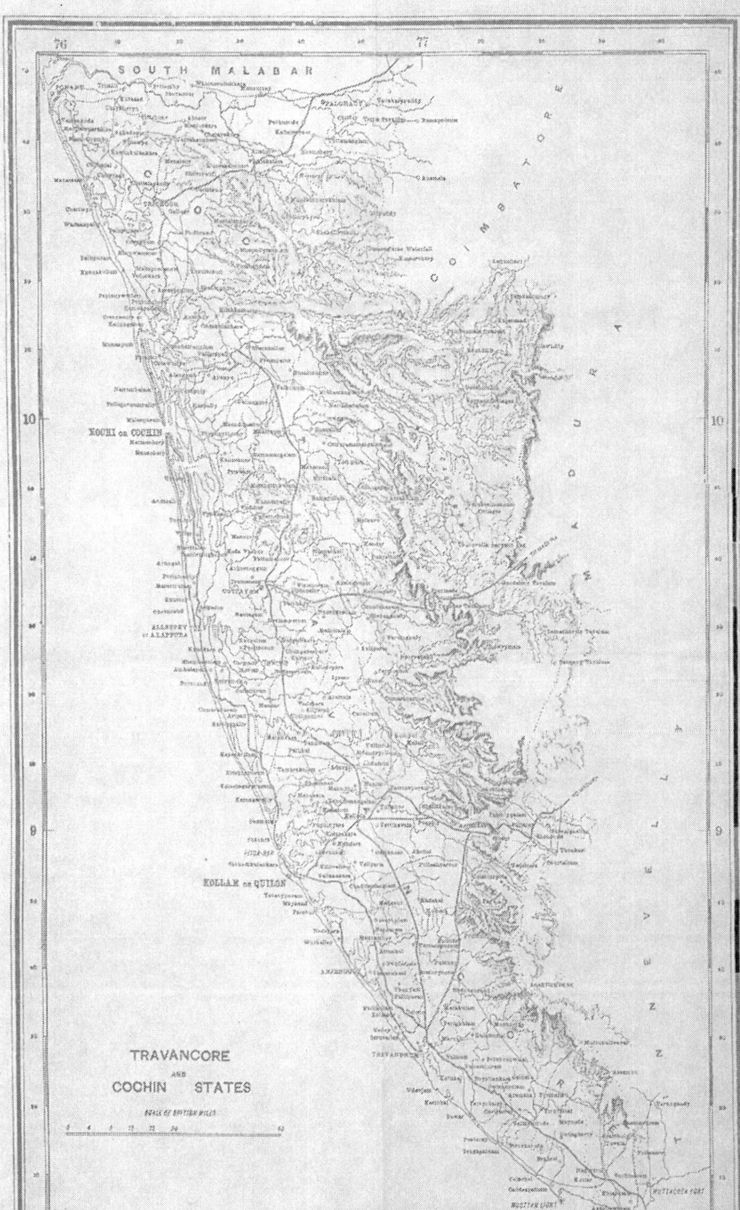

TRAVANCORE
AND
COCHIN STATES
SCALE OF BRITISH MILES
SOUTH MALABAR
COIMBATORE
MADURA
TINNEVELLY
KOCHI or COCHIN
ALLEPPEY or ALAPPUZA
KOTTAYAM
KOLLAM or QUILON
TRIVANDRUM
C. COMORIN
76
77
10
9